Patriots and Proletarians
Politicizing Hungarian Immigrants in Interwar Canada

Most of the Hungarian immigrants who came to Canada in the after-math of the First World War were peasants who had been excluded from political and associational life in Hungary by their poverty and low level of education. Once in Canada, they divided into two mutually exclusive and antagonistic camps, one conservative and nationalistic, the other radical and pro-communist. In *Patriots and Proletarians,* Carmela Patrias shows that the politicization of these peasant immigrants was an integral part of the development of their community institutions and group consciousness in Canada.

The agents of politicization were primarily a small elite of middle-class immigrants, clergy, urban artisans, and Communist party activists, as well as forces outside the Hungarian-Canadian community such as the Hungarian government and the Communist party. Immigrant churches, mutual aid societies, and cultural clubs were created largely because of the efforts of such agents. Cultural artefacts and activities – lectures, discussions, theatrical performances, poetry recitals, singing, and embroidery – formed an important part of these associations and were used to transmit political ideas. Politics thus became intertwined with other elements of Hungarian-Canadian culture. Because ordinary immigrants, marginalized by their status as foreigners and unskilled workers, were forced to rely almost exclusively on ideologies and institutions from within their own communities to analyse and better their situation, the ideologies of the competing groups became an integral part of the self-definition of Hungarian Canadians.

Patrias situates the experience of Hungarian immigrants within the larger context of immigration history and, by exploring the social trans-mission of political ideologies, shows how the social and political dimensions of immigrant groups develop.

CARMELA PATRIAS is an assistant professor of history at Brock University.

McGILL-QUEEN'S STUDIES IN ETHNIC HISTORY
Donald Harman Akenson, Editor

Patriots and Proletarians

Politicizing Hungarian Immigrants in Interwar Canada

CARMELA PATRIAS

McGill-Queen's University Press
Montreal & Kingston • London • Buffalo

© McGill–Queen's University Press 1994
ISBN 0–7735–1174–1

Legal deposit third quarter 1994
Bibliothèque nationale du Québec

Printed in Canada on acid-free paper

This book has been published with the help of a grant from the
Social Science Federation of Canada, using funds provided by the
Social Sciences and Humanities Research Council of Canada.
Publication has also been supported by the Department of Canadian
Heritage, Multiculturalism Programs, and by the Canada Council through
its block grant program.

Canadian Cataloguing in Publication Data

Patrias, Carmela, 1950–
    Patriots and proletarians: politicizing Hungarian immigrants
in interwar Canada
    (McGill-Queen's studies in ethnic history; 19)
    Includes bibliographical references and index.
    ISBN 0-7735-1174-1
    1. Hungarian Canadians – Politics and government. 2. Hungarian
Canadians – Societies, etc. – History. 3. Canada – History –
1918–1939. I. Title. II. Series.
FC106.H95P39 1994   971'.00494511   C94-900172-4
F1035.H8P39 1994

This book was typeset by Typo Litho Composition Inc. in
10/12 Baskerville.

For my parents,
Klára Ács and István Patriász,
twice immigrants

Contents

viii   Contents

Acknowledgments

This book could not have been written without the help of men and women who migrated to Canada from Hungary and the successor states of the Austro-Hungarian Monarchy during the interwar years and who permitted me to interview them and to consult their personal records. Showing remarkable trust and generosity, they welcomed me into their homes in Canada and in Hungary and patiently answered my many questions. Unfortunately, few of them will be able to see the final product. I can only hope that by shedding light on the complexity of the forces that shaped their communities and their political behaviour, this analysis will have redeemed their trust.

The help of the immigrants themselves was indispensable because written sources on the history of Hungarian immigration to Canada between the wars are scattered and often fragmentary. I managed to uncover these sources thanks to the assistance of dozens of archivists and Librarians in Hungary – at the National Archives of Hungary, the Széchényi, Ervin Szabó, and Central Statistical libraries, the Institute for Party History, the World Federation of Hungarians, the Szabolcs-Szatmár County Archives, and the Manuscript Collection of the Sárospatak College of Theology – and in Canada – at the National Archives of Canada (Ottawa), the Archives of Ontario (Toronto), the (Roman Catholic) Archdiocesan Archives of Toronto, the United Church Archives (Toronto), the Presbyterian Church in Canada Archives (Toronto), the Multicultural History Society of Ontario (Toronto), the Glenbow Archives (Calgary), and the Saskatchewan Archives (Regina).

While I worked on this project, first as a graduate student and later as a research fellow and sessional instructor, I benefited from the advice and encouragement of a number of teachers, colleagues, and friends. It is a pleasure to thank them now that the project is complete. No scholar has done more to make this study possible than Julianna Puskás of the History Institute of the Hungarian Academy of Sciences. She introduced me to rural life in Hungary, gave me access to valuable source material which she collected in Hungary and Canada, and shared with me her expertise on the history of Hungary and of Hungarian emigrants. In his capacity as my employer and thesis supervisor, the late Robert Harney encouraged me to return to university and gave me the freedom to pursue this topic as I saw fit. Frances Abele, János Bak, Janet Hamilton, Harvey Mitchell, Danny Vickers, and Fred Weihs, my "shadow committee," read and criticized all or parts of this manuscript, helping immensely to clarify my thinking and improve my writing. Colleagues at the history departments of the University of British Columbia, Wilfrid Laurier University, and Atkinson College of York University helped to keep me engaged in the teaching and writing of history by providing friendship, encouragement, and intellectual stimulation. I would like especially to thank János Bak, Paul Krause, Harvey Mitchell, Roberto Perin, Alan Sinel, Peter Ward, and Suzanne Zeller. Through friendship and example, John Ayre, Jane Brackley, Mary-Ellen Belfiore, Erzsébet Bihari, Mimi Divinsky, Ruth Frager, David Johnstone, Ken Klonsky, Marjory Lang, Donna Lightfoot, Duncan McLaren, Don Rayko, Panni Sardi, and Ron Vida contributed unknowingly to the completion of this manuscript. I should also like to thank John Parry for his thoughtful suggestions and careful copy-editing.

Wayne Thorpe convinced me that the thesis should be turned into a book and helped to make that a reality through his intelligent, gentle criticism of my work, his affectionate encouragement, and his irreverent sense of humour.

The pleasure that should have accompanied the publication of a study so long in the making is not complete, as no celebration will ever be, because Susan and Alex Vida will not share it owing to their tragic and untimely deaths.

This book is dedicated to my parents, Klára Ács and István Patriász. Their love of learning, their decency and courage, which survived all that they experienced in Central Europe during the 1930s, 1940s, and 1950s, have been a constant source of inspiration.

Patriots and Proletarians

INTRODUCTION

MARCH 15, POLITICS, AND HISTORY

Hungarians! My Brothers! My little friends!
We are performing a play for you. For the next hour we have the floor.
Our words are Hungarian, and we express them with Hungarian feelings, so
as to kindle the Hungarian flame in you!
The earth is crying out beneath us, Hungarians! Over our virgin fields, the
tread of wild enemies reverberates! Their sneers and curses cut our faces
like a whip. We, who were once leaders, wherever generous hearts, strong
arms, and proud heads could lead, are now bent over, humiliated,
trampled under foot....
Though we may be telling a story, play acting, setting afloat the magic
carpet of the imagination, we can no longer do so with flighty, empty words.
Not as we did in happier times, when our sun rose over the snowy
Carpathians, to cast its rays over golden streams and to sink contentedly to
sleep in the lap of the gently humming sea. No! Today, the word, the
tone, the will, are different.
Hungarians! My Brothers! My little friends!
We are performing a play for you. Listen to us. Why, what resounds in our
words is what pains you and tears the skies asunder. No! No! This cannot
be! The earth itself will mutiny, and our country, now torn to bits, will live
again. You will be proud again Hungarians, but you must be worthy.[1]

With this impassioned, patriotic declaration, a young boy introduced
Spring Will Come Again to Hungarians assembled at the Welland

Hungarian Self-Culture Society on 15 March 1930. His words, and the
play that followed, expressed outrage at the Treaty of Trianon – the
peace settlement imposed on Hungary in 1920, following the collapse
of the Austro-Hungarian monarchy at the end of the First World War.
The treaty awarded roughly 70 per cent of Hungary's prewar territory,
and 60 per cent of its population, much of which was ethnically
Hungarian, to Czechoslovakia, Romania, and Yugoslavia. Choosing this
theme to mark 15 March, Hungary's national holiday, was an expression of defiance. Celebrations on that day commemorate the start in
Budapest of the revolution of 1848 in which Hungarians fought cour-
ageously but unsuccessfully for constitutional reform and national
independence from Austria. The play linked Hungarians' resistance
in the past to their refusal to accept the dismemberment of their
homeland.

The play takes place in 1922, on the second anniversary of the Treaty
of Trianon, and it is set in Transylvania, one of the major areas lost by
Hungary under the terms of the treaty. The fate of the Nagy family –
to which three of the play's four characters, Ilona, Jani, and Béla,
belong (the fourth is an old gypsy violinist, Dani, whose presence on
stage provides comic relief) – represents the fate of Hungarians in
Transylvania. Formerly the owners of a large estate and a beautiful
manor-house, the Nagys have been reduced to poverty by the
Romanians. The new rulers have also murdered Ilona's brother Ákos,
whom they accused of spying for the Hungarians. Béla, who is in love
with his cousin Ilona, has escaped to Hungary, to avoid Ákos's fate and
to plot the return of Hungarian rule.

The murdered Ákos has become the symbol of resistance to
Romanian rule in the village. On the first anniversary of Trianon, the
Hungarian villagers had expressed their opposition to their nation's
dismemberment by placing flowers on his grave. Resolved to prevent
such insubordination a year later, the Romanians have placed armed
guards around the cemetery. The action of the play revolves around
the determination of Béla and his brother Jani to defy the Romanian
authorities. Twelve-year-old Jani has been selected by the village boys to
place a wreath on the grave under cover of darkness, and Béla has
risked his life to return to place the Hungarian tricolour on Ákos's
grave.

Narrowly escaping Romanian bullets, the boys succeed in carrying
out their acts of defiance. Although Béla must return to Hungary before dawn, the play ends on an optimistic note. The three young actors,
accompanied by Dani, the gypsy, on the violin, sing an irredentist song.
After Béla's departure, Dani hangs his violin on the wall and promises

not to play it again until Transylvania is returned to Hungary once more. As the curtain falls, Jani, Ilona, and Dani sing "Let the good old days return."

In 1931, only a year after this play was staged in Welland, 15 March was marked by a very different performance at the Toronto Workers' club. *Virgin Mary* by émigré communist writer Andor Gábor commemorates in fact less the revolution of 1848 than the defeat of the Hungarian Commune of 1919 – the brief reign of communists in Hungary between 21 March and 1 August, 1919.[3] Never firmly in control, having acceded to power during postwar turmoil, the communists succumbed in the face of domestic opposition and foreign intervention. The play is set immediately following the commune's defeat, in the Zalaegerszeg internment camp, notorious for the brutal treatment of inmates – that is, anyone suspected of having taken part in the commune. The villain of the piece is the camp doctor, whose pretentiously elegant speech patterns place him unmistakably within the ranks of the gentry, or of the gentrified middle classes – the backbone of the counter-revolution of Admiral Nicholas Horthy, who took the title of regent of Hungary. About the baseness of this representative of the Horthy regime, the playwright permits us to have little doubt. His victim, 17-year-old Mary Neuman, has been interned along with her parents because her father is a union activist and a self-confessed communist. Mary, a ravishingly beautiful school teacher, has been nicknamed "Virgin Mary" by camp guards and fellow inmates because of her impeccable conduct. The dignified and virtuous character of this working-class daughter serves to emphasize the spineless, self-seeking, exploitative behaviour of the camp doctor.

The play opens with the arrival of an order from the Ministry of the Interior that internees be examined for venereal disease. Through a discussion between the doctor and his assistant, the audience learns that the camp guards, some of whom have gonorrhoea, have been raping female internees. Since the foreign press has published reports of these goings on, the Ministry of the Interior wants to prove, through the examination, that the accusations against the guards are unfounded and that the promiscuity and immorality of the communist internees themselves are responsible for the epidemic. At the same time, the evil camp doctor intends to use the excuse of an internal examination to take advantage of Mary Neuman, who has until now rebuffed all his advances. His manly pride does not permit him to rape her. Instead, the doctor promises her mother that if she can convince Mary to comply with his wishes, Mr Neuman, who is very ill, will be transferred to a hospital. Needless to say, the doctor has no intention of carrying out his end of the bargain. But Mary, in any event, extricates herself from his lecherous web by committing suicide.

POLITICS AND HUNGARIAN IMMIGRANTS

The commemoration of the 1848 revolution in Hungary – undoubtedly the most important community function of Hungarian immigrants in Canada during the interwar years – served to express and to affirm Hungarian group identity in Canada.[4] This study opens with a description of the radically different ways in which two immigrant associations marked this day to show the two contrasting identities that emerged among Hungarian immigrants in Canada between the two world wars. Indeed, the study's title, *Patriots and Proletarians*, refers to the division of the immigrant group along political lines into two mutually exclusive and antagonistic camps, each with its own organizational structure and ideology. To one camp belonged Hungarian religious and secular organizations whose members supported or at least accepted the established power structures both in Hungary and in Canada. I call this camp the patriotic camp, since its members often described themselves as "hazafias magyarok," or patriotic Hungarians. To the other camp belonged the Hungarian mass organizations of the Communist Party in Canada. As their performance of *Virgin Mary* suggests, the members of this camp were hostile to Admiral Horthy's counterrevolutionary regime. For them the brief reign of the commune was a moment of glory; they celebrated its memory and hoped for its resurrection. I call this camp the proletarian camp, since its members often referred to themselves as "öntudatos munkások," or class-conscious proletarians.

Whether they belonged to the patriotic or the proletarian camp, associations such as the Welland Hungarian Self-Culture Society and the Toronto Workers' club attempted to meet the economic, social, and cultural needs of their members in similar ways: they offered sick and funeral benefits, organized cultural and recreational events, and provided educational opportunities. What distinguished the two camps and pitted them against one another were the differences in their ideologies.

By ideology I mean the more-or-less coherent set of ideas developed within each camp to shape the collective identity of its members and guide their actions as a group. I stress that both patriotic and proletarian ideologies were "more-or-less" coherent, because neither ideology was formally elaborated. Rather, we can discern them from the activities of immigrant associations and from patriotic and proletarian publications. As the 1848 ceremonies illustrate, politics permeated the activities of Hungarian associations in Canada.

For Hungarian immigrants, homeland concerns were not abstract considerations or exercises in nostalgia to be entertained during moments of leisure; they formed an integral part of the quest to define what it meant to be Hungarian in Canada. The symbols of Old World culture and chapters of shared history emphasized within each camp influenced the type of adaptation advocated in the new land. Thus, for example, Hungarian immigrants who celebrated the Hungarian Commune of 1919 accepted communist leadership and analysis of conditions in Canada during the interwar years. Consequently, as we shall see, they lent their support to communist-led unions and other organizations and to militant actions that transcended ethnic boundaries. Immigrants who embraced patriotic ideology not only supported a right-wing government in Hungary, they also rejected communist-led actions, thereby rejecting one of the few avenues of protest open to them between the two world wars.

At first glance, neither the intense politicization of community events nor the preoccupation of Hungarian immigrants in Canada with the Treaty of Trianon or with the Commune of 1919 appears surprising. Outrage at the loss of territory and population that the treaty decreed was widespread among Hungarians at this time, and the Horthy regime did its utmost to intensify the nationalism and irredentism awakened by this outrage. At the same time, reactions to the Hungarian commune were almost as important in defining Hungarian political consciousness. While Horthyist ideologues used the commune as an example of the evils of internationalism, communists, most of them in exile, strove to perpetuate its image as a beneficent popular revolution and yearned to recreate it.

What is intriguing about the nature of the 1848 ceremonies and the highly politicized content of competing group identities that they reflected is that the members of the Welland Hungarian Self-Culture Society and of the Toronto Workers' club were largely agriculturalists from the lowest ranks of Hungarian rural society. Like most of the almost 34,000 Hungarians who came to Canada between the two world wars (see Table A6 in the Appendix), most members of both immigrant organizations had been excluded from political and associational life in Hungary by their poverty and their low level of education. Communism failed to take hold among them in 1919 and so did the counterrevolutionary ideology of the Horthy regime after 1920. Paradoxically, it was in Canada that peasant immigrants rallied around homeland concerns that left them unmoved in Hungary. One of the central arguments of this study is that their politicization was a response to the immigrant experience. The adoption of both proletarian and patriotic ideologies was an integral part of the development of community institutions and group consciousness among Hungarian immigrants in Canada.

The new condition of peasant immigrants as workers and newcomers in Canada, however, can no more explain the group's ideological polarization by itself than can their shared past. Had group consciousness simply developed unmediated out of their common experiences, Hungarian peasant immigrants would have been united. Most of them came from the lower ranks of Hungarian rural society, and in Canada they worked in menial jobs and, at least when they first arrived, lived clustered together in immigrant neighbourhoods. The emergence of rival ideological groupings among them can have come about only as a result of interaction with members of other social groups, either within or outside the immigrant group. Indeed, I intend to show that a small elite, comprised of business people, members of the liberal professions, artisans, skilled workers, and Hungarians who came to Canada after having spent some years in the United States, played a decisive part – out of all proportion to its small size – in the development of Hungarian communities. It laid the foundations of ethnic associations and shaped their ideological substance. But from the very beginning, forces from outside the immigrant group – most notably, Canadian church authorities, clergymen from the United States, the Communist party, and the government in Budapest – also played a crucial role in the world of the immigrants. The representatives of these outside forces sought to gain their allegiance to partisan objectives, in which extra-community concerns had a major share, by attempting to influence community life on an ongoing basis.

I chose to begin this study with *Spring Will Come Again* and *Virgin Mary* because they point to the involvement of outside forces in community life. *Spring Will Come Again*, one of five short plays in a collection entitled *Hazafias Szinpad* (Patriotic Stage), was published in 1928 by the Hungarian National Federation, an organization funded by the regime in Budapest to promote its conservative-nationalist ideology at home and abroad. *Virgin Mary* was written by Andor Gábor, a Hungarian communist writer who took part in the Commune of 1919. Gábor had first-hand experience of Horthyist jails, having been briefly imprisoned following the victory of the counterrevolutionary forces. After his release he emigrated to Vienna, then to Berlin, and following Hitler's advent to power, to Moscow. Throughout his years in emigration, Gábor's plays, novels, poems, and articles were published by the communist press in Europe and America. *Virgin Mary* reached peasant immigrants in Canada as part of the Communist party's campaign to win their support.

These two examples suggest not only that forces from outside the immigrant group attempted to arouse partisan loyalties within it but also that the channels and tools on which they relied to transmit their concerns to Hungarian immigrants were by no means patent and obvious. Indeed, the social transmission of political ideologies is more complex than any example can suggest. The main argument of *Patriots and Proletarians* is that the politicization of group consciousness among Hungarian immigrants was the result of a process of interaction among forces from outside the ethnic group, a handful of artisans, skilled workers, and middle-class people within it; and the men and women from the lower strata of Hungarian rural society who made up the group's rank and file. Immigrant organizations were the major arenas for this interaction, and cultural artifacts and activities – lectures, discussions, theatrical performances, poetry recitals, singing, and embroidery – were the vehicles through which the ideas of the immigrant elite and outside forces were transmitted to the rank and file. To reach ordinary immigrants, however, both members of the elite and representatives of outside forces incorporated elements of popular culture into their programs. Accordingly, while two contrasting identities developed among Hungarians in Canada, each contained elements of the Old World cultures of the educated middle class, of urban and rural artisans, and of peasants, as well as of American-Hungarian culture.

HISTORIANS AND THE POLITICAL DIMENSION OF THE IMMIGRANT EXPERIENCE

I decided to focus on the politicization of Hungarian immigrants, however, not only because politics was of such obvious importance in their community life, but also because the existing literature on immigrant and ethnic groups provides no explanatory model that adequately accounts for the political dimension of their experience.

No doubt because of their relatively small numbers, Hungarian immigrants have received far less attention from scholars than the Irish, the Italians, the Poles, and other larger groups. Julianna Puskás's magisterial study, *Kivándorló magyarok az Egyesült Államokban, 1880–1914* (Hungarian Emigrants in the United States, 1880–1914), published in Budapest in 1982, is the first and only attempt to provide an overview of the Hungarian immigrant experience in the United States in that period. This study does an admirable job of describing the development of associations and political groupings of all shades. Owing to its pioneering and comprehensive nature, however, it cannot provide an analysis of the process of politicization among Hungarian immigrants. *Struggle and Hope: The Hungarian-Canadian Experience* (1982), by N.F. Dreisziger et al., is the only survey of the Hungarian immigrant experience in Canada. Its treatment of the interwar era is necessarily cursory. It is, moreover, descriptive rather than analytical. The authors of this study make little effort to relate their findings to the rich literature on immigration, labour, and social history in North America.[5]

But neglect of the political dimension characterizes studies of other groups of immigrants as well. Conventional descriptive monographs on the history of immigrant and ethnic groups do of course deal with politics. They generally limit their discussions, however, to formal political processes: voting patterns, membership in established parties, the quest for office, or lobbying for group or homeland concerns. Such a narrow definition suffers from several shortcomings. First, it has an inbuilt bias towards immigrant and ethnic groups large enough to muster votes and constitute lobbies of sufficient weight to influence political decisions. Second, because such studies generally fail to take into account that peasant immigrants often became politicized only in the receiving society, they analyse neither the social and economic causes nor the means of politicization among immigrants. Third, and most important, the highly politicized culture evidenced by the 1848 ceremonies in Canada challenges the narrow definition of politics, which clearly cannot account for the complex ways whereby authority is deployed and resisted in society.[6]

This study defines politics more broadly as an interactive process between rulers and ruled that extends beyond explicitly political processes and institutions. Specifically, *Patriots and Proletarians* examines the ways in which the experience of Hungarians in Canadian society combined with their culture – language, community institutions, values, symbols, rituals, interpretations of the group's history, and formulations of its identity in Canada – to legitimize or challenge constituted authority in Hungary and Canada.

If conventional monographs on immigrant groups neglect the social and cultural dimensions of their politics, social histories purporting to offer a total view of the past experience of such groups from southern and eastern Europe have until recently ignored or minimized the political dimension of this experience. This neglect of politics is the result of two related assumptions: first, that the initial and decisive stage of community building was the accomplishment of working-class immigrants, and second, that genuine immigrant or ethnic culture is the culture of those very people. Publications since the mid-1970s by historians such as June Alexander, Josef Barton, John Briggs, Caroline Golab, and Virginia Yans-McLaughlin imply that the new communities grew spontaneously out of the experience that working-class immigrants shared, both in their native lands and in the receiving society.[7] Giving evidence of their group consciousness, ordinary immigrants clustered together in immigrant neighbourhoods on arriving in North America. The development and persistence of these neighbourhoods created arenas for strengthening – and in the case of newcomers united by narrower local and regional ties, for forging – ethnic consciousness among the newcomers. The help that these people received in finding housing and employment, the security that they derived from being surrounded by men and women who spoke their language and shared their traditions, and the kinship and friendship ties that bound them to their neighbours all reinforced ethnic group solidarity. Within these ethnic colonies, moreover, immigrants could maintain many of their characteristic patterns of behaviour, and as the areas matured, establishment of businesses and ethnic institutions that catered to the group's special needs contributed significantly to the persistence of distinct ethnic identities.

Settlement patterns, occupational clustering, and the emergence of informal kinship and friendship networks are all unreflective manifestations of ethnic cohesiveness. Social historians seem to see these patterns of behaviour as the most reliable indicators of group consciousness among immigrants because they are amenable to supposedly objective, quantifiable analysis.

The model of spontaneous generation also extends, however, to the establishment of mutual aid societies, fraternal lodges, and even religious associations. Social historians pay considerable attention to these more self-conscious assertions of immigrant group solidarity because they believe that such associations were, at least at their founding, grass-roots organizations formed to meet the social, economic, and cultural needs of immigrant workers. Such bodies expressed and formalized the shared experiences and needs that had led immigrants to congregate in ethnic neighbourhoods and to set up various informal social networks. Indeed, in the US literature, interpretations of the origins and nature of such voluntary organizations have become a principal measure of the groups' autonomy, of their spirit of initiative and enterprise. Older scholars, such as Herbert Banfield writing in 1974, see peasant immigrants' lack of familiarity with voluntary associations as indicative of backwardness and demoralization caused by poverty.

Banfield maintains that they were incapable of acting collectively and planning ahead. Oscar Handlin's "uprooted" peasants (1951) also lack the impulse for self-improvement in Europe. He sees their founding of associations as a step in their Americanization.[8]

It is in large measure against this characterization that the proponents of the models of spontaneous generation of working-class immigrant culture insist that peasant newcomers were familiar with voluntary organizations when they arrived in North America. They believe that, starting in the late nineteenth century, peasants in Slovak, Romanian, Italian, and Hungarian villages created mutual aid societies, savings and loans associations, consumers' and producers' cooperatives, because they recognized that traditional household, kinship, and communal ties were inadequate to permit individual small producers to succeed in the world of commercialized agriculture. Barton, Bodnar, and Briggs, among others, argue that their Old World experience prepared them to form grass-roots bodies in North America and that these associations, in turn, permitted them a significant degree of autonomy in shaping group identity and adaptation to American society.

The willed, ideological elaboration of group identity, by contrast, receives far less attention in social histories because it did not grow out of the shared experiences of immigrant workers. Attempts to define and provide theoretical justification for the position of the ethnic group in the host society, the relationship between the group and the native land of its members or their ancestors, and the tasks of cultural preservation were generally the work of elites.[9] Having been more fully integrated into national political life in their native lands than their economically and educationally deprived counterparts, they often continued to be engaged with homeland political concerns even after they emigrated. Because of their greater educational and economic resources, moreover, they found it easier to form ties outside their own group than former agriculturalists. They often acted as intermediaries between their co-nationals and the receiving society. By playing down their role, the model of spontaneous generation minimizes the influence of ideas in the formation of ethnic communities. It severs ideology from popular culture.

The most extreme formulation of spontaneous generation, advanced in 1982 by John Bodnar in *Workers' World. Kinship, Community and Protest in an Industrial Society, 1900–1940,* makes no allowance at all for the role of elites in immigrant groups. Bodnar presents the world of newly arrived workers as a completely insular and autonomous "enclave," whose inhabitants were "circumscribed, cut-off from social and political influences, from those of higher social rank and even other workers."[10] Even historians such as Josef Barton, John Briggs, and Virginia Yans-McLaughlin, who acknowledge that elites played a role in immigrant communities, imply that their contribution constituted, at the very most, a secondary phase in community development. Their studies suggest that ordinary immigrants could accept or reject the initiatives of elites, including political initiatives, at will. According to Yans-McLaughlin's 1977 study, the interests of ethnic elites, especially their political interests, were irrelevant to rank-and-file Italians in Buffalo[11], whose political behaviour was determined entirely by pragmatic considerations. John Briggs (1978) suggests that the existence of clearly defined group consciousness permitted them to respond to elite initiatives critically and selectively.[12] Josef Barton argues that ethnic elites built upon the foundations established by the rank and file. Their efforts to unite and lend coherence to the ethnic group on the broadest possible basis, so as to enhance its status and political effectiveness in the host society and to aid in the survival of the group's language and culture, carried forward the work of their less-educated counterparts.[13]

The emphasis on the dignity and resourcefulness of ordinary immigrants, part of a broader movement to study society from "the bottom up," was a necessary corrective to the more traditional and patronizing approach that equated poverty with helplessness and lack of education with absence of plans and ideas. To argue that elites and outside forces were decisive in community building among Hungarian immigrants is to deny neither the initiative and enterprise of peasants in their new land nor their ability to act collectively. *Patriots and Proletarians* merely asserts that the majority of these people, who came from the bottom of rural society, lacked experience in politics and formal organization because of their poverty and limited education. As chapters 1 and 2 make clear, however, both their decision to migrate and their early adaptation in Canada testify to their energy and resourcefulness. The remaining chapters, which describe the emergence of community organizations and life within them, demonstrate that although most peasants gained organizational experience and became politicized only in Canada, they were by no means passive participants in this process. They took an active part first in the building and later in the running of bodies founded and led by elites and outside forces because these associations responded to their needs.

Even if the social composition of other groups of peasant immigrants was different from that of the Hungarians, spontaneous generation still cannot adequately explain the political dimension of their experience. The chief fallacy of the view that group consciousness and community building grew spontaneously out of the shared experiences of socially and economically homogeneous groups is that it suggests that general agreement existed within them as to group interests. This consensus view implies that each group's interests were politically neutral and makes politics appear an external factor. All these versions of spontaneous generation allow only that politics could be placed in the service of ethnicity, not that ethnicity could serve politics.

The limitations of the model become most clear when it is applied to southern and eastern Europeans who, like the Hungarians, became polarized along political lines in North America. The consensus model cannot account for the emergence of radically different strategies of adaptation and interpretations of group interests within immigrant groups at the community level.

A handful of recent social histories examine the political dimension of the social experience of working-class newcomers.[14] The radical departure of this approach from that of earlier social histories is most clearly apparent in the work of John Bodnar. In *The Transplanted: A History of Immigrants in Urban America* (1987), a synthesis of scholarly research on immigrants who settled in American cities, this former proponent of the insularity of working-class immigrants stresses that the experience of these people was in fact shaped by the "interaction of classes, ideologies, and culture within and outside the communities of newcomers."[15] Yet possibly as a legacy of his earlier work, even here Bodnar writes of politics in a fragmented, narrow way, as something imported from outside, that never became fully a part of the world of these workers. He assumes that the penetration of capitalism into the rural world brought with it the growing integration of the peasant into the national state in every respect, but he does not examine peasant politicization.[16] Consequently, he does not consider the possibility that many peasants became politicized only in North America. Nor does he explore the ideological component of immigrant or ethnic culture itself.

The importance of immigrant culture as a path for the transmission of various political ideologies is also obscured in studies that focus exclusively on a particular faction within groups of newcomers. Studies of immigrant radicalism, for example, such as Donald Avery's *Dangerous Foreigners* (1979), touch on the relationship between politics and culture. Noting that the appeal of radical leaders such as Matthew Popovich was greatly enhanced by their ability not only to speak Ukrainian but also to sing Ukrainian songs, Avery does not explain why this was so. His focus on radicalism creates the misleading impression that the marginalization and exploitation of the immigrants invariably led them to become radical. It fails to consider those Ukrainians, Finns, and Jews who, while just as exploited as their radical brethren, adopted conservative ideologies in Canada. Consequently, the importance of immigrant culture itself as a path for the transmission of different, even conflicting political ideologies does not become fully apparent in studies that focus on radicalism alone.[17]

Historians who concentrate on the dominant ideologies within immigrant groups, without giving due consideration to the existence of oppositional expressions of group identity, also obscure the political content of emerging group consciousness. John Zucchi's *Italians in Toronto* (1988), for example, carefully traces how through their urban experience in Canada, and their contacts with Italian and non-Italian clergy and notables, an Italian national consciousness developed among people originally divided by local and regional loyalties.[18] In Zucchi's account, the nationalism of Italian immigrants appears politically neutral.[19] He mentions but does not analyse the opposing socialist and anarchist formulations of group identity. Although these minority alternatives failed to make serious inroads among Toronto's Italians, their existence suffices to show what nationalists themselves sometimes denied – the inevitable political content of their creed. The critical endeavours of socialists and anarchists underscored the existence of political assumptions among purportedly neutral nationalists even before some of them embraced fascism in the 1920s and 1930s. These political assumptions undoubtedly affected the immigrants' perceptions not only of their native land but of Canadian society as well.

Hungarians' ideological division in Canada confirms the need, recognized in Bodnar's *The Transplanted* and in Avery's and Zucchi's work, of reintegrating the social and political dimensions of their experience. By examining the spread of both radical and nationalist ideologies among Hungarians, however, *Patriots and Proletarians* attempts to add a new element to this integrative framework. It emphasizes that ethnicity itself is an ideological construct permeated with political content, and it tries to show how an immigrant group's identity and political ideologies become intertwined.

David Montgomery's 1986 essay "Nationalism, American Patriotism, and Class Consciousness among Immigrant Workers in the United States in the Epoch of World War I" is one of the few studies that considers the impact of conflicting ideologies on ordinary immigrants.[20] Using interviews and records of rank-and-file behaviour during public meetings and demonstrations, Montgomery attempts to discover how working-class newcomers translated the views of groups intent on shaping their attitudes – internationalist socialist organizers, nationalist leaders concerned with developments in their homelands and with community formation in North America, government officials, members of the American Federation of Labor, and others intent on

"Americanizing" the foreign-born – to express their own aspirations and sense of self. What is missing even in this finely textured analysis, however, is an examination of the ways whereby political ideologies were transmitted to these workers.

By paying close attention to the tools and agencies through which ideas of the immigrant elite and outside forces were transmitted to Hungarians new to Canada, I hope to show that immigrant workers were not always in a position to respond critically and selectively to ideologies which they encountered. The extent to which political ideas became enmeshed with other elements of immigrant culture, specifically such activities as drama, poetry, singing, and even embroidery, limited the workers' ability to accept or discard these ideas.

LIMITS OF THIS STUDY, SOURCES, AND METHODS

Some readers might object to the importance accorded here to formal associations, on the grounds that only a minority of most immigrant groups participated in organized community life. According to my estimates, at least one-quarter of Hungarians in central Canada belonged to patriotic and proletarian organizations.[21] By the eve of the Second World War, there was an impressive array of associations. Toronto's Hungarians, numbering approximately 2,200, had four religious congregations and four secular associations. Montreal's 3,450 Hungarians claimed five religious bodies and four secular ones, and Welland's 1,600, three religious and four secular associations. Even if the proportion of participants in organized community life was smaller in other immigrant groups, taken together their numbers represent a notable proportion of newcomers in Canada. Their experience is accordingly worthy of attention. Moreover, the number of people who participated in the activities of such associations, especially in community-wide functions, far exceeded the numbers indicated by membership figures. (The eight tables in the Appendix to this book present various statistics on the almost 34,000 Hungarians who immigrated to Canada between 1923 and 1940).

The interwar period seemed the most appropriate timeframe to study the politicization of Hungarian immigrants in Canada for two reasons. First, and most important, the fact that Canada became the principal destination of people leaving Hungary at this time led to unprecedented involvement of both the Hungarian government and communist émigrés in the group's community life. Second, because these years were ones of exceptional hardship and because immigrants had virtually no access to the sources of power in Canadian society, they relied heavily on their associations and on the ideologies offered within them. Interwar immigration of Hungarians to Canada began in 1923, with the arrival of Hungarians from the successor states of Austro-Hungary, and ended with the outbreak of war in 1939.[22]

The study's focus on central Canada – specifically, Montreal and several cities in Ontario – was determined by the nature of the sources on which it is based. I have made extensive use of material internal to the community: newspapers, almanacs, jubilee publications, minute books of associations, and oral histories. Only a portion of the records of Hungarian organizations was deposited in archives in Canada and Hungary. The gathering or consultation of the rest, and the recording of oral testimonies that supplemented written records, required numerous field trips to various Hungarian-Canadian communities. Time and financial constraints dictated that I limit these field trips to one region of Canada. Since it became the most significant area of settlement for Hungarians during the interwar years, central Canada was the obvious choice.

Patriots and Proletarians has more to say about the agents of politicization and about the means whereby they infused ethnic community life with political content than about the political consciousness of ordinary immigrants. This emphasis was dictated by sources. Inevitably, material about officials and organizations outside the community, and about the more articulate members of the group, was more abundant than material about the rank and file. My use of oral histories and descriptions of the activities of Hungarian organizations did not fully offset this imbalance. The nature of sources, however, should not be confused with the emphasis of my argument. I am not suggesting that the representatives of outside forces, or leading figures within the group, could mould the attitudes and behaviour of Hungarians at will. Politicization was the result of interaction between the rank and file and these agents of political ideologies. Whenever sources permit, I discuss the role of all parties involved in this complex process.

The organization of this book reflects its concern with demonstrating that ethnic identity becomes intertwined with political ideologies because the immigrant experience brings together different social classes and ideologies from within and outside the group. Part 1 has three chapters. Chapter 1 sketches the Old World life of Hungarian immigrants, but it is not simply a "background" chapter. By carefully tracing not only economic circumstances, but also associational and political traditions, it explains why most of these people became familiar with political ideologies and engaged in associational life only in Canada. Chapter 2's discussions of their momentous decision to migrate and their ingenuity and skill in finding employment in Canada are intended to show that while the majority of the newcomers were shackled by poverty and lack of education, they were nevertheless venturesome and resourceful. This chapter also explains why conditions in interwar Canada made Hungarians rely on organizations and ideologies within their own communities. Focusing on the origins of Hungarian communities in central Canada, chapter 3 demonstrates that Hungarians, like other groups of peasant immigrants, settled in distinct neighbourhoods and relied on informal networks of friendship and kinship to make the initial adjustment to the New World. As chapters 4–7 (part II) reveal, however, these networks were essential but not sufficient for the emergence of formal community organizations and the forging of group identity among Hungarians. The leadership and ideologies of members of the group's elite and of outside forces were central in determining the structure and ideological content of community institutions. The study's remaining three chapters (part III) explore the development of group consciousness among Hungarian immigrants in the patriotic and the proletarian camps.

PART ONE

Old World, New World

1 Divided Homeland

Imre Lénart and his wife, tenant farmers in Karcsa, Zemplén county, were stacking hay one day in 1924 when they saw two men approaching the village notary's office. The men called out to them that it was possible to register for work in Canada at the Cunard office in the nearby town of Sátoraljaújhely. The Lénarts stopped working. They rushed home to prepare Imre for the 10-km journey to Sátoraljaújhely, and as soon as they were ready, Imre walked there and applied to go to Canada.[1]

Karcsa was a village so isolated and backward that it did not even have its own post office, nor was it serviced by rail. It seems astonishing at first glance, therefore, that Lénart decided to leave home for a distant land so rapidly and apparently without a moment's hesitation. His behaviour appears less surprising if one considers that Karcsa was located in northeastern Hungary, an area that had witnessed mass emigration before the First World War. Consequently, as Lénart himself explained, he made the decision to go to Canada with some idea of what he would find here: "I heard very much about America. Masses of people from Karcsa had been there, or were still there even when I came back from the war. They were in Argentina, in the United States and in Canada. I had four brothers in the United States. They wrote home that it is possible to earn money there, life isn't as rotten as it is here." But the discrepancy between economic possibilities in Hungary and Canada did not convince Lénart to leave Karcsa permanently. He travelled to Canada twice, in 1924 and in 1930, each time with the intention of improving his position in Hungary. The first time he stayed for four years, long enough to earn the money necessary to buy a house and land in Karcsa. He returned a second time in order to "earn more money, to improve my farm."[2]

These recollections alert us to two significant attributes of Hungarian migration to Canada between the worldwars. First, it was not a new development, for us to consider independently, but rather the resurgence of pre-1914 migration to North America. When the men and women who would reach Canada in the 1920s were growing up, news about "Amerika" and its opportunities had penetrated every corner of the country and left no social stratum unaffected.[3] By the decade before the First World War, many Hungarians, especially in the countryside, had come to view transatlantic migration as an accepted, perhaps the only, means to improve their lot. "It was generally believed," explained one immigrant to Canada, "that there wasn't much likelihood that we could improve our lives if we stayed home. Whoever could should try America."[4] Second, like Imre Lénart, most interwar Hungarian migrants to Canada saw the move as a temporary measure, the means for improving their lives within Hungarian rural society.

The First World War, by halting the flow of international migration, merely forced these prospective migrants to postpone their plans.[5] At war's end, their readiness to go to "America" – North or South – became apparent at once: news of renewed prospects of emigration spread among them "like wild fire."[6] But most Hungarians could no longer migrate to the United States. That country's government placed severe quotas on migration from east-central Europe in 1921 and 1924. Lénart's recollections suggest that prospective migrants readily redirected their hopes to Canada and even Argentina. To him, all three countries appeared to be scarcely distinguishable parts of "America."

Analysing the European background of Hungarian immigrants, this chapter first looks at peasants from Hungary and from the successor states of Austria-Hungary and their situation in an attempt to explain why they undertook transatlantic migration during the interwar years. Next it examines the organizational and political traditions that would shape their behaviour in Canada. Finally, it considers the city-based group of professionals, business people, artisans, and industrial workers who played such a major role in organizing the "patriot" and the "proletarian" camps among the immigrants after they arrived in Canada.

MIGRANTS FROM RURAL SOCIETY

Conditions in Hungary

Like Lénart, the overwhelming majority of Hungarians who migrated to Canada were agriculturalists. According to Hungarian government statistics, 83.5 per cent of the Hungarians who went to Canada between 1928 and 1930 belonged to this category.[7] Their proportion among the emigrants far outweighed their share in Hungary's population: by 1920, Hungarians employed in agriculture constituted 55.7 per cent of the population, but they made up over 80 per cent of those leaving for Canada a few years later. Canada's stated preference for farmers and agricultural labourers from eastern and central Europe undoubtedly inflated this category. Prospective emigrants no longer engaged in the agrarian sector, especially those who had but recently left the countryside, often convinced local officials in Hungary to certify that they were agriculturalists. To ensure that Canadian immigration officials would also accept their newly acquired credentials, city-dwellers devised clever ways to make their hands appear roughened by years of tilling the soil. Yet the number of such impostors cannot account for the disproportionately large number of agriculturalists among the migrants. The propensity of this group to migrate across the Atlantic reflected chronic problems in Hungary's agrarian sector.[8]

Most of the agriculturalists who migrated to Canada between the world wars were concentrated at the bottom of rural society: 69.7 per cent of them were landless farm hands and day labourers, at a time when only 41.4 per cent of Hungary's rural labour force belonged to these ranks; the remainder were independent farmers.[9] Oral recollections and the reports of contemporary observers suggest that many of these landholding peasants also belonged to the lowest strata of rural society: they were either dwarf holders, who owned less than 1 hectare (ha.) – about 2½ acres – of land, or small holders, who owned between 1 and 5 ha. In fact, the distinction between the independent farmers and farm hands and day labourers was not as great as their classification in statistical records would suggest. On the one hand, because of the diminutive size of their holdings, all dwarf holders and many small holders were forced to hire themselves out as labourers in order to support themselves and their families; on the other hand, some of the younger migrants may have been the sons of small or dwarf holders who stood to inherit little pieces of land later in life.[10]

The problems that precipitated migration from the lowest ranks of rural society dated back to the period before 1914. Between the mid-nineteenth century and the outbreak of the First World War, the population of Hungary increased by 54.5 per cent.[11] Largely because of the pattern of land tenure, the agrarian sector, which on the eve of the war still employed more than half of the nation's labour, was incapable of absorbing this rapidly increasing population.[12] Large and medium-sized estates – holdings over 100 ha. – which made up 58.8 per cent of all land under cultivation, remained outside the reach of the peasantry.[13] Accordingly, the burden of the growing populace fell on less

than half of the agricultural land – the area made up of peasant holdings. Under the combined pressures of an expanding population and
a system of partible inheritance, these holdings were increasingly subdivided, often becoming within two generations too small to support a
family .[14]

Because of these unfavourable conditions, not only landless labourers but many dwarf holders, and often even the children of small
holders, were forced to work for others. Yet the employment opportunities within the agrarian sector were limited. The seasonal nature of
agriculture made underemployment endemic. Precisely at the time of
the upsurge in the ranks of agricultural labourers, moreover, increased
mechanization reduced the need for rural labour.[15]

Since the agrarian sector could not accommodate them, large numbers of agriculturalists sought work in the industrial and service sectors,
but opportunities there were also limited. Despite rapid growth in the
decades before the First World War, the industrial sector remained altogether too small to absorb the surplus of rural workers. The number
of emigrants from Hungary during the forty years before 1914 was four
times as large as the total number of industrial workers within the country. Furthermore, rural labourers lacked the skills necessary for heavy
industry, which comprised a significant portion of the nation's industrial sector. Ironically, therefore, even while there were large numbers
of unemployed and underemployed in Hungary, skilled people were
coming from the more industrialized regions of the Austro-Hungarian
monarchy. Brickworks, food processing plants, distilleries, and lumber
mills, which required unskilled labour, offered only seasonal or temporary employment.[16] The jobs that these industries, as well as public
works projects and domestic service, offered were generally badly paid
and socially undesirable.

When the First World War broke out in 1914, emigration had not yet
reached what scholars describe as the "regression stage": neither the
numbers who left for "America", nor the remittances that they sent
home, sufficed to eliminate compelling reasons for transatlantic migration.[17] In fact, the war itself, the dissolution of the Austro-Hungarian
monarchy, and the harsh peace settlement imposed on Hungary aggravated economic problems at home and led to a deterioration in the
condition of domestic agriculturalists.

The war had dislocated and damaged the nation's economy.
Although development of certain branches of heavy industry was actually aided by manufacture of armaments, exclusive concern with production of war materials hurt all other branches of industry. In the
agrarian sector, production was severely limited by the recruitment of
approximately half of the prewar labour force into the army: much
land remained untilled and production of major crops fell.[18]

Domestic political unrest, and the activities of invading armies that followed the defeat of Austria-Hungary, aggravated postwar economic chaos and delayed economic recovery.[19] In the year following the end of the war, Hungary experienced rapid changes in government: Count Károlyi's republican government remained in power for four months only, from 31 October 1918 to 20 March 1919; Béla Kun's Communist government, which took over from Károlyi on 21 March, fled the country on 1 August 1919, in the wake of military defeat, having been in power a mere 133 days; a Social Democratic government led by Gyula Piedl, in power for less than one week, was replaced by the traditional ruling elite on 6 August; and Admiral Horthy did not attain full control of the country until November 1919. Until November, no administration was in power long enough to initiate postwar reconstruction. The presence of Romanian and Yugoslav troops until the nation's final submission – at the palais de Trianon in Versailles on 4 June 1920 – to the terms of the peace settlement, and removal of industrial equipment as a form of reparation by these armies, put additional strains on an already exhausted economy.

The ability of the economy to recover was even further limited by the collapse of the dual monarchy and by the imposition of Trianon, which took away approximately two-thirds of Hungary's prewar territory and three-fifths of its prewar population. Hungarian food processing, which had been the leading branch of industry before the war, suffered primarily from the loss of prewar markets as Austria-Hungary, within which Hungarian food products enjoyed protected status, was broken into new states with protectionist trade policies. The disappearance of protected markets meant that once international trade resumed after the war, Hungarian agricultural products also had to compete with the products of more highly developed nations on the open market.[20] Heavy industry was deprived of essential raw materials by boundary revisions.[21]

Frightened by the turbulence of 1918–19, even the most conservative members of Hungary's ruling circles recognized that some kind of land reform was urgently required to solve problems in the rural sector. They were concerned above all to assuage popular discontent without fundamentally altering the nature of society. This they accomplished. For while the Land Reform Act of 1920 distributed land among small holders, dwarf holders, and landless labourers, no fundamental restructuring of the country's inequitable land distribution occurred between the world wars.[22] Although the beneficiaries and their families numbered 1½-million people, or more than a quarter of the agricultural population, the lands that they received made a barely perceptible dent in the share held in large estates and had no impact at all on middle-sized properties. Since most recipients owned properties of less than 5 ha. at the time of the Reform Act, the parcels of 1.5 or 2 ha. that they acquired under the act were not large enough to alter their status. The land reform thus merely increased the number of tiny holdings in the countryside.[23] Since large landowners not infrequently used the act to get rid of their least desirable land, the new parcels were often unproductive or located at great distances from villages. But even those people who received better pieces lacked the means to maximize production. Yet by creating the illusion that economic independence within the agrarian sector was possible, the reform strengthened the attachment of even the poorest agriculturalists to the land.[24]

In fact, however, the condition of small holders, dwarf holders, and agricultural labourers – the lowest strata of rural society – grew ever more precarious between the world wars. Any modernization during this period took place on large estates. Without the aid of modern technology and fertilizers, owners of small plots were able to produce only minimal surpluses. Yet they were burdened by higher taxation after the war than before it. One indication of their hardship was their high indebtedness throughout the period.[25]

Accordingly, during the 1920s, even more small holders than before 1914 were forced to sell their labour. The end of mass emigration also substantially increased the number of those seeking work in agriculture. But because of agrarian stagnation, there was no growth in demand for agricultural labour.[26] Consequently, the average number of days put in annually by agriculturalists was significantly lower between the wars than before 1914. Indeed, the shortage of agricultural work continued to be the major force that pushed Hungarians to emigrate. During the course of an investigation concerning the rise in emigration from Hungary, officials from Abaúj county, for example, acknowledged that some parts of their county were unable to support their rural population: "The rural population has enough property, but because many families have 6–7 children, dwarf holders are incapable of making an adequate living from their own holdings, while the properties of small holders are subdivided among numerous children, to such an extent that they cannot support a family either. This is why young adults from families of 5–7 siblings, owning 1–8 hectares of land, decide to emigrate, even after they start a family. In this region there are no employment opportunities."[27]

To assume that only those agriculturalists who were underemployed and could not make ends meet decided to seek work overseas, however, would be to underestimate both the enterprise of peasant migrants and the careful calculations that informed their decision to seek employment across the ocean.[28] The residents of the village of Pétervára, in Heves county, for example, could find ample employment on neighbouring estates, and, by their own admission, their wages would have sufficed to support their families as well. But they could not earn enough locally to improve their lot. Accordingly, many of them were attracted across the ocean by the prospect of receiving sufficiently high wages to enable them to improve their situation in Pétervára.[29] In most cases, this meant the attainment of independence through ownership of enough land to permit a comfortable existence.

Others chose emigration to escape what they viewed as exploitation. Having a large surplus of workers at their disposal, landowners were able to dictate the terms of employment. In some instances, in order to be awarded labour contracts workers had to perform some tasks without payment. If they protested, or if employers deemed their demands excessive, they simply brought in labourers from other counties. As a result, agricultural wages were even lower between the wars than during the period of mass emigration, and some workers found this state of affairs unacceptable.[30] György Nóvák, from Végárdó, Zemplén county, decided to emigrate because he believed that he was not receiving a "fair" wage: "When I got married, I got nothing from home, from the small holding of my family. My wife got 2½ hectares. In the mean time, we had two children. I tried share cropping, I undertook hoeing on the estates of Barons Windischgratz and Waldbott in return for payment in kind. To get the hoeing contract, I even had to work in the vineyard for nothing. I could just barely support my family from my own land and the work on the large estates. I did not think that my pay was good enough, considering how hard I worked. Slowly the idea of emigrating began to take hold of me."[31]

A decline in supplementary, non-agrarian work available to the poorer peasants after the First World War also helps to explain why many decided to migrate. As noted above, the food industry, a major employer of unskilled labourers, suffered when the dual monarchy was broken into new states with restrictive trade policies.[32] Employment on public works projects, another major outlet up to 1914, also shrank considerably, as the financially beleaguered government in Budapest cut back on virtually all railway, road, and waterway construction. Building by private contractors also declined.[33]

Among sectors traditionally employing unskilled rural labourers, only mining expanded in the years immediately following the war, when disruption of international trade made it impossible to import coal. Between 1918 and 1924, many small mines were opened in the counties of Borsod, Heves, and Nógrád.[34] But when international trade resumed, Hungarian duties were too low to protect the poorer-quality domestic coal from outside competition, and many of these smaller operations were abandoned.[35] Hundreds of agriculturalists, who had depended on seasonal work there to supplement their income, found their way to the sugar-beet fields of southern Alberta.[36]

Most peasants who worked in mines, factories, and construction sites in Hungary did so, in any case, only out of necessity. Their efforts, poorly paid and seasonal in nature, forced them to leave their families for weeks and even for months at a time.[37] Lőrincz Kovács, for example, from the village of Mátraderecske, in Heves county, was a day labourer on large estates in summer and in neighbouring mines in winter. His work took him away from his wife and child for several weeks at a time, and, as he explained, it "was very hard to live like that, especially for a young man." He moved to Canada hoping to save enough money in three to five years to acquire land in Mátraderecske and thus be freed from having to sell his labour.[38]

The binding forces of rural traditions, moreover, combined with urban prejudice against the peasants, to reinforce their ties to their communities and to agrarian work. Despite hardship, even the poorest agriculturalists displayed fierce attachment to their villages, undoubtedly strengthened by the contempt that they faced elsewhere – for many urban dwellers, the term "büdös" (stinking) was inseparably linked to "paraszt" (peasant). Despite long-standing traditions of migration in search of labour, rural villagers were far from fully integrated into national life.[39]

Describing the interaction between miners and labourers of peasant origin, an ethnographic study of the mountain regions of Bükk, Cserhát, and Mátra in northwestern Hungary sheds light on the deep gulf that separated peasants from the rest of interwar society:

The two strata and the two lifestyles have one point of contact: the work performed in the mines. This does not bring the peasant-miners and the miners closer together, and does not lead to the disappearance of the class differences between them. The peasants, despite the fact that they work for part of each year in the mines, actually still resemble poor peasants much more than miners. The settled miners see the villagers as some kind of inferior breed, a rootless people, made up of clumsy, stupid peasants, not quite belonging to the mines. The rural worker also looks down on the settled miner, because he at least generally owns a house, and may even possess a small property, albeit one divided into narrow strips. Under the influence of rural traditions, the rural worker looks down on wage labour, which he undertook out of necessity, not by choice. As a general rule, not even the precariousness of his existence as a half-peasant, half-miner would lead him to become a miner. On the other hand, he would gladly exchange places with the peasant who owns enough land to guarantee an independent existence.[40]

Studies of pre-1914 migration to the New World suggest that because of the cleavage between rural and urban society in Hungary, peasants found temporary transatlantic migration – seen as the most likely way to preserve their traditional way of life – more acceptable than migration to towns in their own country. Indeed, most of those who returned, the Amerikások, went back to their villages, where they purchased land or livestock or improved properties with their overseas earnings.[41]

This continued to be the motivation of peasants who migrated to Canada after 1918. Whether they went because they could not find enough work at home or because they did not feel adequately rewarded for their efforts, all of them believed that jobs in Canada might improve their lot. As before 1914, migrants generally thought of improvement strictly within the rural world. Asked about their motives for departing, dwarf holders, tenant farmers, and wage labourers who ventured to Canada between the world wars replied that they did so in order to be able to build a house, to buy livestock, and above all to acquire land – in their native country. As one of them explained: "I just wanted land, because the Hungarian needs land."[42]

Conditions in the Successor States

Even the Magyar agriculturalists who migrated to Canada from the successor states of Austria-Hungary shared the motives of their counterparts from Hungary.[43] Steven H., who moved to Canada from Czechoslovakia, for example, fully intended to return home. He had very specific plans for the money that he would save by working abroad for a few years: "Next to me lived a childless couple, advanced in years. They had 15 hectares of land, a stone house, surrounded by a half hectare of land which was full of fruit trees. So I reckoned that I would be able to buy this. I would go to Canada and stay there for 4 years. Two thousand dollars would be enough. Plus one thousand for renovations and livestock. I didn't expect much. I told myself if I can save four thousand dollars, good-bye Canada!"[44]

This similarity of motives is noteworthy, because even scholarly works generally ascribe Magyar migration from the successor states to Canada solely to political reasons.[45] The acrimony surrounding Hungary's loss of territory and population at the end of the First World War still overshadows the fact that the areas awarded to Czechoslovakia, Romania, and Yugoslavia had seen heavy emigration – by all ethnic groups – even when they still formed part of Greater Hungary.

Dislike of the new regimes, uncertainty about the future that awaited Hungarians as a minority group, or specific instances of discrimination certainly contributed to emigration from neighbouring states. Reluctance to serve in the Romanian army, where Hungarians were apparently mistreated, was repeatedly offered in interviews as a reason for emigration. Ambrus Lőrincz from Transylvania, for example, believes

that 50 young men of military age from his village alone left Romania
in order to dodge the draft:

You were asking: why did we come here from Transylvania? Because the
Romanians treated us abominably. I mean then, it was hard on young people.
And they ran away so that they could dodge the draft.... They mistreated us in
the Romanian army and those who came to our village after discharge, one became deaf, they broke the nose of the other. They made them work hard; in
six weeks their clothing became rags and tatters. At that time they didn't dress
them up in soldiers' uniforms. They weren't really soldiers, they had them only
work. Once they drafted them, they made them work for three years. There
were three from our village whom they gave a beating with gun stock, their ear-
drums ruptured during the military service, so we fled.[46]

Close attention to oral testimony discloses, however, that the same emigrants who point emphatically and angrily to the redrawing of the
boundaries as the reason for their emigration frequently also reveal
that economic causes contributed to their decision. Many of them
came from villages with well-established traditions of transatlantic migration by Hungarians. Sándor Zsadányi's father and brother went to
Canada in 1923, from Szapárifalva, in Krassószörény county in
Transylvania. When asked why they did so, he replied without hesitation: "because we did not like the Romanians." Yet his father had been
to the United States twice before 1914, when his native village still
belonged to Hungary.[47]

The age and gender distribution among Hungarian migrants from
Hungary and the successor states suggests their sojourning intentions.
Although many were married and had children, adult males always
comprised more than two-thirds of the group between 1926 and 1929,
the years of heaviest Hungarian migration to Canada.[48] They left their
families behind because they identified thoroughly with their village
world, which they planned to re-enter. What this attachment to birth-
place suggests is that despite their long-standing traditions of local and
transatlantic migration, Hungarian peasant-migrants were still insular
in many respects, and were indeed far from fully integrated into
national life.

ASSOCIATIONAL LIFE
IN THE COUNTRYSIDE

A view of European peasant life as insular is one that many students of
migration reject. Intent on demonstrating that such immigrants from
southern and eastern Europe were rational and enterprising rather

than backward people fleeing poverty, these scholars insist that by the time of mass migration the societies that these villagers left behind were no longer static or isolated. They see the emergence of rural associations in Croatian, Italian, Slovakian, and Ukrainian rural communities as indicative of the penetration of capitalism even to the more remote corners of the European countryside and the concomitant integration of its residents into broader national states. To these scholars, the existence of rural mutual aid societies and religious associations suggests that peasant-migrants acquired the skills to cope with the complexities of the capitalist system even before they left for North America.[49]

Yet the history of rural organizations in Hungary seems to diverge from this pattern. Village mutual aid and religious associations were by and large not expressions of peasant mutualism but agencies of social control. Set up by government officials, members of the religious and landowning elite, and the village intelligentsia to influence peasants behaviour, they did not provide landless labourers and dwarf holders with the training and self-confidence that would have permitted them independently to found self-help organizations in Canada. Unfortunately, the most important source for studying elite involvement with such associations between the wars – the records of the Ministry of Religion and Education – have been destroyed. Moreover, peasant organizations and peasant politics in this period have attracted little attention from scholars. Enough materials exist, however, to indicate both the motivation behind the creation of village associations and the fact that, even where such bodies existed, they offered very little opportunity to poor peasants and rural labourers to gain organizational experience.

The largest associational networks in rural Hungary – Farmers' Circles (gazda körök), credit associations and the Hangya (Ant) Consumer Cooperatives – were formed by the government and large landowners in the wake of social and economic instability in the countryside. Rapid demographic growth, commercialization of agriculture, and improved transportation led not only to mass emigration but also to internal migration and rural unrest. In the 1890s and again in 1905, agricultural labourers struck for higher wages and in some areas even attempted to distribute property. Although these strikes were short-lived and limited to certain regions, they alarmed large landowners because they coincided with domestic and transatlantic labour migration. These landowners and their political representatives set up rural associations to reduce discontent by stabilizing economic conditions and to foster a spirit of cooperation that would act as an antidote to radical and socialist ideas. They established Farmers' Circles to introduce peasants to modern and efficient methods of cultivation through lectures and libraries, formed credit associations to ease the peasants' chronic indebtedness by providing small loans, and founded consumer cooperatives to eliminate the need for middlemen who were depicted as the chief agents of peasant wretchedness.[50]

To state that the majority of village associations were created by outside forces as agencies of social control is not a priori to rule out the possibility that Hungarian peasants, like their Italian counterparts described by John Briggs, found these bodies so useful that they appropriated them for their own purposes. Studies of pre-First World War rural cooperatives suggest, however, that while members came to include even some dwarf holders and landless labourers, local leadership remained in the hands of the community elite – clerics, teachers, and well-to-do peasants.[51] At the national level, direction stayed in the hands of large landowners and financial leaders. Poorer peasants were frequently so far removed from the administration of cooperatives that they knew nothing of their mutualist intent. Even after the war, rural teachers and clerics were still the chief organizers and leaders of the cooperatives, which served the interests of the middle peasantry.[52]

The reasons for the subordinate role of lower strata of rural society are not hard to find. Limited education left poor agriculturalists incapable of handling the administrative duties, accounting, inventories, and correspondence of the cooperatives.[53] Accordingly, although a large number of voluntary associations existed in the countryside, there is no evidence to suggest that they spread the spirit of mutualism among landless labourers and dwarf holders.

After the First World War, as before it, the major impetus for rural associations came not from the peasantry but from government officials, large landowners, and the churches. Alarmed by the turbulence of 1918 and 1919, the ruling elite, like its counterpart around the turn of the century, perceived such bodies as antidotes to radicalism and sought to expand their numbers.[54]

The Horthy regime set up the Village Federation specifically to spread its own conservative-nationalist ideology in the countryside. Ostensibly an umbrella group representing all of the country's rural associations, the federation was in fact established and controlled by a succession of ministers of agriculture and by the representatives of large landowners and the elite-dominated consumer cooperatives. They planned to rally all existing rural bodies behind Horthy's counter-revolutionary regime and to form new conservative and irredentist groups in villages where none existed.[55] The by-laws of the Village Federation alluded only indirectly to these conservative goals: "to ensure the cooperation of all agriculturalists on *a national basis without regard to class, occupation, or language*" (emphasis added). Representative Sándor Csizmadia, speaking in the Hungarian parliament, was more explicit. The federation, he stated, should prevent "those driven to despair by difficult economic conditions from throwing themselves into the arms of the socialists" and ensure that they "listen to us."[56]

Providing a modicum of well-being for the peasants without significantly altering property and power relations was one way whereby the federation hoped to prevent rural unrest. To this end, it provided farmers' circles with livestock, saplings, and agricultural implements at reduced rates and tried to introduce progressive agricultural practices through lectures, radio programs, publications, and agricultural fairs. Relying on the same tools, it also sought to improve the peasants' standards of hygiene and to discourage drinking. Officials such as the subprefect of Zala county believed that the economic advancement of the peasantry through farmers' circles and producers' cooperatives would ensure their loyalty to the government. In his experience, he explained in a letter to Prime Minister Bethlen, "the patriotism of our agriculturalists is based on the economic questions that interest them the most."[57]

The other major plank in the federation's program was cultural. It sought to awaken nationalism and irredentism among agriculturalists, thereby to obtain their support for the Horthy regime's irredentist, Christian, and conservative ideology. The federation employed a variety of cultural artifacts in its attempt to shape popular attitudes. It encouraged the revival of folk culture and the establishment of amateur drama troupes in Hungarian villages. It also published a periodical, *A falu* (The Village), distributed in 3,500 copies to villages throughout the country, and a series of pamphlets for peasant audiences called The Village Library. It used materials published by the Ministry of Religion and Education and by the Hungarian National Federation – the organization funded by the Horthy regime to promote its ideology at home and abroad.[58]

Revival of folk culture was an important component of the federation's program because, as Mihály Bajtay, one of its officials, explained, "the nation's sons who discard national traditions and customs and who shed traditional costumes, also break away from nationalist feelings and thoughts."[59] Through *A falu* and its other publications, the federation disseminated long-used patterns of embroidery, instructions for wood carving, traditional home design and decoration, and the words and melodies of folksongs, all with the intention of convincing peasants to return to the old ways.[60]

But the federation did not insist on *authentic* folk culture as the leaven for nationalist feelings and thoughts among the peasants. It also favoured urban-born, pseudofolk materials, or fakelore.[61] Folk operettas (népszínművek) are perhaps the best example, with their settings, themes, characters, and music supposedly drawn from rural life and folk ways. Written in the 1870s and 1880s to entertain urban audiences, however, they presented an embellished and sentimentalized view of the village; the arduous lives and dire poverty of the vast majority of Hungary's rural inhabitants hardly provided suitable material for light entertainment.[62]

The pictures of thatched cottages and acacia trees that made such pretty backdrops for the operettas were highly stylized renditions of the often pitiful housing of rural inhabitants. The colourful costumes, especially if made of silk and velvet, far surpassed in luxury even the Sunday best of the wealthiest peasants. Even the music was influenced less by the musical heritage of the peasantry than by "art-music" (népies műzene), a type of urban song and dance music, popular since the mid-nineteenth century, which became known as "Hungarian" (magyaros) music, despite the fact that it derived from European melodies.[63] The idyllic ambience that the operettas presented was, in any case, incidental to the preoccupations of their central characters. Their concerns could just as easily have been the concerns of urban dwellers in, or outside, Hungary.

Folk operettas and other fakelore were deemed appropriate fare for village audiences precisely because they bore so little resemblance to rural life. They served to obscure the problems that plagued rural society. Artificially revived folklore would also give an unrealistically healthy glow to the ailing village by creating the illusion that it was home to a vital peasant culture. The flowering of "genuine Hungarian culture" would serve, Horthyist propagandists hoped, to discredit as alien all modern, cosmopolitan values and ideologies antithetical to the regime's conservative orientation. These ranged from the spread of popular music and "immoral" dances to Hungarian villages to internationalist communism, which Horthyist ideologues frequently identified as a Jewish ideology.[64]

Apart from authentic and synthetic folk materials, irredentist works were the most common cultural artifacts distributed and promoted by the Village Federation. Poems, songs, and plays decrying the injustice of Trianon, bemoaning the loss of territories ceded to the successor states, lovingly describing these areas and demanding their return, were just one facet of the intense, bellicose irredentist campaign. Children in schools and adults in public meetings of all kinds daily recited the "Magyar Creed":

I believe in one God,
I believe in one Fatherland,
I believe in one divine eternal Truth,
I believe in the resurrection of Hungary, Amen.

Everywhere, in newspapers, books, and on wall posters, citizens could read the motto of defiance: "No! No! Never!" and see the map of truncated Hungary, with broken off Slovakia, Transylvania, and Vojvodina.[65]

Spring Will Come Again, the play performed at the Hungarian Self-Culture Society in Welland, Ontario, in 1930, and described at the beginning of this study, was typical of the irredentist publications aimed at the village. The Village Federation's officials considered amateur drama troupes especially effective for conveying Horthyist ideology to the peasantry. *A falu,* the federation's periodical, observed: "There are scarcely any more praiseworthy combatants in our homeland for the awakening of national self-awareness, for education through noble entertainment than the small village amateur drama troupes. Since Trianon, no one has outdone village amateur drama troupes in spreading Christian nationalist ideology, awakening of morally noble and artistically beautiful feelings, and implanting these in the soul of the nation...."[66] Works intended specifically for such troupes were written in simple language and could be produced easily and cheaply. Literary merit and educational value were far less important than their ideological message:

It is possible that the plays that appear on this list cannot in all cases stand up to strict dramatic criticism just as amateur dramatic performances and amateur performers do not meet professional dramatic standards. But this is as it should be. We are not speaking of the theatre and theatre arts here, but rather of spiritual cooperation, embracing ideas, the melting together of village society, cooperation. In amateur performances, religious, moral, patriotic, irredentist, social ideals and all other universal human ideals appear clearly and bravely – albeit at times naively and awkwardly – and they are presented in an honest and selfless way. Only those who know amateur drama performances can appreciate that great spiritual value that is generated by them. Most of the short plays are like wild flowers. They live under the open sky, unassuming, but their scent is sweet, they are beautiful and hardy. The village adopts them as its own, because they serve the festive mood of the people, its strength and freshness.

So explained the introduction to a list of plays recommended for rural performances by the Ministry of Religion and Education.[67] The purpose of government officials and of the Village Federation was clearly not education but indoctrination.

But the federation failed in its effort to integrate the peasantry into Hungary's official culture. Neither formation of rural associations nor dissemination of cultural artifacts accomplished the federation's intended aim. Many agriculturalists joined it only because membership was a prerequisite for acquiring livestock, seeds, and saplings at a reduced rate.[68] In any event, only better-off peasants could even think of benefiting from these economic programs. Cultural programs, which did not offer material rewards, were even less successful. Only 31 drama troupes and a few choirs and orchestras were formed under the federation's aegis.[69]

Ironically, the state-initiated associational network that was most successful in penetrating rural Hungary and in reaching even the lower strata of the peasantry was not established specifically for rural areas. The levente was a paramilitary youth organization founded in the 1920s as a partial substitute for conscription, which had been prohibited by Trianon. It had branches in both rural and urban Hungary. According to reports about 44 villages in Abaúj, Borsod, and Zemplén counties compiled in the 1930s and 1940s by students at the Sárospatak Theological College of the Hungarian Reformed Church, for example, 12 had active levente groups. While their activities were oriented towards physical education, they were also used to transmit the government's ideology to young people in city and country alike. They made an especially great impact on village youths, however, precisely because there were so few cultural and social associations in many villages. Young men there enjoyed the opportunity to demonstrate their athletic skills and strength, and once they accepted the levente the cultural activities of the village also frequently came to be centred in them.[70]

Under the influence of Timothy Smith, historians sometimes identify lay participation in church administration and in religious organizations, along with rural voluntary associations, as an area in which prospective peasant-emigrants gained experience that permitted them to establish similar bodies in North America at their own initiative.[71]

While Hungarian rural labourers and dwarf holders were no less devout than other peasants in eastern and southern Europe, they did not, however, help administer church affairs, which was a status symbol monopolized by well-to-do peasants. The history of the council of the Reformed church in the village of Átány, Heves county, illustrates why. In the early 1930s, the church was suffering from a large deficit. Blaming the deficit on the rich peasants who controlled the church council, landless labourers from the village, who worked in town for part of each year, attempted to take over. They managed to get elected to the council, but they remained in office for one term only; they quickly realized that they did not know how to administer complicated church affairs.[72]

Lay associations and devotional societies formed by clerics also did little to promote the self-reliance and independence of poorer agriculturalists. Only in the 1930s (that is, after departure of most migrants to Canada) did reform-minded clerics attempt to use such bodies to bring about fundamental social change. Until then, ecclesiastical authorities set up their own associations in Hungarian villages and encouraged clerics and teachers to become involved in agricultural cooperatives and farmers' circles, with a conservative intent. They wanted not only to smooth the process of modernization in agriculture but also to safeguard the peasantry from what they viewed as pernicious ideological influences. Involvement in village associations, wrote the official organ of the Reformed church in 1909, "is the only way to prevent the intrusion of unpatriotic, irresponsible elements into the ranks of the rural population. This is the only way to prevent unscrupulous demagogues from becoming leaders among the rural people and infecting their souls with false, internationalist doctrines."[73] Roman Catholic officials encouraged the creation of Christian consumers' cooperatives and other rural associations for the same reasons.[74] As Lajos Fekete, a Roman Catholic adviser to the Ministry of Religion and Education, explained in 1930, peasant involvement with informal education such as amateur drama could not only prevent secularization in villages but also protect inhabitants from the danger represented by the "ominous clouds of communism" from the East.[75]

Churches were more successful than the state in creating and maintaining rural associations. Devotional societies proliferated in areas where few voluntary associations existed: the number of Protestant groups was notable in northeastern Hungary and devotional societies were frequently the only formal organizations in the predominantly Roman Catholic villages of Vas and Zala counties. Activities were sometimes limited to Bible-reading and prayer but often extended to reading aloud, listening to the radio, embroidery for girls, and amateur dramatic performances. Some devotional societies also subscribed to religious periodicals and had small libraries; whether Roman Catholic or Protestant, however, they were paternalistic and run by clergy and teachers. Because even the most committed among the leaders had many other duties, cultural programs were of a modest scale. In many villages, for example, amateur drama troupes performed only one play a year.[76]

The only type of rural association that did not originate outside the village was the reading circle. This was a cultural rather than an economic organization, modelled after the kaszinó – a type of group formed several decades earlier by wealthy farmers and by Hungary's rural intelligentsia. As their name suggests, the circles maintained lending libraries for their members. They also served as social centres. In the halls that they rented or owned, members gathered to chat, read newspapers, and play billiards or cards, more often than not while having a drink or two, for many circles served alcoholic beverages. They also held regular dances and banquets and frequently provided amateur theatricals. Revenue from the sale of alcohol and from social functions, as well as income from membership fees, paid for maintenance of club buildings and for acquisition of library books and periodicals.[77]

But reading circles were not evenly distributed through the countryside, and their members did not always include all strata of rural society. They were most popular in the large agrotowns of the Hungarian plain, especially in the three counties of "Stormy Corner" – Békés, Csanád, and Csongrád. The social structure of this region set it apart from the rest of rural Hungary. Artisans were concentrated here in much greater numbers than in smaller villages in other regions. Labourers in these parts, moreover, differed from agricultural labourers elsewhere. They were in fact "navvies," who found employment on large construction projects throughout the country, where they frequently came into contact with industrial workers. Artisans and navvies formed their own reading circles, which were frequently socialist in orientation. In the interwar years, when large-scale road, sewer, and railway construction had come to a halt, and many navvies rejoined the ranks of agriculturalists, these associations weakened considerably. In any event, few inhabitants of this region's agrotowns made their way to Canada after the First World War.[78]

Smaller villages of northeastern Hungary and of the hilly western counties, which would supply a large portion of Hungarian immigrants to Canada between the two world wars, were often too poor to have reading circles. They did not have enough middle-class residents, artisans, or well-to-do peasants to support such groups, while the dwarf holders and landless labourers who comprised the bulk of their population could afford neither to rent or buy halls to house such circles nor to pay for the heat and light that would have been required to make them functional when peasants have some leisure – in winter and evenings.[79] According to the reports by the Sárospatak students, a circle was set up in only one of the 44 villages surveyed. Significantly, it was in Mezőkeresztes, a large, socially diverse village of 5,000.[80]

Between the wars then, most members of the lowest strata of rural society were unfamiliar with associational life. A survey conducted in 1921, only two years before the beginning of migration to Canada, revealed that while every second village in Hungary had a voluntary association, many of these groups existed only on paper. Notaries and teachers dutifully recorded the existence of all of those that had ever operated in their villages, even if they no longer had halls and their libraries were locked away. This was still the case in 1937, which witnessed the next major survey of rural associations. Only about three hundred new bodies had been created since 1921, and, according to a contemporary observer of rural society, most of them were founded by the local intelligentsia and failed to take root.[81]

PEASANT POLITICS

If the exclusion or subordination of landless labourers and dwarf holders from or in rural associations and church councils was largely the unintended outcome of their poverty and low level of education, their exclusion from politics was in no small part the result of government policy. At the village level, landless labourers had been denied the right to serve on local councils even before the First World War. During the Horthy regime, however, more prosperous peasants also lost their voice in local affairs. Under the guise of attempting to curtail inflation, county officials usurped village councils' right to impose certain taxes. The growing complexity of government regulations, moreover, permitted village notaries, who were appointed, not elected, to appropriate more and more control over local affairs. A great increase in the number and powers of the gendarmerie – Hungary's notorious rural police force – accompanied this reduction in peasant participation in local government.[82]

The denial of access to power to the lowest strata of rural society was even more apparent in national politics. In the Hungarian elections of 1920, the Smallholders party, representing property-owning, middle peasants but intent on improving the situation of the lowest strata of rural society as well, received considerable support. This was because the victorious allied powers had insisted on democratic elections, and Hungarian politicians, hoping to get a favourable peace settlement, acquiesced by broadening the franchise and introducing secret balloting even in the countryside. Precisely because the reforms that the Smallholders' party proposed threatened the established order, however, Hungary's prime minister, Count István Bethlen, who presented himself as a great advocate for the peasantry, actually did everything in his power to weaken its party. Along with twenty of his supporters, Bethlen joined the Smallholders in order to dilute their autonomous political strength. The reorganized party was tellingly renamed the Christian, Agriculturalist, Smallholder and Bourgeois party. Bethlen was now in a position to force the leader of the Smallholders, István Nagyatádi Szabó, to accept the ineffectual land reform legislation described above.

To prevent any shifts in the distribution of power that might lead to more radical land reform, Bethlen also narrowed the franchise. In 1920, all literate men and women over the age of 24 who met minimal citizenship and residency requirements had been enfranchised. From 1922, women voters were required to have completed six grades of school and men four. Bethlen thus disenfranchised a large proportion of rural society, since only one in six peasant children between the ages of six and eleven attended school on a regular basis. He also reintroduced open balloting in the countryside, thereby allowing local officials to control the outcome of elections. Small wonder then that peasants were by and large passive or mistrustful towards politics during the interwar years.[83]

Did any of them protest against their disenfranchisement? Did the radicalism of those who joined the proletarian camp in Canada have antecedents in Hungary? The turbulent years of 1918–19 certainly allowed ample opportunity for protest to all strata of society. Unfortunately, however, because the communist regime of post–Second World War Hungary adopted this revolutionary period as its precursor and model, pointing to it as evidence that radicalism had deep roots in the nation's past, there are almost no reliable histories of this period. The behaviour of ordinary citizens, especially peasants, is deliberately neglected or distorted in "authorized" accounts because the 1919 commune was not a broadly based, popular revolution.

The one detailed local study of the immediate postwar period, Ignác Romsics's *A Duna-Tisza köze hatalmi politikai viszonyai, 1918–19-ben* (Political and Power Relations in the Region between the Duna and the

Tisza in 1918–19), published in 1982, suggests that radical ideologies did not enjoy broad support among peasants.[84] Although few peasants migrated from this area to Canada, his conclusions are nevertheless useful for our purposes. If in this region, which was relatively well integrated into political life by virtue of its proximity to the capital, the lower strata of rural society were often unfamiliar with radicalism, then poorer peasants in the peripheral regions that supplied the bulk of emigrants to Canada must have been doubly so. Admittedly, there were widespread rural protests over food shortages throughout Hungary at the end of the war. These protests, however, were generally devoid of political content.[85] Agricultural labourers and dwarf holders in small villages were not well informed about developments in the capital. Few of them voted in the April 1919 elections for local councils, and when they did, they sometimes re-elected the very same notables who controlled village councils before the First World War. Clearly, these rural electors did not plan radically to redistribute political power through the ballot.[86]

This did not mean that landless labourers and dwarf holders were necessarily hostile to the commune from the beginning. Some hoped that it would distribute land from confiscated large estates among them. But the actions of the new government quickly disabused them of their hopes. It decided to nationalize large estates, and, adding insult to injury, it retained the traditional overseers to run them. Labourers who were able to obtain work on these estates – for unemployment was high – received low wages and put in long hours. To their great misfortune, moreover, even these low wages soon became worthless because of a loss of confidence in the commune's currency. Hostility to the commune grew when its soldiers, unable to purchase grain and animals because of the peasants' mistrust of official currency, forcibly requisitioned these, without regard to the social or economic standing of their owners. The commune's anti-clericalism also decreased its appeal for the peasantry. Finally, when the beleaguered commune government announced that flour would be rationed and that conscription would take effect precisely at harvest time, it lost its last vestiges of support in the countryside. Many peasants withdrew into political passivity; others took an active part in the counterrevolution.

Accordingly, only a handful of the peasants arriving in Canada in the 1920s and 1930s had joined their village directories and the red guard because they believed that the commune represented their interests. Moreover, those few peasant radicals who did migrate to Canada were followers rather than leaders. The brevity of the commune's existence and the repressive climate of Horthy's counterrevolutionary regime prevented even the most talented among them from becoming well versed in socialist theory and practice. Consequently, they lacked the experience necessary to establish organizations in Canada on their own initiative.

EMIGRANT LEADERS

Not all Hungarians who emigrated to Canada between the wars were agriculturalists. A small minority, less than 3 per cent according to Hungarian statistics, were members of the liberal professions, independent merchants, independent craftsmen, and industrial workers.[87] Their numbers were probably somewhat greater than such figures would suggest; as mentioned, a few urban men and women succeeded in being classified as agriculturalists to meet Canadian immigration requirements. I group these people together as the immigrants' "elite" because they were all better educated and more fully integrated into national life than the rank and file. Consequently, the members of the group's elite came to play a key role among Hungarians in Canada. To understand their behaviour in Canada, it is important to consider their background and reasons for emigration.

Employment opportunities for members of the Hungarian intelligentsia – civil servants and teachers, in particular – were fewer between the world wars than during the period of mass emigration. Because a career in the civil service was commonly thought to be more "gentlemanly" than involvement in trade, Hungary had a surplus of civil servants even before the First World War.[88] After 1918, however, competition for such jobs intensified considerably, not only because of cutbacks in the civil service but also because a reported 44,253 public employees – judges, prosecutors, court clerks, village notaries, police officers, gendarmes, teachers, and professors – who lost their jobs when Hungarian rule ended in Slovakia, Transylvania, and northern Yugoslavia, now sought employment in post-Trianon Hungary.[89] The ranks of Hungarians who emigrated to Canada between 1923 and 1939 were thus augmented by educated men and women of middle-class background who were unable to find jobs in Hungary; this category included both residents of Trianon Hungary and refugees from the successor states.

According to Hungarian statistics, members of the liberal professions comprised a tiny 0.3 per cent of emigrants. As mentioned, these figures are not entirely reliable. John Kosa's estimate that 2,000, or nearly 7 per cent, of all Hungarian immigrants to Canada between the wars were of middle- or upper-class background seems unduly high.[90]

Both immigrants from this category who became prominent among their brethren in Canada, and Hungarian government officials, repeatedly complained about the paucity of educated men and women among Hungarians in Canada.[91]

During the interwar years, artisans also faced great difficulties both in Hungary and in the successor states. While prior to the First World War, the sole threat to their livelihood came from industry, after the war, when Hungary experienced mass unemployment in industry for the first time, artisans faced additional competition from industrial workers who turned back to independent artisanal production.[92] The period saw the mushrooming of tiny workshops and retail stores. Since demand for their services and goods did not rise, and since they suffered under heavy taxation, many small businesses failed.[93] Consequently, both independent urban craftsmen and small merchants joined the ranks of migrants to Canada.[94]

As Béla Vágó, who immigrated to Canada in 1928, discovered, in these hard times apprenticeship could no longer bring social improvement for rural children trying to get ahead by breaking all ties to the land. He left his village around 1925 to apprentice as a tailor in the town of Szendrő, Borsod county. He was, however, unable to find long-term employment in Hungary, despite the fact that he travelled not only to nearby Miskolc, but even to Budapest to look for work.[95] Even established artisans such as Sándor Birinyi from Czigánd came to see transatlantic migration as a way to improve their situation at home. He hoped to enlarge his cartwright's shop in the village with money earned in Canada.[96]

Hard economic times also convinced artisans from the successor states to migrate to Canada. When asked why he travelled to Canada, Ernő B., from Mezőváros, Székelyudvarhely county, Transylvania, first replied that he did not want to be drafted into the Romanian army. Upon further reflection, however, he added that his poverty while he apprenticed as a harness maker, and his lack of capital to set himself up as an independent craftsman when he completed his apprenticeship, also shaped his decision.[97]

Because of the political turbulence of 1918–19 and the Horthy regime's anti-left and anti-union policies throughout the next two decades, political exiles joined the ranks of those who left Hungary during those years. Hungary's human and material losses in the war had been so immense as to leave virtually no family untouched: 530,965 Hungarians were killed or died, 1,492,000 wounded, and 833,570 captured and imprisoned by enemy forces.[98] Both soldiers and the civilian population, moreover, were exposed to material hardship, because of shortages of food, fuel, and clothing. As mentioned above, Hungary, without being allowed any time to recover from the trauma of war, was subjected to occupation and pillaging by foreign troops and to two years of domestic unrest. The rapid changes in government during 1918 and 1919 were accompanied by violence and bloodshed. Even once Horthy seemed to be firmly in control, moreover, the ascendancy of peace in the Danubian basin could hardly have appeared certain to contemporaries, amid the barrage of bellicose, irredentist propaganda put out by Budapest.

The memoirs of István Markos, who migrated to Canada from Transylvania in 1928, bear witness to the relationship between this ambience and emigration: "Another question kept occurring to me; did not leave me in peace ... while the Hungarian government kept up an unceasing campaign against Romania along the lines of 'everything back,' the Romanian bourgeoisie also kept up its invectives against the Soviet Union. One world conflagration was hardly over; the wounds had not yet healed, the tears had not yet dried, the pain had not yet ceased. Could they be preparing another war? I began to think of leaving the country."[99]

The ranks of political exiles included radicals as well. Most of the commune's leaders managed to escape before the consolidation of Horthy's counterrevolution. They sought refuge in Austria, Czechoslovakia, France, Germany, the Soviet Union, and the United States. The men and women who went to Canada because of their political convictions and activities at home were from the lower ranks of the revolution, those who participated as red guards, or as representatives on village and workers' councils, and who faced severe retribution from the counterrevolutionary forces. Many radicals were killed, others were tortured and imprisoned, and still others lost their jobs and were subjected to continual harassment by local authorities. The Hungarian government's policies made life at home intolerable not only for former supporters of the commune, but also for those who took part in social and political protest after the fall of the commune.[100]

Sándor Greczula, a shoemaker, was among the more experienced radical activists to immigrate to Canada at this time. He became a Bolshevik when he was a prisoner of war in Russia. When he returned to Hungary, Greczula immediately tried to build up opposition to the counterrevolution by organizing fellow workers. Like many communists, he responded to the ban against the Communist party by operating within the Social Democratic party. Although that body was recognized by the Horthy regime, government officials tried to curtail labour activism within it. A court order forbidding Greczula from seeking employment in cities cut short his efforts to organize leather workers in Debrecen. For a few years he continued his organizing activities in the smaller towns of Matészalka and Nyirbátor. In 1928, however, he could no longer tolerate harassment, and he decided to go to Canada. There he would become president of the communist-led Workers' Club in Montreal.[101]

Most radical immigrants, however, were less experienced and less familiar with communist ideology than Greczula. Some of them were the children of agriculturalists who were introduced to radicalism when they left their villages to work in mines or on the railway. József Gaál, for example, the son of landless labourers from Fűzesabony, Heves county, first encountered labour activism as a young boy, when he worked on the railway during the First World War. He started his career with the railway by looking after the stationmaster's pigs but moved up rapidly to the position of railway utility man. He found his wages and working conditions unsatisfactory even in this new position, however, and quite willingly listened to union activists who sought to mobilize railway employees in support of a program of radical social change. Their use of metaphors drawn from the rural world captured Gaál's imagination. Seventy years after the first radical meeting he attended, he still recalled that the union organizers compared workers to oxen, and they argued that if oxen had brains they would not allow a twelve-year-old boy to lead them. Gaál found these arguments sufficiently convincing that he distributed leaflets on behalf of the radicals and began to read radical newspapers. In August 1919, when the commune was defeated, however, Gaál buried his political leaflets, and his radical activism in Hungary came to an end. Only in Canada did participation in the activities of communist-led Hungarian-Canadian organizations, first in Hamilton and later in Montreal, lead him to embrace communist ideology.

Because many of the participants in 1919 came from the most impoverished sectors of society, it is sometimes difficult, if not impossible, to separate their political and their economic motives for emigration. Lajos Koszta, a labourer from the village of Matyus, in Szabolcs county, for example, was certainly an undesirable element by the standards of the Horthy regime. Bitterness at the conduct of the war and the injustices of the prewar regime led him to take part in the commune. He continued clandestine political activity even after the commune's defeat – for instance, by helping to distribute outlawed newspapers published by Hungarian Communists in Czechoslovakia. When describing his decision to emigrate, however, he invoked both political and economic reasons. "I decided to emigrate," he wrote in his memoirs, "because I could not guarantee my family's bread anywhere, and, of course, the gendarmerie was forever on my heels."[102]

József Jenei's motives for emigrating were similar. The son of landless labourers, he took part in the commune as a red guard. Following a brief period of imprisonment at the end of the commune, he was allowed to return to his village. He was, however, forbidden to speak to fellow villagers in the street. He was also prevented from getting work in the community and its surroundings. This treatment drove Jenei to abandon the area and to seek employment in Budapest, but the difficulties of living as a casual labourer in the capital eventually led him to Canada, where he was to continue his involvement with the left.[103]

In contrast to rural labourers and poor peasants, urban craftsmen and skilled workers from Hungary could draw on rich associational traditions. Artisanal guilds in Hungary, as elsewhere in Europe, dated back to the Middle Ages. These bodies not only regulated training, and the quality and prices of artisanal work, but also catered to the social and cultural needs of their members. Even before industrialization, urban workers who did not belong to guilds expressed occupational solidarity by forming religious confraternities. They participated in religious processions and attended funerals as a group. After craft guilds were disbanded in 1872, independent craftsmen voluntarily re-established trade associations that took over many of the functions of guilds. During the same period, skilled workers set up a wide variety of voluntary associations: mutual aid and self-improvement societies, choirs, sports associations, library clubs, and trade unions. While some of these groups restricted their activities to improving the moral and material well-being of their members, others became engaged in politics. Many unions were formally allied to the Social Democratic party.

Middle-class immigrants also had ample opportunity to become familiar with associational traditions. In rural areas, they belonged to the kaszinó. In towns and cities, they formed a wide array of social clubs and cultural, political, and philanthropic organizations. Such middle-class associations could not simply be replicated in Canada, however, given the social structure of the immigrant group. Immigrant associations could survive only if they served the needs of former agriculturalists. Consequently, as we see below, the role of the elite in founding immigrant associations in Canada resembled that of the village intelligentsia in establishing rural organizations in Hungary.

While in Hungary artisans, skilled urban workers, and members of the middle class would not generally have belonged to the same associations as peasants, they arrived in Canada with certain ideas about the peasantry that shaped the interaction of the two groups. Middle-class Hungarians and artisans were receptive to the romanticized view of peasant society promoted by the Horthy regime. In fact, the irredentist, Christian-nationalist propaganda campaign, of which fakelore formed such an essential component, was far more successful among members of the lower middle class than among poor agriculturalists.

Urban Hungarians were responsive to fakelore partly because Hungary, indeed all of central and eastern Europe, has a long tradition of expressing cultural regeneration by turning to folk culture.[104] The romantic nationalism of the late eighteenth and early nineteenth centuries maintained that the unique spirit of every nation resided in the Volk. In Hungary, the acquisition of home rule within the Hapsburg Monarchy in 1867 led to an intensification of this type of nationalism. It was no accident, therefore, that folk operettas became popular among urban audiences in the 1870s and 1880s. During the same period, artisans were also susceptible to peasant romanticism. Harvest balls, inspired by rural celebrations, became widespread among them.[105] Indicative of the importance of fakelore was the inclusion of village replicas, complete with inhabitants in folk costumes supposedly carrying out their daily activities, among the exhibits of the World's Fair held in Budapest in 1896 to mark Hungary's millennium.[106]

Following the dislocation of war and revolution and the blow that Trianon dealt to national pride, not only politicians but a large number of educated people turned to the peasantry and to folklore with renewed interest, in search of symbols and inspiration for healing their wounded national self-esteem. They sought proof of the uniqueness, greatness, and indestructibility of the Magyars in folk culture.[107] Many of them, however, knew only urban-born, romanticized pseudo-folklore. That is why *Süt a Nap* (The Sun Is Shining), a modernized folk operetta by Lajos Zilahy, enjoyed tremendous successes in 1924 in Budapest and provincial towns.[108]

Perhaps the best illustration of the appeal of fakelore in the city was the "pearly bouquet" (gyöngyösbokréta) movement, comprised of peasant dance troupes. Every August between 1931 and 1940, members of these groups donned colourful peasant costumes and travelled to Budapest to demonstrate the beauties of folk culture to residents of the capital and to tourists. On 20 August, the feast of St Stephen, Hungary's patron saint, they participated in a religious procession accompanying his mummified right hand. And for several evenings before and after that day they also appeared on stage, where they performed not only folksongs and dances but also folk customs and rituals that purportedly accompanied various types of work and seasonal celebrations in Hungarian villages.[109]

These customs and rituals were often not part of living culture in Hungarian villages. The creation and preparation of pearly bouquets for the annual performance in the capital were generally the work of village notaries, clerics, and teachers. In the interest of enriching the fare of their troupes, these members of the rural intelligentsia sometimes revived obsolete folk customs. Peasants in fact participated less out of pride in or love for their own traditions than because they not only got a chance to visit Budapest but also received a daily honorarium worth more than their wages for a hard day's labour in their village.

While the movement's founders do not appear to have been influenced by political objectives, politicians and government officials were quick to realize that the pearly bouquets could further their objectives; by its very nature, the movement brought folklore – authentic and synthetic – to life in the countryside. They also recognized that the pearly bouquets could serve their purposes beyond the village, in Hungarian cities and even abroad. By bringing folklore or fakelore to the city, they created the illusion of reducing the split between urban and rural society. Budapest residents – who, according to contemporary accounts, were deeply moved by the performances of the peasant troupes – and even tourists formed an idyllic view of rural life. The existence of such a vibrant peasant culture suggested contentment and leisure in rural Hungary. It helped to obscure the need for social and economic reform. Ernő Csikvándy, a member of parliament, believed that the bouquets enjoyed recognition throughout Europe and could therefore do a great service for the interests of Hungary abroad as well.[110] The government expressed its approval by decreeing that folk troupes, which required state approval, could operate only on the basis of the bouquet movement's principles and plans. By adopting the cause of these nominally "folk" troupes, moreover, the regime would demonstrate its "folk" orientation.

The susceptibility to fakelore of groups whose members would constitute the immigrant elite in Canada helps to explain why these immigrants were so willing to employ Hungarian government propaganda materials in Canada to transmit Horthyist ideology to the rank and file. The immigrant experience, however, was indispensable for the politicization of peasants newly arrived in Canada. It led to collaboration between the elite and the rank and file, and it made peasant immigrants receptive to elite ideologies.

2 Canada: Image and Reality

From emigration	Save us O Lord!
From meatless cabbage	Save us O Lord!
From a sixteen-hour work-day	Save us O Lord!
From hauling heavy loads on our backs	Save us O Lord!
From the tax-collector	Save us O Lord!
From the royal ruler	Save us O Lord!
From the exciseman and the gendarme	Save us O Lord![1]

This version of the "Litany of Widows and Orphans" originated in northeastern Hungary, an area that experienced serious labour unrest at the turn of the century, when rural workers rebelled against starvation wages, heavy taxation, dismal housing, and harsh treatment by overseers. During the same period, thousands of agriculturalists from this region migrated to the New World. Yet despite living and working conditions so unacceptable that they drove workers to organize protest and to seek employment across the Atlantic, the prospect of emigration was evidently far from welcome.

So accustomed are we to hearing about the exaggerated hopes that drew the people of southern and eastern Europe to North America that the inclusion of emigration among the worst afflictions of the rural labourer's life is at first startling. We are more familiar with descriptions of "America" as the "land of promise" or the "golden land," where "the streets are paved with gold" and the "fences made of sausages."

Abundant evidence of transatlantic opportunities was certainly available to prospective emigrants: idealized pictures of the New

World painted in letters from emigrants and in accounts by remigrants; photographs of co-villagers across the Atlantic, dressed in
suits, "like the priest back home at Easter"; remittances; and the houses
constructed and lands purchased with money earned across the
ocean.

Counter-examples, however, were just as plentiful. Nearly half of
those who migrated to the United States from Szabolcs county around
the turn of the century, for example, returned home empty-handed.
Each village in the regions of emigration also harboured the victims of
transatlantic migration: individuals who went back to their village after
being injured overseas and the broken families of men who deserted
their wives and children by going to North America or of women who
committed adultery while their husbands were away. Nor were those
who stayed in the New World necessarily successful. Some died or were
maimed in industrial accidents; hardship and loneliness led others to
drink or to gambling, and they ended their days defeated and demor-
alized in a distant land. Remigrants brought home sad tales of their
fate.[2]

The decision of millions of Europeans to migrate helps to explain
why we are so conscious of the positive images that lured prospective
emigrants, while we pay scant attention to the negative information
that was equally accessible. Yet as this chapter demonstrates, concen-
trating exclusively on the positive image of "America" that pervaded
the European countryside seriously limits our ability to comprehend
the migrants. By disregarding their awareness of the risks and dangers inherent in transatlantic migration, we overlook the ambition,
spirit of enterprise, and self-reliance that fed the decision to migrate.
These people were willing to face the risks of personal failure, family
breakdown, and indebtedness because – in contrast to their own
society – first the United States and then Canada held the promise of
improving their lot. Such initiative was taken even by people who came
from the lowest strata of rural society and consequently did not
possess the education and experience with voluntary associations that
students of migration have used as gauges of peasant initiative and
resourcefulness. It is also essential to understanding their behaviour
in North America to recognize that for many agriculturalists migration across the Atlantic was the sole avenue for ameliorating their
lives.

This chapter juxtaposes the image that inspired migration to Canada
and the reality that the immigrants encountered in the 1920s and
1930s, in an attempt to explain what led immigrants to create their
own communities and to rely almost exclusively on institutions and
ideologies within them.

IMAGE

Few Illusions

Since most immigrants crossed the Atlantic in search of employment, it is not surprising that they were especially intent on gathering information about work in North America. Interviews with men and women from rural Hungary reveal that they had no illusions about "easy money." Whether out of bitterness or out of bravado, most remigrants emphasized how difficult and dangerous was the work performed by Hungarians in the United States. That is how József Fejes, born between the wars in the village of Bodony, Heves county, gathered detailed information about the conditions of industrial employment in the United States without ever having visited it. As a child, on winter evenings, József listened while his father and others reminisced about their experiences in the New World. He got the impression that Hungarians "worked the hardest everywhere … No one could stand it … except the Hungarians. Because they did not have any protective clothing, no asbestos or anything like that." His father's clothes "burned off him" when he worked by the "big furnace." In Bodony and elsewhere in Hungary, the bodies of men maimed by industrial accidents in North America provided incontestable evidence of the veracity of stories about the dangers of industrial work there.[3]

We do not need to rely on a handful of oral testimonies, however, to show that such negative information penetrated the popular imagination. The themes of the crushing burden of work, low wages, and industrial accidents appear in folksongs about North America from virtually every region of Hungary. The songs depict the factories in which immigrants found work as grim places where employees were required to perform heavy duties, for long hours and little pay. In a song from Szatmár county, for example, an emigrant imagines how sad his mother must be, knowing that her beloved son is "languishing" in an American sawmill, while in a song from Veszprém county, a woman imagines her sweetheart working in a "dreadful" American iron foundry from seven in the morning until six at night.[4] Yet another, sung in various parts of Hungary, describes American factories as sapping the life forces of the immigrant and bemoans the low wages that he receives:

Don't be surprised my love, that I have withered;
I have been a grinder for nine years,
I pass the tenth year in the Alber factory,
Grinding iron for the farmers.

The grinder's wages are oh so low,
He sure could use more money for breakfast and dinner;
As soon as I have a little money in my chest,
I too will return to beautiful Hungary.[5]

   Evidence also abounded in Hungarian villages about the tragic consequences that transatlantic migration could have for family life.
Julianna Birinyi, who went to Canada in 1927, lost both her father and
her first husband through migration. She was six months old when her
father departed for the United States, leaving his wife and three youngsters behind. About five years later, when her mother refused to leave
the children with their paternal grandmother in order to join her father, he abandoned the family and remarried. This experience was repeated in Julianna's own life. When she wed, her husband also went to
North America. He wrote and asked her to join him there. But her
mother, by now an elderly woman, begged her not to go. "I want to die
beside you.... I struggled with you until now," she said; "don't leave
me!" Sensitive to the sacrifice that her mother had made, Julianna decided not to go. Soon afterwards, her husband met another woman in
the United States, and they got married. Julianna was left behind in
Páczin with two children. Eventually she remarried, and when her second husband moved to Canada she took no chances. She followed him
to Toronto.[6]
   Even if Mrs Birinyi's experience was not typical, the mere awareness
of such possibilities deepened the anxieties of migrants and their families. In the small village of Hollóháza, Abaúj county, for example, ru-
mours abounded that men were "ruined" in North America, "they
didn't care about their families anymore." That is why Mary Gabura followed her husband to Canada even though he fully intended to return
to Hungary.[7]
   Men were not alone responsible for family breakdown. In the absence of their husbands, some young women in Hungarian villages entered adulterous relationships. They became known as "Canadian wife"
or "American wife."[8] But because such behaviour departed from village
norms, so enormous was the stress felt by such women that some of
them were driven to kill infants conceived after the departure of their
spouses.[9] Though less extreme, the pain in the recollections of cuck-
olded husbands, and the divorces to which adultery by women whose
partners were in North America frequently led, also underscore the dis-
tressing reality of this consequence of transatlantic migration.[10]
   The separation from loved ones and its sometimes tragic results are
by far the most common themes in Hungarian folksongs about emigra-

tion. In a song from Veszprém county, a migrant boarding the ship that will take him to the United States is overwhelmed by sorrow because he will be separated from his wife and homeland for a long time, possibly forever:

When I came to America,
I leaned over the ship's railing
I looked back with tears in my eyes:
My Hungarian homeland, will I see you again?

God be with you beloved wife!
The Lord will help me to return.
Return, return, but I don't know when.
I will be an old man by then![11]

A song from Orosháza, Békés county, conveys the helplessness and frustration that a Hungarian in "America" experiences when he receives a letter from his young bride in Hungary. Mourning his absence, she has been wearing black for three years. She begs him to come home, but he cannot comply:

I would go home, I don't have fifty dollars,
I have nothing to buy the ticket.

Similar sentiments are expressed in a song that Ferenc Magyar, who spent seven years in Canada between the two world wars, sang for me when I visited his village, Ajak, in Szabolcs county:

In northern Canada cold winds blow
My frequent sighs homeward flow
With somnolent eyes I see my beautiful homeland

When I think of you dear little family
I, who can easily tolerate suffering,
When I think of you, my tears flow.[12]

No clear distinction was made in folk tradition between the United States and Canada. Songs about Canada, such as the one sung by Magyar, were simply handed down in the oral tradition of rural Hungary as "Amerikás" songs. In some mournful folksongs originally inspired by experiences in the United States, Canada or Canadian place names were simply substituted for American ones.[13]

Illés Kerekes (right) emigrated to Canada in 1927 from the village of Ajak, Szabolcs county. He returned to Ajak on a visit in 1969.

Illés left behind his wife of six years, Maria, and four children. Only Illés, Jr, who appears here, lived to adulthood. Despite his long absence, Illés wrote to his wife and son every month and sent them as much money as he could.

In 1936, Maria built this house with the money sent by her husband from Canada.

This photograph was the only means young Illés had for introducing his bride to his father.

By the time Illés returned to Hungary, his grandchildren (two appear here adorned with Canadian toques sent by Illés) were adults. Money from him permitted his grandsons to purchase motorcycles and his granddaughter to acquire a fur coat, a washing machine, and a gas stove.

Information and Its Uses

Was information specifically about Canada unavailable to prospective migrants? After all, approximately 13,000 Hungarians migrated to Canada by 1914, when they could have gone instead to the United States. Did their experiences not create a distinctive impression of Canada in Hungary?

Contemporary and historical accounts alike stress that the promise of free land and the prospect of continuing their traditional occupations attracted Hungarians to Canada before the First World War.[14] Indeed, news of 160-acre (64-ha.) homesteads that were still available free of charge to settlers in "America" circulated in the Hungarian countryside, although it could refer only to the Canadian prairie provinces, where most Hungarians arriving in the country up to 1914 actually settled.[15] While some prospective emigrants may have been aware that Canada was distinct from the United States, many knew only that the homesteads were located in "America."

Immigrants to Canada formed a very small portion of the Hungarians who crossed the Atlantic up to 1914. It is therefore not surprising that their experiences should have been overshadowed by those of Hungarian immigrants to the United States. The development of a few successful Hungarian communities in Saskatchewan did not suffice to awaken interest in Canada throughout the Hungarian countryside.[16] Approximately one-quarter of the Hungarians who immigrated to Canada at that time, moreover, did not settle on the land. They found employment in mines in Alberta, British Columbia, and Nova Scotia. In southern Ontario, they worked in construction and manufacturing. Like their compatriots in the United States, they were generally male sojourners who had no intention of remaining. In their view, Canada was probably not much different from the United States. Indeed, some of them moved back and forth between the two countries.[17]

During the interwar years, as the volume of emigration declined, the subject ceased to be a major preoccupation in Hungary. Once Canada emerged as the chief destination, however, conditions there did receive some attention in the press. While Canada was presented as preferable to Latin America – the other main target of transatlantic migration between the world wars – descriptions of conditions were by no means glowing. Hungarian newspapers emphasized that free land was no longer available in Canada and that considerable capital investment was now required by those wishing to farm. They also described the low wages and seasonal employment of agricultural labourers.[18] So negative were such accounts that the Budapest representative of the Canadian Pacific Railway (CPR) described them as "hair raising" when he complained about them to the Hungarian minister of the interior.[19]

It is difficult to say how far such information penetrated into the countryside. Small holders, dwarf holders, and landless labourers, who made up the bulk of emigrants to Canada, did not generally read newspapers. Members of the village intelligentsia – the priest or minister, the notary, the teacher – who did read papers could have conveyed their content to prospective emigrants who frequently sought their advice.[20]

Oral testimony and reports by Hungarian officials suggest that both favourable and unfavourable information about Canada reached even the lowest strata of rural society. Thus, for example, the schemes of sponsored immigration, under which entry into Canada was facilitated by an offer of employment from western farmers, led some prospective migrants to believe that their employment was guaranteed for an indefinite period.[21] Others, such as John Farisz, were assured that work in Canada was plentiful. Unemployed and penniless in 1931, he was to complain to the CPR's Department of Colonization, "it was given to understand to me [sic] that as an ordinary labourer I could earn at least Three Hundred Dollars a year, and that at no time will conditions be such that the above mentioned amount could not be earned."[22]

But many people who planned to go to Canada had been warned by relatives or friends who preceded them that offers in the west were for temporary work. Having discovered that higher wages could be earned in central Canada, these immigrants advised those who followed them to ignore jobs on the prairies, to get off west-bound trains in Montreal or Ontario, and to try their fortune in central Canada. Steven H. recalled that friends had written to him in Czechoslovakia to advise "that if I could, I should sneak off the train in Montreal because if I went west, I would not find work and it would cost money to come back east."[23]

In 1925 and 1926, however, some Hungarian newcomers seemed well pleased with agricultural opportunities in the Canadian west. According to a report on emigration from Heves county, more and more villagers from that county were seeking to go to Canada by 1927, because they saw irrefutable evidence of the success of co-nationals there. The remittances sent by fellow villagers who left only a year or two earlier, and who found employment in western Canada, were sufficiently large not only to repay the money that they had borrowed to finance their journey but also to permit their families to acquire farm machinery, build new homes, and even purchase land.[24]

At the same time, unfavourable reports about Canada also reached the villages of Heves county. A detective commissioned by the Hungarian Ministry of Interior to investigate the causes of rising emigration from this area was informed by the wives of several men who were in Canada that their husbands complained because they were unable to secure employment during winter. These complaints, which undoubtedly reached fellow villagers, did not reduce emigration.[25]

Prospective migrants such as Lőrincz Kovács, a landless labourer from Mátraderecske, Heves county, assimilated information about Canada selectively. When he decided to emigrate in 1928, some of his fellow villagers were already in Canada and were sending money to their relatives at home. But Kovács also heard discouraging reports about prospects in Canada. One of his neighbours, who read newspapers, told him of unemployment. The words of another neighbour, who spent a few months in Canada before the First World War, were also far from reassuring. "There's nothing there," he told Kovács, but "forests, forests and forests and rocks everywhere." "Brother," he cautioned, "after what I saw, I wouldn't go to Canada!" But Kovács did not allow these reports to dissuade him. He wavered only once, after talking to a fellow villager who was deported from Canada for trying, out of desperation, to enter the United States illegally and who reached Mátraderecske when preparations for Kovács's departure were almost complete. In the end, however, Kovács disregarded even the experiences of this man. He decided to focus instead on the example of those villagers who sent money from Canada or even returned with savings. "If he succeeded, perhaps I will succeed too," he reasoned, and he left for Canada. Thinking about his decision half a century later, he added in an apologetic tone, "This little bit of vanity is in everyone, isn't it?"[26]

The experience of András Kocsis, from Makkóshotyka, Zemplén county, offers another illustration of the selective manner in which prospective emigrants assimilated information about Canada. Kocsis became interested in migrating because he could barely support his family on combined earnings from his trade as carpenter and a small piece of land. He walked across the hills of Zemplén to Mikóháza, five villages away, when he heard that a certain Colonel Zágonyi would be speaking there about conditions in Canada.[27]

Zágonyi was a retired army officer who spent 11 months in Canada in 1925, possibly with the intention of settling. However, his experiences convinced him that the country offered little to Hungarian immigrants, and apparently he felt compelled to publicize his views. He wrote a book about the harsh conditions that awaited immigrants. His visit to Mikóháza formed part of a government-sponsored lecture tour in the chief districts of emigration, designed to discourage migration. Not surprisingly, therefore, what he had to say was anything but encouraging. He believed that it was foolish to draw a parallel between conditions that awaited Hungarians in the United States prior to the First World War, and those in Canada in the 1920s. Describing Hungarians in Canada as the "gullible children of our nation on the shores of the Arctic ocean," he stressed that only extreme hardship awaited those who embarked on the journey to this northern land.[28]

When Kocsis realized that Zágonyi's account of conditions was not favourable – he still remembered in 1980 that the retired officer described the low wages and seasonally restricted employment awaiting in Canada – he dismissed the colonel as an agent of a government hostile to emigration and decided not to heed his warning.

Kocsis now preferred to consult "Amerikások" – villagers who had lived and worked in "America" – on his prospects overseas. It was clear from his reminiscences that he looked up to these people. He described them as "experienced men," who knew how to work and how to make money and who dressed in "more intelligent clothes" than their neighbours. The houses that they built and the land that they purchased with money earned across the ocean testified in a concrete form to their success. Descriptions of the New World given by the "Amerikások," more encouraging than Zágonyi's, convinced Kocsis to try his fortune overseas. But although he was inspired by these successful migrants, he was also aware that for other villagers the excursion had ended in failure; some could not even pay for the return trip home. Knowledge of their fate did no more to weaken his resolve to seek employment in Canada than Zágonyi's lecture. He ascribed their failure to laziness, and, confident in his own willingness and ability to work hard, he was certain that such an unhappy outcome could not befall him.[29]

Although peasants intent on migrating in search of labour, such as András Kocsis and Lőrincz Kovács, may have mistrusted newspaper accounts or descriptions by their social superiors of hardships in North America, many, if not most of them must nevertheless have been fully aware of the inherent risks. Yet they repressed or minimized evidence of hardship from their compatriots and of the suffering of those left behind, embracing instead a positive view of "America." When US legislation closed this avenue to them, they simply broadened their image of "America" to encompass Canada and even Argentina, the remaining transatlantic destinations open to them. They clung to this view in order to overcome the fears and tensions inherent in the decision to migrate along the only avenue of social mobility available to most of Hungary's rural population. Their own society denied them the attainment of a dignified existence as a reward for hard labour.[30] Altogether, 33,885 Hungarians emigrated to Canada during the interwar era.[31]

REALITY

"Forced to Become Vagabonds"

Conditions in interwar Canada were ill-suited to meet the expectations of Hungarian immigrants. Although they arrived eager and able to work hard, even between 1924 and 1929, when employment was plentiful, their efforts to save money were all too frequently thwarted by the seasonal nature of the jobs open to them.

Most Hungarians who eventually settled in Ontario and Quebec in the 1920s and 1930s originally headed to the prairie provinces when they arrived in Canada. This initial destination was dictated by the Railway Agreement that governed migration from central and eastern Europe between 1926 and 1930. Under the agreement, the CPR and the Canadian National Railways (CNR) brought agriculturalists from Austria, Czechoslovakia, Estonia, Germany, Hungary, Latvia, Lithuania, Poland, Romania, Russia, and Yugoslavia – all so-called non-preferred countries – ostensibly to settle the prairie west. These agricultural immigrants were divided into three categories: farmers with capital, agricultural labourers, and domestic servants. The vast majority of Magyars from Hungary and from the successor states fell into the second category.[32]

Although the largest number of Hungarian immigrants arrived in Canada in April and May, many of them, as officials of the railway companies knew very well, would not be able to find work in agriculture until harvest in September. Farmers required fewer workers during June, July, and August and fewer still after the harvest. Few of them kept hired hands during winter. According to one estimate, only 15 per cent of the farmers who employed Hungarian labourers during the agricultural season required their services in winter.[33] Even if immigrants managed to find low-season work, however, they were often unwilling to stay on farms because the wages offered in June, July, August, and during winter were low.[34] Weighed down by debts incurred to pay for the journey to Canada, and anxious to be reunited with their families as quickly as possible, most immigrants felt compelled to seek higher wages outside agriculture.[35]

While some of them arrived thinking that they were guaranteed employment in western Canada, others had been warned by friends and relatives not to go west because of the seasonality of agrarian work. Apparently aware of such warnings, the railway companies took precautions to ensure that the newcomers reached the west. Hungarians who arrived in Canada in the 1920s recalled being told that they were legally bound to go west. Some of them were even threatened with deportation should they attempt to leave the train before it reached the prairie provinces. Just in case such warnings proved an insufficient deterrent, however, when immigrant trains pulled into eastern Canadian stations for servicing, not only were passengers warned not to get off but car doors were frequently locked.[36] All "non-preferred" immigrants, moreover, had to deposit twenty-five dollars with company officials, and this money – a substantial sum for most Hungarian immigrants – was returned only upon arrival on the prairies.[37] Not surprisingly, therefore, only a few of them left westbound trains in central Canada. Some crawled out of toilet windows, while others, who managed to walk off the trains, abandoned part of their luggage to create the impression that they would be returning.

The railways were intent on ensuring that the immigrants reached the west for several reasons. First, almost from the Railway Agreement's inception in 1925, the CPR and the CNR were under considerable pressure from organized labour and from nativists to bring only agriculturalists to Canada and to prove that the Canadian economy actually required these immigrants. Unionized workers feared competition, while nativists feared non-Anglo-Celtic immigration. The railway companies, which stood to gain from large-scale immigration, sought to assuage their critics' fears by appearing to place new arrivals on western farms. Of course, since the need for year-round farm help in the west was limited, temporary employment in agriculture did not guarantee that the immigrants would not move to other sectors of the economy. As long as they could claim to be abiding by the terms of the Railway Agreement, however, the companies were not concerned about the fate of immigrant labourers; in fact, they stood to gain from their departure for other walks of life. The more immigrants who left farming each year, the more new ones would be needed the following year. While organized labour and nativists were painfully aware of this ruse, the Railway Agreement was maintained until 1930 because employers in construction, mining, and logging welcomed it. The existence of a pool of surplus labour enabled them to keep wages low and to dismiss workers suspected of radicalism.[38]

Second, the railways wanted the immigrants to reach the west because they themselves needed labourers to do track work in that region. Jobs in the construction and maintenance of tracks in remote locations did not appeal to Canadian-born workers and "preferred" immigrants. Consequently, many newcomers brought to Canada nominally to work in agriculture were in fact sent by the railway companies to man their "extra gangs."[39]

Third and finally, until 1929, seasonal farm workers were desperately needed in the west, especially during harvest season in early fall.[40] But those from "non-preferred" countries were also required to perform other types of agricultural work, as on sugar beets in southern Alberta. Known as "stoop work," because people must kneel or stoop to thin, weed, and harvest the crop, beet work is gruelling. Not only are these operations back-breaking, but in spring and fall they demand 14 to 15 hours a day in the fields. Not surprisingly, native Anglo-Canadians, Americans, British, and Scandinavians, reluctant to engage in farm labour of any type, were particularly averse to employment in the sugar beet fields. Growers, therefore, depended on "non-preferred" immigrants. Thousands of Hungarians were brought to Canada for Alberta's beet fields.[41] Canadian farmers also required immigrants to perform general chores and to help with land clearing and the harvest. Since requests from western farmers determined the number of immigrants that could be transported each year, the railways were eager to satisfy their clients.

For the immigrants, the seasonality of employment in Canada created serious problems. Although, as we have seen, many of them had plenty of opportunity to become acquainted with seasonal employment and underemployment in Hungary, few were prepared for the hardships caused by seasonal fluctuations of the Canadian labour market.[42] Those Hungarians who believed that they were guaranteed employment, such as Ferenc Magyar, were bitterly disappointed. Still full of indignation 46 years after he returned to his native land, he observed that Canada "should be ashamed of itself" for luring people with false promises of work.[43] Unexpected difficulties were in store, however, even for those who knew that they could not expect permanent employment.

Because few Hungarians could imagine the vastness of the country before their arrival, they could not foresee the cost, time, and energy involved in seeking year-round employment. Consequently, while they were working, many of them kept only enough money for subsistence, sending the rest home. When their jobs on western farms or on the railway ended, however, they discovered that winter jobs were scarce in the west. In Alberta, for example, they may have hoped to get work in the coal mines. Some of their compatriots who had arrived in Canada before the First World War were busy there.[44] By the late 1920s, however, only a small proportion of the Hungarian labourers seeking fall and winter employment could secure such positions.

With debts and families in Hungary, sojourners could not afford to stay in the west to await renewed employment in the spring. Accordingly, they were forced to travel great distances in search of work. Because winter jobs were scarce throughout Canada, this was a costly proposition. As István Weszely found out, travel exhausted savings very rapidly. When Weszely arrived in Canada in 1926, he found only short-term work in Saskatchewan, first on a farm and then in construction in Melville. Hoping to find something steadier, he went to Winnipeg. After ten days of searching in vain and sleeping in the railway station, he heard that there was work in Fort Frances, Ontario. Weszely bought a ticket to go there with his last dollars, only to discover that there was nothing in Fort Frances, either. Since he had no more money, he was forced to continue his search by "riding the rods." This mode of travel became such an established part of the immigrants' life in interwar Canada that a "Hunglish" word, derived from the verb jump, was coined for it: "dzsumpolás." But as Weszely discovered, it was not a comfortable way to get around, especially in winter. If migrants were caught, which happened not infrequently, they were forced to disembark and to walk great distances.

Irresponsible employment agents and the railways contributed to the migrants' predicament. In December 1928, for example, an agent of the CPR sent 24 Hungarians to a lumber camp in eastern Ontario, supposedly for long-term employment. Each of the men paid $29 for the trip. Their jobs lasted less than nine days. The Hungarian consul in Montreal reported having records of many similar incidents.[45]

As the memoirs of Lajos Rózsa illustrate, such experiences kindled the indignation of immigrants who already felt cheated and betrayed by Canadian authorities and railway companies. Like so many of his compatriots, Rózsa was employed only for a brief period following his arrival and was then forced to travel extensively to find work. At one point, he was forced off a train because he could not afford the fare. He wished then that he could speak English, so that he could explain to the conductor that he believed that the CPR owed him something. The company had taken all his money, and its officers did not inform him that "we would be forced to become vagabonds here." A small child who waved to him when he was forced to disembark reminded him of his own little daughter, Ica, "fatherless in Hungary, and her father here in 'glorious Canada,' forced to lead the life of a miserable drifter, simply because he would like to find work."[46]

For many Hungarians, the transience dictated by the Canadian labour market, which they repeatedly described as "forced vagabondage," was the worst feature of immigrant life. They criss-crossed the country, from the mines of Nova Scotia to the lumber mills of British Columbia, in search of employment, but the seasonality of unskilled work, their inability to speak English, their unfamiliarity with local conditions, and the low status accorded to foreign workers meant that they could seldom settle into secure positions anywhere. Since for many of them migration was the only possible route of escape from a precarious existence in Hungary as well, it is not difficult to comprehend their anguish.

Although they could not afford to be selective, Hungarians were not oblivious to the undesirability of the positions that they were able to obtain. Their treatment at the hands of some more established members of the host society drove home in a painful way their own low status. One man who began life in Canada typically by working for western farmers believed that despite their reliance on immigrant labour these employers remained suspicious of "foreigners" and treated them "like criminals."[47] A woman whose whole family laboured in the beet fields of southern Alberta for two years before she moved to Hamilton remembered conditions with bitterness: their kitchen was a chicken coop and a granary their bedroom, while they had to work "from dark till dark."[48]

Experience of a lumber camp led one immigrant to describe Canada as "the torturer of man and beast,"[49] while another concluded that only men who killed their own mothers should have to work in lumbering.[50] Unlike the Finns or Swedes, Hungarians were unaccustomed to the cold. Very few of them, moreover, had been in the lumber industry in their native land, and, since lumber companies often paid piece rates rather than monthly wages, inexperience seriously limited their earning capacities. At times, they could make barely enough to cover the cost of the trip to remote camps, the warm clothing that was indispensable, and food and lodgings in the camp. According to an official of the consulate in Montreal, Hungarians proved so inadequate in this industry that employers were reluctant to hire them.[51] The same official also reported, however, that subcontractors in lumber camps frequently paid immigrants less than the wages owed them and then disappeared without a trace. It is a measure of the scarcity of opportunities that, despite their inexperience and even aversion, many Hungarians nevertheless worked in remote lumber camps.

Heading East

The majority of Hungarian immigrants hoped to escape or at least reduce their "forced vagabondage" by finding steadier, more lucrative employment in south-central Canada. Their migration eastwards was part of a broader process, for Canadians of all ethnic backgrounds were gravitating towards Ontario and Quebec. While the country as a whole experienced economic growth between 1925 and 1929, the greatest expansion occurred in its two central provinces: Ontario and Quebec saw a notable increase not only in manufacturing but also in transportation, trade, and finance. Industrial expansion and the concomitant increase in population in turn led to growth for urban centres in central Canada, and with urban development came significant new opportunities in construction.[52] During the 1930s, the calamitous impact of the Depression on the prairies hastened the trek from country to city and from west to east.

The decision of Hungarians to migrate to central Canada seems thus to have been informed by an accurate assessment of economic conditions and employment prospects in various regions. Given that most of them were newcomers who spoke little English, their familiarity with the situation appears surprising. But oral histories help to explain that Old World ties and informal communications networks among migrants combined to disseminate accurate, up-to-date information about opportunities and thereby to shape their secondary distribution in Canada. Most Hungarians headed east on the advice of relatives and friends who wrote from Ontario or Quebec, telling them about specific positions or that prospects were better in central Canada than in the west, and offering to help them. This type of advice spread rapidly, at times through remarkably circuitous routes. Sándor Egyed, for example, was drifting from place to place in 1927, trying in vain to keep working, when he received a letter from Hungary, from his wife, advising him to go to Niagara Falls. Mrs Egyed, who was living in the village of Felnémet, in Heves county, had learned from conversations with neighbours whose husbands were in Canada that immigrants were being hired in that city. Egyed followed his wife's suggestion, which proved so sound that in 1982, at the time of the interview from which this information was taken, he was still living in the border city.[53]

Most of the Hungarians who wandered east during the 1920s did so with the hope of obtaining positions in factories. Some of them, like István Tóth, were attracted by factory work itself. Having been a miner both in Hungary and in western Canada, Tóth was thrilled when he managed to get a job at the Acme Screw and Gear Co. of Toronto, a producer of machine parts, in 1927; he saw it as placing him on the threshold of a new life. Instead of working in "mud, water, poor air, bent in two," he would now be "in a factory, standing upright, near machines."[54] Most Hungarians, however, were drawn to factories above all because they promised good wages and relatively steady employment.

Because few Hungarians had any training or experience in industry, however, their prospects were limited to those types of factory employment for which competition was most intense – unskilled or, at best, semi-skilled work. For although central Canada experienced a manufacturing boom between 1926 and 1929, it also had a surplus of unskilled labourers. Newcomers quickly learned that they would have to mobilize all their energy and ingenuity to obtain jobs in factories. When they arrived in a new city or town, they learned the location of factories employing unskilled labour and wandered from one to another, often on foot to save money, to inquire if men were needed. If there was the slightest likelihood that a factory was about to hire new people, they returned to its gates day after day, each of them hoping to be chosen from the crowd that invariably gathered.[55]

There were always immigrants who did not depend entirely on luck to be chosen. They knew someone inside – a cousin, a brother, or a friend from back home – who had given their name to the foreman, and if the foreman were impressed by the industry and character of the immigrant's "contacts," he might well select him from among those waiting at the factory gates.[56] In a few cases, especially in older Hungarian communities such as Welland and Hamilton, there were even Hungarian foremen who preferred to hire their co-nationals.[57] More often, however, foremen required additional inducements such as money, liquor, or various favours, before they consented to hire immigrants.[58] Some of the interwar migrants, such as Steven H., had learned of this practice even before they arrived in Canada, from "Amerikások." When he was preparing to leave for Canada, his father, who had spent some years in the United States, advised him: "If it's a question of a 'big job' don't begrudge anything to the foreman or the boss."[59] Although they adopted this practice, Hungarians resented having to "buy work."[60]

Immigrants who lacked contacts frequently displayed remarkable ingenuity. When István Tóth heard that Acme Screw and Gear was looking for men with experience, he found out from two Hungarian employees what type of labour performed in the company could be learned most quickly and easily. They advised him to apply for drill work. He did so, claiming to be experienced, and by observing the motions of fellow drillers he managed to learn enough during his first day on the job to convince the foreman to keep him.[61] András Gabura, an agriculturalist, and Béla Vágó, a tailor, learned from their compatriots that the Ontario Malleable Iron Co. in Oshawa hired inexperienced men as moulders – unskilled men could be paid less than experienced ones. So as not to bear the cost of training new workers, the firm paid them only for perfect moulds. Thus, when a man started at the company, he earned next to nothing. Vágó and Gabura were nevertheless willing to submit themselves to this short "apprenticeship" because they hoped to find more lucrative employment elsewhere, once they mastered the moulder's skills.[62]

Despite their ingenuity and their willingness to pay bribes, however, peasant newcomers were still generally forced to take the worst jobs in factories. In light industry, they worked in establishments, such as Welland's Imperial Cotton Mill, that were notorious for underpaying or in chemical plants such as the American Cyanamide Co. in Niagara Falls, where they were exposed to noxious fumes. In the metal industry, they got the hottest, dirtiest jobs. Although they desperately wanted work in industry, former agriculturalists complained about the quality of the air, the ventilation, the noise, and the pace. Pál Krizsán remembered the Nickel Plant in Port Colborne, which employed many Hungarians, as "a factory where you were burning." Ferenc Magyar, who worked in a silk factory in Cornwall, and Sándor Medgyesi, who was hired for the copper smelter in Rouyn-Noranda, actually gave up much-coveted factory jobs because they feared for their health.[63]

Although the immigrants' lack of skills was of course partly responsible for the type of jobs they got, many also blamed ethnic discrimination. When asked about his co-workers, one man from an oil refinery stressed that there were no "English" among them. "The English," he explained, "were unwilling to do such 'bad' work." Another Hungarian explained the preponderance of immigrants at American Cyanamide: "Only immigrant workers work here because a native worker would not be willing to do this life-killing work."[64] The fact that most of them hoped to labour in Canada for only a few years, until they amassed enough money to buy land back home, undoubtedly increased their tolerance of otherwise unacceptable conditions.

The hold of Hungarians remained tenuous, however, even over such undesirable jobs. Production in manufacturing fluctuated according to season and demand, and immigrants, generally unskilled and among the last to be hired, were the first to feel the effects of any slowdown. At best, only their hours were cut; at worst, they were dismissed. With the coming of the Depression, dismissals reached epidemic proportions. Even during the years of prosperity between 1925 and 1929, however, when employers could count on a return to full-scale production at some point each year, they did not generally promise to rehire people who were dismissed in the "off" periods. They knew that when the need arose, they would have no difficulty in recruiting new staff. In any event, Hungarians could not afford to wait around in the hope of being rehired.

Insecurity of tenure made peasant immigrants, Hungarians among them, particularly vulnerable to the arbitrary power of foremen in a pre-union era. Many of them were expected to pay foremen and forewomen weekly or to provide them with liquor merely to hold on to their jobs. On the evening of every pay day, for example, Sándor G.'s foreman at the Ford plant in Windsor awaited the men from his department in front of a local motel. There they had "to stay till midnight and buy him drinks."[65]

Despite their acquiescence in such corrupt practices, despite their eagerness and resourcefulness, many Hungarian immigrants failed altogether to secure factory jobs. Some attributed their failure to ethnic discrimination. Ferenc B., for example, explained that he was forced into construction in Montreal because the "English and French factories hired only natives."[66] George G. also blamed mistrust of immigrants for his inability to get a factory job in Hamilton in 1929.[67]

Thus, although most of them left the prairies because they hoped to find steady industrial work, Hungarians in central Canada were forced to continue in a wide range of non-industrial, often seasonal or temporary, occupations. In cities, the service industries, including domestic and personal services, offered employment to Hungarians who lacked specific skills and training. Men and women became waiters or waitresses, bus boys, dishwashers, janitors, house maids, lift boys, porters, and gardeners. Wages, however, were low, and hours were also much longer than in industry. Many Hungarians disliked this type of work, moreover, because of its low status in their native land. Mary Polyoka, for instance, recalls that she often cried when she was forced to serve as a maid in a small hotel "because at home we looked down on servants, and I kept thinking that I never had to work as a servant in Hungary and here in Canada I had to do it."[68]

Hungarian women were particularly averse to domestic service. As noted in chapter 1, females from rural areas where domestic service had become accepted for young women tended to migrate to Budapest. Relatively few women came to Canada as domestics. Indeed, the proportion of adult women who chose this route of migration was far lower among Hungarians than among any other group of "non-preferred" immigrants. While more than one-half of the Ruthenian women who arrived in Canada, one-half of the Polish, two-fifths of the German, and one-third of the Slovak women came as domestics, only one-fifth of the Hungarian women did do.[69] According to the consul in Montreal, even these agreed to serve as domestics only to gain entry to the country. Most hoped to move to cities as quickly as possible to become seamstresses or salesclerks.[70] Other Hungarian women usually turned to domestic service only if they could find no other employment. During the Depression, for example, some women cleaned houses when their husbands lost their jobs. But several reported with satisfaction that their spouses did not "permit" them to be servants for long.[71]

A building crew constructing a power station near Black River, Quebec, 1928–29. Most of the workers were Slovak or Hungarian. Multicultural History Society of Ontario Collection, Archives of Ontario.

Like other immigrants from rural areas in eastern and southern Europe, Hungarian men frequently turned to outdoor work. They built and repaired roads, sidewalks, and bridges, dug ditches, and worked on building sites. Although they were accustomed to outdoor jobs, these were far less attractive to them than factory work. The recollections of the daughter of a man who worked on the third Welland Canal help to explain why:

I remember when my father worked on the canal, he didn't like the work at all but it was a source of bread on the table. He had to do something. He couldn't get a job in the plant at the time so he had to work outdoors on the canal. It was hard work especially in the cold weather. I remember my father getting dressed to go to his job: everybody sort of helped. He had to put on his big heavy boots, his long black coat, a long home knitted scarf, a thick pair of gloves and a wool hat that covered his ears. Off he would go to dig the canal or at other times help level and landscape or plant trees along the banks. He would come home tired and chilled through, but those were the jobs foreigners had to do; nobody else wanted them.[72]

Outdoor jobs did not tie Hungarian immigrants to any one place. In central Canada as in the west, many continued to move from city to city and from one work site, however remote, to another, in response to news of better prospects or of higher wages.[73] Their forced vagabondage continued.

During the agricultural season, they also worked on farms. Indeed, until 1929, many of them returned to the west each September, taking advantage of the low rates offered by the railways to harvest workers.[74] Throughout the interwar years, moreover, men, women, and even children got employment in the vicinity of the cities where they lived, frequently undertaking "stoop work." Throughout southern Ontario, they picked fruits and vegetables, around Windsor they also worked in sugar beet fields, and in Norfolk and Oxford counties they harvested tobacco.[75]

For women and children, farm work offered a way to supplement family income. But most Hungarians saw it as temporary, to tide them over until they got steady indoor jobs. Agricultural wages were generally too low to permit men either to return to their native villages with savings or to bring their families to Canada. Sándor Gál, who did not succeed in finding any other type of position between the world wars, believed that the life of a migrant agricultural labourer prolonged his separation from his wife and ultimately led to the break-up of his family.[76]

A number of Hungarians who first worked as field hands on southwestern Ontario's tobacco farms, however, decided to stay on. They saw that even during the 1930s the industry was enjoying relative prosperity, and having become painfully aware of their limited prospects in cities, they decided to try farming. They rented land on a sharecropping basis and converted it to tobacco; although growing the plant is a precarious enterprise, many Hungarians in the Delhi-Tillsonbourg area were very successful. By the 1940s, they were able to purchase their own farms and to provide employment for their less fortunate co-nationals.[77]

Other Hungarians whose families were in Canada rented or purchased small farms in Ontario, usually near such towns as Welland, Hamilton, and Brantford. While a few farmed full time, others continued to work in urban industry, whenever they could. They viewed farming as a source of supplementary income, especially useful to tide them over periods of seasonal unemployment in industry.[78]

The Depression[79]

Hungarians who did not save enough money to return to their homeland during the 1920s faced insurmountable obstacles during the

Depression. At a time when thousands of people were being laid off, immigrants were frequently among the first to be let go. Employers generally gave preference to the native-born, sometimes also to naturalized Canadians.[80] It was clear that even fewer Hungarians than before would now obtain factory or any other type of work. Consul-General Károly Winter estimated that early in 1930 about 65 per cent of Hungarians in Canada were unemployed.[81] In desperation, some immigrants entrusted their last pennies to men, usually co-nationals, who claimed to have the right connections to obtain work for them. All too often, these men took the money and disappeared.[82]

Even Hungarians who managed to hang on to their jobs often faced drastically reduced hours. Realizing that their sojourn in Canada would have to be prolonged, some among them who had both work and savings brought their families over. But Canadian authorities required hard proof of economic viability from immigrants who sought to do so. With so many citizens relying on public assistance, the last thing the government wanted was more people dependent on the state. Consequently, few Hungarian women and children gained entry to Canada during the 1930s. Their numbers did not significantly alter the group's gender imbalance.[83]

Family reunification not only satisfied psychological needs, it also brought definite material advantages. If they had obtained citizenship, immigrants with families qualified for municipal relief. Women also stretched and supplemented the household budget. They could sew clothes or alter used clothing for their families. Throughout central Canada, they grew vegetables, "making even unpromising city soil fairly fertile," and canned their produce, as well as food purchased inexpensively in farmers' markets to tide them over the winter months.[84] They also smoked and preserved meats bought wholesale. Women's efforts both in and outside the home assumed unprecedented importance as unemployment grew. Females could still generally find work as domestics, and their labour in agriculture became far more important than it was while their husbands were still more fully employed. In cities, women also took in sewing to increase their families' income.[85]

The willingness of Hungarian women to accept any type of job did not mean that they were not angered by the arduousness or meagre returns. Erzsébet C., who toiled in the sugar beet fields near Windsor, recalled bitterly that "we preferred to crawl on our bellies, rather than go on relief."[86] While some women who were domestics gratefully accepted food and used clothing from their employers, others believed that their employers took advantage of their desperation by paying them unconscionably low wages.

Some of the men who could not afford to bring their families to Canada, or who were unwilling to use up their hard-earned savings without any prospects in sight, began to think of returning to Hungary. By declaring themselves destitute, they could gain free passage home.[87] But others persisted, some because they believed that, despite high unemployment, they still stood a better chance of finding work in Canada than in Hungary, others because they were unwilling to concede that migration – their only chance to improve their situation back home – had ended in failure. Still others feared that in Europe they faced not only poverty but also the prospect of another war. When Steven H. from Czechoslovakia wrote his wife that he was thinking of returning, she advised him to do so only as a last resort, if he were starving. Believing that war was imminent, she argued that any hardship in Canada was preferable to the mortal danger that conscription at home might entail.[88] To men aware of such possibilities, the rounding up of destitute immigrants and their forcible deportation during the 1930s appeared profoundly unjust. One of them even compared the expulsion of immigrants to the lynching of blacks in the American south.[89]

Men whose families were in Hungary were far more vulnerable economically as well as psychologically than their compatriots with wives and children in Canada. The fact that they had families in Hungary who depended on remittances was irrelevant to employers and relief administrators. In Canada, they were classified as "single." When factories gave preference to married employees, men with families in Hungary were let go.[90] Even if they could meet residency requirements and were thus eligible for relief, these "single" unemployed qualified for much more meagre aid than men with families. As a rule, they received one meal a day in a soup kitchen and a place to sleep. Those who had been transient or who failed to become naturalized did not qualify for any assistance at all.

The only option that the federal government offered the single unemployed was a move to remote relief camps, where they would be lodged in barracks, fed, and paid 20 cents a day for "make work" projects. Their designation of these places as "slave camps" illustrates just how unsatisfactory this solution seemed to Hungarian immigrants.[91] Even those among them who in their desperation took this option found it humiliating. Barna Hegedűs wrote to Hungary in 1934 from the relief camp in Frank, Alberta, that he regretted coming to Canada. He acknowledged that life back home had been far from rosy, but at least, he wrote, no one was forced to labour for 20 cents a day and to eat slops.[92] At best, the camps permitted survival. They did not seem like a viable option to men with dependants in Hungary.

These men continued their frantic search for work, riding the rails across Canada and accepting whatever jobs they were offered. Letters from Hungary, informing them of the destitution wrought by the Depression in the countryside there, spurred them on. But so many jobless descended on places that offered opportunities even in the 1930s, such as the tobacco region in southern Ontario, that a great many failed altogether to secure work. Unable to help their families, they were racked by guilt and worry. Sandor Hajas from Hamilton tried to explain to his aged parents why he stopped sending money to them: "I know that you are without help, you cannot expect assistance from anyone.... As long as I was working I helped you as much as I could. I would help now too if I had work. But finding work in this country today is like hoping to find one's lost wealth on the moon."[93]

These migrants' deepest fears must have been aroused when they read newspaper reports such as the one that described the circumstances surrounding the suicide of János Escher's wife, in Hungary. Escher had sold his small holding in order to pay for his trip to Canada. He left behind a wife and two children. He was so ashamed of being unable to find work in Canada that he stopped writing to his family. His wife fell upon the charity of family members, who were themselves struggling to survive the Depression in Hungary. She found this predicament so intolerable that she drowned herself in the well. The description of her fate appeared in the *Kanadai Magyar Ujság* (Winnipeg), the most widely read Hungarian-language paper in Canada, in July 1931.[94]

Some Hungarians in Canada were similarly overcome by despair. Short notices in the press were frequently their only memorial: "Thirty-three-year old John Horvath shot himself in a boarding house in Cooksville, Ontario. He was despondent over failure to obtain work."[95] "Having come from the west to find work and having been unsuccessful, John Kotaszi drowned himself in the Saint Lawrence."[96]

Others survived somehow. Having postponed their return home through the 1930s, they were further prevented from leaving by the Second World War. Many thus became Canadians despite themselves. Asked to explain what made them abandon their plans to return home, why they decided to stay, they pointed time and time again to the Depression. Because their decision was made at a time when Canada was "a bad place for foreigners," it is not surprising that many did not immediately develop strong loyalties to the new land.[97] Almost without exception, they saw their treatment at the hands of Canadian authorities as profoundly unjust. As one of them explained, "no one came to Canada to die of hunger."[98] In their eyes, the federal government, having recruited immigrants to fulfil its labour needs and then failing to provide them with a living through work, owed them something. They believed that it should have supported them some other way.[99] As one immigrant explained, life in Canada was not "what we thought it would be, and maybe if it had been I would have become more Canadian than I am Hungarian but things just didn't work out."

Amid circumstances of hardship and deprivation, Hungarians could turn for comfort and assistance only to their own communities. Neighbours, landlords, storekeepers, fellow villages understood their predicament and tried to help. Various forms of relief also came from formal institutions set up within the community. Ties of kinship and friendship among the immigrants, Hungarian neighbourhoods, and Hungarian institutions, moreover, permitted men and women who saw themselves as victims of exploitation and discrimination in the broader society to reassert their humanity and dignity.

3 Hungarian Communities in Canada

The table was set for us, with 'southern fried chicken' (a Hungarian kind of chicken) and cucumber salad, made the Hungarian way, with sour cream and all Hungarian dishes, all piping hot, just as Hungarian ladies would do this for any man whose family was coming ... The next day, well the next two, three, four days, my father took us, I think to everybody in the Hungarian community to introduce us, so within days we knew dozens of Hungarian immigrants who would come with us to show us where the butcher was, where the grocer was ... where they all spoke Hungarian. The first weekend we were taken to all the Hungarian clubs, churches. So that within two weeks we were integrated, we were part of a community. Mother was on a first name basis with several dozen ladies ... We all lived within the same district. Somebody was visiting somebody. There was no loneliness.[1]

So recalled Margaret Breckner, who arrived, aged nine, in Montreal with her mother in 1931 to rejoin her father, who had left Transylvania two years earlier. Her new "home" was a rented flat in the city's Hungarian quarter.

Margaret's recollections convey some of the essential features and functions of Hungarian neighbourhoods in central Canada, which helped immigrants adjust to the New World. From the moment of their arrival, newcomers such as the Breckners were surrounded by men and women who not only shared their language and traditions but also assisted them in finding their way in an unfamiliar environment. Hungarian neighbourhoods also housed businesses and associations that catered to the immigrants' needs.

The study of such neighbourhoods occupies an important place in historical works on ethnicity and immigration in North America. Scholars stress their importance in the development of group consciousness. They see the very fact that newcomers tended to cluster together in cities as evidence of group consciousness, and they argue that the development of such neighbourhoods created arenas for further strengthening this awareness. The help that newcomers received in finding work and lodgings, the security that they derived from being surrounded by compatriots, and the kinship and friendship ties that bound them to their neighbours all reinforced the group's solidarity. Within their own neighbourhoods, moreover, immigrants could maintain many of their characteristic patterns of behaviour, and as the neighbourhoods matured, the establishment of businesses catering to the group's special needs contributed significantly to the persistence of its distinct identity. Residential concentration also provided these communities with a visible structure and stimulated the development of formal immigrant organizations. The latter expressed and formalized the shared experiences and needs that led newcomers to congregate in such districts and to set up informal social networks.[2]

This chapter examines first the emergence of Hungarian neighbourhoods in central Canada. It considers the significance of these neighbourhoods and looks at some of their characteristic institutions – boarding-houses and small businesses. It thus sketches in the background for the discussion of Hungarian community organizations, which are the focus of the remainder of this study. It analyses as well the role of the immigrant elite in the development of these neighbourhoods. Members of this elite, which included steamship agents and publishers and editors of Hungarian-language commercial newspapers, frequently did not live in these districts, but many of them depended on the growth and persistence of these areas for their livelihood, their prestige, or both. Consequently, as we see below, they lent a measure of stability and cohesion to Hungarian neighbourhoods in central Canada.

THE EMERGENCE OF HUNGARIAN
NEIGHBOURHOODS IN CENTRAL CANADA

Although few of them realized the hope of finding steady, well-paid jobs that attracted them eastwards, most Hungarians decided to stay in central Canada. Between 1921 and 1941, the proportion of Hungarians living in Ontario and Quebec grew from 14 to 48 per cent – 40 per cent in Ontario, and the remaining 8 per cent in Quebec, mostly in Montreal. During the same period, the share of the three prairie provinces declined from 82 to 51 per cent.[3] Increased concentration led to the emergence of distinct communities in central Canada. The nuclei of some of these settlements had in fact been founded by 1914. Employment opportunities, which were opened by rapid economic expansion in southern Ontario between 1905 and 1913, attracted Hungarians both from Hungary and from the United States, and a few of them settled in Welland, Hamilton and Brantford. The arrival of immigrants in the 1920s and 1930s revitalized the small Hungarian colonies in these towns, which had actually begun to decline during the depression that followed the war.[4] The Hungarian population of Hamilton increased by more than ten times, from 200 in 1921 to 2,575 in 1941, while that of Welland rose from 243 in 1921 to 1,648 by 1941 and that of Brantford from 247 to 593.[5] Interwar immigration also led to of sizeable communities of Hungarians in places where few or none had lived prior to 1914. The largest such community in Canada, with a population of 3,457 in 1941, emerged in Montreal, for example, where only a handful of people from Hungary had lived before Canada reopened its gates to immigrants from that country in 1924. Similarly, the number of Hungarians increased by more than twenty times in Toronto, from 83 in 1921 to 2,194 in 1941, and in Windsor, from 86 in 1921 to 1,858 in 1941.[6]

Gender and age distribution suggests that groupings were no longer transitory clusters of sojourners, but increasingly stable communities of immigrants. As migrants began to realize that they would have to stay longer than the three- to five-year sojourn in their original plans, those who could brought wives and children to Canada, while others married here. Yet even in 1931, the imbalance between men and women was greater among Hungarians than among any other group of immigrants except Slovaks.[7] By choice or circumstance, many of the group's members remained sojourners.

Proximity to work and the availability of cheap housing were key factors in determining where immigrants settled. In Welland, for example, Hungarians lived in two neighbourhoods surrounding factories that employed immigrant workers. The larger of the two, extending from King Street in the west to the CNR tracks in the east, and from Lincoln Street in the south to Griffiths and Asher streets in the north, was within walking distance of the Empire Cotton Mills and of the larger metallurgical plants of Page Hersey, Union Carbide, and Electrometallurgical. A smaller cluster lived in Crowland township, north and east of the industrial area.

Montreal's Hungarians lived in the city's ethnic corridor along St Lawrence Boulevard, from the river approximately to Pine Avenue. This same area housed many of the smaller manufacturers that employed immigrants, and it was within easy reach of larger plants in the harbour area, such as the meat-packers that also depended on unskilled workers.

In Toronto, Hungarians were more dispersed. The majority lived in the city's core, in the area bounded roughly by Lake Ontario in the south, College Street in the north, University Avenue in the east, and Bathurst Street in the west. But small clusters inhabited other districts – that extending west from Bathurst Street approximately to Lansdowne, and the one surrounding the industries of the "Junction," where the CPR and the CNR tracks intersected. There were also small groups living east of the city's business core; north of the industrial area along the lakeshore; in the Dupont-Davenport area; in New Toronto; and in Mimico. Each district adjoined one of the city's major industrial areas, and each had older, inexpensive houses suitable for immigrant boarding-houses. Accordingly, the settlement patterns of Hungarians in Toronto, like those of their counterparts in Welland and Montreal, seem to have been shaped largely by the city's industrial structure and its housing stock.

Parochial or National Loyalties?

Students of peasant immigrants from southern and eastern Europe warn us not to assume that settlement patterns were determined by a shared sense of national identity. In his seminal piece, "Contadini in Chicago" (1964), Rudolph Vecoli, for example, showed that while Old World ties were unquestionably strong among Italians in Chicago, these were not national, but parochial. At the time of mass emigration, the spirit of Italian nationalism had not reached the bulk of the peasantry. It was thus the spirit of localism, or campanilismo, Vecoli maintains, that produced 17 separate Italian neighbourhoods in Chicago.[8] Similarly, June Alexander (1980) argued that regional and county loyalties were responsible for distinct neighbourhoods among Slovaks in Pittsburgh.[9] Robert Harney (1981) and John Zucchi (1981) discovered that even within a single ward in Toronto campanilismo shaped settlement patterns among Italians. Rather than settling indiscriminately next to their co-nationals, Italians in the city's St John's ward chose to live next to fellow townsmen.[10]

Hungarian immigrants in Canada, like their Slovak and Italian counterparts in North America, cherished strong village and regional loyalties. The men and women interviewed for this study used the term "földi" – the exact equivalent of the Italian "paesano" – to designate fellow immigrants from their native village or its surroundings. Some of them even described as idegenek, or strangers, newcomers from other parts of Hungary. Particularistic loyalties were very much in evidence in the immigrants' social life; földik gathered together on happy and sad occasions alike. When, for example, an immigrant celebrated the annual name day (the feast day of the Saint after whom he or she was named), fellow villagers were prominent among the guests. When a worker suffered an accident, people from the village visited in the hospital, and if an immigrant died they usually made the funeral arrangements and notified family back home.[11] Hungarian immigrants also preferred to marry a földi. As one of them explained, "family life ... perhaps would unite you more if you knew that, well, both wife and husband, in this big world, got here from the same place."[12] Some even felt the need to assert their local identity publicly within the ethnic group. To express their distinct presence, men and women from the town of Mór, for example, donated a statue to the Hungarian Roman Catholic church of Welland.[13]

Instances of discord within Hungarian-Canadian communities also bear witness to the strength of localism. József Jáger remembered that "there was always discord, disagreements," within the drama troupe of the Hungarian Roman Catholic congregation in Toronto; "people were from all various types of counties from Hungary, all different villages from Hungary, and two took one side, two others took another side, and there was constantly disharmony."[14]

In attempting to discover the nature of group consciousness, moreover, we must consider another potentially divisive factor. Not only did most Hungarian immigrants, like their Slovak and Italian counterparts, come from villages – often small and remote – but they were also divided along religious lines. Indeed, after studying US Hungarians, Timothy Smith concluded that such segmentation actually produced four separate ethnic communities – Catholic, Jewish, Lutheran, and Reformed.[15] Were Hungarians in Canada also divided along regional and religious lines?

Unfortunately, there is a dearth of relevant sources. Quantifiable data about village origins are available only for Montreal, from the records of the Hungarian United Church and those of the Alex Kelen steamship agency.[16] Fortunately, Montreal offers probably the best possible example of Hungarian settlement patterns in Canada. Not only was it the nation's largest Hungarian colony between the world wars, but its inhabitants came from virtually every county in the homeland. And while the relative representation of each county was not identical to its role within the general flow of Hungarians to Canada during the period, the eight counties that supplied the most immigrants to Canada also sent the largest number of Hungarians to Montreal. People from the successor states, moreover, comprised roughly the same proportion of the Hungarians of Montreal as they did of all Hungarians who immigrated to Canada between the wars. The behaviour of Montreal's Hungarians suggests that neither village, nor county, nor religious ties decisively shaped their neighbourhoods. Compatriots from different villages, counties, and religious denominations lived side by side along City Hall, Clarke, Colonial, de Bullion, Demontigny, St Dominique, St Elizabeth, St George, St Lawrence, St Urbain, and other streets of the city's immigrant quarter.

In the absence of more extensive sources, let us glance briefly at marriage patterns to see whether national identity transcended regional and religious segmentation. As noted above, Hungarians, given a choice, preferred to marry someone from their village or county of origin. From the limited statistical records available, it appears, however, that many did not have this choice.[17] The registers of marriages of the Hungarian Presbyterian congregations of Toronto and Hamilton and of the United Church of Montreal show that national rather than local ties determined the choice of partners there. In 86 per cent of the 80 weddings between Hungarian partners recorded by the Hungarian Presbyterian Church of Toronto between 1937 and 1945, partners came from different villages. Sixty per cent of the couples, moreover, were marrying across denominational lines.[18] A high incidence of religious mixing appears for Hamilton and Montreal as well. Forty-five per cent of the weddings documented in the Hamilton church between 1926 and 1934, and 51 per cent of those in the Montreal church between 1926 and 1941, were mixed.[19] Thus, in marriages, national identity overrode parochial loyalties.

There were two main reasons for the readiness of Hungarians from all parts of Hungary and the successor states and from all Christian denominations to intermarry and to settle next to one another in Canadian cities: the group's small size and its nation-wide dispersal as a result of immigration regulations and the labour market. The railways' efforts to direct all "non-preferred" immigrants to the west and the seasonal or intermittent nature of jobs open to newcomers there generally prevented chain migration – the characteristic pattern of peasant migration. Groups of földi could not simply follow one another in a chain and settle next to one another. As we saw in the previous chapter, fellow villagers kept in touch, informing one another about opportunities, and this shared information influenced patterns of migration and settlement. As a rule, however, there were not enough people from any one village or region in any Canadian community to permit them to depend entirely on fellow villagers for the satisfaction of social and cultural needs or for suitable marriage partners.

The exception to this rule was the Székelys – descendants of an ancient Magyar tribe, which settled in southern Transylvania sometime in the early Middle Ages. Though Hungarian-speaking, they differed from the Magyars not just by tribal origin but also by history. When the feudal order first took shape in the region, the Székelys were border guards, not serfs, and although by the seventeenth century the social and economic position of most Székelys had become indistinguishable from that of Magyar serfs, a sense of distinct, even superior, identity lived on in folk memory. The fact that group members faced considerable economic hardship, which forced them to migrate in the Danubian basin as early as the eighteenth century, seemed only to intensify group solidarity. [20] A strong sense of group identity was still evident among the Székelys who migrated to Canada. They sometimes travelled in groups, and they took up residence with, or near, other Székelys in Canada. The fact that there were half-a-dozen families among the earlier Székely settlers in Montreal helped to reinforce this sense of separate identity. Unmarried Székely men, or men whose families were in the old country, boarded with Székely families in Montreal. Strong sub-group loyalties, however, did not preclude identification with the larger immigrant group. As we see below, these people participated fully in Hungarian community life.

A sense of exclusion from the host society reinforced group consciousness among immigrants. Encounters with hostility from members of the host society were by no means limited to the workplace. "It didn't matter if your clothing was made of citizenship papers," complained one immigrant who had clearly been naturalized, "in the eyes of the English and the French you were a 'Hanki'." [21] Another, a cooper from Transylvania, recorded the same impression in his memoirs: "Wherever we came from, and for whatever reasons, we were all the same in one respect: we were homeless, fate-stricken foreigners. Everywhere we turned we encountered expressions of Anglo-Saxon chauvinism." [22] Hungarians "stuck together" because they were poor and because they were not accepted by the "English." [23]

The Meaning of Hungarian Neighbourhoods

But if a sense of national identity shaped the settlement patterns of Hungarians, their small numbers meant that they did not dominate in any of the neighbourhoods in which they chose to live. Proximity to employment and cheap housing, the two other central factors, were not specific to the Hungarians but applied equally to other groups of newcomers whose occupational and residential choices were limited by the absence of specialized skills and a concomitant low income. Consequently, Hungarians generally lived interspersed with other groups of immigrants, in the "foreign quarters" that had emerged in virtually every Canadian urban centre by the 1920s.[24] Even in Welland, where Hungarians comprised 10 per cent of the population, their households alternated with those of Italian, Jewish, and Slavic immigrants. When people who resided in the Hungarian community of Montreal during the interwar era described it as "a veritable Hungarian quarter," in which "everything was Hungarian," they were talking not about ethnic composition so much as a psychic space.[25] Hungarians seemed ubiquitous there because of the practical and psychological role that they fulfilled in one another's lives.

This role began from the moment of arrival in a Canadian settlement. Two Hungarians who migrated to Welland from the west described their encounters immediately after they left the train:

We began walking down the street and I guess we had come about a block when we came upon a group of old ladies sitting under a big tree. The one said to the other in Hungarian 'well I wonder where these people are from. It looks as though they have been travelling for some time.' When we heard this we were really happy. We greeted them in Hungarian and the poor old women were shocked as well as embarrassed. Having told them of our experiences so far and of the fact that we were without money, they offered to take us into their homes immediately.[26]

The old women in this story bear a suspicious resemblance to the archetypical old woman/witch that wandering youths encounter in Hungarian folk tales. If addressed with respect, these frightening old women can become benevolent and beneficent. As the work of ethnologist Linda Degh has shown, the infiltration of traditional folk motifs into the narration of life histories by peasant immigrants is not unusual. Although such narratives belong in the category of folk prose genres, they nevertheless contain essential historical and sociocultural data.[27] Accidental meetings with fellow Hungarians upon arrival in unfamiliar settlements appear time and time again as the first points of stability in accounts of migration to central Canada. More established compatriots directed new arrivals to Hungarian neighbourhoods, even to specific boarding-houses where lodging was available, to Hungarian restaurants, and to potential places of employment. Endowing such meetings with an almost magical quality underscores their significance in helping immigrants find their bearings in an alien environment.

Boarding-houses

The importance of shared ethnicity in satisfying a complex of economic, social, psychological, and cultural needs is also apparent in the most common living arrangement among Hungarian immigrants: the boarding-house. The term "burdos ház" (boarding-house) actually denoted a variety of living arrangements.[28] The term "betyár burd" ("rogue's board") described the practice of a group of men renting a house together and preparing meals for themselves. This type of arrangement was most common during the formative period, when there were very few women among the immigrants. "Rogue's board" was also a characteristic system in outlying areas, where men found seasonal employment, but where few Hungarian women ventured.[29] Hostel-type boarding-houses constituted another type of arrangement before wives joined the men in Canada. These institutions accommodated up to 40 or 50 men. Anywhere from four to eight slept in one room, often two to a bed.[30] Each bed was often occupied around the clock. At night, men who had jobs during the day slept in it, and in the morning, almost as soon as they left for work, those on night shift took their place. As more and more men brought their families to Canada, however, family-run boarding-houses, somewhat less crowded and generally cleaner than hostel-type institutions, became increasingly common.

Boarding suited both boarders and operators. As Mary Gabura discovered, setting up a boarding-house could hasten family reunification. She learned about such places in her native village of Hollóháza, in Abauj county, from women who returned after having spent many years in the United States. They "talked about having boarders and cooking for them. Well, I thought to myself, if they could cook and have boarders and could help out their husbands, why shouldn't I be able to do the same? Why shouldn't our family be reunited?"[31]

While women who kept boarders performed tasks not markedly different from those undertaken by domestic servants – cooking, cleaning, and washing and ironing – they were self-employed. As long as Hungarian immigrants were employed, keeping boarders was perhaps the most lucrative occupation open to Hungarian women in Canadian cities.[32] Some operators, both male and female, of boarding-houses even resorted to moonshining and bootlegging to increase their earnings.[33] Moreover, boarding enabled women with small children to add to their family income while staying at home. It is no wonder, therefore, that Hungarians who arrived in Canada in the 1920s and 1930s believed that married men who brought their wives over were more likely to succeed, because with a woman, "money came into the house."[34]

While the boarding-house was definitely a business undertaking, shared ethnicity could create a special relationship of trust between householders and boarders. Operators often provided room and board on credit for immigrants when they first arrived in a community and had not yet obtained work. As Ferenc Magyar recalled, in the course of wandering through central Canada in search of a job he sometimes took rooms with the "English," but "with them you had to pay ahead. Hungarians sometimes let you stay even for a month before you had to pay." By way of explanation, he added: "The Magyar after all was still a Magyar."[35] During the Depression, some keepers allowed their unemployed boarders to live in their houses free of charge or to leave in search of work with a mere promise that when they could they would settle outstanding bills.[36] Sometimes this trust was based on parochial ties in the old country. Given a choice, immigrants did lodge with people from their village or county. The group's small size and the initial transience of its members meant, however, that even boarders in a Hungarian home did not always come from the same village or from neighbouring villages.

The pervasiveness of the boarding-house indicates that it also satisfied a variety of needs. First and foremost, it provided lodgings and food at a reasonable cost – particularly important to sojourners who wanted to save as much money as possible so as to return home, or bring their families to Canada.[37] But for most of them, the proximity of compatriots who shared their language, traditions, and foodways was also important. Indeed, at times these non-economic considerations seemed to outweigh economic ones in the choice of food and lodgings. Mary Gabura, who became one of the first women to run a boarding-house in Toronto when she joined her husband there in 1926 or 1927, recalled that even men who did not live in her house begged her to cook for them. Parsimonious in every other respect, they were willing to pay generously for the privilege of eating Hungarian food: "We didn't even want to ask so much. I didn't want to cook for more men. It was too much for me. But they paid me more, a dollar for a dinner, just so I would cook for them. They also asked me to give them lunch. They didn't mind, they said, if I made a sandwich from the left-overs. So I couldn't help it, what else could I have done?" More Hungarians wanted to live in her establishment than she could accommodate. "Everybody was happy because same language was together," she explained.[38]

Boarding-houses frequently also served as social centres. At the Bornemisszas' in Welland, for example, boarders frequently celebrated on weekends by drinking and singing to the accompaniment of a local "gypsy" violinist.[39] Music appears to have been an essential part of entertainment in other cities as well. When József Gaál was looking for entertainment on Saturday nights in Montreal, he would look for co-nationals. He had no difficulty locating them: "You could hear

Hungarian singing from the street, that's how you knew where the Hungarians were."[40] Boarding-houses were especially valued in small communities with few or no formal immigrant organizations. György Nóvák recalled, for example, that in the Hungarian house where he boarded in Fort William "young people periodically organized balls, where they danced and sang. We celebrated one another's name day. In the evenings we played cards, not for money but for matches; this way you couldn't lose much."[41]

If we want to understand the circumstances of hardship and deprivation amid which most new arrivals lived during the interwar years, however, we must not romanticize the institution of boarding. Although immigrants derived comfort and security from being surrounded by their compatriots, they were not oblivious to the overcrowding. Joseph Blasko, an employee of Goodyear Tire who lived in a Hungarian boarding-house in New Toronto, found sharing his bed especially distasteful: "When I went home, tired, and crawled into bed, I always smelled the body odor of the man who slept there before me. This was mixed with a very unpleasant smell of fermented beans. Of course the guy who worked the night shift must have had a similar experience when he crawled into bed the next morning."[42]

Nor do operators recall the institution with pleasure. All the women interviewed for this study agreed that indispensable as it was, money received from boarders could not adequately pay for their services. A glance at the timetable of a typical keeper explains why. Up at the crack of dawn to prepare breakfast and perhaps even lunch buckets for those boarders who began work early, she was still in the kitchen at midnight, cleaning up after the men who returned from the late shift. When not preparing meals or washing up, she was doing laundry, often by hand, or ironing. She usually got some help from her husband and from Hungarian or other ethnic grocers and butchers who picked up her food orders and delivered goods to her door. The burden of planning and running the house, however, usually fell to the women, who were simultaneously raising several children.

Living arrangements that brought together a female operator with groups of lonely men who were often under the influence of alcohol inevitably also created sexual tensions. These tensions found a creative outlet in humorous songs, tales, and plays depicting the "star boarder" who enjoyed the special favours of the keeper.[43] In reality, however, for most women these tensions were a source of strain. That is why some migrants such as István Szakszon decided not to bring their wives and children to Canada. To ensure a living for the entire family, his wife would have had to take in boarders, and he did not want to subject her to that fate: "Everyone there [in Hamilton] kept boarders and I didn't think it was right ... One man was like this, another like that, and my wife could not have taken it. One came home more drunk than the other.... You would have needed a lot of guts not to sell booze. If you didn't, you were finished, and if you did then you had to put up with people getting drunk in your house ... I didn't think this was good."[44]

Boarding-houses were transitional institutions, well-suited to the needs of a community comprised overwhelmingly of sojourners. Neither owners nor boarders aspired to preserve such arrangements. Yet the Depression killed the hopes of most operators and boarders to move on. According to Hungarian Consul Károly Winter, in the 1930s many of Montreal's Hungarian homeowners were losing their houses because about three-quarters of boarding co-nationals were unable to pay for food and accommodations.[45]

Other Small Businesses

Boarding-houses were not the only small businesses to emerge among Hungarian communities in central Canada. Each larger neighbourhood also housed Hungarian groceries, butchers, restaurants, barbers, shoemakers, tailors, seamstresses, tobacco shops, and billiard rooms. Not only tradesmen and small businessmen from Hungary but even some former agriculturalists tried their hand at such endeavours, for operating them required neither high levels of literacy nor a large initial capital investment and used the labour only of the owner, his wife, and perhaps his grown children. Economic calculation was linked inseparably to shared ethnicity. Owners, familiar with the circumstances of their compatriots and desirous of having them as customers, frequently extended credit and a host of other services to them. Storekeepers who spoke English and understood the customs of the host society also became mediators between their customers and Canadian society. They helped their clients to fill out forms and write official letters. Because an immigrant store was frequently the most visible institution in Canadian towns and cities, employers seeking immigrant workers often notified proprietors, who willingly passed on such information to their compatriots.[46] These acts of kindness helped to build a loyal clientele and hence were good business practice. Consequently, some storekeepers, especially owners of groceries and butcher stores, became very successful and branched out, buying real estate and opening steamship agencies or banks. Their success brought them prominence within the immigrant elite.

Most of these endeavours, however, remained small and vulnerable. The relationship of trust that advanced such businesses could also has-

ten their demise. When many if not most of their customers were unemployed because of the Depression, a number of them were forced to
close.[47] Helen Süle, whose husband operated a butcher store on
Queen Street in Toronto, recalled that out of loyalty her husband extended credit to his regular customers during the Depression, even
when he knew that they were unemployed. He eventually had to close
his shop. With the return of prosperity, Süle was able to open another
store.[48]

Where small Hungarian businesses survived, however, they provided
focal points in immigrant neighbourhoods. In places such as Toronto
or Welland, where Hungarians lived in several districts, visits to businesses owned by co-nationals helped to bring them together. Although
immigrants did not deal exclusively with Hungarian businesses, they
were attracted to them because they could speak their native tongue,
obtain familiar goods, and receive credit.[49] For many of them, moreover, a visit to the local grocery or barber shop quite often also served
as a social occasion. Billiard halls were also social centres.

THE IMMIGRANT ELITE AND
COMMUNITY FORMATION

Middle-class immigrants contributed a measure of stability and cohesion to Hungarian neighbourhoods. Since their professional qualifications were not recognized in Canada, Hungarian-trained teachers,
lawyers, and army officers, for instance, had to abandon their traditional occupations. While some were forced to become manual
labourers, middle-class immigrants generally tried to find work that
would permit them to retain their class status. Some employed their
specialized skills within the confines of their ethnic group. They recognized that because the vast majority of Hungarians in central Canada
were uneducated and spoke little or no English, they required intermediaries in their dealings with the host society, as well as in their official
and business contacts with their native land. Former engineers, civil
servants, army officers, and businessmen took on the role of mediators
by becoming steamship agents and newspaper publishers and editors.
But Hungarian communities in central Canada were so small and impoverished that they could support only a handful of such go-betweens.

Canadian Protestant churches added to the ranks of these mediators. They were willing to train educated Hungarians as ministers and
to guarantee their salaries. An ecclesiastical career thus offered the
most secure avenue for such people to preserve their class status, and
because so few alternatives were open to them, a number who had not
been prepared for the church back home decided to become clerics in

Canada. Their role in their new communities is analyzed in chapter 5. The analysis of the immigrant elite in this chapter is confined to members who did not receive financial support from outside agencies.

Steamship Agents

The narrowness of opportunities provided by Hungarian communities in central Canada is perhaps most clearly apparent from the fate of steamship agents, whose services were indispensable for their compatriots. During the 1920s and the early 1930s, they derived most of their income from handling immigrants' Old World affairs. They remitted savings to families in Hungary, Czechoslovakia, Romania, and Yugoslavia, and when many of the settlers decided to bring their families to Canada, the agents completed the paperwork and sold them prepaid tickets – often on instalment. Almost all the agencies also handled real-estate transactions in Canada. Not until the late 1930s – when immigration had virtually ended, but the economic condition of Hungarians in Canada began to improve and more and more of them were in a position to purchase homes – were the agencies able to derive substantial income from this branch of their operations.[50] Some agents also offered life insurance, but a number of large insurance companies employed special agents within immigrant communities. Béla Eisner, for example, a lawyer from Slovakia who was to become an influential figure among Hungarians in Canada, worked for the Sun Life Insurance Co. in Montreal.[51] Charles Steinmetz, who became a Presbyterian minister in Toronto, first came in contact with Hungarians in that city as an agent of the New York Life Insurance Co.

Throughout the interwar years, all successful steamship agents also acted as translators, notaries, letter writers, counsellors, and employment agents, and they permitted migrant workers to use their offices as postes restantes. Although they may have charged a small fee for some of these services, agents responded to very real needs primarily in order to build a relationship of trust. Alex Kelen of Montreal, for instance, allowed Hungarians to use his address on Colonial Avenue: "They needed an address, so that they could receive mail from home, because one day they worked here, the next week they were thrown out of that place, from the workshop, the brewery, or wherever, and they were unemployed and they came to beg me to let them use my address. So I built little pigeon holes for them and the unfortunates would begin to guess from the street ... I think I have a letter ... it looks like there's a letter in my box."[52]

Yet, despite the unquestionable need for their services, few steamship agencies survived. In Welland, for instance, seven men embarked on careers as steamship agents and ethnic bankers. Not all of them were of middle-class background, nor were they all engaged solely in remittance and travel. Victor Subosits, for example, was not an educated man. Having settled in Welland before 1914, and having operated a general store there for many years, he felt sufficiently familiar with Canadian conditions to become an ethnic broker for more recent immigrants. Accordingly, he attempted, unsuccessfully, to expand his business by acting as a steamship and real estate agent for Hungarians in Welland and in Niagara Falls. He also published a Hungarian-language newspaper, the *Canadai Magyar Népszava* (Canadian Hungarian People's Voice).[53] Another would-be agent was the printer József Imre, who launched the only commercial Hungarian-language newspaper in Canada that enjoyed a measure of success between the wars. His venture into travel and banking, however, did not enjoy equal success.[54] Indeed, by 1939, not a single Hungarian steamship agency was operating in Welland. The members of the ethnic group probably relied on the services of steamship agents in nearby Hungarian colonies.

Of the six agencies opened by Hungarians in Toronto during the 1920s and 1930s, only one survived by 1940 – the National Travel Agency of Izsó Kennedy, later known as Kennedy Travel. It catered not only to Hungarians in Toronto and its environs but also to those of the growing colony in the tobacco-growing area around Delhi and Tillsonburg.[55] The steamship and remittance business within the ethnic group in Montreal was monopolized by Alex Kelen, who became the most prosperous of all Hungarian steamship agents in Canada. During the interwar period, his office had branches in Hamilton and Port Colborne and for a short time in Kirkland Lake and Rouyn-Noranda as well. Sándor Lukács, manager of the Hamilton branch, eventually became independent of Kelen, and his agency, Lucas and King, controlled the Hungarian business in Hamilton and its vicinity.[56]

Business acumen and a fair amount of capital largely explain these successes. Alex Kelen believes that exceptionally good exchange rates, thanks to his connections with banks in Europe, for money remitted to Hungary helped him a great deal. His ability and willingness to provide credit to clients who bought tickets for their families also contributed. During this period of unemployment and hardship, almost no one was able to pay the full fare at once. Kelen sold tickets for a low down payment, followed by monthly payments at 10 per cent annual interest. The fact that 20 per cent of the clients defaulted indicates that Kelen took a considerable risk. He believes, however, that his credit system led to an ever growing clientele.[57]

Earning the immigrants' trust was as important as business acumen in the small, highly competitive Hungarian market in central Canada. Immigrants were understandably careful in selecting the agent who would send their hard-earned savings to their families. The fact that at least two Hungarian agents in central Canada had embezzled remittance money made it imperative that steamship agents prove their trustworthiness.[58]

Despite the important role of middle-class immigrants in organized community life in Canada, the most notable steamship agents were not central to the social life of the communities. This was because Alex Kelen of Montreal, Izsó Kennedy of Toronto, Sándor Lukács of Hamilton, and Jenő Klein of Windsor were Jewish, or of Jewish background. Hungarian agriculturalists would have found nothing unusual about dealing with Jewish businessmen in Canada. After all, in their native villages, the storekeeper and the innkeeper, who were often also money-lenders, were in all likelihood also Jewish. But the readiness of their non-Jewish compatriots to deal with Jews in the world of business did not necessarily mean that they accepted Jews as bona fide Hungarians. Although Jews in Hungary had repeatedly given evidence of their support for the nationalist movement since its beginning in the early nineteenth century, their position in interwar Society remained tenuous.

An appalling indication that Jews were not fully accepted by Hungarians in Canada either was the expulsion of Jenő Klein from the Windsor and District Hungarian Club. The steamship agent had been one of the club's founding members, yet in 1938 fellow members introduced a new provision to admit only "morally upright Christians," forever barring him from the club.[59] Not all efforts by steamship agents of Jewish background to forge close links with their clients by joining Hungarian associations were rebuffed. Alex Kelen of Montreal belonged to the Székely Club and to the Hungarian United Church congregation. Steamship agents also participated in community events and contributed funds towards the maintenance of Hungarian associations. But none of them played a key role in organized community life. The primary identification of at least one of them, Izsó Kennedy of Toronto, was not with the Hungarian community at all. Kennedy, who had changed his name from Klein, was an observant Jew and belonged to a synagogue. (There were no Hungarian-Jewish synagogues in the city at this time.)

The Hungarian Commercial Press in Canada

Some educated immigrants saw an opportunity to earn a living, while putting their special skills to use and maintaining their class status, either by publishing Hungarian newspapers themselves or by working for those who did. As Robert Park pointed out in *The Immigrant Press and Its Control* (1922), newspapers helped immigrants to adjust to American society. Even men and women who arrived in North America from rural areas, and who had not been in the habit of reading papers in their native land, turned to the ethnic press in order to understand their new environment and to be able to function within it.[60] Ethnic newspapers reported on job opportunities and the arrival of new immigrants from Europe, carried advertisements for ethnic businesses, including larger boarding-houses, and announced the activities of ethnic associations. In larger ethnic groups, therefore, commercial papers had a fairly reliable readership, and their popularity made it worthwhile for business, both from within and from outside the ethnic group, to advertise in them. A significant portion of the income of ethnic publishers, moreover, came from printing wedding invitations, flyers, and announcements for the members of their communities.

But the Hungarian communities of central Canada proved infertile for commercial newspapers. Park's observations apply to Hungarian Canadians: many of them began to read newspapers for the first time in Canada. Their communities, however, were too small to support papers. Not only was the potential readership small, but printing announcements for the community could generate little revenue. Successful Hungarian-Canadian businesses were too scarce to provide substantial additional income through advertising. Being few in number, Hungarians were not sufficiently visible in most Canadian communities to motivate business from outside the ethnic group to advertise in Hungarian-language newspapers.

Of the six secular Hungarian papers that appeared in central Canada during the interwar period, only five were more or less commercial ventures: *Kanadai Magyar Hírlap* (Canadian Hungarian Journal) of Welland (1927–29); *Canadai Magyar Népszava* (Canadian Hungarian People's Voice) of Hamilton (1925–30), *Canadai Kis Ujság* (Little Hungarian News of Canada) of Welland (1931–41), *Híradó* (Hungarian Herald) of Toronto and Hamilton (1935–37), and *Magyarság* (Hungarians) of Toronto (1939). (Although nominally secular, *Egyetértés* [Concord] of Montreal [1931] received subsidies from the Roman Catholic church.)[61] The publishers of the five commercial newspapers did not rely on them entirely for support. As mentioned earlier, József Imre, who published the *Canadai Kis Ujság*, was a printer, and Victor Subosits, publisher of the *Canadai Magyar Népszava*, a grocer, real estate agent, and would-be steamship agent. As well, it is likely that, at least for some publishers, considerations of prestige were as important as the hope of making money. Nevertheless, they seemed to expect that the papers would, at the very least, pay for themselves. Only such expectations can explain why the owners of the *Hírlap* and the *Népszava* employed full-time editors.

Indicative of the limited opportunities that central Canadian colonies offered to middle-class Hungarians, the former army officer Zoltán Molnár, after he failed as a newspaper editor, opened a steamship agency in Niagara Falls. Ferenc Szabolcs of Hamilton also tried his hand, unsuccessfully, both at running a steamship agency and at editing a Hungarian newspaper.[62]

The emergence of Hungarian neighbourhoods in central Canada did much to help immigrants adjust to Canadian life even amid the very difficult circumstances created by the Depression. The sense of collective identity that led ordinary Hungarians to settle in distinct neighbourhoods was an essential, but not the sole, factor that led to the establishment of formal community organizations. The participation of business people, members of the liberal professions, artisans, and skilled workers who made up the immigrant elite was also essential. They possessed the experience and self-confidence required to create formal associations.

What brought them together with the rank and file was their shared condition as immigrants. As newcomers, the small minority of elite background could satisfy social ambitions only by attaining leadership and influence within the group. A sense of exclusion from Canadian society lent new meaning to the language and national history that they shared with the others. But mutuality and interconnectedness had their limits. The involvement of outside forces – such as Canadian church authorities, Hungarian clerics from the United States, the government in Budapest, and the Communist party – in Hungarian communities in central Canada helped divide the immigrants along ideological lines into two antagonistic camps.

PART TWO

Community Organizations and Group Identity

4 Secular Associations

Hungarian-Canadian voluntary associations all sought to give formal expression to the sense of group consciousness that informed the settlement and marriage patterns of Hungarian immigrants in central Canada. To explain why their efforts led to the group's division into two opposing camps is the main objective of *Patriots and Proletarians*, and central to this explanation is the recognition that these associations were not built by the grass roots, set up spontaneously by former agriculturalists. As this chapter shows, the initiative came from artisans, skilled urban workers, and middle-class immigrants, who made up only a minority of Hungarians in Canada, but who brought with them well-developed associational traditions from their homeland. Newcomers who arrived in Canada after having spent some years in the United States, where they were introduced to voluntary associations, also helped found Hungarian groups in Canada.

Former agriculturalists who, for reasons discussed in chapter 1, lacked the skills and self-confidence necessary to launch formal organizations were responsive to these elite initiatives because mutual aid societies and social and cultural clubs fulfilled economic, social, and cultural needs. Voluntary associations thus became important arenas for regular interaction among different social strata among the immigrants. They also became forums for the formal expression of group identity. Precisely because they brought about a relationship between former agriculturalists, artisans, and middle-class immigrants that had no precedent in Hungary, such bodies, whose stated aim was the preservation of Hungarian culture in Canada, in fact created new group identities. Their definitions of what it meant to be Hungarian in Canada contained elements from the culture of various social strata in Hungary but also from the world of North American immigrants.[1]

ORIGINS

The oldest Hungarian-Canadian associations in central Canada were established before the start of post–First World War migration. The First Hungarian Sick Benefit Society of Hamilton was founded in 1907, and the Brantford Hungarian Sick Benefit Society in 1913, as a branch of the Hamilton association. The Brantford group became independent in 1926, and by 1927 it had its own branches in Hamilton, Galt, Guelph, Niagara Falls, and St Catharines.[2] Ten years later, the St Catharines branch ceased to exist, but new branches of the Brantford Hungarian Sick Benefit Society were operating in New Waterford, Toronto, and Welland.[3] Although no documentary evidence is available about establishment of the Hamilton Benefit Society, the oldest living members say that some of the founders came from the United States, while others were skilled workers from Hungary. Indeed, early members included individuals from both categories. István Botos, a machinist, and Joseph Král, a tool- and die-maker, had participated in the labour movement in Hungary. István Morey, a taxi driver, and Ferenc Kristoff, a lathe operator, had been active in the Hungarian socialist movement for some time while still in the United States.[4] A number of the Brantford society's 13 founding members also arrived in Canada only after having spent some years in the United States.[5]

The earliest and most complete written records of the membership of these bodies date from the time of incorporation. As the only Hungarian association in Hamilton, the First Hungarian Sick Benefit Society attracted immigrants from all religious persuasions and all walks of life in 1927, when it was incorporated. Some of its members – Ferenc Szabolcs, a steamship agent, István Morey, the taxi driver named above, who learned to speak English in the United States and acted as an interpreter for Hamilton's Hungarians, William Pope, a grocery-store owner, and K. Binkhart, a clerk – belonged to Hamilton's tiny Hungarian elite. The overwhelming majority of the members were independent craftsman, skilled factory workers, or unskilled labourers. There were two carpenters, a tailor, a shoemaker, a cleaner, two barbers, one tool-maker, ten machinists, ten moulders, and 45 labourers among them. Eleven of the 86 members were women, ten of whom were housewives, while one worked as a domestic.[6]

Not surprisingly, given the nature of Hungarian immigration to Canada, the majority of those who joined the first chapter of the

Brantford Hungarian Sick Benefit Society when it was incorporated in
1926 were also workers: the signatures of 35 labourers, 25 moulders,
two foremen, a machinist, a woodworker, a coremaker, a grocer, and
ten farmers appear on the charter.[7] Yet membership was open to any
individual under 45 years of age who was willing to abide by the group's
regulations, and educated, middle-class Hungarians also had a part in
the Society's development. One of the leaders of the Hamilton branch,
for example, was Dezső Andrássy, a graduate of the Hungarian
Economic Academy, who was the North German Lloyd Co.'s Hamilton
representative.[8] Noteworthy among members of the Toronto branch
was Elemér Izsák. The Canadian-born son of pioneer Hungarian settlers in Bekevar, Saskatchewan, Izsák was the first member of the
Hungarian ethnic group to obtain a law degree in Canada.[9] István
Jánossy, owner of a steamship agency in Toronto, and part owner of the
Hungarian-language newspaper the *Híradó* (Herald), was active in both
the Hamilton and the Toronto branches of the Brantford society.[10]

The Welland Hungarian Self-Culture Society was also established before the post-1918 renewal of immigration, by Hungarians who settled
in Canada prior to the war. In 1924, when the society was formally incorporated, any Hungarian man or woman could become a member
for the modest fee of 25 cents. While labourers constituted the bulk
of the membership, only one of the five directors in 1924 was a
labourer; the others were two merchants, a mason, and a blacksmith.
The adherence, from these early days, of a Hungarian-language newspaper editor, two steamship agents, and several merchants indicated a
relatively stable and prosperous Hungarian settlement in Welland.[11]

The Windsor and District Hungarian Club, like the Brantford
society, was the offspring of the First Hungarian Sick Benefit Society of
Hamilton and Hungarian mutual aid societies in the United States.
Some of the club's founders moved to Windsor from Hamilton, where
they had belonged to that city's society, while others came from the
United States. The club's constitution was modelled along lines suggested in a membership booklet that one of the founding members
brought with him from the United States. The associational traditions
of Hungarian craftsmen also influenced the Windsor club's development, since some of the 47 men who gathered on 17 October 1926 at
the founding meeting were tailors and shoemakers in Hungary, where
they had belonged to craft associations. The proud sense of identity is
evident from the recollections of one of them. "We had brains," he
stated proudly when he explained his group's role in setting up the
club, "because we were artisans." The president between 1931 and
1936 was the Hungarian Jewish steamship agent Jenő Klein, whom we
encountered in chapter 2.[12]

Impetus for the formation of the Hungaria Social Club of Montreal in 1926 also came from a group of artisans and skilled workers, but the organization's chief aim was to unite all Hungarians and Hungarian-speaking immigrants in Montreal. The Hungaria's 88 founding members did, indeed, comprise a representative sample of the city's Hungarian colony. There were Catholics, Protestants, and Jews among them, and while artisans took the initiative to create the club, many, if not most, members were former agriculturalists from Hungary and the successor states. A few educated, middle-class men were also active in club affairs. These included Béla Eisner, a former lawyer from Slovakia, Miklós Jónás, a chiropractor who also owned a large Hungarian bakery in Montreal, Ernő Bartók, a former engineer and editor of Montreal's short-lived Hungarian newspaper, *Egyetértés*, and Louis White, an interior decorator who came to Canada after 23 years in the United States, where he was active in associational life. The Hungarian consul general, Albert de Haydin, and the United Church minister Mihály Fehér, at that time the only Hungarian clergyman in Montreal, were also on hand to applaud the club's formation.[13]

Regional and village ties, which were crucial in the formation of Italian and Slovak associations in North America, did not influence creation of the Hungarian-Canadian bodies described thus far. The social background of the founders was in part responsible for this. By virtue of their occupation, education, and experience, these men were less likely to be bound by strong regional or village ties than agricultural labourers or dwarf holders. But the small size of the ethnic group, which prevented emergence of residential clusters based on villages of origin, also made impossible associations based on local ties. So few immigrants from any one area settled in each Hungarian colony that they could not have set up lasting societies on their own.

There was only one exception to this rule: 88 Székelys founded a group based on regional and ethnic sub-group loyalties in Montreal, on 18 January 1932.[14] The chief aim of the Székely Hungarian Cultural Club was to "unite the Székelys, to contribute to their cultural development, and to establish a Székely home." The association had two distinct classes of membership. All morally upright, Hungarian-speaking individuals could participate as associate members; but only Székelys could become charter members. The holding of office was also restricted to Székelys, because, as one of the founders explained: "a special relationship of trust exists among the Székelys, a handshake between two Székelys is as good as a written contract."[15]

But if the club differed from other secular associations because of the strong sub-group bond among its members, it resembled these bodies in the important role that artisans played in its establishment. The first president, Albert Kibédi, for example, was a butcher in his native Székelykeresztúr. It was thanks to his influence that the constitution and by-laws were modelled after those of the craftsmen's association of Székelykeresztúr.[16]

Sándor Biró, the club's first recording secretary, was selected because he had served as the village "death spy" in Transylvania – an honorary position, which conferred the responsibility of filling out official forms, when a villager passed away, concerning the circumstances of death. Club members, few of whom had much education, thought that his former position gave Biró the qualifications necessary to record the minutes of their meetings.[17]

Hungarian Jews stood in a far more ambivalent relationship to the rest of the immigrant group than did the Székelys. Some of them distinguished themselves from non-Jewish Hungarians. In Toronto, such Jews founded the Toronto Hungarian Jewish Cultural Club.[18] Izsó Kennedy, Toronto's only successful Hungarian steamship agent, was a member.[19] The institutionalization of anti-semitism in Hungary through anti-Jewish laws, starting in 1938,[20] convinced other Jewish immigrants from Hungary to organize independently of their Christian compatriots. Jews in Montreal formed the Benevolent Society of Hungarian Jews, setting assistance to their co-religionists in Hungary as one of their objectives. Ironically, despite the treatment accorded Jews in Hungary, these emigrants still asserted their patriotic loyalty to their native land.[21] Still other Jews, like the unfortunate Jenő Klein, who was abruptly shut out of the Windsor and District Hungarian Club, or like a number of the Hungaria Social Club's founders, identified fully with non-Jewish Hungarians and joined their associations.

Their efforts to become fully integrated into the Hungarian immigrant group, however, were unsuccessful. In the Windsor club, as we have seen, conflict between Klein, who was president 1931–37, and the members assumed an anti-semitic character when they restricted admission to "morally upright Christians."[22] The case of Béla Eisner suggests, however, that Jews were not fully integrated even in associations such as the Hungaria that gave no sign of overt anti-semitism. Eisner, a founder and leader of that club, was not even born a Jew. His family had converted to Christianity before his birth. Yet even he believed that despite his 20 years of active participation in the club and more generally in the patriotic camp in Montreal, he was still not fully accepted as Hungarian. That is why he would not consider becoming president of the Grand Committee of Hungarian Churches and Associations in Montreal, established at the initiative of the Canadian government to unite Hungarians during the Second World War. He explained to a friend in Windsor that, "given the fact that there are a number of intelligent and worthwhile Christian leaders in Montreal, I did not think it appropriate to expose, not so much myself but the whole movement to carping critics, and to provide them with a possible focus for their attacks."[23]

THE NATURE AND FUNCTIONS OF SECULAR ORGANIZATIONS

Mutual Aid

The provision of financial aid for members and their families in the case of illness or death was a major objective of secular associations. The importance of this service before the introduction of state-run social insurance schemes can scarcely be exaggerated. The First Hungarian Sick Benefit Society of Hamilton, the Brantford Hungarian Sick Benefit Society, and the Windsor and District Hungarian Club were first and foremost mutual aid societies. Before the First World War, neither the Hamilton society nor its Brantford branch was incorporated, and money to assist members who fell ill, or to cover funeral expenses, was raised on an ad hoc basis, by imposing a levy on members whenever the need arose.[24]

By 1926, each new member of the Hamilton society paid an initiation fee of one dollar and monthly dues of 75 cents. In return for these payments, members received $7.50 a week in the case of illness. The club also paid $75 to cover funeral expenses.[25] In August 1927, as we shall see in chapter 7, when members voted to affiliate with the Hungarian Workers Mutual Aid and Self-Improvement Society – the Hungarian mass organization of the American Communist party – its benefit plan became more generous still.[26]

The Brantford society did not follow the example of its parent association. It was incorporated separately, to become the largest mutual aid society in the patriotic camp. It subscribed to insurance policies with Northern Life Insurance Co. In 1926, most members paid an initiation fee of $2 and monthly dues of 50 cents, while those whose occupations were considered hazardous were required to pay slightly higher dues. In return, all members were entitled to benefits of $6 a week during the first ten weeks of illness and $3 thereafter, for a period to be determined by the membership. They were also entitled to funeral benefits of $50. By-laws required that all members attend the funerals of fellow members.[27]

At its inception, the Windsor and District Hungarian Club operated as a mutual aid society of the most basic sort: each member paid a membership fee of $1 per month, in return for which he was entitled to receive $6 a week in case of illness. However, the resources that could be raised from dues alone were so meagre that the club was initially too poor to offer funeral benefits. Even to meet the costs of aiding sick members it had to rely on fundraising social events as well. Small wonder, then, that members responded willingly to the agents of the Northern Life Insurance Co., who offered the group an insurance policy. Under the agreement, families of deceased members, even if they were still in Hungary, became eligible to receive $1,000. Such a policy was bound to appeal to men engaged in hard and often dangerous physical labour, who had to contend every day with the possibility of accidents. The fact that many of them contracted debts, and possibly mortgaged their modest holdings, in order to migrate to Canada increased their worries with regard to families left behind.[28]

In contrast to the Hamilton, Brantford, and Windsor associations, the Welland Hungarian Self-Culture Society played down mutual aid. During the first years of operation, the amount paid in case of illness or bereavement was determined by the membership as the need arose. The society's constitution suggests that a wish to present Hungarians in a favourable light to the host society, as well as fraternal concerns, lay behind provision of mutual aid. "If the deceased has no lawful heir in Canada," stated one clause, "the society will take care of the burial, so that the deceased will not become a public charge and thus ruin the reputation of Hungarians living here, in the eyes of Canadian authorities."[29] Eventually, sickness and burial benefit plans became incorporated in the society's constitution. When mutual aid plans were formalized, admission to the society was restricted to men under the age of 45 and women under 40. By 1929, members received one dollar a day for the first 12 weeks of illness and 50 cents a day for the next 12. The society, alone among Hungarian associations in Canada, provided special benefits to female members for two weeks following delivery of a baby. It also selected an English-speaking member to accompany fellow members who spoke no English on their visits to the doctor.[30]

Intent on saving money as quickly as possible and thus shortening their stay in Canada, some immigrants judged the costs of any mutual aid scheme to be too high. Full of youthful energy and confidence, they were not unduly concerned about the possibility of accidents. For this reason, such secular associations as the Oshawa Hungarian Cultural Club and the Székely club in Montreal adopted mutual aid schemes only after they had been in existence for some years, while the

Hungaria Social Club did not adopt one at all during the interwar era. Each time a scheme was proposed, it was turned down by members who argued that the high cost of insurance would simply diminish membership.[31] Even in this club, however, informal aid was provided periodically to members in need.

Social and Cultural Activities

All secular associations sought to unite Hungarians by providing them with meeting places. Men and women in Hungarian neighourhoods had given ample evidence of the desire to socialize with fellow nationals by gathering informally on street corners and in district parks, grocery stores, barber shops, billiard halls, and even crowded boarding-houses. The desire to establish a "home" for Hungarians was intensified by the hardships encountered in unfamiliar Canadian surroundings. As the by-laws of the Székely club explained, the association required its own meeting place "where those who find themselves in an alien environment, or who have lost the capacity to work, or who have no home, will find a true home."[32] The Hungaria Social Club hoped "to make up for the warm family life" that many members left behind in Europe.[33] Ordinary apartments or store fronts could be turned into comfortable social centres relatively inexpensively because members contributed their labour and skills free of charge.[34] Although these centres were supposed to serve the needs of all Hungarians, regardless of creed, in some cases, as we have seen, "Hungarian" was defined in a narrow, exclusivist manner to refer only to Christian immigrants from Hungary and the successor states.[35]

Centres established by secular associations were especially important in communities such as Oshawa and Brantford that were too small to support independent Hungarian-Canadian places of worship. In these two communities, the club-houses of the Oshawa Hungarian Cultural Club and of the Brantford Hungarian Sick Benefit Society, respectively, served as the sole meeting places for patriotic Hungarians.

All Hungarian-Canadian social centres tried to cater to the practical needs of immigrant workers. When Montreal's Hungaria first rented, and later purchased, a two-storey building on St Lawrence Boulevard, in the heart of the Hungarian district, it employed a restaurateur to provide nourishing, inexpensive Hungarian meals. The fact that the opening of the restaurant increased attendance at the club suggests that a need existed for such a service. The premises of the Székely club in Montreal also offered shelter for the unemployed and day care for the children of working women.[36]

These associations also fulfilled important social and recreational needs. The acquisition of liquor licences by some greatly enhanced their appeal; income from the sale of alcoholic beverages became a major source of revenue.[37] Thus even associations that did not normally serve liquor obtained temporary licences when they held balls and banquets in their premises. Taking their cue from the popularity of billiard halls in immigrant neighbourhoods, most clubs also purchased one or two billiard tables for their members. Men who gathered in Hungarian social centres also frequently played cards. Gambling, however – one of the main attractions and sources of revenue for bourgeois clubs in Hungarian cities – was not permitted in Hungarian clubs in Canada.

Social functions such as dances and banquets were organized frequently in secular associations. Stating explicitly that the purpose of social functions was "to entertain members and raise funds," the Windsor and District Hungarian Club held a dance every Saturday night.[38] The entertainment committee of the Welland Hungarian Self-Culture Society also organized balls and banquets at least once a month.[39] The fundraising role of these activities is evident from a clause in the society's constitution that required members to purchase tickets even if they did not intend to take part.[40] During the hot summer months, associations organized outings, or "picnics," to local parks and to nearby lakes; members enjoyed the cool outdoors, while playing games, singing, dancing, and eating.

As suggested by such names as the Welland Hungarian-Self Culture Society, the Oshawa Hungarian Culture Club, and the Székely Hungarian Cultural Club, the mandates of such secular associations in Canada, like those of reading circles and workers' groups in Hungary and of most Hungarian-American bodies, generally included cultural objectives as well. The Hungaria Social Club, for example, proposed "to encourage literary pursuits on behalf of its members and for this purpose to organize a library and hold literary evenings."[41] To fulfil these aims, members set up a choir, an amateur drama troupe, and a youth group. Members who had had formal education in their homeland, moreover, held lectures to enlighten fellow members. After the failure of his venture to reach his compatriots through the pages of *Egyetértés*, former engineer Ernő Bartók gave lectures to Hungaria's members on subjects ranging from Canadian history to "the employment question."[42] The Windsor club similarly planned "to hold and conduct lectures and literary classes for the purpose of promoting English and Hungarian literature."[43]

Amateur drama troupes emerged within virtually all the associations, often launched by individuals from the same social and economic background as the founders of these organizations. In the Windsor club, steamship agent Jenő Klein initiated amateur dramatic performances.[44] János Exner, energetic producer of plays in the Welland society, was a tailor. His counterpart in Oshawa's Hungarian club, István K. Karnay, had belonged to a Hungarian theatre group in Lorrain, Ohio, before he moved to Canada in 1925.[45] The Hungaria's amateur performers benefited for years from guidance by Baroness Csávossy, who had been an actress in Hungary. She was assisted in her endeavours by the interior decorator Louis White.[46] Balázs Orbán and Joseph Kovács, who led the drama troupe of the Székely club, had both received high school education, unlike the majority of Hungarian immigrants.[47] Until 1937, they frequently worked under the direction of Mrs Breckner, who later became the most active amateur director among the Hungarians of Toronto. Breckner, a dressmaker, had attended theatrical performances regularly in her native town of Bejus, in Transylvania, and she grew to love the theatre. According to her daughter, Breckner probably took part in amateur dramatics in her native town as well, but in Canada her involvement intensified because "the purpose of it was to keep the young people together, to keep them close to home, so that they don't go, let's say to the Ukrainians ... The older people had to find ways to keep the younger people within the Hungarian community."[48]

An important motive behind these cultural activities, then, was the desire to express and to preserve a Hungarian identity in Canada. The founders of the Windsor club expressed the hope that because of their endeavours future generations of Hungarian origin in Canada would be able to think back to their forbears with "heads raised high, in the Hungarian spirit and with Hungarian pride."[49] Similarly, members of the Oshawa club wanted to ensure that their children were educated "in the Hungarian spirit, both intellectually and emotionally."[50] The Welland society's raison d'être, according to President Louis Szabó, was to "tend the noble Hungarian feeling, a deep love of our people, and all those age-old Hungarian values which win respect for our name everywhere."[51]

In their letters patent and by-laws, a number of associations emphasized their role as agencies of Canadianization, while playing down preservation of a distinctive ethnic identity. Thus, for example, the Welland society's aims as stated in its letters patent in 1924 were: "To educate Hungarian immigrants in Canada in the laws, languages, and customs of Canada, to conduct and form athletic, literary and other educational clubs and classes, to arrange facilities for social intercourse for Hungarian people, and to erect, own and operate a club house or club houses, to hold social and public entertainments of every kind, and to care for Hungarian and other families in need of assistance and to look after the general welfare of their children."[52] In later Hungarian versions of the society's by-laws, its intention to preserve the Hungarian language and culture, as well as the wish to keep alive the love of its members for their native land, took precedence over adaptation. In 1924, the founders perhaps still felt that their position in Canada was vulnerable because Hungary had fought on the side of the Central Powers during the First World War. Consequently, they formulated their objectives with an eye to placating the host society.

The English version of the Oshawa club's by-laws also neglected to mention that one of the organization's main objectives – specified in the Hungarian-language by-laws – was preservation of that language in Canada.[53] Awareness of anti-alien sentiments that persisted among native Canadians between the world wars and intensified with the coming of the Depression may have prompted this discrepancy.

Although secular associations valued preservation of Hungarian culture, they were not uniformly successful in carrying out this mandate. Thus, for example, while the Welland society was the centre of that city's vibrant Hungarian cultural life, the minute books of the Hungaria, the Windsor club, and the Székely club suggest that these bodies periodically neglected cultural activities.[54] The quality of cultural life seemed to depend on the presence of energetic individuals who were somewhat better educated than rank-and-file members of the ethnic group. In the absence of such people, cultural life within the associations sometimes faltered.

For the rank and file of these clubs, successful cultural programs more often than not meant not preservation of their own culture from Hungary but introduction or at least deeper immersion into Hungarian national culture. Some of the mediators of this culture were members of the immigrant elite. As we see below, however, the nature and content of cultural life within these associations were shaped by outside forces as well. Ordinary immigrants were responsive to the overtures of their social superiors and of these outside forces because of the major economic, social, and cultural needs that their societies fulfilled.

All secular organizations were democratically run. Their officials were elected at annual membership meetings, and they reported to the members at regular intervals. The importance attributed to these meetings by the founders is indicated by the strict rules that governed their conduct. The by-laws of several groups specified that members who attended these meetings inebriated were liable to be suspended. Inclusion of careful and detailed rules of conduct in these by-laws resulted also from the inexperience of many in the rank and file. They had to be instructed, for example, to seek the president's permission before speaking and to remain seated during meetings.[55]

The number of officers was high relative to membership. In 1935, 14 of the Welland society's 151 members were officers.[56] Julianna Puskás has suggested that so many posts were created in American Hungarian associations to permit as many members as possible to partake of the prestige conferred by holding office.[57] At least some Hungarian-Canadian organizations, however, may have been simply imitating their counterparts south of the border in form, without sharing their spirit. For some Hungarians in Canada showed reluctance to hold offices: the Windsor club and the Hungaria periodically found it difficult to fill club offices.[58] Lack of experience and self-confidence may well have been responsible for this situation. By contrast, other immigrants, such as Joseph Kovács of the Székely club, saw the democratic nature of associations as an essential feature. He believes that even members who had no experience with organizational life before arriving in Canada held the club's by-laws as sacrosanct. Attendance at membership meetings was mandatory.[59]

While community life among Hungarians in Canada depended on the interaction of immigrants from a variety of social backgrounds within voluntary associations, this interactive process cannot by itself explain the division of the immigrant group into two antagonistic camps along ideological lines. As the remainder of part II shows, the involvement in community life of three major outside forces – church authorities (chapter 5), the Hungarian government (chapter 6), and the Communist party (chapter 7) – helped polarize the group in significant ways.

5 Bastions of the Hungarian Spirit

Father Jeromos Hédly, the Franciscan priest responsible for laying the foundations of Montreal's Hungarian Roman Catholic church, observed in 1928 that in Canada Hungarian churches were the "bastions of the Hungarian spirit."[1] His comment was accurate insofar as churches were the most influential of Hungarian organizations in Canada. Because of religious segmentation, various Hungarian churches – Roman Catholic, Presbyterian, United Church, Lutheran, and Baptist – were active in most larger Hungarian communities, and they generally had more members than secular organizations. These immigrant churches, moreover, catered not only to the religious but also to the social, cultural, and at times even economic needs of their members. Their influence consequently extended well beyond the religious domain.

But if Hédly was implying that the chief cultural role of immigrant churches was merely defence of Old World values and ideas shared by members in an alien, new environment, then his depiction was inaccurate. Within Hungarian-Canadian churches, a new group identity was being forged. The history of Hungarian churches in central Canada offers us a very clear example that immigrant institutions were not simply the formal expression of group consciousness among ordinary immigrants. In fact, these churches were no less paternalistic than village churches and religious organizations in Hungary. The initiative for their establishment came from Hungarian clerics in the United States and from Canadian church authorities – forces from outside the immigrant group altogether – who were intent on shaping newcomers' adjustment according to their own precepts. Immigrants were responsive to these initiatives because Hungarian clergymen and the churches that they built provided them with much-needed services.

ORIGINS

Roman Catholic Congregations

The attention of Roman Catholic authorities was first drawn to the presence of Hungarian co-religionists in central Canada by Father Biró, pastor of St Elizabeth Hungarian Parish in Buffalo, New York. In 1908, Biró wrote to the archdiocese of Toronto, to obtain permission to carry out missionary work among Hungarians in the Welland area.[2] Hungarian settlers in that region had given evidence of their devotion and of their preference for religious services in their own language by travelling to Buffalo to seek out a Hungarian priest. They also asked Biró to come to Welland to hear their confessions. There is no evidence, however, that they took any steps to set up an independent national parish. For the next 15 years, they attended an English-language church and occasionally received missions from visiting Hungarian-American clergymen.

Once Hungarian priests in the United States became aware of the presence of Hungarians in Canada, they began to worry about the fate of these co-religionists. They feared that in Canada, as in the United States, Protestant missionaries would make inroads even among Hungarian Roman Catholics.[3] In 1923, the Hungarian Franciscan fathers of New York wrote to Archbishop Neil McNeil of Toronto to warn him that unless a Hungarian priest were brought to Ontario, the church would lose Hungarian immigrants to the Protestants. They offered to take charge of the Hungarian parishes in Canada.[4] Despite their offer, no action was taken to create Hungarian parishes in central Canada for the next four years.

High-ranking officials in the Canadian hierarchy seemed anxious to match the work of the Protestant churches among new immigrants. They were also intent on preventing secular radical ideologies, especially communism, from making inroads within immigrant communities. As the Reverend P. Casgrain explained in the *Catholic Register*, ministering to immigrants was of the utmost importance not only to the church but also to the state: "when newcomers cease to practice their religion, they generally become freethinkers and are easily misled by the anti-Christian atheistic propaganda of communist agitators and eventually may become a danger to the state. Their religion is, as a matter of fact, the greatest safeguard for the maintenance of law and order."[5] The Hungarians in central Canada, however, apparently did not yet constitute a sufficient presence in 1923 to attract the attention of the local Catholic authorities.

In 1926, the Hungarian consul general drew Archbishop McNeil's attention to the presence of Hungarians in the Toronto area.[6] In the same year, Father Barron of St Peter's and Paul's Church in Welland, where Hungarians worshipped, requested that a Hungarian priest from the United States be employed to assist him.[7] In response, McNeil turned to the United States to seek a suitable candidate to take up work among Hungarians. Father Lipót Mosonyi, pastor of St Elizabeth's in Buffalo, informed him that Hungarian secular priests in the United States could not even fill the needs of American Hungarians.[8] He nevertheless recommended Father Stephen Nyiri, of Homestead, Pennsylvania, who agreed to go to Welland in order to start building a Hungarian parish there.[9]

The efforts of this clergyman, who had taken part in the founding of a number of us immigrant parishes, provided the impetus for the building of Our Lady of Hungary, the first Hungarian Roman Catholic church in central Canada. As suggested by the comments of the church's first steward, Gáspár Almási, not only Father Nyiri's initiative but the promise of financial aid from Canadian church authorities was necessary to convince the Hungarians of Welland that such an undertaking was feasible: "The father, when he came to us in 1927 to tend to our religious needs, and to take charge of the organization of the parish, asked his parishioners whether they would prefer to continue worshipping at the English Catholic church, or whether we could build an independent Hungarian church. We, the parishioners, consented unanimously to the building of a church, as soon as we found out that the Archbishop of Toronto would help us in every way, and that he would arrange for a long term loan to cover the costs of Church building."[10]

Nine months after his arrival, having ensured that launching of a Hungarian parish was well on its way, Nyiri returned to the United States, but not before he found someone to take charge of the new parish. He recommended to Archbishop McNeil the Franciscan fathers Hédly and Burka, who took over the work in Welland. Nyiri also drew the archbishop's attention to the growth of Hungarian settlement in Toronto, and with the prelate's permission he initiated the correspondence with the primate of Hungary that led to the arrival in Canada of László Forgách, the seminarian who became the first Hungarian Roman Catholic priest in Toronto.[11]

Before Forgách's arrival, Welland's Hungarian priests attempted to cater as best they could to the religious needs of co-nationals in

Toronto. During his stay in Canada, Father Nyiri travelled to Toronto and Oshawa once a month to hear confessions in Hungarian. He also arranged that masses be said for the Hungarians every Sunday at St Patrick's Church, on McCaul Street, by the Redemptorist Fathers. Afterwards, a layman would read aloud from the Bible in Hungarian and lead the singing of Hungarian hymns.[12] After Nyiri's departure, Father Burka continued to visit the Hungarians in Toronto and Oshawa. He initiated the establishment of the Catholic Circle, a religiously based social and cultural association.[13]

In Montreal, the first person to explore the possibility of a Hungarian parish was the Hungarian consul, Albert de Haydin. In 1926, he informed the archbishop of Montreal of the presence of Hungarians in his diocese, and through newspaper advertisements he urged Catholic Hungarians to send him their names and addresses, so that a parish could be established in Montreal.[14]

The actual work of organization was begun, however, by the Franciscan Father Jeromos Hédly, who arrived in Canada in April 1927 with the objective of setting up Hungarian parishes throughout eastern Canada. On 23 April 1927, 30 Hungarians responded to his call, and the foundations of the new parish were laid.[15] When Hédly left to take up the work begun by Nyiri in Welland, he was replaced by Father Joseph Rácz, from Stockholm, Saskatchewan.[16]

In 1933, thanks to the intervention of the Hungarian consul general, Károly Winter, Sister Mary of the Sisters of Social Service order arrived in Montreal. Members of her order had undertaken missionary work in western Canada some ten years earlier, with the aid and encouragement of the government in Budapest. Their presence in Montreal was to provide continuity for the city's Hungarian Roman Catholics, who were served by six priests in succession in the 1920s and 1930s. Their work was especially significant from an ethnic point of view between 1933 and 1935, when the parish priest was the French-Canadian Father Gaboury.[17]

Presbyterian Congregations

The attention of the Board of Home Missions of the Presbyterian Church in Canada was drawn to the presence of Hungarians in southern Ontario by activities in the area of Hungarian missionaries from northern New York state.[18] When the Welland session of the Presbyterian church became aware of the growing Hungarian settlement within its jurisdiction in 1925, it requested that the Hamilton presbytery initiate work among these immigrants.[19] Like the Roman Catholic church, Protestant denominations were also intent on gaining the adherence of newcomers and preventing the spread of radical and anti-clerical ideas among them. In the absence of evangelizing work among them, explained Reverend C.L. Cowan, home mission convener of the Presbyterian church, immigrants would become "the happy hunting ground of all kinds of alien and subversive ideas."[20]

To carry out its non-Anglo-Saxon efforts during the 1920s and 1930s, the Board of Home Missions attempted to employ missionaries who spoke the language of the immigrants. To find a suitable candidate to deal with Hungarians, the presbytery turned to Reverend Blaise Hospodár of Tonawanda, New York, who had been active among Hungarians in Canada. Hospodár recommended Ferenc Kovács.[21] A sculptor from Transylvania, Kovács had received his theological and practical training for the ministry in the United States. He studied at Princeton Theological Seminary and worked among Hungarians in New Jersey for two years before moving to Canada. Through his American work, he became familiar with the practices of Hungarian churches in North America.[22]

As a travelling missionary in southern Ontario, Kovács organized congregations in Brantford, Caledonia, Hamilton, Niagara Falls, Oshawa, Port Colborne, Toronto, and Welland.[23] Only in Toronto did lay initiative play a part. Here a few Calvinists had requested a Hungarian-speaking missionary shortly before Kovács began his fortnightly Sunday services in the city.[24] Because this action was unusual for this area, it is important to note that one of the Toronto congregation's founding members, John Bernath, had lived in the United States for many years, where he was one of the founders of the Hungarian Reformed congregation of Newark, New Jersey. Bernath and two other members of the tiny group were skilled workers and thus differed from the agriculturalists who made up the bulk of the ethnic group in Canada.

Even establishment of the Toronto congregation, however, depended on material aid from the Presbyterian church. The Board of Home Missions paid Kovács's salary, as well as the salaries of all Hungarian Presbyterian ministers who worked among their compatriots between the wars. For years, moreover, English-Canadian churches provided Hungarians with facilities in which to meet and to hold Sunday services. The Board of Home Missions also financed the first issues of *Figyelő* (Hungarian Observer), a monthly published by Kovács, distributed free of charge, and seen as an effective means for gaining adherents from within the ethnic group.[25]

The fact that Kovács organized so many congregations meant that he could not carry on the work by himself. His urgent request that the Hamilton presbytery call other Hungarian-speaking ministers, however, was also motivated by the fact that the United Church of Canada (formed 1925) had commenced to work among Hungarians in southern Ontario, and Kovács feared that it would make gains at the expense of the Presbyterians. His fears were well founded. Hungarian Calvinists had no theological reasons for preferring the Presbyterian to the United Church, and while the latter employed a full-time missionary to minister to Hungarians in Welland, for example, Kovács, overburdened by his responsibilities, could visit Welland only fortnightly.[26]

The Hamilton presbytery complied with Kovács's wishes, and in 1927, upon his recommendation, it invited Reverend István Csutoros to Welland from the United States. The rivalry between the two churches thus increased their involvement with immigrant congregations.[27] The new Presbyterian minister was the son of Dr Elek Csutoros, minister of the Hungarian Reformed Church of Cleveland. The younger Csutoros, born and raised within the Hungarian-American community, received his training in the Bloomfield Theological Seminary in Bloomfield, New Jersey. By calling him to Welland and agreeing to pay his salary, the presbytery unintentionally provided yet another link between the mature organizational traditions of US Hungarians and the nascent associational life of Hungarians in Canada.[28]

The Presbyterian church also assumed responsibility for training educated Hungarians to become ministers. Béla Bucsin, for example, whose studies at Knox College in Toronto were financed by the Presbyterian church while he worked as a student missionary among Toronto's Hungarians, had been a school teacher in his native village. When he arrived in Canada in 1924, he discovered that manual labour was the only career open to him. Not surprisingly, therefore, when Reverend Paulin of St Andrew's Church in Windsor, whom Bucsin met because of his participation in the local Hungarian Presbyterian congregation, offered to recommend him for missionary endeavours among his compatriots, Bucsin was all too happy to accept.[29]

Charles Steinmetz, minister 1932–52 of the Hungarian Presbyterian congregation in Toronto, was another layman trained by the Presbyterian church. Unlike Bucsin, however, he had been making his way quite successfully. At the age of 16, he became a coalminer in West Virginia. By 1928, he had almost completed his studies in architecture at Temple University, in Philadelphia, when his family's economic needs cut short his education. But Steinmetz allowed neither his disappointed hopes, nor grim employment prospects in the United States, to discourage him. After working for a few months as a Fuller Brush man, he was hired as a salesman by the New York Life Insurance Co. It was as that firm's representative that Steinmetz arrived in Toronto, in 1929. He became attracted to a career in the church thanks to the encouragement of his future wife, Beatrice Bernath, who was a Presbyterian deaconess, and to his desire to become a guide to his co-nationals in Toronto. "I felt that the Hungarians needed a leader," he was to explain many years later, "which they sorely lacked."[30]

United Church Congregations

The United Church of Canada started its work among Hungarians in central Canada the year after its founding in 1925. In its search for a suitable clergyman, the church's Board of Home Missions, like its Presbyterian counterpart, turned to the United States. Reverend Mihály Fehér, whom the board invited to take up the task, had arrived in the United States in 1923, as a scholarship student from the theological seminary of the Hungarian Reformed Church in Debrecen. He studied at the Dutch Reformed Seminary in New Brunswick, New Jersey, where he was ordained in 1925, and then proceeded to post-graduate studies at Princeton Theological Seminary. While he studied, Fehér also served as a missionary in Uniontown, New Jersey. Thus, like Kovács, he became acquainted with the ways of Hungarian churches in the United States.[31]

So anxious was the United Church to begin efforts among Hungarians that it invited Fehér to Canada even before its Board of Home Missions had a clear idea where such work could be carried out effectively. When Fehér, who was supposed to begin in the same general areas as Kovács, informed the board that he saw little sense in competing with his Presbyterian colleague, the board sent him to Kingston. Only after he discovered that there were no Hungarians in Kingston, was he allowed to proceed to Montreal.[32]

Popular initiative did not play a part in the inception of the Montreal congregation. When Fehér arrived in the city, in May 1926, he did not even know where to find Hungarian immigrants. At the YMCA, he accidentally encountered two Hungarians: a Lutheran draftsman, János László Papp, and a Roman Catholic sculptor, Béla Zoltványi. With their aid, he proceeded to track down Protestant co-nationals. They visited Hungarian barbershops and restaurants on City Hall, de Bullion, Demontigny, and St Urbain streets, where many Hungarians lived. They also knocked on doors, and on 23 May 1926, ten days after Fehér's arrival, a small group gathered in a German Lutheran hall for a service. Since no other Hungarian Organizations existed in Montreal, some Lutherans and Catholics also joined in early services. Forty Hungarian-speaking Slovaks were also active in the nascent congregation. With the promise of financial assistance from the United Church, this mixed company officially established the Hungarian United Church of Montreal.

Although Fehér's reluctance to divide the ranks of the Hungarian Calvinists in Canada somewhat delayed the competition between the United and the Presbyterian churches for Hungarian adherents in southern Ontario, the former was not long content to leave this field to the latter. In 1926, reluctantly acquiescing to the wishes of his superiors, Fehér recommended Reverend Musznai – a Calvinist minister from Transylvania who was doing postgraduate studies at Princeton – to start ministering to Hungarians in the Niagara presbytery of the United Church.[33] When Musznai returned to Transylvania, he was replaced by a layman, János Papp, the Lutheran draftsman from Montreal. The Board of Home Missions encouraged Papp to study theology at Victoria College in Toronto so that he could be ordained. Papp, however, found the combined load of his studies and his responsibilities as a student missionary too onerous. He also believed that in order to be effective he would have to be ordained at once. When church officials refused to ordain him before he completed his studies, he left the United Church, to become a Lutheran pastor, and, as we shall see, he founded all the Hungarian Lutheran congregations in central Canada.[34]

Charles Farkas, who replaced Papp in the Niagara presbytery, also became a minister under the sponsorship of the Board of Home Missions. A native of Transylvania, he had begun his training at the Calvinist theological academy in Kolozsvár. But after Transylvania was given to Romania by the Treaty of Trianon, opportunities for Hungarian Calvinist ministers there declined, and Farkas decided to emigrate. He arrived in Canada in 1925 and worked as a colonization agent for the CNR in the west until 1929, when he began his studies at St Andrew's College in Saskatoon. Reverend Farkas served the Hungarians of Welland from 1929 until his death in 1965.[35]

Dr Ambrosius Czakó, who became the minister of the Hungarian United Church congregation in Toronto after Papp's departure, was ordained as a Roman Catholic priest, and as a young man he belonged to the Cistercian order. He obtained a doctorate from the University of Budapest and was sent by his order to do postdoctoral work at the universities of Fribourg and Vienna. In 1916, however, Czakó left the Roman Catholic church because publication of his theological writings, which earned high praise from liberal clerics for their intellectual content and integrity, was forbidden by church authorities. He became a secondary school teacher and obtained a minister's diploma from the Calvinist theological college of Debrecen. But apparently dissenting theologians of the calibre of Czakó presented a threat to the conservative Hungarian church establishment, for Admiral Horthy's first minister of education, who was a Roman Catholic priest, forced Czakó's dismissal from his job. Czakó further angered church authorities by translating into Hungarian a work by the Swiss theologian Kutter, which included a strong defence of labour unions.[36]

Czakó was eventually forced to leave Hungary because of his political, not his theological writings. He belonged to the radical republicans who threw their support behind Count Mihály Károlyi in 1918, and in 1921, when the group was proscribed by the government, Czakó published a periodical, *Független Szemle* (Independent Review), which for a time was the sole voice of radical democratic opposition to the counterrevolution. The periodical was suppressed, and Czakó's attempts to produce it under a different title also failed. He eventually left for Vienna in 1925 because he faced imprisonment for attempting to publish subversive material. Efforts by another leading radical democrat, Oszkár Jászi, to gain him entry into the United States failed, and apart from a visit to England at the invitation of the Society of Friends, who admired his work, he lived in dire poverty in Vienna until the United Church, made aware of his predicament by Professor Mincken of Queen's University, invited him to Canada.[37] As we see below, his educational background, his intellectual inclinations, and especially his political leanings isolated him from his fellow Hungarian clerics in Canada and even influenced his relationship with his congregation.

Lutheran Congregations

The origins of Hungarian Lutheran congregations in central Canada offer yet another, striking illustration of the pivotal role of clerics in the foundation of Hungarian congregations in this country. The founder of all Hungarian Lutheran congregations in central Canada was Reverend János László Papp, who, as mentioned above, became a Lutheran minister after falling out with the United Church's Board of Home Missions. In 1928, Papp founded Lutheran congregations both in Toronto and in Windsor, but apparently he found the field in Windsor more promising because he decided to settle there. Yet only two men came to the first meeting he called in order to establish a local congregation. With the help of these two dedicated people, however, Papp recruited additional adherents, so that by the time of the congregation's official establishment it had 45 members.[38]

Reverend Eugene Ruzsa, who became minister of the Hungarian Lutheran Church of Toronto in 1930, received his theological training in Canada, at the Lutheran seminary in Waterloo. He held services for

Lutherans in Welland and Hamilton as well. The history of his Toronto congregation suggests that the lines dividing Hungarian-Canadian Protestant congregations from one another were not all that firm. While most Hungarian Lutherans in North America joined the United Lutheran Church of America, the Toronto congregation, apparently for financial reasons, joined the United Church of Canada and functioned within this denomination for many years.[39]

Baptist Congregations

It is perhaps significant that the only Hungarian congregation in central Canada that owed its origins solely to lay initiative, the Hungarian Baptist Congregation in Toronto, belonged to a church without strong roots in Hungary. Its founder, Julius Nagy, immigrated to the United States before the First World War and became a convert to the Baptist faith in New Jersey. Before his conversion, he was a wild youth; he drank and gambled, and generally – he later came to believe – wasted his life away.[40] So great was Nagy's devotion to the religion that was responsible for changing his life that he set about founding a Hungarian Baptist congregation almost immediately following his arrival in Toronto, in 1924. After work, he would seek out the handful of Hungarians then living in the city and invite them to his home. According to the recollections of those who attended these gatherings, the possibility of meeting their compatriots and talking to them in Hungarian, rather than curiosity about the Baptist faith, attracted them to Nagy's home.[41]

The host convinced some of his guests to join him in forming the nucleus of a congregation. Until 1929, the small group worshipped in the Beverly Street Baptist Church. After the service, they would return to Nagy's home, where they would translate the sermon into Hungarian and listen to Nagy's interpretation of it. They were occasionally visited by the Hungarian Baptist preacher from Buffalo, who instructed them on ways to evangelize their co-nationals, a practice that was virtually unknown in Hungary.[42] By 1929, because of the adherence of local Hungarians as a result of proselytizing and the arrival of more Baptists from Hungary, the congregation was considered strong enough by the Baptist Mission Board to warrant establishment of a Hungarian mission field. The board invited György Balla, a student at the Baptist seminary in East Orange, New Jersey, to serve as the congregation's minister. Balla completed his studies at McMaster University, and he preached not only in Toronto, but also in Guelph, Port Colborne, and Welland.[43]

The Role of the Clergy

By stressing the role of Canadian church authorities and of clergymen in the founding and running of Hungarian-Canadian congregations, I do not intend to minimize the devotion of many rank-and-file immigrants. The case of the Hungarian Roman Catholics from Welland who travelled to Buffalo in search of religious services in their native language is but one example of their piety. Before they had their own congregations, many other Hungarians eagerly sought out visiting Hungarian missionaries from the United States.[44] They also took part in religious services held in Hungarian churches of denominations not their own.[45] Many even attended services in English-Canadian churches or in the churches of other ethnic groups.[46] Not surprisingly, these devout immigrants responded with joy to the founding of Hungarian congregations by Canadian churches.

Nor do I mean to underestimate the contributions of ordinary immigrants to the building of such congregations. While Canadian churches laid the foundations of most such bodies and provided them with indispensable financial assistance, the extent of their support should not be exaggerated. By and large, they assisted only those ethnic congregations that were able to help themselves. The Presbyterian church, for example, terminated Hungarian services in Oshawa in 1937, "on account of the decrease in numbers and finance."[47] Services in Welland were similarly halted in 1941. Thus, Hungarian-Canadian churches were unable to survive without the participation of ordinary immigrants, who made up the largest segment of their membership, and we see below that former agriculturalists and dwarf holders gave generously of their time, energy, and limited financial resources to the upkeep of their churches.

What I am suggesting is that Hungarian clergymen, deaconesses, and nuns – men and women who stood culturally apart from the rank and file – played a decisive role in the life of these churches in the 1920s and 1930s. They not only shaped the structure and formulated the rules for these "bastions of the Hungarian spirit" but also defined the nature of the ethnic identity that developed within them. While historians have analysed the transgressions committed by American and Canadian churches against the integrity of the culture of immigrant groups, they have paid less attention to cultural differences between ethnic clergymen and most of their flock.[48] Yet because of the inexperience of most Hungarian newcomers in managing church affairs, clerics and their assistants fashioned the organizational forms and ideological substance of Hungarian churches in Canada. I thereby imply not that clerics and middle-class immigrants who helped in the cultural and educational programs moulded the attitudes of ordinary immigrants at will but rather that they became leaders precisely because they could and did provide desperately needed services. Immigrant clergymen influenced rank-and-file attitudes more than did their counterparts in Hungary because shared immigrant status created symbiosis between the interests of clergy and those of congregations in Canada that was frequently absent in rural Hungary.

LIFE WITHIN HUNGARIAN-CANADIAN CONGREGATIONS

Cleric-Intermediaries

From the moment that they began their work among Hungarian immigrants, clergymen and the women who worked with them – nuns, ministers' wives, and deaconesses – were called upon to aid the immigrants not only with spiritual but also with worldly affairs. For courageous and inventive as poor peasant and rural labourers from Hungary may have been in facing the traumas of immigrant life, because they did not speak English and were generally unfamiliar with Canadian ways they frequently had to rely on elite intervention in their dealings with the host society. As members of the small group of educated immigrants, who also had formal connections with institutions in the host society, the clergymen and their assistants were an obvious choice to act as intermediaries.

The experiences of Father Forgách, the first Hungarian Roman Catholic priest in Toronto, illustrate how problems that immigrants encountered broadened the tasks of their clergy and the services provided. In 1928, when Forgách, a 20-year-old seminarian, arrived in Toronto, Archbishop McNeil deemed creation of a local Hungarian parish so urgent that he did not want to wait until Forgách's ordination. But when the young seminarian soon set about organizing a parish, he quickly realized that his duties would not be limited to catering to spiritual needs: "the people started immediately to come to me to help them. Within two years I rented five houses, one on Beverly street, just below College. We transformed it into a sort of club house ... I had thirty-six families living in these houses. I undertook to pay the rent. I ... hadn't the slightest idea just how I am going to do it."[49] Because Forgách was neither prosperous nor much more familiar with the ways of Canadian society than his flock, his well-intentioned but hasty forays into community work quickly led him to accumulate debts. He also ran into problems with municipal authorities: so many immigrants took advantage of the shelter that he provided that the houses were soon deemed overcrowded. Fortunately, however, the young seminarian had by then met a number of Canadian priests and prominent lay people who helped him out of these difficulties.

Forgách accepted that part of his role was to help immigrants cope with their new environment. Thus, for example, he visited factories and work sites to seek employment for his parishioners: "you have to lead the people ... it's not only the matter of spiritual life, but those people had to work. So you're spending your whole day looking for jobs for people. Going from one place to the other, to see if you can find any place,"[50] he explained in an interview. Small wonder that he concluded his reminiscences by saying: "Oh, those days were busy days."[51]

Forgách was not the only cleric-intermediary. Priests and ministers served as employment agents and provided character references.[52] They and the women who worked with them acted as translators and interpreters, accompanying immigrants to hospitals and to government agencies. When immigrants encountered emergencies or got into trouble with the law, they frequently sought the help of clerics. Thus, for example, Reverend Ambrosius Czakó, the Hungarian United Church minister, assisted Mary Gabura in 1929. Gabura, the mother of four, also ran a boarding-house. When she fell ill under the pressure of her work, and was hospitalized, her husband was unable to pay the costs. She became a public charge and thus faced deportation. A frightened relative called on Czakó to intervene on her behalf, and the minister was able to convince authorities to stop the proceedings.[53] Similarly, when a Hungarian woman in Montreal discovered her neighbours lying unconscious as a result of a gas leak in their rooming-house, she immediately ran to Reverend Fehér for assistance.[54]

Because of their familiarity with the immigrant community, clerics understood the occasionally cruel implications of Canadian laws. Consequently, at times they even helped their compatriots to circumvent these laws. In Toronto, for example, a deaconess provided Hungarian women with the name of a doctor who performed safe abortions. In Montreal, Sister Mary of the Social Service Order masterminded a scheme which speeded up family reunification despite Canadian regulations. To be permitted to bring their families during the Depression, immigrants were required to prove that they would be able to support them in Canada. As proof, they had to have savings in the bank. Sister Mary, who knew that many Hungarians would thus not be able to see their wives and children for years, organized a community fund for family reunification, to which the community at large contributed. The proceeds were placed in the account of a man who wished to bring out his family. Once his family was safely in Canada, the money was transferred into the account of another man.[55]

Clergymen attempted to familiarize immigrants with Canada's language and customs. Virtually every Hungarian-Canadian congregation offered its members English classes. Reverend Ferenc Kovács of the Hungarian Presbyterian Church in Hamilton even mounted a lecture series for his congregation. He tapped the resources of the area's handful of middle-class Hungarians and even invited English speakers, whose lectures he or his wife translated. Dezső Andrássy, who obtained a degree in economics in Hungary and served as the North German Lloyd Co.'s representative in Hamilton, lectured about "The Hungarians in Canada and Land." Dr István Jánossy, a steamship agent from Toronto, spoke on "How Hungarian Immigrants Can Succeed in Canada." A Canadian lawyer, H.L.G. Westland, discussed the nature of contracts and the acquisition of property. Dr Sole, the only Hungarian doctor in eastern Canada, talked about patent medicines – items advertised regularly in Hungarian-language newspapers – while a Canadian dentist gave a talk on the relationship between healthy teeth and proper diet.[56]

Many of these lectures differed only in language of delivery from the type of lectures that Canadian missionaries would deliver for the edification and improvement of immigrants. Hungarian-Canadian clerics, much like their Canadian colleagues, or for that matter their counterparts in Hungarian villages, viewed Hungarian peasants as culturally deprived, in need of education and enlightenment. Reverend Fehér argued, for example, that the newcomers needed guidance because most of them were "not critically minded,"[57] and despite his many responsibilities, he energetically set out to redress their poor education. Léna Váradi, a member of his congregation, recalled gratefully: "It was the Minister who introduced me to the pleasures of reading. He lent many books from his own library to the Hungarians who lived in Montreal."[58] Reverend Czakó believed that his foremost role was that of a teacher: "I still recall though it is forty years since I said it – that I was not a minister (though I had a Protestant minister's diploma) but a teacher, and teach them I did all the many years I was with them."[59]

Community Service

As Hungarian-Canadian clerics became more established in their new congregations, they tried to anticipate the needs of immigrants and to deal with their problems in a systematic way. Whereas mutual aid societies formed by Italian, Polish, or Slovak immigrants often served as the bases for ethnic churches, clergymen working within Hungarian congregations created by Canadian ecclesiastical authorities attempted to set up sick benefit and burial societies.[60]

Almost all the clerics also opened community centres in Hungarian neighbourhoods. Perhaps the most ambitious was the St Imre Home in Montreal. Opened in 1930, by Father Joseph Rácz, the home attempted to provide for the special needs of transient, unemployed Hungarians, many of whom criss-crossed the country restlessly in search of employment. The top floor of the three-storey building served as a dormitory for single men who needed shelter, while a few rooms were set aside for couples and families in need of temporary accommodation. The residence also provided cheap meals to impoverished immigrants. To the children of women who were fortunate enough to be employed, it offered day care.

The home also served the cultural and recreational needs of local Hungarians. It provided space for community functions such as dances, theatrical performances, and banquets. Immigrants could also take advantage, on a daily basis, of the library, reading room, and billiard table.[61]

Although the services that the home provided were much needed, its maintenance proved to be too costly. Even though Father Rácz received financial aid from prominent Montrealers, the Quebec government, the Society of St Vincent de Paul, and the Hungarian consul general, the home was closed in 1933.[62] Its place was soon taken, however, by a more modest centre for Hungarian Roman Catholics, which was opened by the Sisters of Social Service on St Famille Street. The new centre offered 15 beds to homeless immigrants, day care services and Hungarian-language classes for children, and English classes for adults. It also served as a meeting place for the choir, the women's embroidery and sewing circle, the youth group, and the amateur drama troupe that were organized by the sisters.[63]

The humanitarian work of Hungarian churches assumed tremendous importance during the Depression. In Montreal, provincial and municipal authorities relied on them to transmit assistance to eligible unemployed immigrants, as did the Hungarian consul general.[64] The churches supplemented relief through collections and fundraising events,[65] but only church members were eligible for such aid. The application of 107 Hungarians for membership in the Hungarian Reformed Church in Montreal during a single month in 1931 is indicative of the great need that this relief filled in the immigrant community.[66]

More than humanitarian concern motivated clergymen to become so deeply involved in community work. They knew that catering to immigrants' needs helped them retain the loyalty of their flock and attract new adherents. Hungarian immigrants seem to have viewed community work as an integral part of the clergy's responsibilities. Perhaps the clearest example is the case of Reverend Charles Kovács, who served the Hungarian congregations of Toronto and Oshawa between 1930 and 1932. Although Kovács held impressive academic credentials, having taught theology in Budapest and Transylvania before he took up postgraduate work at the Princeton School of Theology in 1924, he was unable to help his congregations.[67] While poor health partly accounts for his failure, the discrepancy between his views and those of members regarding his duties also contributed to his dismissal. In 1932, for example, Kovács protested to the church elders that it was not his responsibility to act as an employment agent and amateur drama director.[68] So unacceptable were his views that membership dwindled almost to nothing. The congregation was not revitalized until the arrival of Charles Steinmetz, a resourceful, enterprising, and ambitious young man who saw the role of the ethnic clergy as one of overall leadership in the community.[69]

Thus, despite the presence of many devout men and women, the religious impulse did not itself guarantee the growth and development of ethnic congregations. One force that slowed growth of church membership was the transience of immigrant workers. Indeed, in some smaller settlements, such as Oshawa, turnover was so great that it undermined efforts even to establish, let alone expand, Hungarian congregations.[70] But maintenance of viable church bodies was difficult even in larger communities. As Reverend Fehér of the Hungarian United Church in Montreal explained in 1929, "On account of the constant moving of our population, one of my biggest work is to visit constantly the people, and to influence them to take up discontinued relations with the Church."[71] Reports by clergy of other denominations confirm that Hungarians did not spontaneously flock to new parishes. Many had to be convinced to join by clergymen or by church elders, who conducted door-to-door recruitment.[72] Opening of church-affiliated community centres was intended in part to attract immigrants who did not otherwise attend church. As Reverend Ferenc Kovács explained in his report to the General Assembly of the Presbyterian church, "In Toronto, people live very much scattered and unless some centre for social activities develops, it is hard to show greater results at present."[73]

Religious Segmentation

Competition among churches to gain adherents also induced ethnic clergymen to broaden the services offered. For while this competition hastened the establishment of Hungarian congregations, it also under-mined the viability of the very bodies that it helped to create. Hun-garian colonies in central Canada were simply too small to sustain all the congregations formed in their midst.

Because no major doctrinal differences divided them, this competi-tion was most acute between the United Church and Presbyterians. The two denominations did not sponsor rival congregations in all Hungarian colonies in central Canada, possibly because of a shortage of qualified Hungarian ministers. In some settlements, however, the success of one church was conceded by its rival and efforts to create rival congregations were quickly abandoned. Thus, for example, it was probably because of Reverend Fehér's great success in recruiting Hungarian Protestants in Montreal for the United Church that efforts to organize a local Hungarian Presbyterian church came to naught.[74]

In some settlements where both churches were active, however, con-fusion and bitterness within the ethnic group ensued. As the recrimi-nations exchanged by Ferenc Kovács (Presbyterian) and Charles Farkas (United Church) – the two ministers serving in the Niagara presbytery – show, both denominations' claims of affinity with the Reformed Church of Hungary confounded immigrants. Because the Presbyterian church began its work among Welland's Hungarians before its rival, Kovács blamed the latter for the confusion and accused it of using underhanded tactics. "It is very difficult to explain the differences between the two 'Calvinist' churches," he wrote in his 1930 annual report, "and the fact that two Hungarian 'Presbyterian' ministers are as-signed for such a small group of people, and furthermore, it is hard to build a selfrespecting congregation among a comparatively poor group, who are daily reminded that the United Church is not ex-pecting them to contribute regularly."[75] Farkas in turn accused Kovács of deliberately misleading immigrants by telling them that "if they go to the United Church they will cease to be 'Reformed.'"[76] Indeed, so great were the tensions that in 1941 the Presbyterian church decided to end its Hungarian work in Welland and urged Protestant Hungarians to join the United Church congregation.[77]

The strain created by religious segmentation extended beyond Protestant congregations to Hungarian Roman Catholic and Greek Catholic groups as well. When an impostor by the name of Victor Boross, claiming to be a Greek Catholic priest, organized a congrega-tion in Montreal, Sister Mary complained to the director of the Permanent Bureau of the World Congress of Hungarians: "We had and continue to have many difficulties in this respect, because he succeeds in enticing even some of the faithful."[78]

Competition among churches also diversified the social and cultural activities that ethnic clergymen organized. It was in response to the

opening of the United Church mission to the Hungarians of Welland
that the Presbyterian church hastened to open a Hungarian community centre in that city. As Reverend Kovács explained:

the store and large hall behind at 485 Main St., near the Michigan Central station, in the geographical centre of the two large Hungarian groups at Crowland
and Welland, where 80 per cent of them pass daily and is accessible to adults
but especially to children. This step was important in view of the fact that
English classes for adults, and daily vacation Bible school for children should
be opened immediately.... Although we do not intend to pay much attention
to the Methodist mission's fishing tactics, still we are deepening our work and
increasing our activities rather to be positive for our own church and not to be
negative against anyone.[79]

The recollections of Joseph Blaskó, a Hungarian immigrant from
Toronto, suggest just how effective community centres proved to be.
He recalls that in 1926 there was no meeting place for the Hungarians
of Toronto, aside from the bootlegger's, street corners, and billiard
halls, until they discovered the United Church Building near the corner of Queen and Spadina. Here, "Hungarian immigrants were welcomed. The church's leaders were kind people and they did everything
in their power to make us feel comfortable. There was a Hungarian theology student at the church, János Papp, who helped Hungarians to adjust. He conducted English classes which were well attended."[80]
Margaret Wappel, who belonged to the Catholic Circle in Toronto during the 1930s, likened its premises to "the hub of family life," where
"people would go almost every evening. The men who did not work
would also go during the day. It was a place to keep warm ... and possibly also a place to hear about work."[81]

   The establishment of proletarian organizations within the immigrant group and their apparent success further diversified life within
immigrant congregations. Hungarian clerics believed that cultural activities were used by proletarian leaders to transmit radical
propaganda. They thought that similar activities within their churches
would act as an antidote to radicalism.[82]

Finances

Financial considerations also motivated ethnic clergymen to organize
such social functions as banquets, balls, and bazaars, which had not
been part of church life in Hungary. Most Hungarian-Canadian congregations were plagued by financial difficulties throughout the interwar years. Although Canadian church authorities provided financial

aid which was indispensable for the creation of Hungarian congregations, they fully expected these bodies to become self-supporting. To their consternation, no Hungarian churches in central Canada achieved economic independence before the outbreak of the Second World War.

At least one official, Reverend C.L. Cowan of the Presbyterian church, concluded that Hungarians were undeserving of the aid that they received. He believed that their reluctance to pay for the upkeep of their churches bespoke insufficient commitment.[83] Cowan seemed unaware that the high rate of unemployment during the Depression undermined immigrants' ability to assist their churches. The generosity with which many of the same immigrants donated their labour to the repair and even construction of church buildings illustrates a deep commitment to the maintenance of Hungarian churches in Canada. "It is a joy to see them," wrote Sister Mary of the men who were helping to repair the building that housed the Roman Catholic community centre in Montreal, "as they come here day after day to work in their tattered clothing and bad shoes. They go home from work to eat a modest meal and then they come here, joking good naturedly all the while."[84]

Yet Reverend Cowan was not entirely wrong. Some Hungarians were not prepared to make a commitment to ethnic churches because they did not intend to settle in Canada. Furthermore, since in Hungary all officially recognized churches were financed in large part through a church tax, imposed and administered by the state, as taxpayers in Hungary most immigrants were automatically contributing to the upkeep of churches in their native land. Understandably, therefore, the same sojourners who forswore most forms of pleasure and comfort to save their hard-earned cash and thus to hasten their return home were loath to contribute to Canadian churches as well.

But while some immigrants gave up all forms of entertainment, many others flocked to the social and cultural functions organized by ethnic congregations. Some did so because they recognized the contribution that income from banquets, balls, bazaars, picnics, and amateur dramatic performances made to the upkeep of their churches. As Imre S. from Windsor proudly explained, "in the old days we maintained our churches by organizing theatrical performances every two or three weeks."[85] Many others, however, attended church functions to socialize with co-nationals and to partake of Hungarian culture. Whatever the reason for their popularity, church functions became important sources of revenue. In Windsor, for example, Mrs Eugene Molnár, the wife of the minister of the Hungarian Presbyterian congregation who was a music teacher by training, raised a good share of the money to cover the congregation's expenses by organizing choir concerts and social functions with the aid of the women's auxiliary.[86] In Toronto's Hungarian Presbyterian congregation, a Christmas social raised more than four times as much as the collection plate in December 1930, and even in 1943, when most immigrants were gainfully employed, a banquet held in February produced more than the monthly income from the collection plate and membership dues combined.[87]

The success of social functions as fundraising events was only occasionally marred by disputes over their propriety with Canadian church officials and even with Hungarian clergymen. Thus, for example, in the eyes of many immigrants merry-making necessarily involved drinking. When some Hungarian clerics, such as Reverend Nagy of the Hungarian Presbyterian Church of Welland, went along with this popular notion, they occasioned the disapproval of teetotallers, both among their Hungarian colleagues and within the Canadian church hierarchy.[88] The holding of church picnics and other social activities on the Sabbath also elicited criticism.[89]

Cultural Preservation

The need to increase church revenues and to recruit new members, as well as the clergy's paternalistic concern with the welfare and enlightenment of immigrants, thus led to the introduction of a wide range of social and cultural activities into parish life. But Hungarian clerics also ascribed the utmost importance to these activities as vehicles for the preservation of Hungarian identity in Canada. All of them seemed to agree that the expression and affirmation of a distinct ethnic identity were among the main tasks of their churches. Some seemed confident that, with their mediation, a distinct identity would persist in Canada indefinitely: "as long as Hungarian national parishes exist, and are led by clerics who think and feel Hungarian," wrote one of them, "we do not need to worry about the assimilation of our race."[90] Others were more doubtful. Reverend Fehér of Montreal, that active and dedicated promoter of Hungarian culture, confessed in a letter to his father: "No matter how hard we try, our Hungarian work will be temporary.... Sooner or later, complete assimilation awaits us. In America, in this English and French environment, Hungarian Reformed Churches are ... like flower gardens planted on ice-floes."[91] Thus, despite his repeated and impassioned calls for the preservation of the Hungarian spirit in Canada, Reverend Fehér actually seemed to be struggling to ease immigrants into their new environment as painlessly as possible. "We wish to work for the progressive, best and happiest adjustment or amalgamation of our people with Canadian life, customs and institutions," he stated.[92]

The religious services provided by ethnic congregations were vehicles for the preservation of language and culture. Even in Roman Catholic congregations, where services were in Latin, Hungarian immigrants gave evidence of their strong desire to commune with God in their own language by clinging to the singing of hymns in Hungarian. "We cried," recalled Mrs András Szabó of the first mass held by Father Jeromos Hédly in Montreal; "the good Lord had not forgotten us even in these remote parts."[93] In her recollections, Sister Mary gives a moving account of how this wish persisted and came to be expressed by the members of Our Lady of Hungary Roman Catholic parish in Montreal, some time later when the parish priest was the French-Canadian Father Gaboury:

during the first mass which was held in the Hungarian chapel, the singing was in Latin. The people were distressed and saddened. But nothing could be forcibly accomplished. We decided that at the end of the first mass we will sing the Hungarian national anthem. The church was packed. The windows were open. The yard was packed and so was the street outside, and 'God Bless the Hungarian' resounded everywhere. When we went to the parsonage after holy mass, Bishop Duchamp called Father Gaboury and myself and told Father Gaboury: "Since Hungarian singing comes from the very heart, I hereby give permission that during Hungarian mass, singing should be in Hungarian."[94]

Protestant clergymen, possibly in response to confusion and accusations stemming from their affiliation with the United and Presbyterian churches, insisted that their services were absolutely in accordance with the practices of the Hungarian Reformed Church: "The language of the service is, of course, Hungarian. We use the hymnals which are used in Hungary. The ordering of the service and all other practices are absolutely in keeping with old country traditions."[95]

To retain the loyalty of immigrants, the clerics kept alive certain liturgical practices from Hungary that were not characteristic in Canada. Roman Catholic priests, for example, organized religious processions, which served to assert ethnic as well as religious identity. The immigrants who took part in a procession around Our Lady of Hungary in Montreal were dressed in national folk costumes. The men at the head of the ranks carried the Hungarian flag, as well as the Union Jack.[96]

But Hungarian clerics and their assistants also believed that the more worldly social and cultural enterprises that came to form part of parish life were indispensable to ethnic distinctiveness. They viewed the preservation of a Hungarian identity as a major objective behind the setting up of sub-groups within congregations. As the wife of the Hungarian United Church minister in Montreal explained à propos of the congre-

gation's Bethlen Kata Women's Association: "Although the establishment of this association came about with the aid of the Reformed
Church, it is not strictly speaking a church organization, but a
Hungarian women's organization. Its aim is to tend the Hungarian
spirit and to help Hungarian women. Through mothers it hopes to preserve Hungarian feelings and thoughts in Hungarian families."[97] The
clergy encouraged the formation of amateur drama troupes, choirs,
and dance ensembles, not only because performances raised funds for
the church and provided edifying recreation for performers and audiences alike, but also because they believed that such cultural activities
were unusually effective in developing ethnic identity.

This commitment of Hungarian-Canadian clergymen to ethnic preservation combined with cultural and social activities as recruitment and
fundraising agencies to ensure a rich cultural life within their religious
organizations. But what ultimately guaranteed the success of these activities as agencies for the expression of a Hungarian identity was their
popularity within the ethnic group. Sister Mary of Montreal believed
that the formation of an embroidery circle "distracted those who were
crushed by difficult times, and they were thus better able to bear the
burdens of life."[98] The recollections of men and women who were active in such social and cultural groups suggest that Sister Mary's obser-
vation was not only apt but applied to other cultural activities as well.
While preparation for church bazaars, banquets, and performances
laid claim to a considerable portion of the leisure time of church-going
Hungarians, these activities provided an escape from the enormous social and economic difficulties with which most of them were grappling.
As suggested by the recollections of Joseph Jáger, a shoemaker who was
one of the most active members of the drama troupe of Toronto's
Catholic Circle, acting, dancing, singing, designing stage sets, and sewing costumes all permitted immigrants to express their creativity. "I
took all the boots myself," he proudly recalls, "that all the actors had,
they were mainly from the old country. And I put new soles on them
and so they could have new boots for the play. The britches that we had
which were so characteristic of what we had in the old country, we tried
to keep up all the time, we kept them in good condition and we tried
to dress in the characteristic Hungarian style. If Hussar dress was necessary, then twenty or thirty of us would get together led by the tailors
in the group, and we bought cheap material and we worked all night
and by morning we had as many Hussar uniforms as were necessary."[99]

Helping to build vital, self-supporting ethnic parishes filled the rank-
and-file members with pride, and their participation strengthened
their sense of community and their loyalty to Hungarian churches in
the New World. Hungarian-Canadian congregations thus became the

most powerful agencies for the creation and maintenance of a distinct Hungarian identity in Canada. Ironically, these bastions of ethnic distinctiveness operated within, and were financially assisted by, Canadian churches with a history of promoting assimilation. How can this curious development be explained?

Immigrant Churches and Canadian Church Authorities

Since the church played a major role in the development of virtually all immigrant communities, the relationship between Canadian churches and immigrant congregations is a subject of great importance in the study of immigration and ethnicity. Unfortunately, no studies of the attitude of Canadian church officials to immigrants during the interwar years have yet been undertaken. The authorities' dealings with Hungarians suggest that Canadian churches had gained at least tactical awareness of the distinctive heritage of immigrants, if not sensitivity to the role of tradition in the lives of newcomers. Church officials recognized that immigrants could be reached only by clergymen who spoke their language.

The Roman Catholic church seemed more concerned with retaining the loyalty of new immigrants to the faith, by preventing Protestant churches and radical political movements from gaining followers among the immigrants, than with hastening assimilation.[100] Its officials sought to bring Hungarian-speaking priests to Canada whenever possible, and once they arrived here, these priests seem to have been given considerable autonomy. As suggested by Our Lady of Hungary in Montreal, under Father Gaboury,[101] even parishes with francophone and anglophone priests tried to enable immigrants to preserve their language and some of their traditional religious practices. In this respect, the Sisters of Social Service played a significant role.

Like the Roman Catholic church, Protestant denominations were also intent on preventing the spread of radical and anti-clerical ideas among immigrants.[102] At the same time, however, the United and Presbyterian churches actively promoted Canadianization,[103] while recognizing that overly aggressive policies would alienate newcomers. "Canadianization," stressed a United Church publication, ought not to be "a narrow nationalism that necessitates a ruthless severing of all ties with the old world."[104] Indeed, public statements made by church officials in the 1920s and 1930s suggest that they accepted ethnic pluralism. "Your coming to us as one of over sixty nationalities," Reverend W.R. Cruikshank told Hungarians at the opening service of the Hungarian Congregation of the Church of All Nations in Montreal in 1930, "are [sic] like so many tributaries flowing into the great stream

of Canadian life and bringing to us so many and so different qualities
to share with your new co-workers and companions here that a new nation shall emerge possessing we hope the virtues of all, but none of
their vices."[105] Willingness to allow immigrants to retain a special identity is even more apparent in a letter written by the Canadian minister
of All People's Mission in the Niagara presbytery of the United Church
to the office of the Hungarian consul general in Montreal. Thanking
the consul for the flags and almanacs that he sent to the mission,
Reverend Harvey Forster wrote: "Our Hungarian people are mostly
Canadians now, but we want them to feel that they are Hungarians as
well, and to keep alive in their souls a deep and profound love for the
land of their birth. Accordingly, we try to observe all Hungarian national holidays and in other ways to rekindle that love of country without which a man ceases to be a man."[106]

Judging by their official communications with their superiors, the
objectives of Hungarian clerics were entirely compatible with those of
Canadian church authorities. "It is quite obvious," reported Reverend
Fehér of Montreal to the Board of Missions of the United Church, "that
our church as any church has a definite obligation to work for a perfect
unity, a spiritual, cultural and even physical unity of a certain land that
we call country."[107]

Yet this apparent consensus actually masked a discrepancy between
the plans of Canadian church officials and those of Hungarian clerics.
Thus, for example, the United Church deliberately brought together
a number of ethnic groups in such congregations as the Church of All
Nations in Toronto, in order to aid assimilation:

It was manifestly impossible to establish churches for each racial group and
probably unwise, even if possible, to encourage the separateness which would
result from such a policy. 'Would it not be better' it was thought, 'more eco-
nomical, and more likely to make for national unity, as well as Christian unity,
to establish here and there fairly large centres, adequately staffed and
equipped, where a number of groups might worship, where they might meet
as units for their own worship under their own language ministers and for whatever else might be helpful, but where a certain amount of mingling would be
inevitable?'[108]

By contrast, Hungarian clergymen, who, as we have seen, used the facilities provided for them by Canadian churches, generally viewed
membership in such multiethnic institutions as a temporary arrangement, necessitated by the poverty of their congregations. Most of them
planned to set up independent Hungarian churches precisely because
they hoped thereby to ensure the preservation of a distinct identity in

Canada. "We have built the first Hungarian Church in Toronto," announced the Hungarian Presbyterian minister of Toronto with great pride to the consul general in Montreal; "[it] announces to the world at large that Hungarians live here ... and that they want to survive!"[109]

The differences between statements made by ethnic clergymen to Canadian church officials and those that they made to their compatriots should not be seen as hypocritical. Genuine confusion seems to lie behind them. Clerics were uncertain about the fate of their homeland and about the permanence of Hungarian settlement in Canada. Most of them, as we shall see, hoped for the restoration of Greater Hungary and believed that a redrawing of their homeland's boundaries and an improvement of economic conditions there would lead many immigrants to return. While they all advocated ethnic preservation, some may have doubted the likelihood of the persistence of Hungarian culture in Canada.

This divergence in plans notwithstanding, Hungarian Protestant clergymen, like their Roman Catholic counterparts, were by and large permitted to carry on their work as they saw fit. Some of them earned the esteem of their Canadian colleagues, and their advice was sought in devising church policy towards immigrants. When the Hamilton presbytery of the Presbyterian church wanted to evaluate its work among Ukrainian immigrants, for example, it asked Reverend Ferenc Kovács to prepare a careful survey of the field.[110]

In the course of my research, I discovered only one instance – that of the Hungarian United Church congregation in Montreal – when differences between Canadian church officials and an ethnic clergyman led to outright conflict. This conflict emerged over the question of Sunday school education for the children of Hungarian immigrants. Canadian church officials wanted these young people to attend classes in English, jointly with children from other immigrant groups, whereas Reverend Fehér believed that this plan threatened not only the survival of his congregation but also harmony within the families in his flock. Hasty Canadianization, he argued, "would result in a superiority complex on the part of the children and the consequent loss of parental control on the part of the parents, which again means confusion and disintegration of the family and the breeding of a generation of law breakers."[111] Fehér's anger was more apparent when he informed his congregation about the plans of the Board of Home Missions. He spoke of attempts to "entice" young Hungarians with "honeyed words and many other forms of flattery" and emphasized the urgency of escaping financial dependence on Canadian churches.[112]

Despite the assimilationist goals of the churches that sponsored their formation, Hungarian Protestant congregations, along with their

Roman Catholic counterparts, were among the most important agencies for the preservation of Hungarian ethnic identity in Canada during the years between the world wars. The ethnic identity that emerged within these organizations transcended denominational segmentation and united religious associations with a group of secular bodies to form the patriotic camp.

6 Wooing Hungarians Abroad for the National Cause

SERVICES FOR EMIGRANTS

The government in Budapest directed its attention to Canada in the early 1920s when it realized that the northern half of the North American Continent had become the most likely destination of Hungarian emigrants who were barred from entering and settling in the United States by that nation's quota system.[1] In 1922, the government of Hungary sent out Armand de Hann to set up and open a consulate general in Montreal. In 1924, shortly after Canada had reopened its gates to allow in Hungarian immigrants and it had become apparent that most of these newcomers would seek to settle in the western part of the country, the Hungarian government established the Canadian Hungarian Immigrant Aid Bureau in Winnipeg; in 1927 it also set up a consulate in the Manitoba capital.[2]

The Canadian Hungarian Aid Bureau was created as a branch of the Emigrants and Remigrants Protection Bureau, which had been founded in Budapest by the government in 1921. As its name suggests, the Budapest agency's function was to protect both emigrants and remigrants from unscrupulous agents by helping them through the maze of regulations that governed international migration. The bureau was to provide information concerning economic conditions and rules of immigration in the countries to which people proposed to travel and to help them with the complex, expensive, and time-consuming task of obtaining all the required tickets and documents. People already living abroad and intending to return to Hungary were to receive information about economic opportunities in their homeland; the bureau also offered to assist them in finding employment and purchasing land. To accommodate emigrants, remigrants, and tourists of Hungarian origin who were passing through the Hungarian capital, the bureau operated a hostel, right next to one of the city's largest railway stations. It also undertook to aid Hungarians living abroad with all legal and financial transactions that they wished to conduct in their native land. The activities of the bureau, as of all organizations involved in matters of emigration, were financed by the Emigration Foundation, which received government allocations, as well as funds raised through the imposition of taxes on the issuing of passports to prospective emigrants and permits to the shipping companies that transported them. [3]

In Winnipeg, the Immigrant Aid Bureau held mail for Hungarian migrants and helped them to find employment and housing and to purchase land. The bureau's employees acted as translators and interpreters and interceded on behalf of Hungarians in cases of disputes or problems with Canadian employers and authorities. Through the parent organization, they also assisted immigrants in settling personal or family legal and financial problems that arose back home during their absence. [4]

The bureau had a commercial arm as well – a travel, remittance, and trade agency called the Pannonia Co. The justification for the firm's creation was that it would conduct commercial transactions on behalf of the immigrants more scrupulously and cheaply than privately owned agencies. In reality, however, Hungarian officials also hoped that the costs of operating the Immigrant Aid Bureau would be at least partially offset by profits from the sale of steamship tickets, the remittances of emigrants' savings to their families, and the sale of Hungarian goods in Canada. [5] However, this business venture proved unsuccessful, and the bureau continued to rely on subsidies from Budapest.

More than paternalistic concern with the welfare of immigrants motivated establishment of the bureau in Winnipeg, however, and convinced Hungarian officials to aid it financially. The bureau's employees were to unite and to lead Hungarians in Canada so as to counteract any tendency towards assimilation and to recruit their services on behalf of their afflicted homeland. [6] Hungarian officials spoke of providing nationals abroad with "spiritual guidance" – that is, "placing the masses living abroad in the service of Hungarian national, economic, and cultural interests." [7] Expatriates could help by investing their savings in Hungary and thereby sending much-needed foreign currency to that country; by buying and promoting the consumption of Hungarian goods abroad, thereby encouraging trade; and by visiting their homeland themselves and urging their non-Hungarian friends to follow

their example, thereby assisting tourism.[8] But their most important service, Horthyist officials believed, was political: they could sway international public opinion in favour of the revision of the Treaty of Trianon,
by familiarizing the people among whom they lived with the injustices
inherent in the treaty and by gaining their respect and support for the
Hungarian nation in general and for the Horthy regime in particular.[9]
They could also sway the governments of their adoptive countries to
support Horthyist aims. As Consul Schefbeck explained, if Hungarians
in Canada employed their rights as citizens in the New World on behalf
of their native land, they would constitute a Hungarian fortification
pushed far abroad.[10]

Since the activities of communist émigrés from Hungary threatened
to dissuade both expatriates and their new neighbours from rallying
behind Horthy's government, the regime, which was in any case virulently anti-communist, made a concerted effort to discredit communism among emigrants.[11] The need to prevent the communists from
making inroads seemed all the more important since many expatriates
planned to return to Hungary.

Because it kept in touch with emigrants and provided them with useful services, the Immigrant Aid Bureau was ideally suited to fulfilling
propagandistic goals. But suspecting that their political activities would
anger Canadians, the bureau's employees kept silent about this aspect
of their work. Indeed, Canadian authorities viewed the agency's operations with suspicion: "the department should keep track of an organization of this kind," warned the chief commissioner of the CPR, "as it
is quite evident that their purpose is to encourage their nationals to retain their citizenship and to send their money back to Hungary for
investment there."[12]

Aware that authorities in the countries where Hungarians settled would
not look with favour on the machinations of a foreign government
within their boundaries, Budapest conducted its entire propaganda
campaign among emigrants through nominally independent associations. Between 1920 and 1925, the League of Hungarians Abroad was
in charge of rallying expatriates behind their homeland. The league's
activities were carried on between 1929 and 1938 by the Permanent
Bureau of the World Congress of Hungarians and after 1938 by the
World Federation of Hungarians, which replaced it. The publicly stated
objectives of these organizations were politically neutral, because, as a
brief to the director of the Permanent Bureau stated, "If we acknowledge publicly that the Congress Office wants to win every Hungarian
abroad for the Hungarian national cause, the countries of immigration
would try to counteract our work even more aggressively."[13] Thus the

stated aims of the World Federation of Hungarians were: "to support any activity which is aimed at preserving and developing the Hungarian language and culture among Hungarians abroad; to foster solidarity among Hungarians abroad; to strengthen ties between Hungarians abroad; to keep track of the activities and accomplishments of Hungarians abroad."[14]

In fact, these bodies were responsible for exporting to Hungarians abroad the Christian-nationalist and revisionist propaganda that the regime disseminated at home, especially in the countryside.[15] Indeed, the close relationship that officials saw between their campaign among peasants at home and the one aimed at nationals abroad is suggested by the Hungarian World Federation's plan to organize expatriates into "Hungarian villages."[16] Although this plan was abandoned, some of the same organizations that were in charge of spreading Christian-nationalist ideology in the countryside, especially the Hungarian National Federation, were also expected to win expatriates for the national cause. The federation, it will be recalled, had been founded to give shelter under its neutral name to the small revisionist leagues supposedly disbanded at the request of the victorious entente powers. While it understandably played down its revisionist orientation, the federation openly stated its support for the "Hungarian national and Christian idea."[17] Its president, Baron Zsigmond Perényi, was also director of the Permanent Bureau of the World Congress, and for a time he headed the Emigration Council as well.

KANADAI MAGYAR UJSÁG

Control from Budapest

In Canada, the Horthy regime's chief propaganda tool was the *Kanadai Magyar Ujság* (Canadian Hungarian News), a newspaper based in Winnipeg and founded in 1924 by Iván Hordossy, director of the Immigrant Aid Bureau in the same city. A journalist by profession, before being sent to Canada by the Hungarian government, Hordossy was a correspondent in the foreign affairs section of the pro-Horthy *Nemzeti Ujság* (National News).[18] Under his direction, two earlier, unsuccessful papers, the *Kanadai Magyar Néplap* and the *Kanadai Magyarság*, joined to form the *Ujság*. One of the *Néplap*'s former editors, Father István Soós, and the Istvánffy brothers, businessmen who owned and edited the *Kanadai Magyarság*, joined the staff of the *Ujság*, as did István Jánossy, Hordossy's assistant at the bureau.[19]

Initially, the paper operated as a joint stock company – the Canadian-Hungarian News Co. Ltd. The controlling, 52 per cent share in the firm was owned by the Hungarian government, and the remaining shares by Baron Lipót Bornemissza, an agent of the Cunard and White Star steamship lines.[20] In 1929, however, Budapest took full control of the *Ujság*.[21]

Not only did the Hungarian government own the *Ujság*, it also provided annual subsidies. Until 1929, the paper received "tens of thousands" of dollars per year, and after that year, because of the government's own financial difficulties, aid was reduced to $4,800 per year.[22] Even this modest sum, however, exceeded the paper's income from independent sources. In 1936–37, for example, its income amounted to $3,790 – $2,503 from subscriptions, $1,190 from advertisements, and $97 from the paper's printing shop. This amount fell short of covering the *Ujság*'s annual expenditures of $9,000. Accordingly, however modest the subsidies, they were indispensable for the paper's survival.[23]

The regime continued to support the *Ujság* because of reassurances from its representatives in Canada that the newspaper was a most effective tool for retaining the loyalty of emigrants.[24] These men, who were familiar with conditions in Canada, saw aid to the paper as especially urgent when they realized that the Communist party was making inroads within Hungarian-Canadian communities.[25] Officials also hoped to supply the Canadian press with information favourable to the regime through the *Ujság*'s wire services. They believed that the "little entente" powers (Czechoslovakia, Romania, and Yugoslavia) supplied the international press with propaganda that compromised Hungary in the eyes of the world.[26]

Since it was deemed impolitic to acknowledge that control of a Hungarian-Canadian newspaper was in the hands of a foreign government, the *Ujság*'s ownership and its reliance on subsidies were kept hidden even from its own readers. Editorials insisted on its independence. On its first anniversary, for example, the *Ujság*'s financial hardships were compared to the trials of Hungarian pioneers in western Canada around the turn of the century; not a word was said about substantial aid from external sources.[27] When the government took complete control of the paper in 1929, Baron Perényi, in his capacity as president of the Hungarian National Federation, was the nominal buyer, and his wish to free the paper from dependence on private commercial interests was offered as an explanation for the purchase.[28] Once again, neither the fact that the new owner was far from being a disinterested participant in dealings with the diaspora, nor his control over the paper's editorial policy and its news material from Hungary, was made public.

Perényi and Hungarian government representatives in Canada were instrumental in selecting the *Ujság*'s editors. Béla Payerle, a Saskatchewan farmer, who had studied agriculture in Hungary and who wrote the paper's agricultural columns until he replaced Hordossy as editor in 1929, and Gusztáv Nemes, the paper's printer, who became its editor in 1938, shared the views and aims of the Horthy regime.[29]

Catering to Its Audience

Although the Hungarian government thus exerted complete control over the *Ujság*, with the intention of using it to shape the attitudes of expatriates in Canada, both officials in Budapest and the paper's editors recognized that the paper, in order to make inroads, would have to satisfy the tastes and needs of immigrants. Accordingly, the *Ujság* was deliberately written in a language accessible to workers and peasants with little education,[30] whom the editors and their Hungarian advisers correctly identified as the majority of their readers. This perception of the tastes and capabilities of their audience was undoubtedly also responsible for the *Ujság*'s strong resemblance, in format and in content, to the popular press back home.

The *Ujság*'s content was far from being limited to political propaganda. Sensationalist stories of scandalous and bizarre events, which occupied an important place in the Hungarian yellow press, also made up a considerable portion of the *Ujság*'s coverage of news from Hungary. Even the members of the lowest strata of rural society, who did not generally read newspapers in their native land, had developed a taste for this type of material through reading "penny dreadfuls" and almanacs, the most popular reading materials in the Hungarian countryside.[31]

Almanacs, which contained pictures, rhymed weather forecasts based on astrological charts, advice to agriculturalists, and informative articles on a wide variety of subjects, as well as sensationalist stories, were especially prized by the Hungarian peasantry. Their popularity prompted the Hungarian ethnologist Gyula Ortutay to refer to the peasants as "almanac readers."[32] Frequently the only reading matter in peasant homes, apart from the Bible and prayer books, they were read bit by bit throughout the year, and while by the interwar years peasants may not have taken such features as the rhymed weather forecasts seriously, these features, along with the almanacs themselves, had become part of rural folklore. It was thus probably with the intention of broadening their readership to include as many "almanac readers" as possible that Hungarian newspapers issued their own almanacs – a practice that was adopted by the *Ujság* in Canada. The format, and even the name – *Illustrated Great Almanac* – of the *Ujság*'s publication were identical to those of almanacs that immigrants would have read in their native villages. Not even the rhymed weather forecasts were missing.

Since it was catering to people in a new and unfamiliar environment, however, the *Ujság* did not limit itself to reproduction of Old World practices. Rather, it tried to enhance its appeal by providing its readers with different types of information designed to facilitate adaptation to their new surroundings. For the benefit of those who did not understand English, it offered English lessons, translated and explained Canadian laws and regulations, and periodically even described Canadian customs and institutions. An agricultural column introduced western settlers to methods of cultivation appropriate to conditions and practices in this region. As urban Hungarian communities grew, moreover, and as unemployment increased, a column on the conditions of labour, employment opportunities, and relief measures throughout Canada became a regular feature. The paper also provided detailed information about patriotic secular and religious associations, as well as Hungarian businesses, throughout Canada.

The *Ujság* tried also to satisfy some of its readers' psychological needs. In an attempt to bridge the gap between the Old and the New worlds, it published stories, poems, and the lyrics of folksongs relevant to the immigrants' experience. Readers could identify with, and gain solace from reading about, the hardships and homesickness generated by the Canadian experience and described in these forms. At the same time, however, the *Ujság* also reported the achievements of immigrants in a manner to generate hope and pride among group members.

Intent on preserving a distinctive Hungarian identity in Canada, *Ujság*'s editors tried to appeal to the children of immigrants as well, first through special columns in English and, from 1937, through an English-language publication, the *Young Magyar American*. Hungarian officials supported this publication because through it they hoped not only to aid ethnic preservation but also to influence "English" public opinion.[33] This attempt to reach the children of immigrants proved completely ineffectual. The *Young Magyar American* survived for a bare two years. But the press was unquestionably influential in shaping the attitudes of the immigrant generation itself.

The *Ujság* was actively supported by patriotic leaders. Clergymen and other educated immigrants wrote columns for the paper on all aspects of Hungarian life in Canada, and commercial newspapers such as the *Canadai Kis Ujság* relied on its news service. But the *Ujság*'s influence extended beyond the ranks of the ethnic group's educated members. Patriotic associations subscribed to it and used its pages to inform the ethnic group at large about their activities and aims. As mentioned above, even poor peasants and rural labourers who never read newspapers in Hungary began to do so in Canada.[34] Many of them turned to the *Ujság*'s reports to familiarize themselves with their new society. As one reader explained in a letter to the editor: "we can understand this [Canadian regulations] only if people who are better educated than we can translate them for us into Hungarian"; $2.50, the cost of an annual subscription, he added, was not too much to pay for this service.[35] Indeed, so responsive were immigrants to the offer by the *Ujság*'s staff to act as intermediaries on their behalf that they inundated the paper's offices with letters requesting aid with practical affairs.[36]

Not only the *Ujság*'s practical advice, but also its attempts to bridge the gap between the Old and the New worlds, struck a responsive chord. Editorial calculations with regard to the popular appeal of both content and form seem to have borne fruit. Thus, for example, Mrs Helen Süle of Toronto showed me a handwritten copy of a poem by János Mező, entitled "I Ask a Bird," 50 years after the poem appeared in the *Ujság*. So apt did the poem, which expressed homesickness, seem to her, that she copied it when she came to Canada and still treasured it after all these years. A letter from Trail, British Columbia, gives us some idea of the immigrant response to the paper's almanac. "I do not know how the rest of you feel about it," she wrote, "but I simply cannot survive without an almanac." Acknowledging that she no longer had any practical use for the weather reports that appeared in these volumes, she explained that she got accustomed to reading versified weather reports "back home," and she proceeded, with unmistakable pleasure and nostalgia, to compare the content of the forecasts in the *Ujság*'s almanac with similar forecasts in Hungary.[37] Amateur drama troupes performed the plays that appeared in the pages of the *Ujság*'s almanacs.[38] The letters of congratulations that the paper received on its anniversaries indicate just how important it had become to its readers. Mihály Papp of Welland wrote on the first anniversary that he had become so attached to the *Ujság* that he could not even go to the factory where he worked without taking a copy with him.[39]

Thus, the smallness of the Hungarian community in Canada, as well as the transience and poverty of its members, rather than lack of interest in Hungarian newspapers, explains why the *Ujság* was unable to survive on income from subscriptions. Immigrants in isolated areas could gain access to the paper only by subscribing to it, and some of them could not afford the annual subscription of $2.50.[40] The paper's small staff, moreover, found it impossible to keep up with highly mobile readers, who in turn often failed to renew their subscriptions.[41] Competition from American Hungarian newspapers that were distributed in larger Hungarian settlements in Canada as well may also have undercut the *Ujság*.

Despite these difficulties, the *Ujság* had a fairly wide readership. In 1937, for example, it had 3,033 subscribers – approximately 10 per

cent of the Hungarians in Canada.[42] Many other immigrants purchased individual copies, which were distributed through Hungarian
businesses in larger colonies throughout Canada. Each copy, moreover, was undoubtedly read by more than one immigrant.

The virtual absence of competition from patriotically oriented
Hungarian-Canadian newspapers helps to account for the *Ujság*'s appeal, for, as we saw, commercial newspaper ventures were largely
unsuccessful.

BUDAPEST AND HUNGARIAN ASSOCIATIONS IN CANADA

Confident as it may have been in the power of the press to transmit its
views and aims to emigrants, and possibly even to native Canadians, the
Hungarian government also sought other avenues to gain support for
its irredentist campaign abroad. Government-sponsored tours by digni-
taries such as Baron Zsigmond Perényi, president of the Hungarian
National Federation, were seen as a means both for fostering stronger
ties with expatriates and for publicizing abroad the nation's plight. In
1928, during his meetings with Canadian politicians, which received
coverage in the English-language press, Perényi spoke at length about
the injustice of the Treaty of Trianon. Visiting virtually every Hungarian settlement and addressing Hungarian-Canadian associations,
he also took steps to unite expatraites in Canada behind the Horthy
regime and its revisionist ideology. He encouraged everyone whom he
met to turn to him personally if they needed any assistance in their
dealings with their homeland.[43]

Letters written by immigrants to Perényi, while he was president of
the World Congress of Hungarians, which functioned from 1929 to
1938, suggest that his show of goodwill did not fail to make an impression among his compatriots in Canada. Turning to him for assistance,
they all referred to the offer of help that he made during his visit. Thus,
for example, when John Czank, a barber from Welland, was unable to
find Hungarian sheet music for his son, who played the violin, he
turned to Perényi for help. In his letter of November 1938, he introduced his request with these words: "First of all, please forgive me for
troubling you, but when you were here, at the Welland Hungarian Self-
Culture Society, you were kind enough to say that I should turn to your
honour with any problems I may have."[44] Perényi's intervention was responsible, as we see below, for mending the rift in the Canadian
Hungarian Association, the first nation-wide organization founded by
Hungarians in Canada during the interwar years.

Another method used by the Horthy regime to present itself and its
irredentist aims in a favourable light was to check the content of books

dealing with Hungary. The Ministry of Foreign Affairs instructed its representatives in Canada to report on any materials that they deemed prejudicial to the national interest.[45] These representatives in turn enlisted Hungarian-Canadian leaders in their campaign. They believed that protest against biased coverage would be more effective if it came from men who were not officially connected with the government.[46]

Trusted local leaders were also asked to place in Canadian libraries books in English and French that were favourable to the Horthy regime and to revision. The volumes placed by Reverend Hoffman in the library of the University of Saskatchewan in Saskatoon, for example, had such titles as *The Treaty of Trianon, Dismembered Hungary; Revision of Peace; Trianon Hungary; La réforme agraire sur les territoires arrachés à la Hongrie*; and *Misère et ruine sociale des 11 millions d'hommes arrachés par le traité de paix à l'ancienne Hongrie.*[47]

Pre–First World War involvement with compatriots in the United States had taught Hungarian officials that ethnic associations constituted an avenue for reaching emigrants. Immigrant churches in particular were seen as effective agencies for the propagation of nationalism among such people.[48] In the case of new communities, where few or no organizations had been set up by immigrants, officials in charge of relations with expatriates were authorized to create associations.[49] In keeping with this policy, when post-1918 immigration to Canada was just beginning, the Ministry of Foreign Affairs, which was in charge of relations with Hungarians abroad, proposed a community centre in Winnipeg. Since almost all new arrivals passed through the city, officials believed that they could reach most of their compatriots through an establishment of this type. By 1926, however, when he realized just how dispersed Hungarian settlement in Canada was to be, the consul general, Albert de Haydin, advised against a community centre.[50]

The consul general decided that Hungarians in Canada could be united most effectively through a nation-wide federation. But he believed that such a large organization could be formed only when viable ethnic associations existed in all settlements. Accordingly, he decided that support for individual associations was the best short-term plan for preserving Hungarian culture in Canada as well as continuing loyalty to the native land.[51] The consul general also believed that support for "decent" lay associations and for churches would curb the influence of Communists within the immigrant group.[52]

In principle, Hungarian government representatives were authorized to aid religious and secular associations financially, provided that they were patriotic in orientation.[53] Because of severe financial constraints in the 1920s and 1930s, however, apart from the *Ujság*, no institutions received substantial financial aid from Budapest. Thus, for

Hungarian flag, gift of the Hungarian government, being presented by Dr István Jánossy, a Toronto steamship agent, to Rev. Charles Steinmetz, pastor of the Hungarian Presbyterian Church of Toronto; Knox College, June 1933. Multicultural History Society of Ontario Collection, Archives of Ontario.

example, despite the fact that the consul general recognized the importance of the St Imre Home of Montreal, both for the social services that it provided and for its promotion of Hungarian culture, he was unable to save it by providing the necessary financial aid. He himself could offer a mere $200, and his efforts to enlist the aid of Canadian charitable organizations also proved inadequate.[54]

By far the most important contribution that the Horthy regime made to the development of a patriotic camp in Canada was to supply emigrants and their associations with various materials – novels, plays, poetry books, books on Hungarian history and geography, readers for children, sheet music, embroidery books, dance manuals, periodicals, flags, posters, maps, and even films. In fact, this cultural aid was an extension of the propaganda campaign mounted at home in Hungarian villages. Consul General de Haydin maintained that although providing these cultural artifacts would tax the limited budget available for Hungarians abroad, this effort would unite the immigrants and ensure the preservation of their culture in Canada. The consul general put special emphasis on the distribution of folk operettas, which, as we shall see, were favoured as tools for ethnic preservation by Hungarian Canadians as well.[55] The cultural artifacts sent to Canada were, in any case, the same materials on which governmental and church authorities relied to integrate the peasantry into Hungary's dominant culture. Indeed, some of them, such as embroidery books, were sent in response to Canadian requests.[56]

These materials were exported under the auspices of the League of Hungarians Abroad, the Permanent Bureau of the World Congress of Hungarians, and the World Federation of Hungarians. In a manner characteristic of their dealings with co-nationals abroad, officials in Budapest seemed intent on hiding the fact that the government was responsible for providing these cultural materials. Thus, for example, the director of the World Congress chastised Reverend Charles Steinmetz for claiming during the flag dedication ceremony of the Hungarian Presbyterian Church of Toronto that the congregation received its Hungarian flag from the Hungarian government, rather than from the Permanent Bureau of the World Congress.[57] Careful to disguise the propagandistic intentions of the regime's cultural campaign, moreover, the consul general advised officials back home that they should send only films whose "propagandistic or political nature is not obvious."[58] In requesting greater financial aid from the Ministry of Foreign Affairs, Baron Perényi of the World Federation of Hungarians reasoned that his association "carries out those tasks which the Ministry of Foreign Affairs cannot carry out officially."[59]

Although we do not have complete figures, a report on the activities of the Permanent Bureau of the World Congress of Hungarians between 1929 and 1935 provides us with some idea of the volume of cultural materials exported. During that period, the bureau sent 10,000 readers, 19,000 works of fiction, 20,000 copies of a work by Andor Kun entitled *Do You Know What the World Owes to Hungarians?*, 4,000 copies of the proceedings of the 1929 gathering of the World Congress, 32,000 pieces of assorted printed matter, and several thousand periodicals.[60] Although most of these publications were donated free of charge, some of them may have been provided at substantially reduced rates, at the request of immigrant associations.[61] The agencies set up by Budapest to maintain close relations with expatriates also transmitted to them religious materials. In 1938, for example, they forwarded hundreds of almanacs of the Hungarian Reformed Church to expatri-

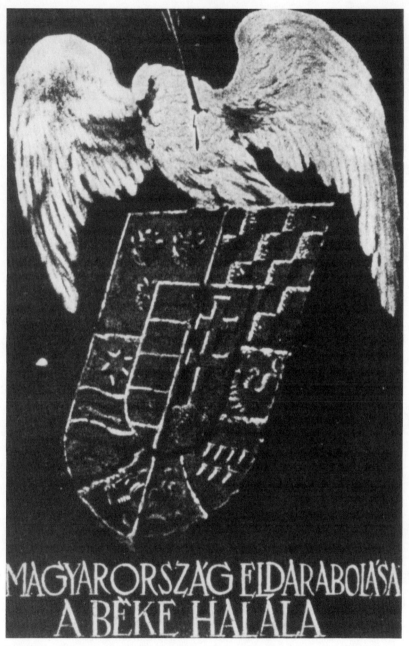

Postcard published and disseminated among emigrants by the Hungarian National Federation. "The fragmentation of Hungary, the death of peace."

ate Protestants in Canada.[62] In this cultural campaign, individual Hungarian-Canadian associations received shipments ranging from 50 to 200 books on several occasions during the interwar years.

These shipments may appear modest. Indeed, they did not always satisfy the needs of the recipient associations.[63] Because of financial limitations and the priority placed on propaganda activities in the successor states, few funds were available for Canadian Hungarians.[64] Yet those patriotic associations in Canada that did receive cultural materials depended on them for recreational reading, entertainment, and educating their children in Hungarian. It is clear from the letters that they sent to Hungary that because of their poverty, they could not afford to obtain books, flags, plays, music, and films from any other source. Even the officers of the Hungarian Self-Culture Society of Welland, perhaps the most prosperous Hungarian-Canadian association in central Canada, complained to the World Congress that their society's cultural work was impeded by its poverty: "our library is small, our plays few," wrote János Exner in 1930; "we can make little progress in the field of self-improvement because our association is poor."[65]

Small wonder that the society's director valued the shipments of books and plays from the congress. "In the letter that you sent us," he wrote to the president, "you say that the books you sent us are a mere nothing, but for us the shipment is a veritable treasure and we will always be grateful to you, who ... honoured our Self-Culture Society with such a magnificent gift." "This shipment," he added, "will greatly help us even far away from our home, in alien surroundings, to preserve unblemished our Hungarian identity and our loyalty to our native land."[66] The president of the Oshawa Hungarian Cultural Club gratefully acknowledged that, because of financial difficulties, the club would have been unable to carry out its mandate "for the preservation of our nationality, for our homeland, and for the dissemination of Hungarian culture," but for help from the World Congress.[67]

Poverty alone, however, does not explain the appeal of the exported cultural artifacts. The promoters of cultural activities within patriotic associations sympathized with the objectives of the Horthy regime and were happy to promote them in Canada. Reverend Fehér, for example, solicited the materials of the Hungarian National Federation from Baron Perényi, because he wanted to help spread the "Hungarian Truth" abroad.[68] Father Forgách assured Hungary's minister of religion and education that in Canada he did everything in his power to contribute to the coming of "the great Hungarian spring."[69]

As we saw above, leaders such as Fehér and Forgách exerted considerable influence over immigrants in Canada.[70] But the condition of former agriculturalists and dwarf holders as immigrants in an unfamiliar and often unfriendly new land also greatly enhanced their receptivity to the material disseminated by Budapest. Indeed, Horthyist propaganda efforts were more successful in Canada than in Hungary. While amateur drama troupes in Hungarian villages – whose activities the regime actively promoted – performed only two or three times a year, some theatre groups in Canada put on a different play every two or three weeks.[71]

The difficulties that most immigrants encountered in their adoptive land intensified their longings for their native land and hence their patriotism. When József Jáger could no longer tolerate the fact that French-Canadian workers in Montreal, who viewed the Hungarians as competitors for scarce jobs, referred to them as "maudits Pollacks," and even threatened to beat them up, he went to the consul to seek advice and consolation. He was able to draw new strength from the diplomat's words: "You are Hungarians, don't let it happen." Following this visit, Jáger went looking for work accompanied by a group of his compatriots, and, thus united, he and his co-nationals no longer felt threatened by the insults and threats of French Canadians.[72]

While, as we see below, difficult economic conditions and a sense of exclusion, radicalized some immigrants, disappointed hopes led others to become intensely patriotic. Their patriotism surged when the World Federation of Hungarians supplied Canadian associations with the Hungarian tricolour. In a 1939 letter of thanks to the federation, István Szalontay, president of the Hungarian Christian Burial Association in Niagara Falls, described the gift as one that "only a mother can give her child." "I was shaking all over when I began to unfold it," he added, "and by the time I held one corner of the unfolded flag and my wife the other, we looked at one another and our eyes clouded, only a few moments later could I see clearly the noble tricolour."[73] The members of the Hungaria Social Club in Montreal expressed their joy upon the receipt of the flag with loud hurrays and applause.[74]

Some immigrants came to idealize the world that they had left behind. John Burkus, who requested and received a shipment of books from the World Congress, wrote in his letter of thanks that he could not understand what moved him to leave his home. As a result of forced unemployment in Canada, his work as an agriculturalist in Szabolcs county, one of Hungary's poorest areas, now seemed appealing.[75] Mátyás Lissauer, a waiter in a Montreal restaurant, who worked 16 hours a day, including Sundays, believed that no one back home had to suffer the humiliation of arduous labour to which immigrants were exposed. "In Canada," he argued, "they make people work as we did oxen back home." Like Burkus, he too longed to return to Hungary.[76]

Nostalgia for their homeland seemed to intensify the desire of immigrants to hold on to Hungarian culture and to transmit it to their children. As one of them explained in a letter to the Hungarian consul in Winnipeg: "I, namely, Imre Furka, the father of 3 children, turn to you because I would like to teach them Hungarian so that love for the homeland will awaken in them too. I tell them a great deal about the homeland but they would still need the Hungarian word, because a happier and more beautiful future may still come when these wandering swallows will set off to find their old neglected nest where they lived many happy days this hope lives in their hearts that we will return home again."[77] While making for awkward reading, the lack of punctuation – an indication of the writer's limited education – inadvertently underscores the sincerity and intensity of his patriotic out-pouring. His letter also suggests that many immigrants continued to cherish the hope of returning home. In their alien, often hostile new environment, they found comfort in the familiar, albeit idealized representation of Hungary that was promoted by Horthy's regime among expatriates. Immigrants drew solace from their nation's heroic past, and they wanted to come to its aid.

7 The Communist Party and the Origins of the Proletarian Camp

Launching the Benefit Federation

The Communist party embarked on a systematic campaign to bring Hungarian immigrants in Canada within its orbit a little later than the Hungarian government and almost simultaneously with Canadian churches. Sometime in 1925 it sent Hungarian organizers from the United States to Canada, and a year later the first Hungarian faction of the Communist party was established in Ontario. [1] Its members, led by organizers from the United States, were charged with creating a communist-led organization among Hungarians in Canada. The Canadian organization was to be a branch of the Hungarian Workers' Mutual Aid and Self-Improvement Society (Workers' Society), the Hungarian mass organization of the American Communist party. It would assume the name Canadian Hungarian Mutual Benefit Federation (Benefit Federation).

The first to undertake this task in the spring of 1926 was Lajos Kövess. Kövess, first editor of the *Új Előre* (New Forward), the official organ of the Hungarian national bureau of the American Communist party, was one of a group of young participants in the Hungarian Soviet Republic of 1919 who escaped from the homeland following its defeat. Other members of the group such as János Gyetvai and Emil Gárdos, who became leaders among US Hungarian communists, also helped to organize the proletarian camp in Canada. These young radicals maintained close ties with fellow émigrés in Paris, Vienna, Kassa (Kosice), Berlin, and above all Moscow. Under their direction, the *Új Előre* followed the Comintern's instructions closely.[2]

The Hungarian communists who came from the United States to Canada to help found the Benefit Federation maintained that the impetus for organizing Hungarians in Canada under the communist banner came from the Communist International, via the National Hungarian Bureau of the US Communist party.[3] Their accounts suggest that by the mid-1920s Hungarian communist leaders realized that Canada had become the chief destination of emigrants, and they saw a unique opportunity for gaining adherents to communist-led organizations among the newly arrived, as yet unorganized immigrants there.[4] According to the Benefit Federation's official history, however, the idea of joining the Workers' Society was conceived in Canada, by radical workers involved with the First Hungarian Sick Benefit Society of Hamilton. Most prominent among them were two men who had been active in the Hungarian labour movement – István Botos, a machinist, and Joseph Král, a tool- and die-maker – and two men who arrived in Canada by way of the United States, where they had belonged to the Hungarian socialist movement – a taxi driver named István Morey and a lathe operator named Ferenc Kristoff.[5] They, and dozens of the group's members, in Hamilton and throughout the Niagara Peninsula were readers of the *Új Előre*.[6]

The communist paper's Canadian readers demonstrated their endorsement of its principles by carrying out subscription campaigns on its behalf. More than once, Canadian readers led in competitions for subscription sales. The paper's editors in turn gave increasing attention to events in Canada. Whereas in the early 1920s references to this country were made only infrequently, by the late 1920s the paper dedicated a whole page to news from Canada. It discussed both issues of general importance to the left and the affairs of Hungarians in Canada. The *Új Előre* attracted immigrants such as István Márkos to the left. Márkos got his first copy of the paper in 1926 from an uncle in the United States: "This was the first time that I obtained written material of the type which I had long sought, and for which there was a great need – a newspaper which educated, taught, led and helped in the struggle. It was the organizer of the working-class in a distant foreign land."[7]

According to the official history of the Benefit Federation, the *Új Előre*'s Canadian readers became acquainted with the US-based Workers' Society through the pages of the paper, which also served as the society's official organ. Canadian readers were so impressed by the nature and scope of the American organization's activities that they wanted to set up a similar mutual aid society, and they requested that the Workers' Society send an organizer to help them with this task.[8]

Since the sources for the history of the Comintern and its world-wide operations constitute politically sensitive material, and access to them in Canada and in Hungary remains limited, it is not possible to establish which of the two versions of the founding of the Benefit Federation is accurate.

American Assistance

It is clear, however, that Hungarians in central Canada who were sympathetic to the Communist party believed that they required aid from the more mature Hungarian communist movement south of the border.[9] These men and women, who were to prove their deep commitment to the communist cause throughout the 1920s and 1930s, did not feel themselves to be qualified organizers. They lacked experience with writing, public speaking, and administration. Many of them, moreover, were unable to communicate effectively in English. As late as 1930–31, the leaders of the Hungarian bureau of the Communist party in Canada complained to the party plenum: "we have not at our disposal sufficient numbers of comrades with organizing ability, especially when it comes to speaking." Given the proximity of a more mature Hungarian communist movement in the United States, it is understandable that Canadian Hungarian radicals turned to their US counterparts for guidance. If their work was to succeed, insisted the Hungarian bureau's members, "steps must be taken to secure an English-speaking Hungarian comrade from the US."[10]

Consequently, Kövess was only the first in a long line of organizers sent north by the US Hungarian movement. It was a measure of the commitment of the Hungarian section of the Comintern to organizing expatriates in Canada that the men whom they sent were the highest-ranking and most capable of the US Hungarian communists. These men, who had been politically active in Hungary and elsewhere in Europe before their arrival in North America, came to Canada with a clearly drawn plan for organizational structure. They were able to shape the development of the proletarian camp in Canada because they stood at its head until the mid-1930s. As bureau secretaries in Canada, they served as intermediaries with the central committee of the Canadian party. They edited the Hungarian-Canadian communist paper, the *Kanadai Magyar Munkás* (Canadian Hungarian Worker), until the mid-1930s.[11] Thanks to their participation, both the organizational framework and the ideological substance of the nascent proletarian camp closely resembled those of communist mass movements throughout North America and Europe. In keeping with communist practice, all members were to be mobilized to support the Communist party's causes, but only the most capable were to be educated and en-

couraged to become members of the party itself. As a first step towards
creating this mass organization, Kövess attempted to convince existing
Hungarian-Canadian associations to affiliate with the Workers' Society,
the Hungarian mass organization of the American Communist party. [12]

But while Kövess's campaign thus had clearly defined political objectives from the start, he concealed his own and the Workers' Society's
links to the Communist party. Having worked as a communist organizer in Hungary and in the United States, Kövess must have known
that open acknowledgment of the Workers' Society's political orientation was bound to unleash a concerted anti-communist campaign
within the community. A campaign of this sort could prevent the
Communist party from gaining a solid base among Hungarian immigrants. The handful of Hungarian radicals in Canada who would be attracted to the Workers' Society precisely by its politics were readers of
the *Új Előre* and were thus aware of the links with the Communist party.

The uniformly favourable reception that Kövess's campaign enjoyed
at its outset confirmed the adroitness of this strategy. Even the *Kanadai
Magyar Ujság* (Canadian Hungarian News), which was subsidized by the
Horthy regime, promoted his efforts. Similarly, Zoltán Molnár, who as
editor of the *Kanadai Magyar Hírlap* was one of the leading patriotic
spokesmen in central Canada, initially endorsed Kövess's campaign
enthusiastically. [13]

The ability of the mature American organization – it had 136
branches and 5,124 members in 1928 – to offer a generous and reliable benefit plan to prospective members undoubtedly enhanced its
appeal. [14] Although its monthly dues were twice those of the First
Hungarian Sick Benefit Society of Hamilton, for example, the
Workers' Society's insurance plan offered higher benefits for a longer
period than the pioneering Canadian society. [15]

The Workers' Society's political colouring, however, could not long
remain hidden. Hungarians in Canada had too many links to US
co-nationals, and strong anti-communist sentiments existed among
Hungarians in both countries. Once patriotic Hungarians in Canada
discovered the association's links to the Communist party, they did
everything in their power to prevent it from making inroads within the
immigrant group. Consequently, Kövess's campaign soon led to strife
within virtually every Hungarian association in central Canada.

PUTTING DOWN ROOTS

Conflict in Montreal

The minute books of the Hungaria Social Club of Montreal bear witness to how bitter and drawn-out such strife within the community

could be. Kövess arrived in Montreal to promote affiliation with the Workers' Society in March 1927, just three months after the club was founded. By the beginning of April, the *Új Előre* confidently announced that at its next meeting the Hungaria would ratify affiliation with the Workers' Society. Since the club's officers favoured such a move, the paper's confidence seemed well founded.[16] But the prospect of fusion with a communist-led organization mobilized a powerful opposition group, comprised of the best-educated and most articulate members, and only two days after the *Új Előre*'s announcement appeared, affiliation was rejected.[17] The Hungaria's president and vice-president resigned in protest, and under their leadership a separate branch of the American-based organization was established in Montreal.[18]

While the founding of this association institutionalized the ideological split among Montreal's Hungarians, political conflict within the Hungaria continued for another year. Some members continued the campaign to bring the club within the orbit of the Communist party. Their efforts were finally thwarted in April 1928 with passage of a motion stating that "the Hungaria Social Club is a nationalist, apolitical organization."[19]

The tactical maladroitness of the Hungaria's radical members may well have been responsible for the patriots' victory. In sharp contrast to the organizational astuteness that characterized Kövess's campaign in Canada, the arguments raised by radical members were ill-suited to winning over their politically uncommitted fellows. They attempted to show that the patriots' revisionist stance was pernicious by depicting it as part of a capitalist plot to unleash an imperialist war against the Soviet Union. This argument was in keeping with the Comintern's latest directive. But while the radicals may actually have developed a strong sense of loyalty to the "fatherland of the world proletariat," in their eagerness to follow the party line they lost sight of the nature of their audience. The fate of the Soviet Union was evidently far removed from the concerns of most other members.

Politically uncommitted club members could identify far more readily with the revisionist campaign that formed the core of the patriotic stance. Hungary, after all, was their native land, and even if many of them felt resentful when the impossibility of ameliorating their situation in Hungary drove them to emigrate, distance, time, and the harshness of conditions in Canada often tempered their resentment, and their anger gradually gave way to homesickness. Some of the Hungaria's members, moreover, came from areas given to the successor states by the Treaty of Trianon. As we see below, the patriotic depiction of truncated Hungary as a wounded motherland crying out to her far-flung children for help appeared especially poignant to them.[20] Just in case the patriotic appeal failed to convince the club's adherents,

however, Béla Eisner, a former lawyer from the area given to
Czechoslovakia, and one of the club's leading members, also threatened that "if the club does not adopt a nationalist orientation, in which
case it will adopt an internationalist orientation," he would do everything in his power "to place obstacles in the club's way, and relying on
his legal knowledge, to close down the club and to have its charter
taken away."[21]

Turmoil Elsewhere

Affiliation with the American mutual aid society elicited lengthy debate
within the Welland Hungarian Self-Culture Society as well. In 1928, the
society decided against affiliation.[22] Thereupon, as in Montreal, Kövess
organized a separate section of the Benefit Federation, which served as
the nucleus of the local proletarian camp. But even after the Benefit
Federation's Welland branch was established, proletarian leaders continued their efforts to draw the Welland Hungarian Self-Culture
Society into the proletarian camp. In 1929, some of the society's members were still sufficiently interested in the left to worry the editor of
Hírlap, the local patriotic paper. He attempted to dissuade them by stating that anyone joining the association would be deported.[23] This
scare tactic apparently worked, but members of the communist mass
organization continued to infiltrate the Self-Culture Society. To protect the latter, its patriotic members suggested as late as 1935 that people who belonged to the Workers' Society be prohibited from
joining.[24]

In the First Hungarian Sick Benefit Society of Hamilton, as noted at
the beginning of this chapter, the proponents of affiliation with the
Workers' Society were victorious. Their victory is not surprising. After
all, radicals in that city were the earliest and most active promoters of
the American association's campaign in Canada. Even in the Hamilton
society, however, affiliation was not achieved without friction. In an attempt to retain a foothold for the patriots, Ferenc Szabolcs, a local steamship agent, ran for secretary in 1928. The club's radical members were
sufficiently influential, however, not only to gain control of all offices
but also to oust Szabolcs from the club altogether.

The decision of the Hungarian Society of Toronto to affiliate with
the Workers' Society is more surprising. The Toronto body was
founded in 1927 by János Papp, a student missionary for the United
Church, and it operated under the aegis of that church.[25] Because of
this connection, affiliation with a communist-led association would
have appeared unlikely. Papp, who was vehemently anti-communist,
tried in vain, however, to dissuade members from linking up with the
Workers' Society.[26] Apparently, many of the men who were attracted

to the Hungarian Society of Toronto as a social centre did not have strong loyalties to the United Church or to its missionary.

Breaking with the Americans

In 1927, the Benefit Federation severed its ties to the US-based Workers' Society.[27] The patriotic campaign against the American society's organizational drive in Canada was probably responsible for this. The Benefit Federation's affairs were now administered by a grand council made up of seven members who were elected annually at a general meeting. The council was based in Hamilton until 1931, when it moved to Toronto. The affairs of each branch of the federation were governed by a committee of eight officers, also chosen annually and responsible to the grand council.[28] The federation's rank and file were informed about the proceedings of grand council meetings and about the federation's financial standing through the *Úttörő* (Pioneer), the federation's monthly bulletin.

Separation from the (American) Workers' Society created serious financial problems for the fledgling Canadian body. This occurred despite the fact that the American organization returned to its Canadian section the initiation and membership fees that it had paid into the Workers' Society fund. At first, the Benefit Federation attempted to stop the depletion of its funds by raising membership fees and by discontinuing payment of funeral benefits to its members and their families. Eventually, however, like the Windsor and District Hungarian Club and the Brantford Hungarian Sick Benefit Society, the federation also took out an insurance policy from a private firm – the Northern Life Insurance Co.[29]

Separation from the Workers' Society did not alter the objectives of the Benefit Federation. Nominally, the Canadian association remained apolitical, but its leaders continued to view it as an agency for developing proletarian consciousness among Hungarian immigrants. The federation's objectives, as specified in its new charter, included the social, moral, and intellectual education of members, and, as we shall see, the association's leaders made sure that this education had very specific political content.[30]

A Canadian Newspaper

In 1929, Joseph Fehér, an American communist operating in Canada under the name of Joseph Dohány, called a meeting to launch the *Kanadai Magyar Munkás* (Canadian Hungarian Worker, henceforth *Munkás*).[31] The decision to publish an independent, Hungarian-language communist paper in Canada was the consequence of a successful campaign by anti-communists to ban distribution of the *Új Előre* in Canada on the grounds that it contained subversive material.[32] US Hungarian communists initially reacted to the ban by printing special copies of the *Új Előre* for circulation in Canada under the name *A Jövő* (Future).[33] This course of action was, however, soon abandoned in favour of publishing a separate communist paper in Canada.

Indicative of the initially narrow base of radicalism among Hungarians in Canada, many of the men active in setting up the Benefit Federation also attended the founding meeting for the *Munkás*. The 24 people who were present demonstrated their deep commitment to the appearance of a radical Hungarian newspaper in Canada by agreeing to donate a whole week's wages to create the capital necessary to print the first issue,[34] which appeared on 16 July 1929.

Dedicated as these men were, however, not one of them had the knowledge or experience required to publish a newspaper. Consequently, as Sándor Vörös, who came from New York in 1929 to edit the *Munkás*, discovered, they were very much dependent on American organizers. He waited in vain for local leaders in Hamilton to open his first official meeting with them: "A short discussion made it clear that they expected me to do that, the comrade sent from the States had always been the Secretary of the Bureau and the leader of the Canadian Hungarian movement."[35]

Contrary to accusations made by its patriotic opponents, the paper received very little financial assistance from the Communist party. Although it operated on a shoestring budget, its existence was precarious in its first decade. In his memoirs, Vörös describes the primitive conditions under which the paper was first published in Hamilton:

The editorial office of the *Worker*, for that's what that basement was, had only one window the top of which was level with the sidewalk, affording no other view than an occasional dog or the legs of the passers-by. It was lighted by two large unshaded bulbs, whitewash on the damp walls was flaky and green in patches. The centre of the room was taken up by a crudely nailed, twelve foot table with two benches made of unpainted roughly planed fir. That, with a leather couch, some crude shelving made of discarded orange crates, comprised all the furniture. There was no desk, typewriter, filing cabinet – there was nothing in that room to indicate even remotely that it was an editorial office.[36]

The poverty of Hungarian immigrants during the 1930s made even this modest operation difficult to maintain. One member of the proletarian camp recounted proudly that he once managed to collect $15 for the *Munkás* from individual donors. Acknowledging that the sum may not appear impressive, he explained that the biggest single donation amounted to 55 cents.[37] On one occasion, when there was no

Cartoon published 13 July 1933 to mark the fourth anniversary of the
Kanadai Magyar Munkás (Canadian Hungarian Worker). "The Munkás
is four years old in the class struggle."

money at all to publish the paper and it urgently requested assistance
from the Communist party secretariat, it did receive $10. Soon after-
wards, however, the editor was informed that the party could not provide $50 to ensure that the *Munkás* would appear on 1 May 1931.[38]

Workers' Clubs

The need to create a solid financial base for the *Munkás* provided the
impetus for establishment of a network of organizations, known first as
Workers' clubs, later (as part of the Communist party's campaign to recruit farmers) as Workers' and Farmers' clubs, and finally, after 1939,
as the Canadian Federation of Democratic Hungarians.[39] The first of
the Workers' clubs was set up in Hamilton on 28 January 1931, and by
1934, 26 were operating among Hungarian immigrants throughout
Canada.[40] Subscription drives for the *Munkás* now took place under
the aegis of the clubs. But much like their patriotic counterparts,
members also organized dinners, dances, teas, picnics, and dramatic

performances in order to raise funds. The financial success of these schemes was apparent almost at once: by 1932, social functions constituted the single largest source of revenue for the *Munkás*.[41] Nevertheless, shortage of funds prevented publication of several issues during the early 1930s.

From the outset, however, communist organizers saw the educational role of these clubs as equal in importance to their fundraising activities. As an article in the *Munkás* stated: "workers should establish Workers' clubs, to find within their framework the possibility of acquiring knowledge harmonious with the vital interests of the working class. The objective is to learn and to teach. Our cultural tools are: lecture series, plays, and discussion groups in which workers' problems are solved, and the causes of the disorder in present day economic life, the historical inevitability of the future society and its advantages for humanity are discussed, strictly in the spirit of the working class."[42]

Creation of the Workers' clubs meant that two communist led organizational networks were active within the ethnic group. What was the relationship between the Benefit Federation and the Workers' clubs? Theoretically, they were quite distinct, each with its own mandate, funds, and officials, but even the official portrayal of the Benefit Federation as the proletarian movement's economic arm, and the Workers' clubs as its cultural arm, betrayed the close links between the two networks.[43] In fact, through their connection to the Communist party, the two organizations were linked at the top. They even held their annual conventions together.[44] On the local level, memberships overlapped: at the outset, members of the Workers' clubs were the most active, if not the total, membership of the Benefit Federation's branches. In the depths of the Depression, however, when many adherents of the Benefit Federation were unable to keep up payment of their monthly dues, membership in the Workers' clubs far outstripped that of the federation.[45] Not even the functions of the two networks were clearly differentiated. As mentioned above, although the Benefit Federation was nominally apolitical, Communist party organizers used its branches, as well as the Workers' clubs, in their efforts to raise class consciousness. Similarly, the Benefit Federation provided support for the *Munkás*, and the federation's bulletin, the *Úttörő*, was published by the *Munkás* press.

Not surprisingly, rank and file members were at times confused about the relationship between the two associations. Some even wondered why more than one "progressive" Hungarian organization was necessary.[46] But party organizers believed that the existence of two associational networks increased the possibilities of reaching immigrants and enlisting them into the proletarian camp. Accordingly, they established district committees in an attempt to regulate and coordinate local activities of the Benefit Federation and the Workers' clubs.[47]

A Solid Institutional Framework

Despite periodic organizational problems, however, the Benefit Federation, the Workers' clubs, and the *Munkás* together provided a solid institutional framework for the proletarian camp. They offered members all but the religious services that competing religious and secular associations offered patriotic Hungarians. Proletarian associations rented, purchased, and on occasion even built halls that served as community centres for members. In these halls, Hungarians met informally, to chat, to exchange gossip and information about the host society, and to play cards and billiards. Dances, banquets, and cultural evenings were held both to entertain and to raise funds. Dance groups, choirs, orchestras, drama groups, and athletic groups were also active within proletarian associations. Moreover, these bodies offered educational opportunities to immigrants of all ages: English and adult-education classes to grown men and women, and Hungarian-language classes to children. And if because of their politics proletarian leaders were unable to help the members of their camp to find employment, they could offer legal aid to people who fell afoul of the law because of their radicalism, and they tried to prevent deportations.

It is difficult to say exactly what portion of those Hungarians who were active in organized community life belonged to proletarian associations. Judging from the fragmentary data available, membership in the largest proletarian associations compared favourably with that in patriotic secular organizations. Thus, for example, in 1935 the Workers' club in Hamilton had approximately 280 members, while its patriotic counterpart, the Hamilton branch of the Brantford Sick Benefit Society, had only 95. In Welland in 1931, the Workers' club had 120 members, while the largest patriotic secular association, the Welland Hungarian Self-Culture Society, had 138.[48]

A somewhat better-documented measure of the Communist party's influence is the readership of the *Munkás*. The paper's circulation compared favourably with that of the leading patriotic newspaper, the *Kanadai Magyar Ujság*, even though the communist paper did not enjoy the type of subsidies that the Hungarian government provided for the *Ujság*.[49] In 1937, the *Ujság* had 3,033 subscribers,[50] while the *Munkás*'s readership, at its lowest, was 2,862. Admittedly, because subscriptions to the *Munkás* were sold on a monthly basis, readership could fluctuate by several hundred from month to month. From 1935 on, however, it always had more than 2,000 readers.[51] The circulation of the *Munkás* seems considerable if we compare it to that of the *Új Elöre* in the United States. In 1925, the American communist paper sold only 9,000 copies on average,[52] even though there were approximately 17 times as many Hungarians in that country as in Canada.

WHY SOME HUNGARIANS RESPONDED

In one of the very few efforts to explain why communism appealed to some members within an immigrant group in Canada and not to others, Anthony Rasporich has suggested that among Croatian immigrants only sojourning males without families, who were employed in outlying areas, joined the Communist party. Such was not the case among Hungarians.[53] Admittedly, men far outnumbered women in the Benefit Federation. In 1931, it had 800 male and only 28 female members.[54] As a consequence of a deliberate effort to recruit women, however, their numbers in Workers' clubs increased during the 1930s. By 1934, in Hamilton, for example, 27 per cent of adherents were women, while women made up approximately 39 per cent of adult Hungarians in the city.[55]

The influence of the Communist party among Hungarians must be viewed within the context of the unprecedented growth of the Communist party of Canada during the 1930s, which was itself a facet of the temporary radicalization of large segments of North American society. The variety of radical parties and protest groups that emerged in Canada and in the United States suggests that harsh economic conditions convinced large numbers of people of all ethnic backgrounds of the need for fundamental social and economic change.[56] Because immigrants were generally among the lowest-paid and least steadily employed workers, they suffered disproportionately from the Depression and had even more reason to protest than native-born workers.

The testimony of Sándor Egyed, to cite one particularly poignant example, permits us to see how economic hardship could radicalize a formerly apolitical and devout person. Egyed, father of two and owner of a small plot of land in Felnémet, Heves county, migrated to Canada in 1927 with the modest aspiration of earning enough in two or three years to rebuild his house in Hungary. But his experiences in Canada were disappointing from the start. For a whole month following his arrival, he was unable to find work, and after that he found only temporary employment, less and less frequently as the Depression closed in. A growing awareness of the injustice inherent in his situation led Egyed, formerly a devout Roman Catholic, to lose faith in God:

When it became so that there was nothing to eat, and on some occasions I had to go to bed hungry, I began to think. I thought things over. Being Roman Catholic, I compared God to a good father, and I realized, what kind of a father is one, who has four or five children, and he selects one of them and gives him everything, and he gives the rest nothing, and lets them starve. What kind of God is that. As a Roman Catholic I learned from the Bible, that's how I understood the Bible, that God could do anything, so everything depended on him. So then, when God the Father rejoices at the suffering of his children, he is not a father.[57]

His loss of his faith, which had been the foundation of his worldview, led to a revolution in Egyed's thinking. He who "spat on the communists" in Hungary and called them "dirty commies" remembered that in 1919 they distributed firewood to the poor for nothing, whereas after the Hungarian Soviet Republic was defeated, the forest was still there, but the poor had no more firewood.

Chances are that Egyed would have joined the proletarian camp even if his new-found admiration for the action of the Hungarian bolsheviks in 1919 had not pointed him towards the communists. There were virtually no other avenues of protest open to him, or to most other Hungarians in Canada. Most of them were employed in sectors of the economy outside the reach of labour unions, and, in any case, as job opportunities declined, organized labour, with the notable exception of communist-led unions, grew increasingly hostile to immigrants. Political protest groups in central Canada, moreover, made no effort to recruit immigrant workers, who were prevented by a language barrier from joining these groups on their own initiative. The Communist party, in contrast, sought out foreign-born workers, and its willingness and ability to provide them with an avenue of protest help to explain the preponderance of immigrants within its ranks.[58]

But the relationship between economic hardship and political radicalism is by no means simple. While immigrant workers from "non-preferred" countries were all subject to exploitation and deprivation they did not all flock to the mass organizations of the Communist party.[59] Similarly, only a fraction, albeit a significant one, of Hungarian newcomers were radicalized by their Canadian experiences. An even larger fraction resisted communist overtures; the religious and secular associations to which they belonged formed the patriotic camp.

At least until the Second World War, joining the patriotic camp was the safe choice for Hungarians. Many patriotic leaders – most notably, clergymen – had traditionally held positions of authority in Hungarian society. Even after such people emigrated authorities back home continued to view and support them as the best leaders of their less-educated compatriots. For some immigrants, their status and authority in Canada were legitimized by the support that they received from Canadian officials and high-ranking clergymen and by their ties to the representatives of the Hungarian government. Patriotic ideology, as we shall see, drew on symbols and assumptions that were familiar to the immigrants.

Commitment to the communist cause, by contrast, as the case of Sándor Egyed indicates, entailed a revolution in the thinking of the rank and file. We shall explore the nature of this radical ideology and its appeal in chapters 9 and 10. By joining the proletarian camp, immigrants risked much more, however, than loss of reassurance from traditional symbols and beliefs. They were defying both traditional figures of authority, such as the clergy and Budapest's representatives, and Canadian officials. Members of the proletarian camp knew that their radicalism jeopardized even the minimal chances of finding employment that existed in the 1930s. They had to forgo the assistance of patriotic leaders, clergymen in particular, who often had connections in the host society that they used to help members of the patriotic camp to find employment.[60]

These immigrants also knew that employers tended not to hire anyone with a reputation for radicalism.[61] The Empire Cotton Mill in Welland, for example, fired workers in 1934 for their "violent Russian red sympathies." Only those Hungarian men and women who could produce a character reference from their clergymen could hope to get a job in the mill.[62] Merely being seen in a communist-led demonstration sufficed at times to disqualify workers from being hired, and some patriots, in their eagerness to eliminate competition for scarce jobs, did not hesitate to inform prospective employers of the suspect political activities of their rivals.[63] Fearful for their jobs, many people who were fortunate enough to be employed stayed away from Workers' clubs.[64] John Sipos, who made no secret of his communist sympathies even during the Depression, recalls that in the 1930s, when he was living in Port Colborne, some Hungarians were so worried about being found guilty by association that they crossed to the other side of the street when they saw him coming.[65] Even immigrants who were in sympathy with proletarian objectives were seemingly deterred by fear from becoming active. In the fundraising campaigns for the *Munkás*, for example, there were always anonymous donors, and the paper even had some subscribers who had their copies delivered to post office boxes.[66]

In an effort to combat what they saw as a dangerous rise in radical activism during the Depression, the Canadian authorities clamped down on the Communist party. In 1931, the party was proscribed, ten of its leaders were tried, and many non-naturalized immigrants who belonged to the party were deported.[67] Hungarian proletarians also felt the consequences of this campaign.

The Ontario attorney general's office kept files on, and considered bringing charges against, the *Munkás* and the *Úttörő*. But the articles selected and translated for Canadian officials could not be considered seditious or disloyal and therefore did not warrant prosecution.[68]

The Royal Canadian Mounted Police (RCMP) also kept some of the leaders of Hungarian mass organizations under surveillance.[69] When John Farkas of Oshawa made a speech to the local Unemployed Workers' Association in 1932, he was arrested under section 98 of the Criminal Code for advocating "the overthrow by force or by violence of constituted law and authority." Farkas was convicted and deported.[70]

Several men and women from the proletarian camp were refused citizenship in the 1930s because of suspected affiliation with the Communist party.[71] Members of proletarian organizations were also occasionally arrested for distributing communist leaflets and for organizing meetings deemed treasonable or dangerous to public safety.[72] Indeed, proletarian activists came to expect unpleasant encounters with the police whenever they were distributing literature on behalf of their associations. As one of them recalls, "each time we went out I had a story all thought out ahead of time, just in case the police would catch us. It's true they would probably only have imprisoned us so that they could milk the movement of 20 or 25 dollars."[73]

Patriotic Hungarians, as we see below, eagerly joined in this anti-red campaign. When the Communist party was proscribed, for example, Károly Winter, the Hungarian consul general, sent a clipping of an article from the *Munkás*, "How Shall We Become Members of the Communist Party" to Ontario's attorney general. Drawing attention to the propagandistic activities of communists among Hungarians, the consul attempted to protect the image of the immigrant group by playing down the influence of the left within it: "I deem it my duty to call your attention to this propaganda, because of its possible influence on Hungarian immigrants in Canada. So far the latter have shown no inclination to follow Communistic leadership, but in their present condition, out of work, and suffering want, it is to be feared that a number of them might be misled by such agitation."[74] Patriotic newspapers and leaders publicized and even exaggerated the dangers that faced immigrants who supported the communist cause.[75]

The Communist party made an effort to protect its supporters, but its ability to do so was limited. The communists had very few elected representatives, but radical immigrants with some command of English could turn to them for help. Bernát Hoó, for example, went to Joe

Salsberg in Toronto when he was trying to obtain relief.[76] Lawyers working with the Canadian Labour Defense League (CLDL) tried to prevent the deportation and incarceration of immigrant radicals.

Faced with such determined opposition, the Communist party could not rely on the power of ideas alone to make inroads within the ethnic group. The party's success among Hungarians depended at least as much on the activities of capable and energetic organizers as on the appeal of radical views during a period of extreme hardship.[77]

Organizational astuteness was, for example, largely responsible for the ability of the proletarians to establish a nation-wide mutual aid society – a task which, as we see below, was undertaken in vain by the patriotic Canadian Hungarian Association.[78] The patriotic scheme was administered strictly as a business proposition. It did not provide a sense of participation in a mutual aid venture. The Canadian Hungarian Mutual Benefit Federation, by contrast, permitted the elected officers of its local branches to help administer the mutual aid fund through its federative structure. Because social and cultural functions were inseparably linked to economic ones within the branches of the Benefit Federation, its members developed strong loyalties to the proletarian association.

From the beginning, moreover, the federation's officers included a paid organizer, whose task it was to travel to every Hungarian settlement, no matter how remote, in order to set up new branches and to oversee the activities of existing branches and to help them with any problems they might have.[79] The results of the organizational drive of 1934–35 best illustrate the crucial role of these organizers in the development of the federation. In 1933, the federation's leaders seriously doubted its ability to survive. Because of the Depression, 75 per cent of its members were unable to pay their monthly dues, and despite a temporary reduction in fees membership declined from 1,204 in 1929 to 523 in 1933.[80] In an effort to remedy this seemingly hopeless situation, Joseph Magyar, the federation's newly elected organizer, embarked on a nation-wide drive. Over the next two years, with the help of local branches, he recruited 1,067 new members.[81]

The branches of the Benefit Federation that itinerant organizers established, moreover, were often the only Hungarian organizations in areas where immigrants settled. Thus, for example, the first Hungarian organization in the Delhi-Tillsonburg tobacco district of Ontario, where settlement by Hungarians began around 1930, was the Vanessa branch of the Benefit Federation, founded by Joseph Magyar during his 1934–35 organizing tour. The first patriotic association in this area was not formed until 1949. To notify immigrants living scattered throughout the tobacco district, Magyar asked Pál Osztács, who delivered bread in the area, to distribute leaflets announcing the federation's organizational meeting. And although the branch had only 17 members when it was founded, in the absence of a competing patriotic body the social functions arranged by this small group attracted many, if not most, of the Hungarians who lived and worked in this area.[82] Even immigrants opposed to the proletarian camp acknowledge that the Benefit Federation exerted considerable influence among immigrants in the region.[83]

The patriotic press, dismayed at the success of these recruitment drives, denounced proletarian organizers as bolshevik agents paid by "rubles rolling" from Moscow. Admittedly, the American Hungarian communists who were the first itinerant organizers in Canada were paid by the National Hungarian Bureau of the US Communist party, and at a time when the proletarian movement in Canada had no financial base at all this contribution, however modest, was indispensable. Once the Benefit Federation was incorporated, however, organizers were paid out of its general expenses fund, and the modest salaries that they received can scarcely have been responsible for the energy and dedication with which they performed their arduous task.[84] In 1933, the federation's expenses fund could not cover even the travel costs of József Tirpák, the organizer for western Canada. Tirpák was therefore forced to travel from one Hungarian settlement to another on a "Columbus Ticket" – that is, by stealing aboard freight trains.[85] It was in order to permit organizers to travel somewhat more comfortably that the federation's secretary, Joseph Blaskó, urged each member to contribute five cents a month towards a travel fund, a measure formally incorporated into the constitution in 1933.[86]

The Workers' clubs, which also had organizers, were no better equipped to pay them. When an organizer was sent to Port Colborne in 1934, in response to the club's request, he received an allowance of $1.50 a week, but just until he managed to get onto local relief rolls.[87] Only the deep commitment of these organizers to the communist cause can explain their unremitting efforts on behalf of the proletarian camp.

Why did some immigrants turn to radical thought and action in order to ameliorate their situation in Canada while others adhered to traditional ideas, leaders, and institutions? The complexity of this question perhaps explains why it has not received the attention that it deserves. My own sense is that only a large number of in-depth studies of individuals could suggest an answer. The following three chapters, which make up part III of this book, embark on a much more modest task.

By examining the ideology and activities of patriotic and proletarian associations, they try to explain what specific attributes of each camp appealed to Hungarian immigrants. These chapters also attempt to show how political ideologies were transmitted within the ethnic group. By stressing that politicization was occurring simultaneously within both the avowedly radical proletarian camp and the nominally apolitical patriotic camp, I hope to show that in the social milieu of immigrants in interwar Canada ethnicity could be placed in the service of politics. By adopting this comparative approach, I hope also to show that in certain important respects the proletarianization of peasant immigrants – that is, the development of an awareness among them of their shared status as workers in an industrial society – resembles ethnicization – the emergence of recognition of shared values and goals based on a common cultural background distinct from the culture of the dominant society.

PART THREE

Patriots and Proletarians

8 Patriots

PATRIOTIC ASSOCIATIONS AND THEIR PROGRAMS

Although they emerged independently of one another, and they owed their inception to a variety of forces and traditions, Hungarian-Canadian religious associations and all those secular bodies that refused to join the communist-led Benefit Federation made up a distinct sector within the ethnic group. Because their members frequently referred to themselves as "hazafias magyarok" (patriotic Hungarians), I call them patriotic associations. All such organizations espoused one goal that surpassed their specific social and economic aims. This goal – which in principle at least transcended particularistic religious loyalties as well – was the creation and maintenance of a Hungarian identity in Canada that would unite members of the ethnic group and ensure its survival. For the spokesmen of patriotic groups, this program meant preservation not only of their native language but also of what they most often described as "szellem" (the Hungarian spirit).[1] The fact that they did not find it necessary to elaborate on what this spirit meant suggests the currency of the term among them.

Closer examination of their statements and of the programs and activities of their associations reveals that this concept embraced three different, but complementary elements of nationalist ideology. First, in wanting to safeguard the Hungarian spirit – described alternately as the Hungarian "feeling" (érzés) or as "genuine Hungarianness" (igazi magyarság) – patriots were inspired by nationalist ideology to reproduce specific parts of their nation's history and culture as the most suitable means for the expression and affirmation of ethnic identity in Canada. Second, the patriotic program of ethnic preservation also implied the maintenance of loyalty to their native land. Third, persistence of the national spirit in Canada depended as well on the place that immigrants would carve for themselves in their new society. Thus patriotic plans for preservation of the Hungarian spirit embodied all facets of the ideological elaboration of ethnic group identity: they prescribed the tasks of cultural preservation and group survival, the relationship of members to their homeland, and the group's position in Canadian society.

Patriotic spokesmen insisted that their program was apolitical. The motion passed by Montreal's Hungaria Social Club in 1928 in response to the attempted takeover by communist sympathizers exemplified this claim to neutrality – the club stood "on a nationalist base without any politics."[2] Indeed, patriotic leaders and the patriotic press generally refrained from expressing support for either Hungarian or Canadian political parties. Yet the patriotic program, as I try to show, had definite political underpinnings. The patriots' interpretation of Hungarian history, their choice of symbols and metaphors to characterize group identity in Canada, their selection of cultural artifacts for the expression of this identity, their attitude to their homeland, and their perceptions of Canadian society and their own position within it all had distinct political implications.

Yet the patriots could dispense with an explicit political platform for two reasons. First, because the patriotic definition of identity was largely an extension of the official culture of Horthyist Hungary, this definition rested on concepts, images, and assumptions that were current at the very least among better-educated Hungarians. Accordingly, in sharp contrast with proletarian leaders who, as we see below, were bent on transforming the thinking of immigrants, patriotic leaders did not feel a need to spell out their own ideological assumptions. Not only the ideological content but even the tools on which they relied bore a remarkable resemblance to the Horthyist program for assimilation of the peasantry to that regime's official culture. Second, patriotic spokesmen were, by and large, willing to accept the status quo in both countries. Their task, as they saw it, was limited to fostering strong links between Hungarian immigrants in Canada and their native land and to carving out a place for the ethnic group within the social, economic, and political order that prevailed in their adoptive land.

The political dimensions of patriotic ideology generally crystallized in response to the challenge from the proletarian camp. The assertion of political neutrality was, in fact, a facet of the patriots' claim that only they represented "genuine" Hungarian interests in Canada.

To point to the social and political implications of the patriotic plan, and to the similarities between this plan and the Horthyist program for spreading the Christian-nationalist ideology among Hungarian peasants, is not to suggest that patriotic leaders in Canada deliberately manipulated cultural artifacts in order to blind the rank and file to social and economic realities back home. Such an argument could more appropriately be made with regard to Horthyist officials in Hungary. But the promoters of cultural activities within the ethnic group – the clergymen and their assistants and middle-class immigrants and artisans – were apparently so fully immersed in Hungary's dominant culture that they themselves believed the programs of the patriotic camp to be the expression of the common, indeed the only, valid interests of their conationals in Canada. But the fact that they transmitted social and political views to the rank and file through cultural activities without perhaps being fully conscious of what they were doing in no way diminishes the political implications of their program of ethnic preservation.

Folklore and the Hungarian Spirit

Patriotic leaders subscribed to the romantic nationalist idea that every nation had a unique spirit (Geist) worth preserving and that this spirit resided in the Volk. They maintained that folk culture was exceptionally well suited for the expression and affirmation of Hungarian ethnic identity in Canada. Pride in its uniqueness and beauty would unite the immigrant generation, convince children that their parents' language and culture were well worth preserving, and ensure continuing loyalty of all members of the ethnic group to their native land.[3] Patriotic leaders also expressed the hope that they could win the admiration and goodwill of members of the host society by introducing them to Hungarian singing, dancing, and embroidery.[4]

Since most members of the ethnic group were former peasants, the choice of rural folk culture for the expression of group identity seems most fitting. But the cultural artifacts on which the guardians of the national spirit relied for the development of ethnic culture in Canada were, for the most part, not generated by peasant creativity. They were the very same ones selected by Horthyists to spread conservative-nationalist ideology in the Hungarian countryside. They fell into two general categories – urban-born, "folksy" materials, supposedly inspired by rural folk culture, and elements of genuine folk culture artificially revived among immigrants.

For ethnic leaders, these urban-born folk materials were interchangeable with genuine folk culture: both were effective in uniting the ethnic group and displaying its creative abilities. But since the traditions of folk dancing, singing, and embroidery did not seem to be alive among the interwar immigrants, the people in charge of cultural activities within patriotic associations – who did not generally come from the ranks of the peasantry – took it upon themselves to revive these elements of rural folk culture in Canada. Thus, for example, relying on books sent from Hungary, nuns and wives of Hungarian Protestant clergymen taught female peasant compatriots how to embroider traditional folk patterns.[5] As suggested above, the meetings of embroidery groups created a sense of community among the immigrant women, and their colourful products not only sold well in church bazaars but also received attention in the women's pages of the Canadian daily press.[6] The wife of a Hungarian clergyman from Montreal believed that through the embroideries prepared for a church bazaar the "artistic and cultural values which lie hidden in the Hungarian people" found expression.[7] Sister Mary, who formed an embroidery group among Hungarian Roman Catholic women in Montreal, saw in the wish expressed by group members "to show Canadians what Hungarian women are capable of accomplishing" proof that folk embroidery "helped to preserve the Hungarian idea" in Canada.[8] The president of the Petőfi choir of Montreal observed: "While we are singing Hungarian songs our souls fly home to the small villages we left behind and we relive the happy years of our youth."[9]

In Canada, as in Hungary, folk operettas were among the most widely used of the "folksy" materials designed to arouse popular nationalism. Ethnic leaders considered them unusually effective for the development of ethnic identity in Canada, precisely because the settings, themes, characters, and music were supposedly drawn from rural life and folk traditions back home. They believed that the staging of these works aided the preservation of the Hungarian language and of songs, dances, customs, and rituals among immigrants and their children.[10] Indeed, folk operettas enjoyed tremendous popularity among immigrants. They were the most frequently performed items in the repertoires of the drama troupes set up within patriotic associations. Hungarians enjoyed acting in these "good old village pieces," and, according to the highly favourable reviews invariably received in the Hungarian-Canadian press, the key to their success was their recreation of the ambience of the village, so that their audiences could, for a brief moment, imagine that they were back in their native land.[11]

Both artificially revived folklore and synthetic folk materials served to obscure the problems that plagued contemporary Hungarian society; the former, by creating the illusion of a vital peasant culture to which only a healthy peasant society could have given birth, and the latter, by presenting an idyllic view of village life. By lessening awareness of the urgency of social and economic reform in the countryside, these

Young performer in *A Falu Rossza* (The Village Scamp), Toronto,
1930s. Because the settings, themes, characters, and music of such folk
operettas were supposedly drawn from rural life and folk traditions
in Hungary, patriotic leaders considered them unusually effective for
development of ethnic identity in Canada. Multicultural History
Society of Ontario Collection, Archives of Ontario.

materials lent credibility to the Horthy regime; they concealed the discrepancy between the regime's glorification of the peasantry and its
failure to introduce any meaningful reforms to aid the peasants.

Hungarian History and the Patriotic Camp

The time-honoured political and religious traditions of the homeland
were additional manifestations of the Hungarian "spirit" that patriotic

leaders sought to preserve and to bring to the attention of Canadians. To achieve these goals, they relied on historical interpretations and symbols that had formed part of the nationalist patrimony since the nineteenth century.

The statements of these leaders, as well as the poems recited and the plays performed in patriotic associations, frequently referred to "our thousand year old nation," thereby emphasizing that the foundations of Hungary's national sovereignty, its constitutionality, and its Christianity had been laid at the beginning of the eleventh century by St Stephen, the nation's first king.[12] The insistence on Hungary's fully developed political traditions, which were at times contrasted to the immaturity of Canada's, may be interpreted as a defensive reaction of an alienated minority.[13] But this reaction served to legitimize the politics of the Horthy regime. By suggesting that their native land was politically more advanced than their adoptive home, patriotic leaders were obscuring the fact that the franchise was actually being restricted in Hungary. As we have seen, those strata of society from which the majority of immigrants came lost political freedom when open balloting was reintroduced in rural society.

Another, no less defensive variation of this emphasis on antiquity was the argument that the religious and political character with which St Stephen endowed Hungary gave it a proud place among Western nations. Indeed, St Stephen provided his nation with the mission of protecting Western Christendom against onslaughts from the East. Having been subjected to attacks first by the Tatars and Mongols and later by the Turks, Hungary, because of its geographical situation, served as a buffer for the rest of Europe. The Magyars thus, according to this argument, made possible the flowering of Western civilization by spilling their blood in the struggle with the eastern hordes.[14]

Religion formed an essential component of the Hungarian spirit as defined by the patriots. Hungarian-Canadian clerics were, of course, most insistent upon this feature of ethnic identity. "To be good Hungarians," stated one of them, "we must also be good Christians."[15] The inseparability of religion and national identity, at least in principle, provided common ground for all church-going Hungarians. But the patriotic press and secular associations also seemed to accept the religious dimension of ethnic identity. In the eyes of some Hungarians the religious content of the national spirit was strictly Christian. Despite their repeated assertions of patriotism, Jewish compatriots could by definition not be "pure" or "genuine" Hungarians.[16]

As was the case with other aspects of patriotic ideology, its religious components crystallized in reaction to the emergence of the proletarian camp, which was virulently anti-clerical. "Don't listen to the renegades who have abandoned their faith ... who announce that they don't need God, that they don't need priests," wrote one of the *Hírlap*'s readers; "infidelity and the denial of God are unworthy of the Magyar nation's thousand year old history. We Magyars bled for centuries in destructive wars and our true faith alone saved us from ruination."[17]

The revolution of 1848 was another chapter of their nation's history to which Hungarian patriots in Canada paid considerable attention. This was not suprising, given the fact that the Magyars' struggle to become independent of Hapsburg rule was a symbol of modern nationalists. Among immigrants in Canada, the annual celebration of 15 March, as we see below, was the high point of community life. The ideological dimensions of the patriotic interpretation of the events of 1848 surfaced in reaction to the proletarian camp. Fear of the revolutionary doctrines of communist mass organizations led patriotic spokesmen such as Father Wesselényi of Montreal to insist that 1848 was not a revolution but a war of national liberation in which patriotic Hungarians of all classes united to fight against foreign oppression.[18] Reverend Ferenc Kovács of Hamilton declared that the nobility had voluntarily given up its special privileges in 1848, so that the nation could fight united for its rights.[19] Gusztáv Nemes, editor of the *Kanadai Magyar Ujság*, argued that the proletarian camp had no right to celebrate 1848, since the leaders of the Hungarian War of Independence, Kossuth, Petőfi, and Széchenyi, had no intention of promoting "red" principles or of denying God. Let it celebrate the birthday of Lenin or Stalin, he suggested.[20]

Proud as patriots may have been of the antiquity of their constitutional and religious heritage and of the Magyars' spirit of independence, their reflections on the course of Hungarian history were also infused with pathos. Owing to its distinct culture, their small state was isolated in east-central Europe, in the midst of powerful and hostile Germanic and Slavic nations, and no other country, they believed, had suffered misfortunes of equal magnitude, with "the gross injustice" of the Treaty of Trianon of 1920 being the most painful, by virtue of its immediacy: "We, the sons of our fate-stricken Magyar home feel our isolation, our condition as orphan-pariahs especially intensely. We are poorer, sicker, more isolated, less protected, more unfortunate, and more tormented than any other nation. Our loss, our uncertain future is more exasperating than the political and economic problems of any other nation."[21]

Trianon and Patriotic Immigrants

Revision of the Treaty of Trianon was unquestionably one of the central preoccupations of patriotic spokesmen in Canada. "There is one goal before us all," stated one of them, "and that is the unceasing fight for the revision of the Treaty of Trianon." They believed that the dismembered motherland, "bleeding from her wounds," needed the aid of her far-flung children, and it was the foremost duty of Hungarians everywhere to respond to her call.[22]

All discussions in the patriotic camp seemed in some way to be linked to revision. Concern with Hungary's past was elicited not simply by a wish to remember a shared heritage in an alien environment, or by the desire to gain recognition in the host society, but also by a need to find arguments for revision and inspiration for the revisionist campaign. Thus, for example, patriotic leaders based arguments for the revision of the treaty on the rights of the crown of St Stephen – the gold crown sent by the Pope in 1000 to crown him as Hungary's first king. According to traditional legal thought, this diadem was imbued with mystical qualities and symbolized the indivisibility of Greater Hungary, or the lands of the crown of St Stephen.[23] From the resilience of the Magyars in face of their various enemies, patriots drew confidence in the eventual resurrection of Greater Hungary and inspiration for the campaign towards this goal.

Social and cultural activities within the patriotic camp were also designed to aid revision. Explaining his reasons for establishing the St Imre Home in Montreal, Father Joseph Rácz stated that he was hoping to counteract the propaganda of Czechs, Romanians, Serbs, and Swabians by showing how constructive and self-reliant Hungarians could be.[24] Other patriotic spokesmen were convinced that once their children got to know the beauties of their parents' culture through folk operettas and plays, "they will become acquainted with the spirit of the Hungarian nation, and having become acquainted with this spirit they will be able to join the protest against the oppression of our brothers across the ocean, and to raise their voice for justice for Hungary."[25] Faith in the "resurrection of Hungary" was fervently expressed in Canada as the members of patriotic organizations recited the "Magyar Creed." Revisionist plays, poems, and songs formed part of every public event in patriotic associations. Although these overtly political materials did not necessarily have any real or pretended connection to the rural world or to folk tradition, they drew on "genuine Hungarian" culture. Not surprisingly, therefore, they quite often resembled such "folksy" materials as folk operettas. Irredentist songs were in the tradition of "art music," rustic images were common in irredentist poems, and plays dealing with irredentist themes were often set in Hungarian villages, especially in the areas lost at the end of the First World War. Patriots embraced these materials as an integral part of the Hungarian spirit which they sought to preserve in Canada.

The revisionist statements of patriotic spokesmen abounded with re-

ligious invocations. Reverend Fehér of the Montreal United Church
believed that God himself favoured revision:

Today there are Hungarians in every corner of the world, whose very presence
broadcasts the criminal outrage of the Treaty of Trianon. Our awareness of this
fact strengthens our conviction that God had a purpose in dispersing us. He
sent us far and wide to publicize this mockery of justice and the suffering of our
native land. We must ensure that those who are in a position to heal, to correct
what was mendaciously inflicted upon us in the name of world peace and democracy, should become aware of our affliction, our wound, which is also the
bleeding wound of Europe and of the civilized world.[26]

So firmly convinced were these spokesmen of the justness of their demands that they denounced any immigrant who did not support the revisionist campaign as "un-Hungarian," a traitor to the homeland.[27] In
this respect, too, the main target of patriotic denunciations was the proletarian camp. While the Communist party did not accept any part of
the 1919 peace settlement, as we see in the following chapter, its supporters among Hungarians in Canada argued that to the disinherited
the redrawing of boundaries only changed the nationality of their exploiters. Since they believed that, by fanning the flames of patriotism
among workers and peasants in Hungary and in Canada, the revisionist
campaign diverted their attention from social and economic inequalities, thus perpetuating the oppression of the working class, proletarian
leaders openly criticized the revisionist campaign,[28] and the patriots
struck back. The *Kanadai Magyar Ujság* remarked: "a man who tries to
stab his own brother in the back, at a time when the brother is struggling for the liberation of millions of unfortunate Hungarians who lan-
guish under foreign oppression, is worse than the worst hooligan. Such
a man does not deserve to be called Hungarian."[29] Members of the
Hungarian Reformed Church of Montreal also condemned the "unpatriotic" behaviour of radical co-nationals.[30]

That many of the Hungarian-Canadian clergymen and immigrants
of middle-class background – the chief promoters of cultural activity
within patriotic associations – came to Canada from the areas ceded to
successor states helps to explain the intense preoccupation with revision. Approximately one-quarter of all Hungarian-speaking immigrants
were also from these territories,[31] and the words of one of them, a
Székely from Transylvania, illustrate how deeply committed they were
to revision: "every Székely," he declared, "would be willing to give his
last drop of blood," to see Transylvania returned to Hungary.[32] Many
immigrants from Hungary proper came from villages immediately next
to the new boundaries, and some of them were also adversely affected

by the treaty. József Jáger, for example, lost some land as a result of the peace settlement, and he recalls – his bitterness tinged with humour – that the new boundary was set on the basis of the Czechs' claim that the little puddle next to the village of Páczin was a navigable river.[33] It is not surprising, therefore, that the irredentist preoccupations of patriotic leaders were shared by large numbers of ordinary immigrants.

The Horthy regime's fervent championing of revision did much to enhance its prestige among patriots. The role of revanchism in earning approval for the regime among expatriates is most clearly apparent from the reaction of patriotic associations to Hungary's reannexation of southern Slovakia and Ruthenia in 1938 and northern Transylvania in 1940. Both events were greeted with jubilation, and patriotic organizations showered Admiral Horthy with messages of thanks and congratulations. Géza Kertész, for example, who came to Canada from that part of Abaúj-Torna county that was given to Czechoslovakia, congratulated the World Federation of Hungarians following the reannexation in 1938 and added: "I and thousands upon thousands of my Magyar brothers and sisters would like to hear that the Hungarian word resounds once more in our beautiful Transylvania."[34] After the 1940 reannexation, Hungarian Roman Catholics in Montreal conducted a special service to thank God for Horthy's twenty-year reign.[35] Before Canada's entry into the Second World War, shared dissatisfaction over the peace settlement of 1919 – and the Axis powers' support for Hungary's reannexation of southern Slovakia and Ruthenia – lent legitimacy even to Mussolini and Hitler in the eyes of some patriotic Hungarians.[36]

Indignation over the treaty also served to legitimize the Horthy regime in another way. Laying the blame for the social and economic problems that plagued interwar Hungary on a settlement dictated by foreigners helped to obscure the regime's failure to institute meaningful reforms. While, as was suggested in chapter 1, inequitable land distribution was a major cause of emigration between the world wars, much as it had been prior to 1914, patriotic representatives invariably blamed Trianon for forcing them to emigrate.[37] Our clearest illustration of how irredentism and folk themes were combined to conceal the real causes of rural misery is a message published in the *Ujság* from the Pro Hungaria International Women's Federation, an irredentist organization, to female compatriots in Canada. The federation's urban-based president explained to her sisters abroad that to be Magyar was "to love a thatched-roofed cottage, fields with poppies, the church steeple of a small village, the steep-pole well (gémes kút) and to love poverty because we have spent all our wealth on the defense of our beloved Hungary."[38]

MEGHIVÓ

Magyar mozielőadás Torontoban
Április 13-án, csütörtökön
este 7 és 9 órai kezdettel
a Labor Lyceumban, Spadina Ave.
a Re-ta Filmtársaság bemutatja a

MAGYAR
FELTÁMADÁS

CIMÜ ÖTEZER LÁB HOSSZU MAGYAR BESZÉLÓ FILMET MEGELÓZVE AZ AMERI-KAI BEMUTATÓKAT, VAGYIS EGYIDÓBEN A BUDAPESTI BEMUTATÓKKAL.

A mai nemzedék előtt zajlik le ez a pompázó magyar film, melyet bátran és joggal mondhatunk a magyar filmek koronájának. Megrázó nyiltsággal tárja elénk e film a most visszacsatolt Felvidék lakosságának szenvedéseit. Ott látjuk a képen a husz év előtti cseh megszállást. Ott látjuk, amikor a csellel huzott trianoni határ kettészelt egy addig békében élő falut. Ott látjuk, amikor az iskolába igyekvő gyermekeket egy sorompó választ el az iskolától, a tanitótól, láthatjuk, amikor a megszállt területi magyar tanitó a magyar himnusz éneklésére tanitja titokban a gyermekeket és láthatjuk a magyar zászlók elásását stb. Láthatjuk amikor a szerelmeseket egy tákolt sorompó választja el egymástól. Láthatjuk a trianoni sorompó lerombolását és csapataink bevonulását a Felvidékre. Magyar ember nem állja ki ezt a képet könnyezés nélkül. Kiss Ferenc, Csortos Gyula, Makláry Zoltán, és Tőkés Anna oly kitünő, pompás alakitást nyujtanak, mint még eddig soha egyetlen filmben sem. Kiss Ferenc egy hazatérő orosz hadifoglyot alakit, kinek lakását a csehek lefoglalták és családját elüzték. A fogságból szabadult magyart saját lakásából a csehek kiutasitják, felesége fényképét kigunyolják, mire a magyart elragadja az elkeseredés és a cseh tisztet megüti. Hadbiróság elé állitják és 15 évi börtönre itélik. Itt kezdődik aztán a magyar kálvária egész napjainkig. Szinte kergetik egymást a szebbnél szebb jelenetek. Ezt a filmet megnézni hazafias kötelessége minden magyarnak, aki magyarnak vallja magát.

E FILMET KÉRJÜK NEM ÖSSZETÉVESZTENI AZ "ÉSZAK FELÉ" CIMÜ KÉPPEL!

RENDES HELYARAK

Flyer announcing the showing of *Hungarian Resurrection*, Toronto, 1939. The film celebrated the awarding of the Felvidék (the predominantly Magyar-inhabited fringe of southern Slovakia and Ruthenia) to Hungary by Germany and Italy in November 1938. It was "the patriotic duty of every Hungarian to see this film." (See p. 201, showing proletarian reaction to the same film.) Multicultural History Society of Ontario Collection, Archives of Ontario.

Anti-Communism and the Patriotic Camp

It should by now be apparent that anti-communism, along with revisionism, was a central tenet of patriotic ideology. The frequency and virulence of attacks on communism in general, and on the mass organizations of the Communist party in Canada in particular, indicate the degree to which patriotic leaders felt threatened by the emergence of the proletarian camp. Indeed, anti-communism was a major centrifugal force within the patriotic camp.

As we have seen, one of the tactics employed by communist organizers was to attempt to convince existing Hungarian organizations to join the proletarian camp.[39] It was often in response to such overtures that patriotic orientation, hitherto unstated, surfaced. Thus, for example, it was in reaction to a move by some of its leading members to join the communist-led Benefit Federation that the Hungaria Social Club of Montreal passed a motion to the effect that it was a "national, apolitical organization."[40] The Welland Hungarian Self-Culture Society denied admission to two prospective members on the grounds that they belonged to an "internationalist" association and prohibited its members from joining such bodies.[41] In Toronto, the fact that no strong secular association emerged to counteract the advances made by communist mass organizations was probably responsible for the establishment of the local branch of the Brantford Hungarian Sick Benefit Society. In an effort to promote the new branch among Hungarians, the *Híradó*, the body's official organ, described the Brantford society as "one of those associations which kept its distance from all communist propaganda, and remained on a pure Hungarian, national basis."[42] The threat of communist domination in Toronto was also behind the movement for a Hungarian House in that city.[43]

Given the anti-clerical component of communist ideology, Hungarian-Canadian clergymen were especially worried about the communist "menace" and consequently became the most outspoken critics of the proletarian camp. In 1934, Reverend Charles Steinmetz of Toronto went so far as to say that Hungarians "are lost to Christian influence because they are carried away with the tide of communism from their childhood faith to no faith."[44] He estimated that approximately half of his compatriots in Canada became communists, and he described those who so converted the immigrants as "criminals," with "unbalanced minds."[45] Father László Forgách saw the "work of Satan" behind communist activities among Hungarians.[46] Clerics withheld aid that they normally extended to immigrants from members of communist mass organizations. During the depths of the Depression, one of them, Ferenc Nagy from Welland, even pointed out in the local Hungarian newspaper that the communists did not find jobs for workers, that they in fact did nothing for their supposed constituency. Competition from these organizations, as well as rivalry from other denominations, led clergymen to broaden the services that they offered to immigrants. In this respect, they had the full backing of Canadian churches, whose support for home missions was in part motivated by fear of communism.[47] Indeed, the threat of "godless" communism was so great that it led Hungarian clerics to reach across denominational lines.[48]

Patriotic newspapers also took an active part in the struggle against communism. They tried to counteract the appeal of the proletarian camp by publicizing the danger of fines, arrests, and, worst of all, deportation that awaited immigrants who belonged to the Communist party. An editorial in the *Híradó* denounced the communists for trying to eliminate true Magyar identity in Canada.[49] The *Hírlap* accused them of reviling everything that was held sacred by Hungarians: "God, homeland, king, law, respect for parents, national and individual honour...."[50] The *Őrszem*, Father Hédly's newspaper, the *Hírlap*, and the *Ujság* even adopted anti-semitism as part of their anti-bolshevik campaign. The *Őrszem* argued that only confused Magyars, who had neither brains nor character, failed to notice that "communist godlessness is nothing but Jewish and Free Masonic eye wash."[51] The *Hírlap* and the *Ujság* alluded to the existence of a Jewish-communist conspiracy. The *Ujság* suggested, for example, that the *Új Előre*, the US Hungarian communist newspaper, which also served as the organ of the proletarian camp in Canada until 1929, was edited by "Galician Jews with side locks" who were subsidized by Moscow.[52] In the same spirit, Hungarian clerics in Windsor blamed Jenő Klein, the local Hungarian Jewish steamship agent, for communist activities.[53] These accusations were no doubt designed to awaken the hostility of peasants and workers who had been taught to blame postwar difficulties in Hungary on a supposed Jewish-communist conspiracy.

When Canadian authorities embarked on an anti-communist campaign in the 1920s, patriotic leaders were eager to assist them. They informed these authorities about the links between the Benefit Federation and the Communist party and advocated deportation of communists.[54] Fear and hatred of communism even led patriotic leaders to act as informers for Budapest. István Jánossy, former employee of the Immigrant Aid Bureau and the *Ujság*, who became editor of the *Híradó* and was active in the Brantford Hungarian Sick Benefit Society, Béla Bucsin of the Presbyterian church, and János László Papp of the Lutheran church collaborated with Hungarian officials in Canada and in Hungary in monitoring the activities and movements of known and suspected communists, taking special care to alert officials if any of these individuals planned to make trips to the homeland.[55] Although they lived abroad, these patriots apparently shared the fear of officials at home that radicalized emigrants would return with the explicit purpose of "infecting" compatriots who stayed behind.

Canadian Society and the Place of Hungarians

The preservation of the Hungarian spirit in Canada depended very much on the adaptation of immigrants to their adoptive land, and patriotic leaders believed that ethnic group interests would be best served by accommodation to the prevailing social and political order and values. At least until the Depression, they believed Canada to be a land of opportunity because of its vastness, its great material wealth, and its small population.[56]

This is not to say that they were oblivious to the difficulties faced by Hungarians who arrived in Canada in the 1920s. They acknowledged that it was extremely difficult for new arrivals to find steady jobs. They also admitted that immigrants were most often employed in arduous and dangerous work. Nevertheless, they urged compatriots not to be fussy about the type of employment they accepted upon arrival.[57] They suggested, moreover, that staying in one place, even if this meant living on one's savings during intervals of unemployment, was wiser than wandering across Canada in desperate search for work. Patriotic leaders believed that perseverance and industry would eventually be rewarded. In Canada, argued Ferenc Szabolcs, a steamship agent from Hamilton who was also a leading member of the Brantford Hungarian Sick Benefit Society and a contributor to the patriotic press, "honest labour bears fruit."[58]

Patriotic leaders were even more optimistic about opportunities for the children of immigrants. In their adoptive country, the offspring of peasants and manual workers could become doctors, lawyers, teachers, and clergymen. Consequently, patriotic spokesmen urged parents to make sacrifices in order to provide their children with education and they promoted scholarships for capable young members of the ethnic group.[59]

The notion that immigrant workers must reconcile themselves to the conditions that they encountered in Canada – however arduous these might be – as well as the belief in the inevitable rewards of honest labour and in the possibilities of upward mobility reflected acceptance of a class society. Some patriotic representatives stressed that social inequality was inevitable: "There is much inequality on earth! There are rich and poor people. There are agriculturalists and educated men. Some men earn their family's bread through long years of arduous labour, while others spend long years studying so that they will be able to improve the life of their fellows through knowledge and science. There are intellectual and physical workers. One group earns more than the other. One completes the other with its work and knowledge.

This is all true, but it does not mean that one group must hate the other, the members of both groups are God's creatures."[60]

In reaction to the theory of class conflict that was being disseminated by proletarian leaders, patriotic spokesmen also insisted on the possibility, indeed the desirability, of class cooperation. Thus, for example, the leaders of the Hungaria Social Club rejected the arguments of radical members by insisting that the interests of intellectuals and of manual workers were the same.[61] Similarly, Reverend Ferenc Kovács of Hamilton appealed to immigrants not to listen to those who "would promote class hatred." He insisted that in the interest of preserving the Hungarian spirit in Canada, Hungarians of all classes had to cooperate.[62] Reverend Mihály Fehér of Montreal also advocated class cooperation. "Employer love thy brother the worker as thyself," he urged, "and you 'proletarian,' love thy brother the employer as thyself."[63]

In marked contrast to the proletarian leaders, who argued that only through the victory of the working class would the condition of Hungarian workers in Canada improve, patriotic leaders believed that their task consisted of carving out a place for members of the ethnic group within the established order. The main objective of their accommodationist program was to improve the status of Hungarians in Canadian society and thereby to increase the opportunities open to them. They wanted above all to erase the stigma of the "non-preferred" classification of Hungarian immigrants.[64]

To this end, they were intent on proving that Hungarians were exceptionally well suited to become productive and loyal citizens of Canada. People from Hungary were exactly the type of hard-working immigrants required by a developing economy. In light of Canada's need for agricultural labourers, the patriots insisted in particular on the fact that most Hungarian immigrants were agriculturalists.[65] They also stressed that the participation of Hungarian "pioneers" in opening the Canadian west had given ample evidence of the abilities and industry of this class of immigrants.[66] As mentioned above, they insisted on the piety of their co-nationals and on their age-old familiarity with constitutional government, in order to demonstrate that Hungary, like Canada, was an advanced Western nation, and that Hungarians would therefore have no difficulties whatsoever with becoming responsible Canadian citizens.[67]

The by-laws of virtually every patriotic association expressed the intention of members to become loyal citizens of Canada,[68] and their leaders cited the willingness of Hungarians to learn English and to become naturalized as illustrations of their commitment to their adoptive home.[69] Aware of Canadian suspicion of ethnic exclusivism, they insisted, moreover, that the devotion of the immigrants to their native land was proof that they would become equally devoted citizens of Canada.[70]

Similarly, they argued that no conflict existed between the intention of Hungarian Canadians to build a strong and united community and their commitment to Canada. They believed that Canadians would be favourably impressed by a cohesive and organized ethnic group.[71] A strong community would also permit immigrants to be self-reliant and thus not to become a burden on the host society. As we saw above, this was an important consideration in the establishment of mutual aid schemes within patriotic associations.[72]

The accommodationist attitude of patriotic spokesmen is apparent not only from their programs for adaptation but also from their responses whenever immigrants departed from socially accepted behaviour. Their greatest concern was that gambling, visible destitution, and criminal acts would earn the censure of Canadians and "tarnish the image of Hungarians." An oft-raised objection to the activities of the Hungarian-Canadian left was that it brought the disapprobation of Canadian officials on the ethnic community as a whole, thus reducing Hungarians' chances of gaining employment and earning the respect of members of the host society.[73] A Hungarian Presbyterian minister in Welland, Reverend Ferenc Nagy, condemned Hungarian radicals whose protests against conditions in Canada he likened to "stabbing in the back the nation that had received them with open arms."[74] He suggested to the town council that such radicals be deported.[75]

The Depression, which forced Canadians of all ethnic backgrounds to acknowledge fundamental social and economic problems, influenced patriotic Hungarians as well. Some of them now protested against social and economic inequalities in Canada.[76] Father László Forgách even sided with Hungarian workers who took part in a strike against the Empire Cotton Mills in Welland in the winter of 1936–37. Although the salary that he received from the church was by no means substantial, he turned down $1,000 offered to him by the company's manager, Nelson Batchelder, in exchange for talking the Hungarians into breaking the strike.[77] Working conditions in the cotton mill were so notorious that – as the *Ujság*, which also supported the strikers, noted – even high-ranking politicians were on the workers' side.[78] Significantly, however, the *Ujság* did not protest when, after the strike's defeat, the mill prohibited formation of a union by its employees.[79] And Father Forgách went to Batchelder on his "hands and knees" to plead with him to reinstate Hungarians fired because of their role in the strike.

Because of communist gains within the ethnic group resulting from the unprecedented hardship, patriotic critics of Canadian society were careful to distance themselves from the radicalism of the proletarian camp.[80] They adopted only such programs as were unlikely to make them targets of anti-alien sentiments. They insisted that changes could be brought about only through gradual reform, and they suggested that Canadian authorities were trying to help destitute immigrants.

While recognizing the need for social change, moreover, certain patriotic leaders continued to place the bulk of the responsibility for surviving these hard times on the individual, depicting endurance as a measure of personal worth. One clergyman described the despair and suicidal tendencies of Hungarians faced with the prospect of long-term unemployment and destitution as a sign of moral weakness, of insufficient faith in God. "Have stronger faith, more confidence, greater optimism," he urged. "The storm will pass, our dark overcast skies will clear and once again the blessed day of His love will glow."[81]

ATTEMPTS TO CREATE NATION-WIDE ASSOCIATIONS

Contrary to the claim of political neutrality, then, virtually all aspects of patriotic ideology had quite specific political content. Patriotic Hungarians generally supported the Horthy regime and its irredentist aims, their attitude to Canadian society was accommodationist, and they were vehemently anti-communist. Were these shared ideological concerns sufficient to unite all Hungarians who belonged to patriotic associations? Could patriotic ideology override the acrimony that resulted from competition among religious denominations?

The Canadian Hungarian Association (1928–31)

The interwar years saw two formal attempts to unite patriotic Hungarians throughout Canada. The first was made in 1928, with the establishment of the Canadian Hungarian Association in Winnipeg.[82] The impetus for the new body came from western Canada, apparently in response to the re-establishment of diplomatic relations between Canada and Hungary and the concomitant renewal of immigration possibilities. Reverend János Kovács, minister of the Hungarian Presbyterian Church of Bekevar, first proposed such an organization.[83] His idea was endorsed almost immediately by Hungarians who had settled in the west before the First World War, and who had wanted to bring out friends and relatives from Hungary at the end of the war.

Steamship agents, who had an obvious interest in renewed immigration, Protestant ministers, and Hungarian government representatives in Canada also responded enthusiastically.[84] In central Canada, most existing patriotic groups supported the movement. The Hungarian United Church of Montreal, the Toronto Hungarian Association and the Hungarian Presbyterian and Lutheran churches in Toronto, the First Hungarian Mutual Benefit Association and the Hungarian Presbyterian Church of Hamilton, the Brantford Hungarian Presbyterian Church and the Brantford Sick Benefit Society, the Welland Hungarian Presbyterian Church and the Welland Hungarian Self-Culture Society, and the Windsor Hungarian Presbyterian Church, as well as a number of associations in smaller Ontario settlements, were all to send representatives to the opening convention in Winnipeg.[85] Delegates included such prominent patriotic Hungarians as Reverend Ferenc Kovács, Reverend János László Papp, Reverend Eugene Molnár, Presbyterian Church missionary Béla Bucsin, and steamship agent Ferenc Szabolcs. Throughout the country, moreover, the organizational drive led to the creation of new associations, formed to unite Hungarians and select delegates to the convention.

In a manner characteristic of patriotic organizations, the new umbrella group claimed to be apolitical. It professed to unite all Hungarian immigrants, regardless of political, religious, or social differences.[86] Indeed, the stated aims were indisputably in the interest of the ethnic group as a whole. The association proposed to familiarize new immigrants with conditions in Canada and to help them with finding employment or with acquiring land; to support existing mutual aid societies and encourage formation of new ones, including the association's own mutual aid scheme; to make scholarships available to students of Hungarian origin who attended institutions of higher learning; and to keep an accurate statistical record of Hungarians in Canada. Eventually, the association even hoped to establish a Hungarian hospital.[87]

Not only concern with the welfare of immigrants but also a desire to enhance the status of the ethnic group informed the body's policies. Its founders wanted to remove the stigma of being "non-preferred" immigrants and believed that the less Hungarian newcomers depended on the host society for employment or social assistance, the more willing Canadian officials would be to re-evaluate group status.[88]

Thus, from the outset, the association's program for integrating the ethnic group was accommodationist. Despite disclaimers, moreover, its patriotic orientation had political dimensions from the planning phases on. Independently of any encouragement from Budapest, the founders – some of whom had not themselves experienced the conse-

quences of Trianon at first hand, having emigrated by 1914 – believed
that the fight for the treaty's revision was the patriotic duty of all
Hungarians in Canada.[89] The new association was also resolutely anti-
communist.[90] Because of its connection with Hungarian representatives in Canada and its revisionist policies, it was subjected to relentless
attacks first in the *Új Előre* – the American-Hungarian communist
paper, which in 1928, as we saw, still served as the organ of left-wing
Hungarians in Canada as well – and from 1929 in the *Munkás*.[91] The
association's organizers were thus quite correct in identifying the
Communist party as a threat to their own efforts.

In February 1928, the Canadian Hungarian Association was off to a
promising start. Its opening convention – attended by delegates from
across the nation – took place amid great fanfare. It even received attention from the English-language press and from Canadian politicians.[92] Despite its espousing objectives that were shared by all
patriotic organizations in Canada and its apparently broad support, it
survived for only three years. Competition among immigrants of elite
background for leadership helped bring about its quick demise.

Individuals who competed for power and influence within the association tried to legitimize their positions by exploiting divisions within
the ethnic group. Reverend János Kovács of Bekevar, for example, pro-
testing against the election of János Ujváry – a Hungarian physician
who became a steamship agent in Saskatoon and who was a relative
newcomer to Canada – claimed to speak for "old Canadians" as a
group.[93] Yet the conflict seems to have been between the two men,
rather than between the two waves of immigrants, for a group of old
settlers repudiated Kovács's arguments.[94] Father Paul Sántha, from
Eszterhazy-Kaposvar, Saskatchewan, attempted to exploit religious segmentation when he claimed that the association represented the interests of Hungarian Protestants only.[95] But since other Roman Catholic
clergymen did support the organization, again personalities in conflict,
rather than broad divisions, seem to have been the real basis of dis-
unity. In Toronto, a would-be leader protested against the election of
Ernő Zola, a Hungarian Jewish businessman, as treasurer of the local
branch. The Jews were opportunists, he maintained, lacking commitment to any cause. "Yesterday they were still on the side of the communists," he argued, no doubt alluding to the prominence of Jews in the
1919 commune, "but today they are genuine Hungarians. After all
business is business." All "genuine" Hungarians, he added, were upset
by Zola's election.[96]

Even representatives of Budapest became embroiled in factional disputes. The *Ujság* supported Reverend Kovács in the dispute with Ujváry.
István Schefbeck, the consul in Winnipeg, believed that the steamship

agents among the association's founders were in the employ of two rival Canadian railway companies. The consul held that men such as Ujváry, "who lived off the body of the Hungarian nation," supported the association, "so that they should receive such and such an amount of money from interested parties, because the sole concern of the illustrious gentlemen is to be able to hand over [to the railways] so many bodies."[97] The steamship agents and the secretary general of the association responded by claiming that the Hungarian government's representatives feared that the Canadian Hungarian Association would impinge upon the influence of the *Ujság* and Budapest's Immigrant Aid Bureau (in Winnipeg) among expatriates.[98] So deep did the divisions become that almost immediately a rival umbrella organization, Hungarian Relief of Western Canada, was founded.

Ultimately, however, both disputes among leaders and disagreements with Budapest's representatives proved surmountable. The warring factions within the association were reconciled with the aid of Baron Zsigmond Perényi, on the occasion of his visit to Canada, and a new president, Baron József Csávossy, who seemed to satisfy all parties, was selected.[99] Unlike Ujváry, Csávossy, a prosperous Alberta farmer, could not be accused of seeking office for personal gain.[100] The association thus having gained a new lease on life, Csávossy travelled in 1929 to Hungary, where he conferred with high-ranking officials, including the prime minister, Count István Bethlen, about the future of co-nationals in Canada.[101] But plans for the association's future were never to materialize. Despite renewed efforts, it accomplished little during the remaining two years of its existence.

Poor planning and organization seem to have been the primary causes of failure. The body did not make inroads within the ethnic group. Although delegates to the founding convention had been elected, their selection apparently occurred at the instigation of local leaders, who usually sought to be chosen themselves. Ordinary immigrants do not seem to have adopted the federative movement as their own. Furthermore, it was established without due consideration for financing, and, as a result, even its single paid employee, Nicholas Istvánffy, went unpaid for many months. Money for his salary had to be raised through loans from the association's more prosperous leaders.[102]

The association's mutual aid scheme was set up as an afterthought, in an effort both to deepen roots among immigrants and to provide a financial base.[103] But the scheme was administered strictly as a business proposition. Although the insurance plan was nominally linked to local chapters, the chapters existed, by and large, in name only. The general secretary administered the plan from Winnipeg, and he appointed individuals in each settlement to sell policies in return for a small commission.[104] Subscription to the scheme did not provide immigrants with the sense of participating in a mutual aid venture.

The Hungarian Canadian National Federation (1936)

The next attempt to form a nation-wide federation came from central Canada, more precisely from Toronto, where patriotic leaders founded the Hungarian Canadian National Federation in 1936. The initiative seems to have come from a group of immigrants of elite background. Toronto steamship agent István Jánossy, formerly an employee of the Immigrant Aid Bureau and part-owner of the *Híradó*, Reverend Steinmetz, of the First Hungarian Presbyterian Church; Lutheran ministers Eugene Ruzsa and János Papp; the Hungarian artist Nicholas Hornyánszky; and Dr Lesko, a dentist and founding member of the Hungarian Roman Catholic congregation in Toronto, were instrumental in establishing the federation.[105]

In its aims, the National Federation closely resembled the Canadian Hungarian Association. Like its precursor, it hoped to unite all Hungarians in Canada, to guide them along patriotic and religious lines, and thus to counteract growing communist influence. The federation also sought to foster closer ties with the homeland and to improve the status of immigrants in Canada. In response to the extreme economic hardship brought about by the Depression, it emphasized its concern for the welfare of immigrants. As a way to combat massive unemployment, it proposed, rather naively, to establish a Hungarian handicraft workshop.[106]

Despite these lofty, if at times impractical aims, however, the federation was even less successful than the Canadian Hungarian Association. Its organizational efforts never extended beyond Ontario, and not even in that province did it take root. Reverend Ruzsa ascribed the federation's failure to the poverty and demoralization of immigrants.[107] While these factors undoubtedly made the task more difficult, during the same period communist organizers set up a nation-wide organization among Hungarians. The federation, in contrast, did not get off the ground; it seems to have had no real existence beyond the ideas and intentions of its founders.

Attempts were made formally to unite patriotic Hungarians locally, as well as nationally. In 1935, leaders of the Hungaria Social Club, the Székely Club, and the Hungarian United Church started a movement to unite co-nationals in Montreal and to open a Hungarian House, or community centre, in the city.[108] Their movement had the support of

local consular officials.[109] In a manner characteristic of patriotic associations, the leaders saw their movement as "loyal to the Hungarian national idea." Consequently, communist mass organizations, whose
anti-clericalism and internationalism the patriots saw as inimical to the
national idea, were prevented from participating.[110]

Despite exclusion of proletarian groups, however, the attempt to
unite Montreal's patriotic associations failed. The patriots evidently felt
stronger loyalty to their individual organizations than to a joint community project, and during the 1930s, when so many of them were unemployed, they found it impossible even to pay the costs of maintaining
individual religious and secular associations.[111] Not until the eve of the
Second World War did their economic situation improve sufficiently to
allow them to consider greater financial obligations. By then, however,
United Church members and Roman Catholics decided that their
movement might draw unfavourable public attention to the ethnic
group, and the plan to open a Hungarian House was suspended.

INFORMAL LINKS AMONG PATRIOTIC ASSOCIATIONS

These abortive attempts to unite patriotic Hungarians locally and nationally should not, however, be seen as proof that patriotic ideology
was ineffectual in uniting Hungarians outside Toronto. Patriotic associations were united by various informal links in almost all settlements.
Membership frequently overlapped in patriotic secular and in religious
associations. Precisely because of the deep ideological divisions within
the ethnic group, similar overlapping between ethnic congregations
and the Communist party's mass organizations was inconceivable.

Because many immigrants belonged both to secular patriotic associations and to Hungarian churches, these two types of groups frequently
aided one another. The Hungaria Social Club, for example, allowed
the Hungarian Lutheran congregation of Montreal to use its club-
house free of charge to show a religious film.[112] On another occasion,
the club-house was rented to the Hungarian Roman Catholic women
for a social function, while the request of the Workers' club to rent the
premises was turned down.[113] Similarly, the Welland Hungarian Self-
Culture Society permitted the local Hungarian Catholic congregation
to hold its social functions in the society's hall.[114] The significance of
sharing facilities did not escape patriotic Hungarians. A member of the
Petőfi choir of the Hungarian United Church, for example, remarked,
"Our heart, our soul, our song and all our feelings are first and foremost Hungarian. In this we feel united with the Roman Catholics who
lent us their hall this evening."[115]

Patriotic organizations sometimes even shared services and offered financial assistance towards one another's development. The Székely Hungarian Cultural Club contributed to the church building fund of the Hungarian Lutheran congregation in Montreal and to the upkeep of the Hungarian-language school of the United Church.[116] When the Welland Hungarian Self-Culture Society was organizing a procession, the local Hungarian Presbyterian congregation donated $50 to help defray costs.[117] The relative rarity and modesty of such donations were the consequence of poverty, not of indifference. The care that such groups took to avoid scheduling their fundraising social and cultural events at the same times revealed their recognition of shared interests and appeal; deliberate timing of patriotic functions to compete with proletarian events was also revealing.[118]

If competition among churches to attract immigrants occasionally led to conflict, there are also many examples of cooperation, and clerics encouraged such efforts on the basis of shared loyalty to Hungary and to its culture. The leaders, if not the members, of all denominations were usually present at the opening ceremonies of any Hungarian church, and events of national interest within individual churches also brought together the patriotic community at large. When the Hamilton Presbyterian church dedicated the Hungarian tricolour, a gift from the World Federation of Hungarians, and the Union Jack, given by the Canadian Club, Father Forgách came from Toronto in honour of the occasion, and both the local Hungarian rabbi and the Lutheran minister were also in attendance.[119] This ecumenical spirit was the product of strong nationalism. As Father Forgách explained at the farewell party for Reverend Nagy of the Hungarian Presbyterian congregation in Welland, "his Hungarian heart, and his Hungarian blood brought him to the celebration."[120] At the same event, the Lutheran minister, Reverend Ruzsa, consoled Hungarian Presbyterians in Welland by saying that they should not feel forlorn, because "Father Forgách will be staying, the noble hearted priest of the Roman Catholics, who is first and foremost the helper and protector of every Hungarian."[121]

The joint celebration of Hungarian national holidays by patriotic associations shows even more clearly than the many informal ties that shared objectives did forge a sense of unity among patriotic secular and religious associations. Hungarian patriots gathered to commemorate the Revolution of 1848 – in which their compatriots fought heroically but unsuccessfully for national autonomy and constitutional rights – twice each year. They held joyous celebrations on 15 March to mark the rallying of the people of Budapest behind demands for liberal reforms and greater autonomy within the Hapsburg Empire – the beginning of the revolution. The gathering on 6 October was funereal, for on that day, in 1849, 13 Hungarian generals who led the fight against Austria were executed, symbolizing the defeat of the War of Independence.

These two days saw addresses by community leaders, poetry recitals, dramatic performances, singing, and dancing. They involved participation by large segments of the ethnic group and required weeks of preparation. Members of patriotic drama troupes, dance ensembles, choirs, and children's groups spent weekends and evenings excitedly preparing for their performances, while other immigrants were busy sewing costumes and building stage sets and still others got food ready for the banquets that frequently followed the ceremonies. Drawn by announcements posted in Hungarian groceries, in butcher and barber stores, and in associational halls, even Hungarians who were not otherwise active in community life often attended.[122]

Commemoration of the events of 1848–49, perhaps more than any other occasions in the life of the communities, served to express and to affirm group identity. For these ceremonies, as for all their cultural activities, patriots generally relied on the plays, songs, and poems sent to them by the Horthy regime. Thus *Spring Will Come Again,* described at the beginning of this study, came to form the cornerstone for celebrations on 15 March 1930 in Welland. According to one observer, the revisionist play moved the assembled immigrants to tears; "it awakened dormant Hungarians."[123]

A week or two before planned ceremonies, the patriotic press would announce where and when they would be held. The *Canadai Kis Ujság, Egyetértés,* the *Híradó,* the *Hírlap,* and the *Kanadai Magyar Ujság,* as well as the bulletins of Hungarian congregations, used these occasions to present the patriotic interpretation of 1848. The themes of their articles were reiterated by clergymen and by better-educated community members who gave the keynote addresses during the 15 March and 6 October ceremonies.

In addition to promoting unity and providing a focus for group loyalty, the events that pulled together patriotic associations also symbolically defined the place of the ethnic group vis-à-vis the host society. In Port Colborne, for example, Hungarians paraded through the streets behind a band on 15 March, bearing high the tricolour, to let the whole town know that they were celebrating.[124] Similarly, when immigrants from every colony in Ontario gathered in Welland in the late summer of 1935 to celebrate Hungarian Day – a patriotic ceremony observed less regularly than the two national holidays mentioned above – they sought to announce their presence and their unity to other residents. Accordingly, they began their event by parading through the city's streets. The parade was led by a car decorated with tricolour streamers. Behind it followed a group of girls dressed in national costumes; two of them carried a map of Greater Hungary, and two others, a map of dismembered Hungary.[125]

9 Proletarian Ideology

Proletarian ideology, in sharp contrast to the accommodationist stance of the patriotic camp, assaulted the very foundations of the established order. Unlike patriotic leaders, whose fear of radicalism led them to assuage the frustration and anger that immigrants felt in response to the difficulties that they experienced, proletarian spokesmen acknowledged these feelings as legitimate reactions to intolerable conditions. Indeed, they tried to focus and harness the immigrants' anger. Through their speeches, the pages of the *Munkás*, and the activities of proletarian associations, communist organizers attempted to explain the causes of the newcomers' plight and to hold out to them a program for radical change.

EXPLAINING THE NEWCOMERS' PLIGHT

Canadian Society and Immigrant Workers

Bringing the whole capitalist system to task, proletarian leaders did not hesitate to point accusingly at those agents of the system whom they considered most directly responsible for the predicament of the immigrants.[1] Among these culprits, Canadian "railway barons" figured prominently. The Canadian railways, explained the *Munkás* in 1930, benefited most from the exploitation of immigrants. As shareholders in steamship companies, they made profits on steamship tickets sold to them. They profited even more from the sale of railway tickets to these same people, who were forced to travel thousands of kilometres to the west, following their arrival in Canada. The railway magnates continued to exploit the newcomers even after they reached their destination: "On the tremendous expansion of railway lines, which were being extended ever northward, there was a need for cheap labour. Slave labour. To this, immigrant workers who were unfamiliar with the local language and customs, were an easy prey. In the absence of militant labour organizations, they fell defenseless into the clutches of the railway barons." The railway owners also stood to gain from the policy of directing immigrants to the agrarian sector. By breaking the soil, and making it more fertile, as homesteaders or as agricultural labourers, newcomers raised the value of lands owned by the railways. Moreover, these companies also reaped a profit from transporting the product of their labour.[2]

Thus, far from being, as the patriots would have it, the last remaining sector in which immigrants could still find a place under the approving gaze of Canadian authorities, the agrarian sector was just another part of the exploitative capitalist system. Small farmers in Canada, argued proletarian spokesmen, were every bit as exploited as rural labourers and urban workers. They "were the prey of tax collectors, bank collectors, various usurers and a whole swarm of other profiteers and exploiters," and even when their crops were bountiful they could not always provide the barest necessities for their families.[3]

In its discussions of the agrarian sector, the proletarian press paid special attention to the "stoop jobs" in which many Hungarians were engaged. The *Új Előre*, for example, described the exploitation of sugar beet workers, referring specifically to a Hungarian steamship agent, Joseph Schwartz of the Colonists' Service Association in Calgary, whom hundreds of his co-nationals would have encountered during their search for labour: "A Hungarian goes to see him: 'Mr. Schwartz, I heard that you can place beet workers.' 'Yes,' answers the hyena. 'What are the conditions?' 'They are as follows: you have to prepare the soil, buy the seed, do the planting, hoeing, harvesting and cleaning, then transport the produce and perhaps you'll get half of it.' "[4] In the 1930s, when large numbers of Hungarians were forced to seek seasonal agricultural work in central Canada as well, the *Munkás* gave increasing attention to beet and especially tobacco work in southern Ontario.[5]

To convince Hungarians that they would face the injustices of the capitalist system no matter where they turned, the *Új Előre* and the *Munkás* talked about the difficulty of finding work throughout Canada. They explained that the system created a reserve army of unemployed, which permitted it the better to exploit workers.[6] The papers described and condemned practices, such as speed-ups and having to bribe the básc (boss) in order to obtain jobs, to which immigrants were forced to acquiesce if they wanted to keep working.[7] They stressed that because of discrimination by employers, immigrants faced greater difficulties than the "English" and "French": "Because we are in a strange land, and we are unfamiliar with its language and customs, our situation is far worse than that of those who are native born or who have lived here for decades. Factory owners know about our vulnerability. When they give us work it is the worst, least well paid, most dangerous work."[8] Proletarian publications carried descriptions of oppressive conditions and low wages in mining, logging camps, construction, factories, and domestic service – all the areas where newcomers were likely to find employment. They paid special attention to the wage-work that women performed at home, "imprisoned" away from fellow workers.[9] These descriptions were unabashedly partisan, calculated to appeal to the emotions:

At the American Seinement Company of Niagara Falls, a chemical and artificial fertilizer plant, shocking conditions reign. The bodies of the men who work there are being infected by the dust and noxious fumes that the chemicals emit, and scorched by the heat. The municipal authorities want to force the plant to relocate because of the noxious fumes that it emits. In order to put an end to the emission of these fumes, however, the management simply shut off the ventilation system which had removed the gases from the factory, so now the workers breathe in the killer gases. There are absolutely no safety devices, or only very primitive ones which offer no real protection. To acquire new ones would cost money and the company which makes millions of dollars in profits, would rather sacrifice workers than see its millions diminish by a few dollars.[10]

Proletarian leaders also addressed crowded living conditions in Hungarian boarding-houses. Adam Schaeffer, one of the local editors of the *Munkás*, observed that everywhere in Canada's wealthy cities he had seen immigrants sleeping four to a bed. Undoubtedly with the intention of directing their discontent against the patriotic camp, he added, "I heard one of the Hungarian priests say, about the residents of these boardinghouses, that they should be ashamed of themselves, because they ruin the reputation of the Hungarians in the eyes of English speaking people."[11]

A description of a working-class neighbourhood in Hamilton by Joseph Dohány, the communist organizer who launched the *Munkás*, shows that even experienced proletarian writers did not shy away from exaggeration in order to drive their points home:

I stand in a corner observing the dilapidated shanties. Gaping doors reveal the dirty interiors of these makeshift structures, with broken windows, which are called houses. The abandoned building over there signals that this is the city of Hamilton's working-class quarter. One end of the building is collapsing, while several families live in the other. Their neighbours are the rats, who promenade through the building's abandoned section. I draw closer, so as to be able to take a look among the ruins. The air is stifling. The smell of mold mixes in with the smell of oil which prevails in the area. Among the ruins, working-class children play 'house.' Just as I approach, one of the girls is saying to the little boy beside her, who appears to be about 6 years old: 'Why are you so lazy? Why do you sleep so much? Now you are late for work.'[12]

The paper's partisan approach struck a responsive chord. Béla Vágó, for example, decided to join the proletarian camp because of the *Munkás*'s treatment of the condition of workers in Canada: "it spoke explicitly about unemployment and the exploitation of the worker," he explained, "which many of us recognized in time, and therefore we supported the *Munkás* with great enthusiasm.... Of course, it was not a paper that I couldn't understand because of its high level, but what we needed."[13] According to Helen Czukár, one of the oldest members of the proletarian camp in Hamilton, the *Munkás* "was a teacher to the people, who were simple people, they had more time here than back home, they picked up newspapers for the first time and compared them, and they ended up here [in the proletarian camp]. This was their newspaper."[14] Mary Kisko recalled that during the Depression unemployed Hungarians would crowd into the Workers' hall in Welland to read the *Munkás*. Some of them read with such difficulty that it took them hours to finish a single page, she added, but "they sure remembered what they read."[15] Looking back on the role that the paper's explanations played in the lives of Hungarians, another Hungarian-Canadian proletarian explained: "naturally it wrote in such a way as to teach the worker. In my opinion, those who read the *Munkás* developed, and learned to see the world differently from those who did not read our paper."[16]

For if proletarian reporting was more polemical than objective, much of it showed considerable psychological insight. However exaggerated their style, proletarian leaders, through their speeches and writings, communicated their empathy with the plight of immigrant workers. They recognized that a radical explanation of the sources of contemporary ills could mitigate not only the frustration and anger but even the humiliation and helplessness of newcomers unable to make a living. Such analyses of the social and economic problems that racked the capitalist system were especially important during the Depression.

Through stories and letters, the *Munkás* conveyed an understanding of the predicament of unemployed and underemployed immigrants whose relatives in Hungary, not understanding why they stopped sending money home, continued to beg them for financial assistance. The hero of a story that appeared in the *Munkás* almanac in 1936 is János, the native of a small village on the banks of the Tisza, who is forced to migrate to Canada by his family's indebtedness. His father and uncle assume new debts to pay for the journey, but once János gets to Canada he finds work only intermittently, and his meagre earnings are all eaten up by the cost of travelling in search of new work and by the cost of boarding during periods of unemployment. Consequently, he is unable to reimburse his father and uncle. Soon his relatives begin to send him letters full of complaints. After he waits in vain for two years to be repaid, his father's letters become bitter. "You don't want to work," he writes, "because if you wanted to, you would have money. You have probably become a rake in the midst of plenty ... but you should know, that soon all our possessions will be auctioned off, and in our old age we will be homeless." János's uncle warns him that he will drive his father to his grave. János, who has not yet joined the proletarian camp, simply despairs. His father commits suicide, leaving behind an accusing note, which János's relatives forward to him in Canada.[17]

In a fictitious letter that appeared in the *Munkás*, another young Hungarian finds himself in a similar situation. Unlike János, however, this man is acquainted with proletarian ideology. He is therefore able to explain to his mother why he is unemployed: "because in their eyes I am a lousy worker, the scum of this social order which rests on the exploitation of workers. I have less value than a dog, although they maintain their thieving reign through my, and our, that is the workers', sweat and blood. Because inner economic problems, the warning signs of the collapse of capitalism, which is on its last legs, require that their regime, condemned to extinction by historical development, be injected with my misery, my hunger and my being thrown out on the street."[18]

Just how closely these didactic, melodramatic accounts reflected the plight of unemployed workers with families in Hungary is illustrated by the similarity between János's letter and that of Sándor Hajas to his aged parents in Böhönye, Somogy county, which was confiscated by the Hungarian Ministry of the Interior.[19] As we saw in chapter 2, the letter conveys the pain and guilt that Hajas felt because he was unable to help his parents. It also shows that some newcomers found deliverance from guilt and despair by adopting the explanations that proletarian leaders

"This is how government relief provides for unemployed workers." *Kanadai Magyar Munkás*, 13 July 1933.

offered. Hajas tells his parents that his "world view in its entirety has completely changed." He offers a rather confused description of the workings of the capitalist system and of the causes of the Depression, revealing that the change in his thinking was brought about by contact with communist ideas. Hajas's letter suggests that even if he did not have a very thorough understanding of these ideas, they did provide him with hope. He concludes by assuring his parents: "we are getting closer and closer to liberation by the day."[20]

World Affairs

In keeping with the Communist party's internationalist line, proletarian leaders placed discussion of the class struggle, and of the Depression as the ultimate manifestation of the inherent instability of capitalism, in a global context. The *Munkás* relied on the *Új Előre* and on the English-language communist press for its coverage of international affairs.[21] The paper, the speeches of proletarian leaders, and discussions in proletarian associations dutifully followed the party line in their treatment of world events.

Until 1935, in keeping with Comintern directives, proletarian leaders were bent on demonstrating to Hungarians that capitalist states were attempting to unleash an imperialist war to destroy the Soviet Union and with it the hopes of workers everywhere.[22] After 1935, when the Comintern's Popular Front policy was officially proclaimed, differences between Western democracies and the USSR were minimized and the need for all anti-fascist forces to cooperate against Hitler was stressed.[23]

While it raged, the Spanish Civil War dominated the international concerns of the proletarians. Leaders explained that the Republican forces in Spain were at the forefront of the struggle against fascism, and they attempted to mobilize the Hungarians behind them. One hundred and ten young immigrants responded by going to fight – 12 of them to die – for the Republican cause.[24]

The participation of the young volunteers heightened proletarian awareness of the struggle against fascism. The civil war became one of the main subjects of discussion within Workers' clubs.[25] Committees were established within all proletarian organizations to aid the Republicans, and the pages of the *Munkás* were filled with letters from the volunteers who were fighting in Spain.[26]

The signing of the Nazi-Soviet pact in August 1939 placed proletarian leaders, like all communists in the West, in an awkward position. They had to explain how the "fatherland of the proletariat" could conclude a treaty of friendship and non-aggression with the world's leading fascist power. The *Munkás* played down the importance of the pact and continued to print anti-fascist articles. In contrast to the Popular Front days, however, it now minimized the differences between Hitler's Germany and western European democracies. It dubbed Britain and France the "Munichist" powers and claimed that their readiness to betray the Soviet Union forced it to conclude the pact with Hitler.[27]

Horthyist Hungary

But while Hungarian immigrants were thus exposed to communist analysis of world events, examples of the evils of capitalism were still most commonly situated in Canada or in Hungary, the two countries with which they were most immediately concerned. We have already seen how some of those aspects of Canadian society that were of special relevance to immigrant workers were treated by the proletarian leaders. For more general discussions of politics and current events, they relied on their English-Canadian comrades. The *Munkás*'s staff, for example, regularly borrowed articles from the *Worker*, the English-language newspaper of the Communist party in Canada, and translated them into Hungarian.[28]

Vigyázzatok — VÉRES!

Magyar Testvérek!
A „MAGYAR FELTÁMADÁS" című film — történelmi HAMISÍTVÁNY! A Felvidék magyarsága — sajnos! — nem támadt fel, hanem a KISEBB bajból a NAGYOBBA esett. A TŰRHETŐBB csehszlovákiai kisebbségi sorsból, a DEMOKRÁCIÁBÓL beleesett, belezuhant a TŰRHETETLENBE, a fojtogató FASIZMUS karmaiba!

SAJÁT véreitek leveleinek hisztek-e inkább, vagy a hazaáruló labanc HORTHYNAK és az ő ügynökségének: a RE-TA filmtársaságnak?

VÉREITEK panaszkodnak!

„CSALÓDÁS ÉS KESERÜSÉG LETT AZ, AMINEK ÖRÖMNEK KELLETT VOLNA LENNIE!"

Horthy meghozta a „feltámadást"? A magyar és szlovák urak egymásra uszították a magyar és szlovák népet. GYILKOLTÁK és GYILKOLJÁK őket!

Bombáztatták KASSÁT, ROZSNYÓT, IGLÓT!

S mi lett a vége? HITLER marsolt be a FELVIDÉKRE! Ezért kellett a csehszlovák demokráciát szétrobbantani? Ezért kellett a revízió? EZÉRT! Mert úgy parancsolta Hitler és Mussolini a magyarul csak gagyogó Horthynak!

HORTHY csak eszköze, BÉRENCE — Hitler-Mussolininek!

Magyarországot KI AKARJÁK FOSZTANI! Már fosztják is!

A magyar népet KENŐCSNEK SZÁNTÁK a fasiszta tengelyre!

Ne higyj (demokratikus) magyar a (fasiszta) németnek!

Magyarországnak DEMOKRÁCIA és SZABADSÁG kell! — Kanadának is!

KIK vannak a RE-TA mögött? Kérdezzétek meg a wellandi szövőgyári munkásokat és akiket miattuk kidobtak a munkából. Pacsuta András a kanadai királyi biztosság által is leleplezett éhbérek és sorvasztó munkaviszonyok miatt indított szövősztrájk elárulója, a „nem-sztrájkolók" elnöke volt 1937-ben. Imre József, a „filmtársaság" ügynöke e hetekben jött vissza Magyarországból, 1937-ben a szövőbárók rendelkezésére bocsájtotta Kis Ujságját a sztrájkoló katolikusok, reformátusok és a többiek ellen!

LE A FASIZMUSSAL! — KI INNEN AZ ÜGYNÖKEIVEL!

Ne türjük a magyar név és becsület beszennyezését!

VÉDJÜK MEG A KANADAI DEMOKRÁCIÁT

a Torontói Magyar Kultúr Klub.

●

The RE-TA is showing a FASCIST film!

This film is glorifying the killing of czechoslovak democracy! Horthy as the "Saviour" of the Hungarian people!

HORTHY is a TRAITER!

He is a hireling, a dirty tool of

HITLER and MUSSOLINI!

Imre and Pacsuta of the Re-Ta were the breakers of the wavers' strike in Welland, 1937. Imre just come back from Budapest.

DOWN WITH FASCISM! — OUT WITH IT'S AGENTS!

DEFEND THE CANADIAN DEMOCRACY!

The Hungarian Cultural Club of Toronto.

Proletarian flyer denouncing *Hungarian Resurrection*, Toronto, 1939.
(See p. 179 for patriotic promotion of the film.)

The proletarian movement's relentless criticism of Horthyist Hungary formed an integral part of its competition with the patriotic camp for the hearts and minds of immigrants. Proletarian leaders feared that under the combined impact of homesickness and the revisionist campaign of the Horthyist regime, expatriates would forget the harsh conditions that forced them to emigrate and would ally themselves to the patriotic camp.[29]

By refuting the argument that the Treaty of Trianon was the main cause of social and economic problems in interwar Hungary, and hence also of emigration, proletarian spokesmen struck at the central tenet of the patriotic camp. They reminded the newcomers that even before the First World War the lives of workers and peasants in Greater Hungary, whatever their ethnic origin, had been extremely difficult.[30] To the disinherited, they argued, the redrawing of borders changed only the nationality of their exploiters. The condition of workers in the successor states was no worse than that of their brothers and sisters in Hungary.[31] Those seriously affected by the nation's loss of two-thirds of its prewar territory belonged to the upper and middle classes – large landowners, whose estates now fell under the jurisdiction of foreign governments, and civil servants in the employ of the government when it lost control of Slovakia and Transylvania. According to proletarian leaders, these groups, hiding under the guise of patriotism, but motivated entirely by self-interest, were partly responsible for the launching of the revanchist campaign.[32] Their bellicose propaganda was intended to convince workers to shed their blood for the capitalists and landowners in the eventuality of war with the successor states, just as they had done during the First World War.

Proletarian spokesmen further claimed that the campaign for revision of Trianon served the interests of landlords and industrialists whose properties fell entirely within post-Trianon Hungary. According to them, the ruling classes promoted revisionism because, by fanning the flames of lower-class patriotism, they could distract workers and peasants from terrible economic oppression.[33] Not only were urban and rural workers paid poorly, argued the *Munkás*, but they also carried almost the total weight of the nation's taxes.[34] Even small holders were fast sinking into the ranks of the proletariat under that burden.[35] Their great poverty led peasant women to seek abortions, and although this step was the product of necessity, not choice, they were nevertheless liable to severe punishment if caught.[36]

According to the *Munkás*, the Hungarian system was so unjust that the ruling class could not rely solely on the promotion of patriotism among the lower classes to safeguard capitalism. Consequently, it deliberately kept workers and peasants ignorant by depriving them of proper education. The Horthy regime, moreover, ruthlessly crushed any individual or group for attempting to enlighten them about the unfairness of their predicament and to encourage them to struggle against the oppressor.[37]

Not Trianon, argued proletarian spokesmen, but economic exploitation, reinforced by political oppression, forced emigration: "We are here because for the past 15 years the Hungarian ruling class, the executioners of the Hungarian people, have been spilling the blood of our brothers, and keeping thousands of them behind somber prison walls. Those who are not in jail, are starved, overtaxed, surrounded by stool pigeons and punished harshly for crimes they did not commit. They banished us from our native land by depriving us of our livelihood, by oppression, by inequity and by tyranny."[38] Relatives and friends who remained at home, argued the proletarians, were still subject to these intolerable conditions.[39]

This analysis was readily accepted by some Hungarian immigrants and convinced them to join the proletarian camp. George Palotás, drawn to the Montreal Workers' Club by a need for companionship, began to pay close attention to the political discussions held in the evenings. Members spoke about conditions prior to emigration: "they spoke about how we were exploited, like three million beggars in Hungary, and until then I never heard this, and that there was great poverty in Hungary and so on ... and how the Hungarian bourgeoisie exploited us, and about the war, the orphans, and I was one."[40]

The Patriotic Camp

According to the leaders of the proletarian camp, the activities of patriotic leaders in Canada constituted a mere extension of the efforts by Hungary's ruling class to manipulate and exploit workers and peasants in the homeland.[41] Not only Budapest's official representatives in Canada, but also patriotic leaders, editors of patriotic newspapers, and clergymen, acted as the regime's agents. Through the pages of the *Új Előre* and the *Munkás*, and through their speeches, proletarian leaders purported to reveal the methods and institutions whereby these "Horthyist agents" tried to manipulate Hungarians in Canada. They correctly identified the *Kanadai Magyar Ujság*,[42] books and flags sent by the Hungarian government to immigrant associations in Canada, and such promotional activities as the Perényi tour, the erection of the Kossuth statue in the United States, and the organization of international congresses for expatriates as means devised by the regime to transmit its propaganda to co-nationals abroad.[43] But the proletarians readily saw the hands of Budapest even behind such patriotic institutions as the non-subsidized patriotic press, and the Canadian Hungarian Association, which were actually founded by members of the ethnic group.[44]

Some immigrants, such as István Tóth, welcomed this analysis. Before he discovered the *Munkás*, Tóth had stopped reading Hungarian newspapers in Canada because "they did nothing but praise Hungary – the country which we were forced to leave by the thousand." The *Munkás's* analysis of Hungarian society was one of the factors that drew him into the proletarian camp.[45]

Proletarian leaders believed that patriotic ideology was itself manipulative. The patriots claimed to be politically neutral in order to gain immigrants' support for objectives with distinct political content, while they denounced as political, and hence somehow reprehensible, everything done on behalf of the working class.[46] According to their opponents, moreover, the patriots were willing enough to appropriate and use folk culture in order to arouse public sympathy for Hungary in Canada, but they deliberately neglected to explain to Canadians under what conditions the creators of this folk culture were forced to live in their native land.[47]

Proletarian critics also rejected the patriots' accommodationism. In response to a call from Reverend Ferenc Nagy of Welland for lawful, orderly behaviour, the *Munkás* wrote bitterly: "that we are being kicked out of factories, that we are being deported, that doctors do not make house calls to the unemployed, all of this is nothing. We should forget it and be good citizens."[48] The condition of immigrant workers defied accommodation to the status quo. Proletarians saw in Ottawa's policy of deporting indigent immigrant workers the clearest example that Hungarians would be acquiescing in victimization and exploitation if they followed the advice of patriotic leaders. Their only salvation was to organize and demand unemployment insurance.[49]

Proletarian accounts claimed, moreover, that economic, as well as ideological, considerations moved members of Hungary's ruling class to follow immigrants to Canada. Former army officers, gendarmes, and bureaucrats accompanied them on their journey because they recognized that in the New World these people would easily fall prey to their machinations because of their inability to speak English and their ignorance of Canadian laws and customs. In Canada, these men, whom the *Új Előre* described as "hyenas,"[50] served as the newcomers' bankers, notaries, employment agents, and steamship and real estate agents, all the while robbing their unsuspecting customers. Proletarian spokesmen were not above levelling unfounded accusations against steamship agents who in fact acted in keeping with accepted business practices. Despite explicit proletarian criticism of anti-semitism, some members even used anti-semitic slurs in an effort to discredit steamship agents.[51] The fact that these agents, most of whom also sold life insurance, presented direct competition to the Canadian Hungarian Mutual Benefit Federation undoubtedly contributed to the acrimony of the denunciations. Yet the proletarians argued that these "class enemies" of the ordinary immigrant, motivated by gain, were alone responsible for dividing the newcomers. Vehement opposition to the left was fuelled by recognition that radicals "stood in their way to the workers' pockets."[52]

Of all attacks against the patriots by the proletarians, however, the most relentless were those against the clergy. Indeed, proletarian anti-clericalism was so ruthless that even some members of that camp found it offensive.[53] But their leaders persisted. Their anti-clericalism had its roots in the anti-religious traditions of the left. The virulence of this campaign, however, which equalled that of the patriots' anti-communist efforts, suggests that this element was also an integral part of the competition with the patriots to win over the immigrants. Communist organizers recognized that within the ethnic group clerics were their most formidable opponents. Consequently, in trying to discredit these "agents who trafficked in heavenly peace,"[54] no attacks seemed too ungentlemanly. Proletarians accused the clergy of appropriating funds collected by the church and of performing religious and social services only in return for hefty fees.[55] Since proletarian leaders knew that Hungarian clergymen in Canada received their salaries from Canadian churches, they also accused them of having entered the service of domestic capitalism. Behind the readiness of the churches to train Hungarian missionaries, to pay their salaries, and to subsidize their newspapers, they saw the hand of Ottawa anxious to train leaders who could "pacify, calm and quiet down the bankrupt, hungry, dissatisfied masses."[56]

PROPOSALS FOR CHANGE

Women were seen as the chief victims of manipulation by the clergy, and hence as the principal purveyors of "reactionary" attitudes within the ethnic group. Accordingly, communist organizers, in their campaign to raise class consciousness, paid special attention to the re-education of women. "We working-class mothers are doubly exploited under the capitalist system, first as wives and mothers and secondly as breadwinners," argued the *Munkás*.[57] Women were encouraged to participate as equals in all the activities of proletarian associations, "to get away from their enslavement in the kitchen."[58] To free them to do so, the *Munkás* urged Hungarian men to begin their political activism in their homes, to make their households "democratic" by helping with domestic chores.[59] Through the press and pamphlets, proletarian leaders attempted to introduce Hungarian women to the writings of

such prominent members of the communist movement as Alexandra
Kollontai and Klara Zetkin.[60]

Unfortunately, the vagaries of party line rather than deep conviction
seemed to inform the proletarian approach to women's issues. In 1934,
the *Munkás* firmly supported women's right to abortions, pointing out
that laws against it were class legislation: bourgeois women with money
could obtain safe abortions despite the laws, whereas working-class
women were forced to go to back-alley abortionists and many died as
a consequence. By late 1936, when a new ruling made abortions illegal
in the Soviet Union, the *Munkás* also reversed its position.[61]

The proletarian analysis of the evils of capitalism in Canada and in
Hungary, of the machinations of its agents within the ethnic group,
and of the oppression of women were counterbalanced by highly idealized accounts of life in the USSR. The preoccupation with the USSR was
undoubtedly a response to the Comintern's directive that workers all
over the world should be mobilized in support of the "fatherland of the
proletariat," which stood in grave danger from the bellicose, imperialist designs of the world's capitalist nations.[62] But stories about full employment, short workdays, excellent working conditions, full equality
between the sexes, free medical care, paid vacations, and the like in the
Soviet Union, also served to underline the inequities of capitalism, and
to provide more clearly defined dimensions to the type of alternative
system that workers should strive to bring about.[63]

If proletarian leaders were circumspect concerning the relationship
between their organizations and the Communist party, they stated
quite openly that immigrants could hasten the advent of a Soviet-type
society both in Canada and in Hungary by supporting that party.[64] In
this respect, as in all others, Hungarian communists in Canada consci-
entiously followed the party line.

Until 1934, when communists everywhere took the first steps
towards creating a Popular Front against fascist forces, Hungarian communist organizers in Canada argued that in this country only the
Communist party represented the interests of the working class, and
they denounced as "social fascists" more moderate, reformist parties
such as the Co-operative Commonwealth Federation (CCF).[65] They
urged Hungarians to join only unions that belonged to the communist-
led Workers' Unity League (WUL).[66] Trades and Labour Congress
(TLC) unions, these organizers argued, only pretended to represent
workers; in reality they acted on behalf of employers.[67] Since, of all the
areas in which WUL unions were active, Hungarians were represented
in significant numbers only in mining, much of the proletarian discussion of the relative merits of the two types of unions centred on a com-

parison between the Mine Workers' Union of Canada and the United Mine Workers of America. The former was denounced as a fascist organization that discriminated against "foreigners."[68] The proletarians' campaign to organize immigrant workers extended to the unemployed. They urged unemployed Hungarians to join the Unemployed Workers' Association, explaining that participation did not increase the threat of deportation, since indigence, as well as radicalism, was grounds for such action.

Similarly, until introduction of the Popular Front policy, the proletarian camp in Canada accepted only the small, illegal Hungarian Communist party as the legitimate and sincere defender of the interest of workers and peasants in the homeland.[69] Accordingly, the arrests and trials of communists in Hungary received extensive coverage in the *Munkás*, as did the campaigns organized by the International Red Aid on behalf of these imprisoned communists.[70] Members of proletarian groups in Canada participated actively in these campaigns, by raising funds for the defence of the prisoners, by circulating petitions demanding their release, and by sending letters of protest to Hungarian authorities.[71] The most intensive effort focused on Mátyás Rákosi. Arrested and imprisoned in 1925 for his role in the Communist party, Rákosi, a member of the Hungarian party's Central Committee, was retried in 1934, just as his first sentence was about to come to an end, and he was reincarcerated. The illegality of this treatment aroused international protest.[72]

Following introduction in 1934 of the Popular Front policy, however, support for reformist parties, and for non-communist trade unions, suddenly became permissible and even encouraged.[73] Communist organizers now encouraged Hungarians in Canada to collaborate with the CCF and to join the mainstream of the Canadian labour movement, and after 1937 they threw their full support behind the American-based Committee for Industrial Organization (CIO).[74]

The proletarian view of politics in the homeland also changed. After the Communist party there allied itself with the populist movement, which advocated radical agrarian reform among other goals, the *Munkás* frequently published articles by and about populist writers.[75] In the late 1930s, when the financial situation of their organizations was improving, proletarian leaders also printed and disseminated copies of books and pamphlets by such leading Hungarian populists as József Darvas, Gyula Illyés, and Péter Veres.

In an effort to comply with the Popular Front policy, proletarian leaders even tried for rapprochement with the patriots. They approached patriotic associations, asking them to participate in protests against unemployment.[76] On a number of occasions they also sought joint commemoration of Hungarian national holidays.[77] Within the ethnic group, however, the reversal in attitudes that the Comintern's new policy required was not very successful. Despite their conciliatory gestures, proletarian leaders apparently found it impossible to suppress their hostility. In the proletarian press, for example, attacks on the clergy persisted even while proletarian delegates visited Hungarian-Canadian congregations and asked for their cooperation.[78] Not surprisingly, the patriots viewed the abrupt change with suspicion and generally rejected these overtures.[79]

Whatever the vagaries of party line, however, the proletarians' program ultimately implied transcendence of ethnic boundaries. Proletarian leaders apparently saw no contradiction between promoting the preservation of the Hungarian language and encouraging collaboration with workers from other ethnic groups. "The cultivation of our language and culture [is a question] of life and death for Hungarian Canadians," argued one leader. Rank and file members stated that the company of fellow nationals and speeches and performances in their own language were among the features that inspired them to join the proletarians.[80] Like the patriots, they too feared that unless their children were taught their language and culture, generational conflict would develop.[81] Yet, as we see below, Hungarians were mobilized through the Benefit Federation and through the Workers' clubs to become involved in the struggle of the working class alongside people from other ethnic groups, as well as the Canadian-born.[82]

The internationalism of proletarian ideology, like its anti-clericalism and its revolutionary attitude towards women and the family, exemplifies the radical reorientation in thought that communist organizers hoped to bring about among Hungarian immigrants. They recognized that the newcomers might initially be more responsive to the patriotic call for ethnic preservation than to proletarian internationalism. The *Munkás* stated: "The majority of Hungarian workers ... find it difficult to understand that they must join the same organization as other immigrant workers and native workers and that united we must take up the struggle against the attacks of organized capitalism. The majority of Hungarian immigrant workers are chauvinistic, filled with patriotic feelings, which obscure from their view the suffering of workers who speak different languages."[83]

But the communist organizers sent from the United States were not deterred by the formidable task of convincing immigrants to abandon their traditional views. Indeed, because of their involvement in the oppositionary, and at times illegal, socialist and communist movements,

these organizers were well prepared to carry out programs of recruitment and politicization under adverse conditions.

10 Proletarian Funerals, Red Sundays, and March 15

RADICALIZING IMMIGRANT WORKERS

In May 1935, when Ferenc Stolc, a 31-year-old Hungarian worker suffering from tuberculosis – a disease, the *Munkás* later pointed out in its obituary, that "owing to the lack of proper treatment causes millions of workers to perish" – felt his end approaching, he requested a proletarian funeral "befitting a worker."[1] Instead of a clergyman, one of Montreal's most respected and articulate proletarian leaders would deliver an oration by his graveside. The surviving fragment of George Marczi's address shows that this emotionally charged event served as a forum to drive home to the assembled Hungarian immigrants with unparalleled intensity the central tenets of the proletarian creed: "He did not live to see the great day of liberation for which he struggled. He left it to us, the living, to accomplish what he could not, having been broken by the murderous onslaught that Capitalism directs against us all. But we will carry on the flag that he dropped, onto the final liberation."[2]

Proletarian funerals offer the most dramatic example of the purposeful politicization that characterized virtually all activities within the proletarian camp. The communist campaign to instil class consciousness among Hungarian immigrants was all-encompassing by necessity. As we have just seen, adoption of proletarian ideology required a revolution in the thinking of the proletarian rank and file. It called for abandonment of familiar customs and symbols and for rejection of traditional figures of authority both in the domestic and in the public realms. This radical reversal, as the leaders well knew, was not easily accomplished. It required a relentless campaign on all fronts.

Even if by the interwar years Hungarian peasants were no longer all deeply religious, the traditional rites that marked the most important occasions in their lives – births, marriages, and deaths – still tied them to the church. Accordingly, if party organizers wanted to draw former agriculturalists completely away from any contact with the church, thus to integrate them fully into the proletarian camp, they would have to supplant Christian rites with ones more in keeping with communist ideology.

Radicals seemed able to dispense with church weddings and christenings without too much difficulty. Generally, secular merry-making, which had in any case formed an important part of these celebrations, sufficed. We have evidence of only a few, spontaneous attempts to turn weddings and christenings into proletarian events. At one wedding, for example, money collected during the so-called bridal dance, destined for the newly married couple according to rural traditions, was instead donated to the *Munkás.*[3] Another proletarian wedding ceremony began with the singing of the "Internationale."[4] Similarly, the christenings of "proletarian" babies occasionally doubled as fundraisers for the paper.[5]

It was the mournful occasion of death, however, that seemed to call for solemn, distinctive ritual. By unveiling the harsh reality of the human condition, death created a need to affirm transcendental aims even in the secular world of communist mass organizations. The unmistakably messianic ring of Marczi's words at Stolc's funeral, and the unintentional parody of church ritual that characterized proletarian funerals in general, suggest that these sombre ceremonies fulfilled people's deeply felt needs. That is why proletarian funerals became widespread among them.

The vehemence with which patriotic leaders resisted the spread of this practice underscores the significance of this departure from tradition. In 1933, Father Horváth, a Hungarian priest from Welland, laid charges of interfering with a dead human body against Nicholas Pásztor, a shoemaker from Guelph and a proletarian leader, for delivering an oration by the graveside of John Stefan at the Port Colborne cemetery. Members of the local Workers' club, to which Stefan had belonged, raised most of the money for his funeral and invited Pásztor to officiate. Apparently unaware of these arrangements, and unheeding of the fact that Stefan had not been a churchgoer, some men from his boarding-house invited Horváth to conduct the last rites. Both Pásztor and Horváth spoke without incident at the boarding-house where the coffin was laid out. But when en route to the cemetery the procession entered the Ukrainian Labour Temple, which also served as a meeting place for the Hungarian Workers' club, and Pásztor again spoke about the deceased, Horváth became angry. Objecting to Pásztor's analysis of the conditions that drove Stefan to emigrate, the priest called the mourners "boot-wearing peasants" who had not even heard of neck-ties in their native land and berated them for expressing dissatisfaction with Canada, where they could afford to wear ties and shoes. When the procession finally reached the cemetery, Horváth spoke by the grave-side. But when Pásztor, who had not originally intended to speak there, tried to respond to his comments, Horváth called the police and laid charges against him.[6]

Proletarian funerals, like all the tools and agencies employed to rad-icalize Hungarian peasants in Canada, did not emerge spontaneously within the immigrant group. They were modelled after socialist rituals and programs that the Communist party adopted or developed inter-nationally to instil its ideology among the masses. Practices that helped politicize Hungarian immigrants in Canada, such as "Red Sundays," "worker correspondents," use of drama to transmit communist ideol-ogy, and organizing the unemployed, all had their counterparts in other ethnic and immigrant groups in Canada and in other countries where communists were active.

But proletarian leaders were no more able to mould the thinking of Hungarian immigrants at will than were their patriotic counterparts. Accordingly, as we see below, both the character of rank-and-file mem-bers of proletarian associations and the activities of competing patriotic associations influenced the campaign of proletarian politicization.

CENTRAL PLANNING AND DISCIPLINE

Thanks to the centralized institutional framework that they had built, communist organizers were better equipped than patriotic leaders to coordinate plans for the transmission of their views to Hungarian im-migrants. Programs for turning these newcomers into class-conscious proletarians were made by the central committee of the Benefit Federation and by that of the Workers' clubs network.[7] Members of the committees, who belonged to the Communist party as well, could thus guide the activities of mass organizations in accordance with the party line.

Like the Horthy regime, communist organizers also relied on books, pamphlets, plays, song books, and curricula and reading materials for Hungarian classes to transmit their ideas to the immigrants. Most of these materials were donated by or purchased from the us Hungarian communist movement. The publications of Hungarian communist émigrés living in Germany, Czechoslovakia, and the Soviet Union reached proletarian associations in Canada via the United States.[8] As the Depression began to recede and the financial situation of the proletarian camp began to improve, some books and pamphlets deemed ideologically suitable were printed in Toronto. Employing their centralized and disciplined organizational structure, the Central Committee of the Workers' clubs supplied local branches with books, periodicals, plays, song books, and readers. To ensure that these publications reached as many immigrants as possible, proletarian leaders suggested that each Workers' club establish a special committee for their dissemination.[9]

The central committees prescribed what other types of groups should be active within each branch of the mass organizations as well. In 1934, for example, the Central Committee of the Workers' clubs suggested that each branch establish a school for children, a self-improvement group, a newspaper committee, worker correspondents, a sports club, a cultural committee, a women's organization, and a committee to aid in the defence of the imprisoned Hungarian communists Imre Sallai and Sándor Fürst.[10] Most of the same bodies were set up within other groups of radical immigrants as well.

But party organizers made some concessions to the distinct national backgrounds of their immigrant supporters. Thus while all groups were expected to make a contribution to the International Red Aid, formed to defend and aid imprisoned communists throughout the world, each ethnic group could do so by helping prisoners in its country of origin. Hungarians directed their efforts to helping Sándor Fürst, Imre Sallai, and above all Mátyás Rákosi, the future Stalinist dictator of Hungary.

The types of activities undertaken by these groups were also prescribed by the party, down to the very topics that would be discussed. Semi-literate agriculturalists in Fort William discussed "Social Development and Marxist Economics," "The Condition of Workers in Capitalist Countries, Especially under the Present Depression, and the Conditions of Workers in Socialist Countries," and "What Is the Difference between the Communist Party and the Treacherous Social Democratic Party?"[11]

Although most members of the proletarian associations did not belong to the Communist party, the communist leadership had the authority to take disciplinary action against them if they openly opposed the party's programs. Ideological disagreements arose primarily within the Workers' clubs – the political arm of the proletarian faction. Sometimes disciplinary procedures were initiated at the local level and seemed to arise out of personal animosities.[12] But members accused of holding unacceptable political views could be expelled from proletarian associations or at least forced to give up their offices.[13] Recalcitrant members were on occasion even subjected to "mass trials," in front of "proletarian tribunals." The trials were announced in advance in the *Munkás*, and all workers were encouraged to attend them. The tribunals consisted of three judges assigned by the party, and the prosecution and the defendant each had its own lawyers. In one such hearing, two members of the Toronto Workers' club were condemned for holding Trotskyist views and ousted. Judging by the report in the *Munkás*, their Trotsykism consisted of criticizing the Communist party.[14]

SOCIAL AND CULTURAL ACTIVITIES

Red Sundays

"Red Sundays" were one method that communist organizers were using by 1933 to transmit their ideology to Hungarians in Canada. The term referred to Sundays on which the immigrants conducted campaigns to increase the readership of the *Munkás* and in the process to win new recruits for the proletarian camp. Organizers had deliberately chosen to mount these campaigns on the day when patriots were encouraged to attend church. Members of Workers' clubs were instructed to visit all Hungarian households, to introduce their compatriots to the *Munkás's* political orientation, and to convince them to choose proletarian politics of protest over the accommodationism, and irredentism of the patriotic press.[15]

Since many of the rank and file were not well versed in politics when they first became active, subscription campaigns for the *Munkás* also served to deepen their understanding of the communist cause. Leaders taught club members not only what arguments to use to gain new readers but also how to deliver their points convincingly.[16] After each recruitment drive, campaigners reported back to local leaders and analysed with them the effectiveness of their tactics. Members were also encouraged to return to those homes that showed interest and to urge people who agreed to subscribe to the *Munkás* to join the Benefit Federation and the local Workers' club.[17] It was no doubt to the dual function of the *Munkás* – as a medium for transmitting communist ideology and as an agency for mobilizing immigrants inside and outside the proletarian camp – that the editors referred when they described their paper as "a weapon" in the struggle against capitalism.[18]

Some of the drives proved remarkably effective. Thus, for example,

Cartoons accompanying call to recruit new members to the proletarian camp by selling them subscriptions to the *Munkás*. They suggest that approaching factory workers is far more appropriate than arguing with priests. *Kanadai Magyar Munkás*, 11 January 1936.

at the end of a ten-week campaign in 1935, the paper gained 1,379 new readers.[19] Because the subscriptions sold during these campaigns were monthly, in view of the poverty of Hungarian immigrants, it was necessary to repeat the campaign every few months throughout the interwar years.

Worker Correspondents

The *Munkás*'s practice, as early as 1929, of relying on "worker correspondents" for reports about working and living conditions in all Hungarian communities in Canada is another example of use of the techniques developed by Russian bolsheviks, but used by communists everywhere, to get the rank and file active in communist-led movements, even as they were learning about ideology.[20] All Workers' clubs were encouraged by their central committee to establish groups of worker correspondents.[21] But because Hungarian settlers generally had had only the most rudimentary education, they needed considerable prompting and guidance to submit articles to the paper. By providing this guidance, leaders could ensure that the articles submitted followed the party line.

The aspiring correspondent received the following list of subjects worthy of attention: working conditions, cutbacks in wages, the difficulty of work, unemployment, slave-driving practices, and bad housing conditions. On another occasion, guidelines were more evidently manipulative. Correspondents were asked to write whether "the traitorous A.F. of L. or social fascists" were active in their workplace and to describe the workers' view of their activities and whether they were fighting against the "Canadian fascists and their cronies the Hungarian fascists."[22] Once the letters were written, they were read aloud to other aspiring correspondents in the club and subjected to criticism. From the letters sent to the *Munkás* offices, those considered most relevant and informative were selected and often subjected to further editing before they finally appeared in the paper, under the heading "Munkás Levelezök" (Worker Correspondents).[23]

Despite these rigid controls, the *Munkás*'s readers responded enthusiastically. The editors complained that they received far more letters than they could publish and that some of them were eight to ten pages long. Contrary to the suggested guidelines, however, many correspondents expressed their loyalty to the proletarian camp by repeating newly learned radical slogans rather than by describing relevant details about their working lives.[24] By relying on reports from worker correspondents, the penurious paper was nevertheless able not only to offer extensive coverage of news of immediate concern to its readers but also to create a sense of participation. Such reports, as one loyal reader from the era recalled, "were written by simple people, and all those letters from workers appeared in the paper. This brought people together. They knew about each other, where others were, what they are doing and what working conditions are like."[25]

Almanacs

By contrast, publication of almanacs by the *Munkás*, and by the *Új Előre* before it, represented a concession to the reading habits of immigrants from rural Hungary. The *Munkás*'s almanacs, however, resembled those in the Hungarian countryside far less than did those published by the *Ujság*. The proletarian publications omitted the traditional soothsayer's section, for example, presumably because it was superstitious. Nevertheless they did preserve some outward resemblance to the traditional format and, like patriotic versions, used those similarities to convey aspects of their ideology. Thus, like almanacs in Hungary, they began with a calendar section, but beside each date were noted not weather forecasts and tips to agriculturalists but momentous events in the history of radical and labour movements. This practice had earlier been adopted by the almanacs of the *Népszava* (People's Voice), the Hungarian Social Democratic newspaper.

Theatre

Communist organizers also used dramatic performances to politicize Hungarian immigrants – actors and audiences alike. The repertoire of the Workers' drama troupes included plays that carried a distinct political message, such as *The Earth Moved*, about harvest strikes in Hungary in 1926; *The Jail of Margit Boulevard*, about imprisoned radicals; and a one-acter entitled simply *Karl Marx*. As an article in the first *Munkás* almanac explained: "The proletariat also uses drama as a weapon in the class struggle. From the stage it shows the various manifestations of oppression and exploitation. It makes the need for united struggle against the crumbling system accessible to the workers. It makes this need comprehensible to the masses through revolutionary plays."[26]

The practice of using drama (agitprop) to arouse popular support for communist ideology was well established by the 1920s. It caught the imagination of radical playwrights and directors, who helped to refine it as a propaganda tool and wrote ideologically committed short plays especially for working-class actors to perform for working-class audiences.[27] Andor Gábor – author of *Virgin Mary*, mentioned at the beginning of this study – was just one of a handful of émigré Hungarian playwrights in Germany, the Soviet Union, and the United States, who wrote for agitprop troupes. The revolutionary plays performed by the Hungarian Workers' drama troupes in Canada were prepared by these émigrés or translated by them from other languages.[28]

Even after they joined the proletarian camp, however, many immigrants were apparently more receptive to folk operettas and to light, entertaining comedies than to dramas about the working class. Consequently, arguments abounded about how many proletarian plays to include in the repertoires of amateur drama troupes. Hard-line leaders believed that only plays about workers were suitable;[29] they saw as opportunistic attempts to cater to popular tastes by performing plays without an explicit political message. Their views were more prevalent in the early 1930s. Other proletarians, however, feared that too much working-class drama would alienate immigrants; they favoured gradual exposure. According to J. Natko of Montreal, for example, only a moderate program could teach workers to appreciate the superiority of proletarian drama: "The proper program and proper distribution of plays will enable us to reawaken the aesthetic sensibility of the people, which has been damaged by the arduousness of their lives, and through this reawakened sensibility to guide them toward class consciousness. To reach this aim, bourgeois plays must always be properly introduced and the performances of working class dramas must be gradually increased."[30]

In recruitment drives, proletarian theatre groups frequently relied on the folk operettas that their patriotic counterparts put on for fund-raising, entertainment, and education. Such reliance illustrates the concessions made by communist organizers to immigrant tastes. "When bourgeois plays with attractive sounding names are staged," wrote one of them in the first *Munkás* almanac, "even those who remained unmoved by revolutionary plays come to see them ... Many workers have remained within our ranks who were first drawn to us by dramatic performances."[31] If certain lines within these "bourgeois" plays were deemed unpalatably reactionary, they were rewritten or simply omitted. All religious invocations and references, for example, were either replaced by secular expressions or eliminated. Thus, in one operetta, "I am trembling, God give me strength!" became "I am cold," and "Thank God!" was replaced by "Good."[32] At each of these performances, moreover, proletarian leaders attempted to recruit new members during intermission.[33]

By mounting playwriting competitions, party organizers encouraged immigrants to develop their own plays. These dramas were supposed to reflect experience and to give expression to the thoughts and feelings of grass-roots members. Coming from the supposed champions of working-class creativity, the guidelines provided by the competition's organizers, however, appear rather rigid: "The play in three acts: should concern itself with working class families and the life of capitalists, a parallel must be drawn between the two classes. The role of the police, agents, priests, judges and stool pigeons must be shown. How under the present system they try to hoodwink workers. The destitution and exploitation of working class families should be stressed. The exploitation of working class girls and women by the capitalists, etc. These plays should be dramatic."[34] These instructions, and similar ones for one- and two-act plays, show yet again how party organizers attempted to mould proletarian consciousness. All that survives from that period are lists of the names of aspiring dramatists who responded and the titles of their plays.[35]

Social Gatherings

Banquets and balls were also used to recruit new members and to raise funds for proletarian associations, and here, as in the patriotic camp, such gatherings were frequently modelled after traditional seasonal festivals in Hungary. In the fall, for example, the Hamilton Workers' club held a harvest festival. In addition to a dinner and dance, grapes were pressed on location and the fresh grape juice was sold for five cents a glass. Club members, dressed as Hungarian villagers, wandered among the crowd. István Weszely, dressed as an old Jewish pedlar, sold ribbons and trinkets to increase revenue. In the winter, members celebrated the festival of pig-killing. Although fundraising was one of the main reasons for these events, during the Depression there was a policy of "pay as you can," and single men on relief, who received little assistance, took advantage of such functions to get a decent meal.[37]

In summer, much of the club's social life was transferred outdoors. On weekends, members, like their patriotic counterparts, held picnics at parks in the Hamilton area. "Picnic" was a new word for most Hungarians, but the function resembled both the Hungarian "majális," a type of picnic and dance held in May, and the "búcsú," a parish feast, generally accompanied by a fair. At the Hamilton Workers' club picnics, as at Hungarian fairs, mystery display tents were set up. István Weszely laughingly recalls that gullible members paid five cents to enter a tent bearing the sign "The Entrance of the Hungarians." Once inside, they were greeted by an empty tent and another sign, "The Exit of the Hungarians." He modelled the display after one that he had seen at a fair in his native town of Pécs.[38]

Whatever the season, communist organizers addressed the immigrants gathered at social functions and urged them to join the proletarian camp.

Women's Groups

Proletarian women's groups, like patriotic ones, prepared and served food at social functions, embroidered articles for auctions, and sewed costumes for amateur drama troupes. But these groups were also designed to educate women politically and to provide them with the necessary writing and public speaking experience to participate as equals in the struggle of the working class. The central committee of the Workers' clubs, which had no women members when this program was undertaken, recommended that, at the beginning of each meeting of the women's groups, more experienced members give a 15-minute talk.[39] There were to follow discussions on such topics as "The Double Exploitation of Women under Capitalism" and "The Condition of Women in the USSR."[40]

As membership grew during the 1930s, the programs produced radical women, some of them, like Mrs Lancsa, with little education and no previous political experience. This former day-labourer and domestic servant distributed a pamphlet entitled *The Role of Women in Communism* door to door among Windsor's Hungarians.[41]

Children's Language Classes

Like the patriots, proletarian associations also offered Hungarian classes for the children of immigrants. Indeed, competition with the patriots was an important reason for establishing these classes. Recognizing that language preservation was important for immigrants, proletarian leaders feared that if they did not provide such classes even parents from their own camp would rely on patriotic associations, where young people would pick up antagonistic views.[42] More than competition, however, was responsible for these programs. Despite their internationalist stand, proletarian leaders, like patriotic ones, believed in preserving the Hungarian language in Canada. They gave attention to programs of language maintenance especially after 1934, when they adopted a more conciliatory attitude towards the patriots.[43] Like patriotic leaders, proletarians too feared that failure to teach the children the language and culture of their parents would result in generational conflict.[44]

As in the patriotic camp, Hungarian-language classes also transmitted political values. If patriotic youngsters learned about the anguish of truncated Hungary and the nobility of patriotic sentiments, proletarian children learned about social injustice and the nobility of the working class, as well as about the need for inter-ethnic cooperation as they were learning the language and history of their parents.[45] The political content of the instruction was more openly acknowledged by the protetarians, for their leaders viewed themselves and their followers as a beleaguered minority, facing opposition not only from within but also from outside the ethnic group. Their children, they believed, had to be protected not only from the teachings of the patriots but also from the ideas disseminated through public, "bourgeois" education.

As the writer of a women's column in the *Munkás* stated: "We must not entrust our children's education to the bourgeoisie, because they will turn our children against us. If we are not careful, we will discover, all of a sudden, that they hate us, their own parents."[46] Consequently, children's groups were named after communist leaders such as Béla Kun, and each meeting had some time allocated to political education.[47]

ORGANIZATIONAL ACTION

Training Leaders

In addition to fostering class consciousness, the social and cultural activities mounted by the branches of the Benefit Federation and the

Workers' clubs also acted as training and selection grounds for new leaders. Despite proletarian associations' being highly centralized and disciplined, the American organizers who led the movement in Canada and the handful of more experienced Canadian Hungarian radicals who assisted them could not by themselves ensure the smooth functioning of local branches. They believed that the absence of capable leadership was responsible for financial problems in some branches of the Benefit Federation and for the movement's loss of members. As an article in the *Munkás* explained: "the membership of our clubs is largely comprised of rural labourers, who despite their dedication and good intentions were not able to fill leadership roles, nor to lead the rest of the members, nor to discipline organizational life."[48] Consequently, the leaders selected the most talented worker correspondents and drama directors, the ablest public speakers, and the best canvassers in proletarian associations and sent them to Communist party schools, to be trained for leadership.

The men thus selected received training either in Canada or in the United States. The curricula of party schools in both countries were more or less the same. They were designed to provide students with a more sophisticated understanding of communist ideology and of the party's organizational practices than they could gain from involvement in mass organizations. Some subjects, such as Marxist economics, and the history of the International, remained unaltered throughout the 1920s and 1930s, while others changed in accordance with the policies of the Comintern. In 1935, for example, in keeping with the new policy of collaboration with anti-fascist forces, Hungarian leadership students were given a course on Popular Front tactics.[49] Our only indication of the numbers attending such schools is that in 1932 18 Hungarian organizers graduated from a Communist party training session.[50]

Leadership recruitment practices permitted immigrants with little formal education and no previous political or organizational experience to rise to leading positions in the proletarian camp. István Tóth, for example, who joined the editorial board of the *Munkás* in 1942, was a landless labourer turned miner, who completed only four grades of school in Hungary and had not taken part in any kind of associational life or political activity before he became involved in the proletarian camp in Canada in 1929. He was introduced to the left when a fellow immigrant sold him a subscription to the *Munkás*. In his autobiography, Tóth describes his reaction: "The *Kanadai Magyar Munkás* was born on July 16, 1929, and on that day I was also reborn. On that day I started to be aware of why things around me were as they were, and of how things could be altered, and much improved."[51] Inspired by the paper, Tóth, who like so many other Hungarians wandered across

Canada in search of employment, became active in proletarian associations wherever he sojourned. In Alberta, for instance, he became an activist in the communist-led Mine Workers' Union of Canada. He also contributed regularly to the *Munkás*, as a worker correspondent. Tóth was asked to join the editorial board when, having been forced to give up mining by poor health, he moved to Toronto.

Alex Medgyesi was another prominent member of the Hungarian-Canadian left who received all his political education and training after he joined the proletarian camp in Canada. Medgyesi first attended a meeting of the Hamilton Workers' club at the invitation of friends, without having a clear idea of the organization's political orientation. He became active in the association because of his interest in drama. A tailor by trade, for a few years Medgyesi had earned his living in his native Slovakia by sewing costumes for an itinerant theatre troupe, and so he was happy to work with amateur proletarian performers in Hamilton and Toronto. But he also became interested in proletarian politics. He read communist literature and eagerly attended lectures by Canadian and Hungarian communist leaders. His political judgment was soon considered sufficiently mature that he was placed in charge of selecting plays for proletarian drama groups to put on for working-class audiences. He directed plays and translated some from English into Hungarian.

Like Tóth, Medgyesi also wrote for the *Munkás* as a worker correspondent, and in this capacity he came to the attention of János Gyetvai, a leading American Hungarian communist who was editor of the paper in 1934. When Gyetvai asked him to become correspondence editor and circulation manager, Medgyesi initially hesitated. He told Gyetvai that he was not familiar with such things. But the American communist replied: "Medgyesi, our kind of work is not taught at universities." But it was taught at party schools, and Medgyesi attended such an institution in the United States. Having completed his training, he joined the *Munkás* staff and looked after administrative and financial affairs. The former tailor also had his own column in the paper. He modelled his writing after that of Andor Gábor, with whose material he had become acquainted in the proletarian camp.[52]

Promoting Internationalism

With their ranks thus expanded by newly recruited communist cadres, proletarian leaders could carry on their campaign for the radicalization of Hungarian immigrants more effectively within proletarian organizations. While it was important that their programs be implemented in Hungarian, since many immigrants did not speak English, translation of the Communist party's internationalist orientation into practice would require collaboration with workers from other ethnic groups.

Hungarian party organizers were not content to wait until their arguments alone convinced immigrants to adopt an internationalist stance. They attempted to promote such an attitude through organizational measures. The establishment of Hungarian branches of the Canadian Labour Defense League, for example, was intended not only to raise funds for individuals in Canada who got into trouble with the law because of their support for communist causes but also to foster a feeling of international brotherhood among Hungarian workers.[53] Hungarian members of the league tried to help communists and sympathizers from other ethnic groups, and fundraising often brought them together with branches active in these groups.[54]

Proletarian leaders also encouraged immigrants to support communist-led unions. The Hungarians were too dispersed geographically and occupationally to be very visible in Canadian strikes and other union activities directed by the Communist party. Two members of the strike committee elected during the 1929 walkout at the National Steel Car Co. in Hamilton, however, were Hungarian communists. One of them, Joseph Dohány, was the American organizer who founded the *Munkás*.[55] When communist organizer Alex Welsh tried to recruit the striking workers of the Empire Cotton Mill in Welland to the United Textile Workers' Union, one of his most influential supporters was "the Passionaria of Welland," Mary Jary, a woman of Hungarian origin. Another Hungarian proletarian leader, by the name of Sproha, helped to organize tobacco workers from his homeland. They hoisted a red flag with the hammer and sickle on the tallest tree in the vicinity of their shanty town outside Delhi. He urged them on by pointing out that under that flag "liberation had been attained on one-sixth of the earth."[56] Hungarian proletarians also helped organize drives and strikes among tobacco and cannery workers elsewhere in southern Ontario and among shoemakers in Montreal.[57]

During the Depression, neighbourhood councils, set up to provide a grass-roots infrastructure for the communist-led National Unemployed Workers' Association, provided another arena for collaboration between ethnic groups. Each neighbourhood council was made up of a group of ethnic street councils, linked to each other by captains. The idea of creating separate councils for each language group came from a member of the proletarian camp, who believed that only in this way could immigrants who did not speak English be recruited. Communist organizers, who initially opposed this plan, were forced to concede its correctness, and Hungarian street councils were established in Montreal and Hamilton.[58] By 1933, such bodies in

224 Patriots and Proletarians

Montreal had 300 members.[59] Council supporters looked up and determined the needs of every unemployed Hungarian who lived on their
street. Their captains often interceded on behalf of these people with
Canadian authorities, helping to obtain relief for them and to speed up
the hospitalization of seriously ill but destitute workers. Collaboration
with members of other ethnic groups occurred when landlords threatened to evict tenants unable to pay their rent. Mobilized through the
neighbourhood council, a large group of unemployed workers of various backgrounds would occupy the apartment of tenants about to be
tossed out, and their mere presence on occasion sufficed to prevent
eviction.[60]

By far the most ambitious organizational venture to promote
inter-ethnic collaboration was the transformation of the Canadian
Hungarian Mutual Benefit Federation into the multi-ethnic Independent
Mutual Benefit Federation in 1934. Creation of such a fraternal association, modelled after the American International Workers' Order,
the largest US communist mass organization, was discussed among
Hungarian proletarians as early as 1931.[61] The party's plan at that time
was to unite the Benefit Federation with two of the largest ethnic mass
bodies in Canada – the Ukrainian Labour Temple Association and the
United Jewish People's Order.[62] Immediate practical considerations
and the desire to promote international cooperation lay behind this
move. Organizers hoped to buttress smaller, poorer ethnic mass organizations, whose existence during the Depression was precarious, by
uniting them with their larger, more prosperous counterparts. They
also believed that the existence of one large body would reduce administrative costs.[63] They hoped as well that a large, multi-ethnic mass organization would attract not only immigrants but also Canadian-born
workers.[64] When these plans failed, however, the Benefit Federation,
apparently the strongest and most prosperous of the mass organizations operating among the smaller ethnic groups, became the nucleus
for the multi-ethnic fraternal organization.[65]

At its establishment, the Hungarian representatives of the International
Workers' Order were on hand to aid Hungarian proletarian leaders in
Canada.[66] Initially, Hungarian organizers, some of whom also spoke
other languages, attempted to recruit from other ethnic groups. Joseph
Magyar, for example, was of Danube Swabian origin, spoke German, and
founded some German sections. Eventually, however, other ethnic
groups provided their own organizers. By 1935, in addition to its
Hungarian branches, the Independent Mutual Benefit Federation
also had eleven Slovak, nine German, and two Polish branches, as well
as a Jewish, a French-Canadian, an Italian, and an English-Canadian
branch.[67] All groups within the federation operated in their own lan-

guages at the branch level and retained considerable autonomy.[68] The massive propaganda campaign that accompanied the launching of the multi-ethnic body, however, enabled proletarian leaders to promote the internationalist aims that inspired the organization's founding. The federation also increased leisure-time contact among members of the various ethnic groups. The smaller, non-Hungarian groups often used the club-houses of Hungarian branches, and proletarian leaders encouraged multi-ethnic participation in social activities and in ceremonial occasions.

Proletarians and Patriots

In the proletarian as in the patriotic camp, commemoration of major historical events formed the high point of community life. Such occasions served to express and to affirm group identity. The proletarian calendar reflected the duality inherent in leftist Hungarians' view of proletarian consciousness: it marked both events in the history of the Hungarian people and turning points in the development of the international socialist movement. In addition to the Revolution of 1848, the proletarian camp also commemorated the Hungarian Soviet Republic of 1919, the Russian Revolution, the Paris Commune of 1871, International Women's Day, and, of course, 1 May.

The celebration of 15 March, however, was the most important occasion for the proletarians, as for the patriots. In form, the events in both camps were similar – addresses from community leaders, plays, poetry readings and the performance of Hungarian songs and dances. On both sides, children's groups, choirs, and dance and drama troupes rehearsed every year, amid great excitement. But content differend drastically in the two camps.

The most significant attribute of the events of 1848–49, according to the proletarians, was their revolutionary character. Their leaders saw 1848 as a bourgeois uprising, the harbinger of a revolutionary process, which would culminate with the victory of the proletariat and a socialist society.[69] They viewed the Hungarian revolution of 1919 as part of the same process and hence often commemorated the two uprisings jointly, either on 15 March or on 21 March.[70] Addresses, poems, plays, and songs to mark these anniversaries all described the revolutionary character of the events of 1848 (and 1919) – precisely that aspect that patriots tried to deny. Indeed, proletarian leaders publicly denounced the patriotic interpretation: "The revolution of 1848, even if it was not a revolution of workers and poor peasants, was a battle against tyranny. And the Horthyist oppressors have no right to exploit and misrepresent the great events of 1848 by spreading irredentist propaganda."[71]

Party organizers also used the March celebrations to affirm internationalism. In their version of the events of 1848–49, Kossuth, leader of the Hungarian nationalists, emerged as the champion of internationalism. They emphasized his concessions to the ethnic minorities during the final phase of the revolution to show that Kossuth, like proletarian leaders in Canada, was a great believer in inter-ethnic cooperation.[72] On occasion, they attempted to make Hungarian immigrants aware of the relationship which, according to communist theory, existed between revolutions everywhere, by commemorating the Paris Commune of 1871, as well as the Hungarian revolutions.[73] They also invited members of communist mass organizations from other ethnic groups to participate in the proletarian celebrations of 1848 and 1919.[74] The commemoration of the 1919 commune in Toronto in 1934, for example, opened with the playing of the "Internationale" by the Ukrainian Workers' Orchestra.[75]

The irreconcilable difference between the proletarian and patriotic interpretations of 1848–49 came sharply into focus in Montreal in 1934, when the two camps celebrated 15 March together. This exceptional collaboration took place at the initiative of proletarian leaders, who were apparently trying to unite the Hungarian immigrants in order to create a broad popular movement against fascism, in accordance with the latest party directives. The patriots in Montreal who, unlike those in Welland, for example, accepted proletarian overtures were to regret their decision.[76] János Papp, one of the proletarian performers, recited the poem "Villa and Hut" by Hungary's most celebrated poet, Sándor Petőfi, also one of the leaders of 1848:

Where did your owner gain the money
which makes a nothing into all?
Where the hawk
rends a bird on whose blood
he puffs up, and the young
cry in the neighbouring bush
for the mother who will not return.

Brag
about your loot, arrogant house.
Show off, it will not be for long.
Your days are numbered.
And I want to see you fall quickly,
the bones of your
wretched habitants beneath the ruins!

I cross the holy threshold
of straw huts
where great men are born
and redeemers sent.
Whoever gives himself to the world
comes from the poor.
And yet contempt and poverty
for the common everywhere.

Do not despair,
happier days will come.
If the past and present are not yours,
the infinite future is.
I kneel
in these narrow holy walls.
Give me your blessing,
and let me give you mine.[77]

As he was reciting Petőfi's revolutionary poem, Papp lifted a broken cross and broken chains from under his feet and displayed them triumphantly to the assembled immigrants, and to Károly Winter, the Hungarian consul general, the Montreal community's guest of honour on this ceremonial occasion. According to the *Munkás*, when Winter witnessed Papp's symbolic gesture his eyes flashed with anger. The patriots tried to prevent the Workers' club from performing two additional numbers that evening. All the club's subsequent attempts to participate in community events along with patriotic associations were blocked by the patriots.[78]

These events illustrate that rather than developing a collective identity based upon a common background in Europe and experiences shared in Canada, Hungarian immigrants had become deeply divided as a result of their politicization in Canada.

Conclusion

The ideological polarity that characterized the Hungarian immigrant group in Canada during the 1920s and 1930s, and the intensely politicized life within it, arose out of circumstances peculiar to this period. Political turmoil in Hungary after the First World War produced the chief agents that politicized community life in Canada. The defeat of the Commune of 1919 led to the emigration of Hungarian communists, who became the mediators between the Communist party and peasant immigrants in Canada. The intensification of Hungarian nationalism generated by the imposition of the harsh Treaty of Trianon explains the receptivity of patriotic leaders to Horthyist propaganda. The post-First World War fear of radicalism in North America hastened the involvement of Canadian Churches in the establishment of immigrant congregations in Canada.

Communist party organizers, clergymen, businessmen, professionals, urban artisans, and immigrants who came to Canada after having spent some years in the United States laid the foundations of two opposing camps within the immigrant group. While both patriotic and proletarian associations attempted to meet the needs of Hungarian immigrants, their activities, infused with political content, acted as channels for the transmission of ideologies to the peasant immigrants who made up the bulk of the membership.

Politicization within the patriotic camp was not entirely deliberate. Patriotic associations did rely on cultural artifacts produced and distributed by the Horthy regime expressly to spread its revisionism and its conservative, nationalist, Christian ideology. The clerics, middle-class immigrants, and urban artisans who organized social and cultural activities within this camp, however, were so fully integrated into Hungary's official culture that they transmitted social and political views to the rank and file without being fully conscious of what they were doing. Their conviction that patriotic goals were the only legitimate aims for immigrants led them to see as apolitical programs for the preservation of Hungarian identity in Canada that rested on acceptance of both the Horthy regime in the homeland and the status quo in Canada.

Within the proletarian camp, politicization was more deliberate. To rally immigrants to the communist movement, its leaders – Hungarian communist organizers – employed agitational and propaganda techniques developed within the international communist movement. While their aims were internationalist, to communicate these ideals to the immigrants they relied not only on the Hungarian language, but also on aspects of shared culture and fellow-feeling. Thus programs for radicalization necessarily had an important ethnic component. The fact that communist organizers, like their patriotic counterparts, relied on cultural activities to spread their views meant that even in the proletarian camp the transmission of political ideology was not always patent and obvious.

Neither the agents of the Communist party nor those of the Horthy regime would have succeeded in infusing group consciousness among Hungarians in Canada with political content had their ideologies, and the institutions that they created and supported, not responded to the needs of immigrants. Circumstances of exceptional deprivation during the interwar years made the rank and file receptive to the initiatives of the agents of politicization. For landless labourers and dwarf holders in interwar Hungary, transatlantic migration represented an accepted, if not the sole avenue for ameliorating their lives. Yet circumstances in Canada at this time were ill-suited to fulfilling their expectations. After a few years of sporadic work at low-paid, difficult jobs, most of them were thrust into unemployment. They suffered years of joblessness, often away from their families, without assistance from institutions that did provide some aid to Anglo-Celtic workers. Unskilled and unemployed, most immigrants did not belong to labour unions. Itinerant, and with many of their number non-naturalized, they did not qualify for aid offered to the unemployed by various levels of government. They had to rely almost exclusively on ideologies and institutions within their ethnic communities to analyse their predicament, offer them assistance and advice, and give them a sense of belonging and a modicum of dignity in their new surroundings.

Proletarian ideology not only acknowledged the legitimacy of the immigrant workers' anger, it tried to focus and harness this anger. While it did not hesitate to provide specific targets by pointing accusingly at railways and steamship lines, employers of immigrant labour, priests and ministers, and steamship agents as their exploiters, proletarian ideology also offered a broader interpretation of their predicament by putting forth simple explanations of the workings and crises of the capitalist economy. Immigrants who accepted these analyses were absolved from feeling responsible for their plight. They could also draw solace from communist predictions that the end of the capitalist system was near. Looking expectantly to the spread of socialism outside the Soviet Union, these immigrants supported the programs that communist organizers initiated in their midst.

Ironically, the same conditions of privation and hopelessness help to explain why interwar immigrants were receptive to patriotic ideology. Using traditional assumptions and familiar images and symbols to draw a rosy vision of their homeland and to recount a heroic version of Hungarian history, it offered to the lonely, alienated, disappointed newcomers a sense of rootedness and belonging. To understand the appeal of patriotic ideology, however, we must also consider the Treaty of Trianon. Since a large segment of the group was directly affected by the treaty, because members lived in areas given to the successor states or immediately next to the new boundaries, the Horthy regime's revisionism did much to enhance its prestige among expatriates. The immigrants' reaction of outrage to the unjust treaty, moreover, undoubtedly acquired special meaning and intensity because of their indignation over their own plight in Canada. Support for the Horthy regime and its revisionism within patriotic ideology was compatible with an accommodationist stance to Canadian society.

The coming of war in 1939 altered the position of Hungarian workers in Canada. Wartime production finally provided immigrants who had suffered long years of under- or unemployment with relatively secure jobs. Many of them, moreover, found work in industry at much higher wages than they received during the 1920s and 1930s. Since their absorption into the industrial labour force coincided with an unprecedented expansion of the Canadian labour movement, Hungarian immigrants also had the opportunity to join labour unions. For the first time since their arrival, therefore, they began to have access to some of the sources of power in Canadian society.

A number of programs instituted by the state during the 1940s also aided the integration of Hungarians into the host society. The provision of unemployment insurance and family allowances offered a measure of social security to them, as to other Canadian workers. In addition to these social welfare measures, created for Canadians at large, more specific programs were initiated to assist immigrants. With the establishment of the Nationality Branch and the Committee on Co-operation in Canadian Citizenship within the Department of National War Services in 1942, the authorities for the first time actively sought to aid the integration of the foreign-born, or at least immigrants of European background, into Canadian society.[1] While the general programs of this organization have not yet been studied by historians, we do know that its representative among Hungarian immigrants, Béla Eisner, undertook to ensure that his co-nationals would not be subject to discrimination in the workplace.[2]

Although circumstances peculiar to the interwar period shaped community life among Hungarian immigrants, this analysis of their experience nevertheless raises several considerations important to the study of immigrants more generally. The politicization of Hungarians who arrived in Canada between the two world wars suggests that even immigrant communities comprised largely of semi-literate peasants and rural labourers should not necessarily be seen as enclaves, cut off from outside influences. Nor should it be assumed that emerging group consciousness was unreflective, devoid of ideological content. Even a handful of better-educated immigrants can exert a crucial influence on community development by infusing it with ideological content and by linking the group to political concerns in the homeland and in the receiving society. Indeed, the experience of Hungarian immigrants suggests that community development and the emergence of group consciousness can be understood only as the products of interaction among the rank and file, key elements within the ethnic group, and forces from outside. Since the organizations and functions that provided the arenas for such contacts had their equivalents among other immigrant and ethnic groups, it is surely worth investigating whether such bodies and events do not act as agencies for the transmission of political ideologies within those other groups as well.

The recognition of the complexity of social structure and interaction within immigrant groups has particular relevance for the student of the Canadian working class. This recognition, it seems to me, is essential for bringing about cross-fertilization between labour and immigration studies. Perhaps the absence of careful analyses of various groups of newcomers has permitted labour historians too frequently to regard study of the working-class segment of these communities as sufficient for their purposes. But to set such parameters for research is implicitly to assume that the proletarian condition of most immigrants – the experiences that they shared among themselves and with workers of other nationalities – was more important to the development of group consciousness than what they shared with other social strata within their own ethnic group. It is to assume, in short, that common class position is invariably more decisive than shared ethnicity in forming group consciousness. The analysis here of the experiences of Hungarian immigrants, by contrast, has shown that membership in an immigrant group – implying recognition both of shared ethnicity and of a sense of "foreignness" in the receiving society – is a powerful force in shaping values, beliefs, and aspirations. It provides a connection among disparate social strata and acts as a conduit for political ideas. While the two types of collective identification are not mutually exclusive, in some historical contexts ethnic consciousness can be more influential in determining political behaviour than class consciousness.

The possibility that seemingly apolitical activities within ethnic and immigrant communities are in fact charged with political content leads me to raise a final speculative point, one that follows from my investigation of community life among Hungarian Canadians during the interwar years but that may suggest a new perspective on the fate of ethnicity in Canada in more recent decades. If cultural activities further politicization among other ethnic and immigrant groups, and not only among Hungarian Canadians, then some of the arguments concerning the policy of multiculturalism will have to be reconsidered. A number of the policy's early critics described it as meaningless, or worse still as manipulative, because while it claims to recognize the collective rights of ethnic minorities, it in fact allows them only "to sing their ethnic songs, dance their ethnic dances, eat their ethnic foods and (otherwise) engage in ethnic exotica – provided that none of these activities contravenes prevailing Canadian laws."[3] Would the case of these critics not be stronger if they realized that the ethnic exotica promoted and subsidized by the government are far from being politically neutral?

Appendix

Table A1
Ethnic Composition of Immigrants to Canada from Hungary, 1926–40

Year	Magyar (%)	German (%)	Hebrew (%)	Slovak (%)	Other (%)	Total (%)
1926–27	3,775	558	16	5	113	4,467
	(84.5)	(12.5)	(0.4)	(0.1)	(2.5)	(100.0)
1927–28	3,949	316	10	4	41	4,320
	(91.4)	(7.3)	(0.2)	(0.1)	(1.0)	(100.0)
1928–29	4,721	411	12	4	29	5,177
	(91.2)	(7.9)	(0.2)	(0.1)	(0.6)	(100.0)
1929–30	4,311	565	13	1	24	4,914
	(87.7)	(11.5)	(0.3)	(0)	(0.5)	(100.0)
1930–31	1,876	225	14	2	11	2,128
	(88.1)	(10.6)	(0.7)	(0.1)	(0.5)	(100.0)
1931–32	296	53	0	3	0	352
	(84.1)	(15.1)	(0)	(0.8)	(0)	(100.0)
1932–33	301	13	1	0	3	318
	(94.7)	(4.1)	(0.3)	(0)	(0.9)	(100.0)
1933–34	401	32	3	0	0	436
	(92.0)	(7.3)	(0.7)	(0)	(0)	(100.0)
1934–35	305	27	0	0	0	332
	(91.9)	(8.1)	(0)	(0)	(0)	(100.0)
1935–36	211	8	0	0	1	220
	(95.9)	(3.6)	(0)	(0)	(0.5)	(100.0)
1936–37	248	20	0	1	1	270
	(91.8)	(7.4)	(0)	(0.4)	(0.4)	(100.0)
1937–38	421	21	1	0	2	445
	(94.6)	(4.7)	(0.2)	(0)	(0.5)	(100.0)
1938–39	359	11	10	0	1	381
	(94.2)	(2.9)	(2.6)	(0)	(0.3)	(100.0)
1939–40	290	5	54	1	14	364
	(79.7)	(1.4)	(14.8)	(0.3)	(3.8)	(100.0)
Total	21,464	2,265	134	21	240	24,124
	(89.0)	(9.4)	(0.5)	(0.1)	(1.0)	(100.0)

Sources: Figures compiled from Canada, Department of Immigration and Colonization, *Annual Departmental Report* (1926–36), and Canada, Department of Mines and Resources, Immigration Branch, *Annual Report*, 1936–40.

Table A2

Occupational breakdown of Hungarian Immigrants to Canada, 1928–30

Occupation	%
Farm hands and day labourers	69.74
Independent farmers	13.76
Other and unspecified branches	9.85
Unskilled industrial workers and day labourers	2.08
Unspecified day labourers	2.08
Domestic servants	1.06
Independent craftsmen	0.91
Professionals	0.31
Miners and mineworkers	0.28
Independent merchants	0.06
Total	100.00

Sources: Figures compiled from Hungary, Hungarian Bureau of Statistics, *Annual Report*, 1928–30.

Table A3
Ethnic Hungarian (Magyar) immigration to Canada from Hungary and successor states, 1926–40

Year	Hungary (%)	Czecho- slovakia (%)	Romania (%)	Yugo- slavia (%)	Total (%)
1926–27	3,775 (78)	531 (11)	423 (9)	100 (2)	4,829 (100)
1927–28	3,949 (75)	610 (11)	469 (9)	250 (5)	5,278 (100)
1928–29	4,721 (76)	613 (10)	689 (11)	199 (3)	6,222 (100)
1929–30	4,311 (76)	435 (8)	699 (12)	197 (4)	5,642 (100)
1930–31	1,876 (79)	186 (8)	237 (10)	90 (3)	2,389 (100)
1931–32	296 (75)	27 (7)	48 (12)	22 (6)	393 (100)
1932–33	301 (84)	27 (8)	23 (6)	8 (2)	359 (100)
1933–34	401 (80)	42 (8)	44 (9)	17 (3)	504 (100)
1934–35	305 (83)	33 (9)	15 (4)	3 (1)	364 (100)
1935–36	211 (69)	32 (10)	49 (16)	19 (6)	311 (100)
1936–37	248 (76)	38 (12)	26 (8)	12 (4)	324 (100)
1937–38	421 (69)	69 (11)	81 (13)	43 (7)	614 (100)
1938–39	366 (68)	64 (12)	49 (9)	56 (11)	535 (100)
1939–40	290 (90)	13 (4)	16 (5)	2 (1)	321 (100)
Total	21,471 (76)	2,720 (10)	2,868 (10)	1,018 (4)	28,077 (100)

Sources: Figures compiled from Canada, Department of Immigration and Colonization, *Annual Departmental Report,* 1926–36, and Department of Mines and Resources, Immigration Branch, *Annual Report, 1936–40.*

Table A4
Ethnic Hungarian immigrants to Canada, by age and sex, 1925–40

Year	Adult male (%)	Adult female (%)	Children (%)	Total
1925–26	3,295 (80.1)	409 (9.9)	408 (10.0)	4,112
1926–27	3,480 (71.6)	720 (14.8)	663 (13.6)	4,863
1927–28	3,673 (69.1)	850 (16.0)	795 (14.9)	5,318
1928–29	4,179 (66.9)	1,077 (17.3)	986 (15.8)	6,242
1929–30	2,621 (46.1)	1,555 (27.3)	1,512 (26.6)	5,688
1930–31	838 (34.9)	832 (34.7)	731 (30.4)	2,401
1931–32	4 (1.0)	162 (40.8)	231 (58.2)	397
1932–33	3 (0.8)	156 (42.9)	205 (56.3)	364
1933–34	11 (2.2)	232 (45.6)	266 (52.3)	509
1934–35	3 (0.8)	148 (40.9)	211 (58.3)	362
1935–36	10 (3.2)	121 (38.5)	183 (58.3)	314
1936–37	14 (4.1)	130 (38.4)	195 (57.5)	339
1937–38	42 6.5)	258 (39.9)	346 (53.6)	646
1938–39	52 (9.4)	234 (42.2)	268 (48.4)	554
1939–40	46 (14.0)	142 (43.2)	141 (42.8)	329
Totals	18,271 (56.3)	7,026 (21.7)	7,141 (22.0)	32,438

Sources: Compiled from data in Canada, Department of Immigration and Colonization, Annual Departmental Report, 1925–40.

Table A5
Religious composition of Hungarian immigrants to Canada, 1928–30

Religion	1928 (%)	1929 (%)	1930 (%)	Totals
Calvinist	957	941	489	2,387
	(20.6)	(19.4)	(19.7)	(19.9)
Greek Catholic	611	464	247	1,322
	(13.2)	(9.6)	(10.0)	(11.0)
Greek Orthodox	11	211	6	228
	(0.2)	(4.4)	(0.2)	(1.9)
Jewish	29	31	39	99
	(0.6)	(0.6)	(1.6)	(0.8)
Lutheran	239	295	157	691
	(5.1)	(6.1)	(6.3)	(5.8)
Roman Catholic	2,783	2,882	1,522	7,187
	(59.9)	(59.3)	(61.4)	(60.0)
Unitarian	0	2	0	2
	(0)	(0)	(0)	(0)
Other	19	31	19	69
	(0.4)	(0.6)	(0.8)	(0.6)
Totals	4,649	4,857	2,479	11,985
	(38.8)	(40.5)	(20.7)	(100.0)

Sources: Compiled from Hungary, Hungarian Bureau of Statistics, Annual Report, 1928–30.

Table A6
Hungarian immigration to Canada, 1920–40

Year	No. of immigrants
1920	23
1921	41
1922	26
1923	123
1924	1,107
1925	2,741
1926	5,182
1927	5,781
1928	6,265
1929	5,375
1930	3,279
1931	493
1932	311
1933	484
1934	427
1935	319
1936	320
1937	555
1938	596
1939	360
1940	77
Total	33,885

Source: Canada, Employment and Immigration Canada, Immigration Statistics Division, "Immigrants Admitted to Canada by Ethnic Group."

Table A7
Hungarians in urban centres in western Canada

City	1921	1931	1941
Calgary	14	688	631
Edmonton	55	119	237
Lethbridge	45	278	521
Regina	277	822	1,144
Saskatoon	41	328	257
Vancouver	25	227	550
Winnipeg	344	966	976
Totals	801	3,428	4,316

Sources: *Census of Canada*, 1921, 1931, 1941.

Table A8
Hungarians in Montreal and metropolitan areas in Ontario

City	1921	1931	1941
Montreal	67	3,541	3,457
Brantford	247	449	593
Galt	5	122	284
Guelph	0	127	196
Hamilton	200	2,651	2,575
Kitchener	0	402	466
Niagara Falls	6	339	451
Oshawa	0	236	351
St Catharines	14	185	225
Toronto	49	1,354	2,194
Welland (Crowland)	234	1,141	1,648
Windsor	86	1,078	1,858
Total	902	11,625	14,298

Sources: *Census of Canada*, 1921, 1931, 1941.

Notes

INTRODUCTION

1 The play appeared in *Hazafias Szinpad* (Patriotic Stage), published by the Hungarian National Federation in 1928.
2 János Exner, Welland Hungarian Self-Culture Society, to Baron Zsigmond Perényi, President of the Hungarian World Federation, 28 March 1930, Records of the Hungarian World Federation (Federation records), P 975, Ka 23, National Archives of Hungary (NAH), Budapest.
3 *Kanadai Magyar Munkás* (*Munkás*) (Hamilton and Toronto), 19 March 1931.
4 Unless otherwise indicated, "Hungarian" in this study refers to ethnic Hungarians (Magyars) from Hungary and the successor states – Czechoslovakia, Romania and Yugoslavia. Immigrants from Hungary also included a substantial number of German-speaking Danube Swabians. Generally, however, this group did not become part of Hungarian ethnic communities in Canada. For the ethnic composition of immigrants from Hungary see Table A1, in the Appendix.
5 Puskás, *Kivándorló magyarok*; Dreisziger et al., *Struggle and Hope.*
6 This problem is discussed with reference to the "new" social history in Fox Genovese and Genovese, "Political Crisis." The authors criticize this history for failing to consider that authority is deployed "through a myriad of tributaries that saturate the social terrain. Culture in all its manifestations, particularly language, standards of education, rituals of deference, patterns of urban space, celebrations of human values, religious practice, social form, all contribute to the plenitude of the authority enjoyed by the ruling class" (p. 216).

7 Barton, *Peasants and Strangers*; Yans-McLaughlin, *Family and Community*;
   Golab, *Immigrant Destinations*; Briggs, *An Italian Passage* and
   Alexander, "The Immigrant Church."
8 Banfield, *The Unheavenly City*, 65–8. Handlin, *The Uprooted.*
9 On this subject, see Higham, ed., *Ethnic Leadership.*
10 Bodnar, *Workers' World*, 63. See also his *Immigration and Industrialization.*
11 Yans-McLaughlin, *Family and Community*, 119, 121.
12 Briggs, *An Italian Passage*, 136, 162.
13 Barton, "Eastern and Southern Europeans".
14 See, for example, Bodnar, *The Transplanted*; Bukowczyk, *And My Children*;
   Gabaccia, *Militants and Migrants.*
15 Bodnar, *The Transplanted*, xvii.
16 Ibid., 47.
17 Avery, *Dangerous Foreigners*, 121 and passim.
18 Zucchi, *Italians in Toronto.*
19 This assumption of the political neutrality of nationalism permits Zucchi
   to observe in his conclusion: "political ideology was never an issue
   for the vast majority of the immigrants. Patriotism was." Ibid., 197.
20 Montgomery, "Nationalism." Some students of Finns in North America
   have also studied the impact of conflicting ideologies on this group.
   See, for example, Puotinen, *Finnish Radicals*, and Lindstrom-Best, "The
   Unbreachable Gulf." On political divisions among Ukrainians, see
   Martynowych, *Ukrainians*; Swyripa, *Wedded*; and Kuropas, *The Ukrainian
   Americans.* On political divisions among working-class Jews in
   Toronto, see Frager, *Sweatshop Strife.* These three studies appeared too
   late to be analysed for purposes of this introduction.
21 My estimate is based on figures – the most complete available to me –
   on membership in Hungarian associations in Montreal between 1939
   and 1944. During this period the members of Montreal's United Church
   (257 in 1940) and Roman Catholic (208 in 1941) congregations,
   the Hungaria Social Club (164), and Workers' club (86 in 1943) accounted for 21 per cent of the city's Hungarians (715 of 3,451).
   These were only four – albeit the largest – of Montreal's ten Hungarian
   associations. Moreover, while in 1941 approximately one-quarter of
   the city's Hungarians were under the age of 19, children were not always
   included in associational membership figures. United Church:
   Minutes, 21 January 1941, Records of the First Hungarian Reformed
   Church of Montreal, M-6481, National Archives (NA); Reports
   1940–41, MG 8, V 76, Vol. 3, NA. Roman Catholic: Records of Our Lady
   of Hungary Parish, Montreal. Hungaria: Minutes. Workers' Club:
   Puskás Collection, Multicultural History Society of Ontario (MHSO),
   Toronto.
     In Toronto, 147 Presbyterians and 262 Workers' club members alone
   accounted for 19 per cent of local Hungarians in 1944. Given as well

the Roman Catholic and the smaller Baptist, Lutheran, and United Church congregations and the Brantford Sick Benefit Society, participation in local associations would seem to have involved much more than one quarter of the population. In the same year, in Hamilton, the Workers' club and the Presbyterian church accounted for 27 per cent of the local Hungarian community.

22 Those few Hungarians who arrived between 1920 and 1923 must have come from the United States. See Table A6 in the Appendix to this book.

CHAPTER ONE

1 Interview with Imre Lénart, 10 November 1968, Karcsa, Hungary, Collection of Julianna Puskás (Puskás collection), MHSO.

2 Ibid.

3 Rácz, "Parasztok elvándorlása a faluból"; Puskás, *Emigration from Hungary*, 61.

4 Interview with Léna Váradi, 22 September 1968, Karcsa, Hungary, Collection of Julianna Puskás (Puskás collection), Budapest.

5 Thirring, "Hungarian Migration," 433.

6 Interview with Béla Vágó, September 1980, Toronto.

7 See Table A2 in the Appendix.

8 For the best recent discussion of the Hungarian peasantry between the world wars, see Gunst, *A paraszti társadalom*. The stratification of peasant society is discussed in chap. 1.

9 Figures compiled from Hungary, Hungarian Bureau of Statistics, *Annual Report*, 1928–30. See Table A2 in the Appendix.

10 Orosz, "A differenciálódás és kisajátitás," 118–19, 143.

11 Puskás, *Kivándorló magyarok az Egyesült Államokban*, 87.

12 Figure based on the 1910 census, reported by Gunst, *A paraszti társadalom* 13.

13 Orosz, "A differenciálódás és kisajátitás," 9–107.

14 Racz, *A paraszti migráció*, 90.

15 Puskás, *Emigration*, 11.

16 Ibid., 52.

17 On European intercontinental emigration, see Gould, "European Inter-Continental Emigration." For diffusion of the idea of transatlantic migration in Hungary specifically see Puskás, *Emigration*, 60, and "Process."

18 Berend and Ránki, *Magyarország gazdasága*, 18–19, and *Hungary*, 92–3.

19 Berend and Ránki, "Economic Problems," 92–3.

20 Berend and Ránki, *Magyarország gazdasága*, 36, 371; Berend and Ránki, *Hungary*, 126–7.

21 Berend and Ránki, *Magyarország gazdasága*, 371. Rothschild, *East Central Europe*, 156.

22 Held, "The Interwar Years," 217, 240–1; Berend and Ránki, *Hungary*, 126; Gunst, *A paraszti társadalom*, 31–2.

23 Berend and Ránki, *Hungary*, 126; Szabó, *A tardi helyzet*, 26–7; Puskás, "A földtulajdonosok és a földet bérlők társadalmi rétegeződésének módosulásai," 452–65.

24 Gunst, *A paraszti társadalom*, 31–2.

25 Held, "Some Aspects," 214–15; Incze and Petőcz, *A dolgozó parasztság helyzete az ellenforradalmi rendszerben*, 14; Weis, *A mai magyar társadalom*, 180.

26 Berend and Ránki, *Magyarország gazdasága*, 415.

27 Report to the Minister of Interior on the causes of emigration to Canada from Abaúj County, 21 October 1927, Records of the Ministry of Agriculture (Agriculture records), FM 1927-62-54.702, NAH.

28 For a discussion of calculations behind the decision to migrate see Morawska, *For Bread with Butter*, chap. 2.

29 Report by Detective Béla Rada, 10 March 1927, Agriculture records, FM 1927-62-54.709, NAH.

30 Berend and Ránki, *Magyarország gazdasága*, 408; Mitnitzky, "Economic and Social Effects," 474.

31 Interview with György Nóvák, n.d., Végárdó, Hungary, Puskás collection.

32 Berend and Ránki, *Magyarország gazdasága*, 371.

33 Ibid., 274, 348–50. Gunst, *A paraszti társadalom*, 21.

34 Eckstein, "Economic Development," 28.

35 Berend and Ránki, *Magyarország gazdasága*, 303.

36 *Szabadság* (Cleveland), 29 March 1926, 30 April 1928; *Új Előre* (New York), 2 April 1926.

37 Berend and Ránki, *Magyarország gazdasága*, 415.

38 Interview with Lőrincz Kovács, 3 March 1980, Welland.

39 Gunst, *A paraszti társadalom*. M. Mitnitzky writes in "Economic and Social Effects," 473: "Many Hungarian workers possess dwarf holdings, which are usually not even sufficiently large to keep the family supplied with vegetables, but the owners do not wish to give up their land or abandon the hope of becoming peasants at some future date. The attitude of mind of this rural proletariat is entirely agricultural, and their economic hopes find expression in terms of units of land rather than in terms of money."

40 Szabó, *Cifra nyomorúság*, 135.

41 Puskás, *Emigration*, 14.

42 Interview with I.L., Tape 33/2, Collection of Linda Degh and Andrew Vázsonyi, Folk Studies Centre, Museum of Civilization, Hull, Quebec (Degh-Vázsonyi collection).

43 For the scale of Hungarian immigration to Canada from the successor states, see Table A3 in the Appendix.

44 Interview with Steven H., Tape 51/1, Degh-Vázsonyi collection.

45 See, for example, Dreisziger et al., eds., *Struggle and Hope*, 44–6.

46 Degh, *People*, 235.

47 Interview with Sándor Zsadányi, March 1980, Caledonia, Ontario.

48 See Table A4 in the Appendix. A clear indication of the marital status of migrants may be obtained from the records of Alexander A. Kelen, the most successful Hungarian steamship agent in Canada during the interwar years. See Records of Kelen, Alexander A., Ltd., NA.

49 Bodnar, *The Transplanted*, 46–9; Barton, *Peasants and Strangers*, 64–9, Briggs, *An Italian Passage*, 15–36.

50 Balogh, "A paraszti művelödés," 487–565; Gyimesi, "A parasztság," 619–20, 628.

51 Gyimesi, "A parasztság," 647–8; Szabad, "A hitelviszonyok," 230.

52 Gyimesi, "A parasztság," 652. Gunst, *A paraszti társadalom*, 131.

53 Vörös, "The Age of Preparation"; Gyimesi, "A parasztság," 647.

54 See Records of the Prime Minister's Office (PM records), K 28 ME-1923-T4, NAH.

55 *A falu*, 15 July 1920, 29.

56 21 January 1925, *Nemzetgyülési Napló*, 181. Cited in Kiss, "Gazdakörök," 181.

57 "Zala megyei társadalmi, gazdasági szervek és sajtó ügyek," PM records, K 28 ME-1923-T-4-16369, NAH.

58 See above, 9.

59 Mihály Bajtay, *A Faluszövetség ismertetése*, 22. See also *A falu*, 15 September 1920, 66.

60 According to Tamás Hofer, the irony in the flowering of these folk arts was that they were recent and the result of the capitalist transformation of rural society. See Hofer, "Creation."

61 The concept of fakelore is used and discussed by Dorson, *Folklore and Fakelore*.

62 Galamb, *A magyar dráma története 1867-töl 1896-ig*.

63 Kodály, *Folk Music of Hungary*.

64 See, for example, *A falu*, 15 September 1920, 15 November 1920, and especially 20 December 1920, 1. Here Ottokár Prohászka contrasts the contentment of modest peasant homes with the palaces occupied by "Galicians" – that is, Jews – in Budapest. For a general discussion of Hungarian nationalism between the two world wars, see Barany, "Hungary."

65 See Barany, "Hungary," 288.

66 *A falu*, 6 June 1919, 1; 6 June 1928, 1.

67 *Műkedvelők szinműtára*, vi.

68 Kiss, "Gazdakörök," 189; Bodor, *Falusi egyletek*, 46.
69 Kiss, "Gazdakörök," 189. See also Gunst," A paraszti társadalom,"131; he believes that peasants were mistrustful of this organization precisely because it was imposed from above.
70 Gergely and Kiss, *Horthy leventéi*, 97 and passim.
71 For the religious composition of immigrants from Hungary, see Table A5 in the Appendix.
72 Fél and Hofer, *Proper Peasants*, 309.
73 Balogh, "A paraszti művelődés," 557.
74 Gyimesi, "A parasztság," 630.
75 Balogh, *A parasztság művelődése*, 84.
76 Reports by students, Manuscript collection, Sárospatak College of Theology, Sárospatak, Hungary.
77 Balogh, "A paraszti művelődés," 553–6. Mrs István Papp, "Adalékok az alföldi olvasókörök és népkönyvtárak történetéhez"; Hajdú, *Vásárhelyi egyletek és könyvtárak*; Fél and Hofer, *Proper Peasants*, 321, 357.
78 *Magyarország Története, 1890–1918*, 135–7. Veres, *Számadás*.
79 Kiss, "Gazdakörök," 181; Gunst, *A paraszti társadalom*, 129–30.
80 Student reports, Sárospatak.
81 Bodor, *Falusi egyletek*; *Országos Mezőgazdasági Cimtár*; Kiss, "Gazdakörök," 174–81; Weis, *A magyar falu*, 64.
82 Degré, "A községi képviselőtestület," 23–32; Gunst, *A paraszti társadalom*, 140.
83 Romsics, *Ellenforradalom és konszolidáció*, 166ff, 222, and *A Duna-Tisza köze hatalmi-politikai viszonyai*, 138–9.
84 Romsics, *A Duna-Tisza köze hatalmi-politikai viszonyai*.
85 Ibid., 32.
86 Ibid., 81–7.
87 See Table A2 in the Appendix.
88 Szabolcs, *Munka nélküli diplomások a Horthy-rendszerben*.
89 Mócsy, "Partition," 494–5.
90 John Kosa, "Immigration and Adjustment of Hungarians in Canada" (ms., c. 1955), cited in Dreisziger et al., eds., *Stuggle and Hope*, 101.
91 Rev. Charles Steinmetz to Rev. W.A. Cameron, 4 April 1940, Reverend Charles Steinmetz papers; MHSO; Vörös, *American Commissar. Kanadai Magyar Munkás (Munkás)* (Hamilton and Toronto), 29 June, 13 July 1933, 19 July 1934, 8 March 1935.
92 Berend and Ránki, *Magyarország gazdasága*, 402; see also their *Development*, 110.
93 Berend and Ránki, *Magyarország gazdasága*, 277–8; *Hungary*, 145; Weis, *A mai magyar társadalom*, 173.
94 Interviews with Alexander Birinyi, a cartwright from Cigánd, November 1976, Toronto; Joseph Süle and Helen Süle, small merchants from Orosháza, January 1977, Toronto.

95　Interview with Béla Vágó, September 1980, Toronto.

96　Interview with Sándor Birinyi, November 1976, Toronto.

97　Interview with Ernő B., Windsor, Tape 28, Degh-Vázsonyi collection.

98　*Az első világháború*, 472.

99　Memoirs of István Márkos, István Szőke papers, Puskás collection, Budapest. See also interview with J.N., Tape 36/2, Degh-Vázsonyi collection.

100　Information on this category of emigrants from Hungary is based largely on interviews and the memoirs of immigrants who were involved with the Hungarian left. These can be found in three collections in Budapest – the papers of István Szőke (editor of the *Munkás*), Puskás collection; the collection of memoirs of the World Federation of Hungarians, and Memoirs of Hungarians Communists Abroad, both in the Institute for Party History (IPH).

101　Sándor Greczula, Memoirs, Puskás collection, Budapest.

102　Recollections of Lajos Koszta, H-k-201, IPH.

103　Recollections of József Jenei, H-j-27, IPH; Memoirs, "Struggle for Life in Hungary and Canada," Szőke papers.

104　Hofer, "Creation"; Lackó, "Kulturális megújulás és népművészet."

105　Hofer, "Creation," 116.

106　Pálfi, "A gyöngyösbokréta története," 115–16.

107　Ibid., 116.

108　Balogh, *A parasztság művelődése*, 13–14.

109　For a discussion of the history of the Pearly Bouquet movement, see Pálfi, "A gyöngyösbokréta története," and Vally, "A gyöngyösbokréta indulása." The movement also had its own publications: a periodical, *Bokrétások Lapja*, and jubilee volumes.

110　Csaba Pálfi, "A gyöngyösbokréta története," 125.

CHAPTER TWO

1　*Magyarország története, 1890–1918*, vol. 7.1, 202.

2　Szászi, *Az Amerikába irányuló kivándorlás Szabolcs megyéből*, 101; Rácz, "Parasztok," 480. Interview with Mary Gabura, Toronto, 1977.

3　Interview with József Fejes, Bodony, Hungary, summer 1980. For a more general discussion, see Rácz, "Parasztok," 480.

4　Ortutay and Katona, eds., *Magyar népdalok*, vol. 2, 604, 606.

5　See, for example, ibid., 603.

6　Interview with Julianna Birinyi, Toronto, 1976.

7　Interview with Mary Gabura, Toronto, 1977.

8　Gunda, "America," 410.

9　See, for example, *Szabadság* (Cleveland), 16 September 1926, 14 January, 14 March 1927.

10　Report dated 12 September 1928 from Montreal Consul, Records of the Consulate General of Hungary, Montreal (Montreal consulate records), K 128, 1/4-15-cs., NAH; interview with J.S., January 1977, Toronto; Pál Stonk to World Federation of Hungarians, n.d., Records of the World Federation of Hungarians (Federation records), P 975, K 153, NAH; H.S. Kent to Van Scoy, 30 July 1929, CPR 830, Colonization Records of the Canadian Pacific Railway Company (CPR records), Glenbow Institute, Calgary.

11 Ortutay and Katona, eds., *Magyar népdalok*, vol. 2, 604.

12 Interview with Ferenc Magyar, August 1980, Ajak, Hungary.

13 See, for example, interview with Mrs J.D., Tape 49, Degh-Vázsonyi collection; Gunda, "America," 411.

14 Faragó, "A magyar kivándorlók Kanadában," 814; Rácz, *A paraszti migráció*, 200, 463; Kovacs, "Searching."

15 Szászi, *Az Amerikába*, 37.

16 On Hungarian migration to Saskatchewan, see Dreisziger et al., eds., *Struggle and Hope*, chap. 3.

17 See *Census of Canada*, 1921, vol. 1, 356–7; Bődy, "Travel Reports," 23; *Kanadai Magyarság* (Winnipeg), 1 May 1908, 30 April 1909, 16 October 1908.

18 See, for example, 8 *Órai Ujság*, 6 March 1924; *Pesti Napló*, 19 April 1925; *Magyarság*, 24 April 1926; *Köztelek*, 23 May 1926; *Nemzeti Ujság*, 4 December 1926; *Magyar Szövetkezés*, 26 February 1927; *Pesti Hírlap*, 8 March 1928; all in Press Archives, Records of the Ministry of Foreign Affairs, 1914–44, K608, 609, NAH. The ministry kept a file of reports that appeared in the Hungarian press on emigration and on conditions in the countries of immigration.

19 Géza Braun Belatin to Dr. Iván Rakovszky, 15 February 1926, Records of the Ministry of Foreign Affairs, Division in Charge of Hungarians Abroad (Hungarians Abroad), K 71, 1931-I/1, NAH.

20 Interview with István Szakszon, July 1980, Ajak, Hungary.

21 Report on the subject of irregularities experienced in connection with emigration to Canada, 29 January 1929, Minute book of the Hungarian Cabinet, in *Iratok az ellenforradalom történetéhez*, vol. 5, 299; John Farisz, an unemployed Hungarian immigrant, to J.S. Kent, Department of Colonization of the CPR, 23 July 1931, file 860, and István Schefbeck, Hungarian Consul in Winnipeg, to J.S. Kent, 24 March 1932, CP-860, CPR records, Glenbow.

22 John Farisz to R.H. Kent, 23 July 1931, CPR 8160, "Correspondence 1932," CPR records.

23 Interview with Steven H., Tape 51, Degh-Vázsonyi collection.

24 Report by Detective Béla Rada, 10 March 1927, Agriculture records, FM 1927-62-54.709, NAH.

25 Ibid.

26 Interview with Lőrincz Kovács, 3 March 1980, Welland.

27 Interview with András Kocsis, August 1980, Makkóshotyka, Hungary.

28 On Zágonyi's views, see Zágonyi, *Kanada,* and see a report of the talk given by Zágonyi to the Emigration Council, 4 December 1926, PM records, Division of Nationalities and Minorities, K 28 ME-1927-A, NAH. On his speaking tour in northeastern Hungary, see an account of   .
the content of his lecture and a letter from Zágonyi to local administrators in Szabolcs-Ung county, v.b. XII, 1927/180-7005/927, and directive of the alispán (head of county administration) to district magistrates and the Mayor of Nyíregyháza, March 1927, v.b. XIII/1927/1890/3417, Records of the alispán, Szabolcs-Szatmár County Archives, Nyíregyháza, Hungary.

29 Interview with András Kocsis, August 1980.

30 On the myth of "America" among Italian peasants, see Levi, *Christ Stopped at Eboli,* 120–32, and Bianco, *The Two Rosetos,* 34–70.

31 See Table A6 in the Appendix.

32 Béla Lipthay to J.S. McGowan, Records of the Canadian National Railways (CNR records), RG 30, vol. 5630, file 5142-1, NA; *Otthon* (Saskatoon), January 1925.

33 *Kanadai Magyar Ujság* (Winnipeg), 27 November 1926.

34 J. Colley to C.A. Van Scoy, 16 January 1928, CP-729, CPR records; *Minutes of the Proceedings and Evidence of the Select Standing Committee on Agriculture and Colonization,* 358.

35 Report by Consul General A. de Haydin, Montreal, Consulate records, K 128 I/4-cs.-15, NAH; Report on the subject of irregularities experienced in connection with emigration to Canada, 29 January 1929, Minute book of the Hungarian Cabinet, in *Iratok az ellenforradalom történetéhez,* vol. 5, 299.

36 Interview with George Palotás, July 1980, Szamosszeg, Hungary.

37 Interview with Lajos Biró, n.d., Montreal, Collection of Reverend Aladár Komjáthy.

38 See Avery, *Dangerous Foreigners,* for an excellent examination of the forces that shaped Canada's immigration policy between the wars. For a more detailed analysis of the impact of the Railway Agreement on Hungarian immigration, see Patrias, "Patriots and Proletarians", chap. 3.

39 Tóth, *23 év,* 104. See also Avery, *Dangerous Foreigners,* 102–3.

40 Report of Deputy Minister, W.J. Egan, Department of Immigration and Colonization, *Annual Report* 2 (1928–29), 5–9; Marsh, "Mobility," 24–5.

41 See the records of the Colonist's Service Association, CPR records. See also Patrias, "Patriots and Proletarians," chap. 3.

42 See above, chap. 1.

43 Interview with Ferenc Magyar, July 1980, Ajak, Hungary. See also Report by the Hungarian Consul in Winnipeg in Montreal consulate records, K 128 I/4-cs.-15, NAH.

44 *Kanadai Magyar Ujság,* 23 January 1926, 5 February 1927; Tóth, *23 év,* 88–9; Palmer and Palmer, "Hungarian Experience," 154, 170–3.

45 Report of Consul General Károly Winter, 3 May 1929, Montreal consulate records, K 128 I/4-15-cs., NAH.

46 Memoirs of Lajos Rózsa, handwritten manuscript (Rózsa memoirs), Collection of memoirs, World Federation of Hungarians, Budapest.

47 Interview with Ernő B., Tape 28, Degh-Vázsonyi collection; see also Tape 49.

48 Interview with Mary Polyoka, 26 February 1980, Hamilton.

49 Rózsa memoirs.

50 Interview with István Szakszon, July 1980, Ajak, Hungary.

51 Interview with Alex Kelen, September 1980, Montreal; Report from Lajos Vaczek, Consular Official, Hungarian Consulate General, Montreal, 6 March 1930, Hungarians Abroad, K 71 1931-1/1-20630, NAH.

52 Mackintosh, *Economic Background,* 97–8. For Hungarian settlement in cities in western and in central Canada, see Tables A7 and A8 in the Appendix.

53 Interview with Sándor Egyed, June 1982, Niagara Falls, Puskás collection, Toronto.

54 Tóth, *23 év,* 153.

55 Interview with János Ragány, July 1980, Ajak, Hungary; Tóth, *23 év,* 152–3.

56 Interview with "uncle" Mátyás, June 1980, Bodony, Hungary.

57 Interviews with M.B., November 1986, Welland, and with Alex Kelen, September 1980, Montreal.

58 Interview with Lőrincz Kovács, 3 March 1980, Welland. *Munkás,* 5 March 1931.

59 Interview with Steven H., Tape 51, Degh-Vázsonyi collection.

60 Interviews with Wilma Lőrincz, Hamilton, June 1982, Puskás collection, Toronto, and Sándor G., Tape 30, Degh-Vázsonyi collection.

61 Tóth, *23 év,* 153.

62 Interviews with Mary Gabura, 31 January 1977, Toronto, and with Béla Vágó, November 1976, Toronto.

63 Interviews with József Magyar, July 1980, Ajak, Hungary, and with Sándor Megyesi, August 1980, Budapest.

64 *Munkás,* 10 December 1931.

65 Interview with Sándor G., Tape 30, Degh-Vázsonyi collection. See also interview with L. Szabó, Puskás collection, MHSO.

66 Interview with Ferenc B., Tape 40, Degh-Vázsonyi collection.

67 Interview with George G., Tape 60, ibid.

68 Interview with Mary Polyoka, 26 February 1980, Hamilton.
69 Figures from Canada, Department of Immigration and Colonization, *Annual Report*, various years.
70 Report on the migration of women domestics to Western Canada, 28 May 1930, Winnipeg consulate records, K 139 1930-2320, NAH.
71 Interviews with Mary Gabura, January 1977 and January 1980, Toronto, and Ilona Kósa, July 1980, Szamosszeg, Hungary.
72 Cited in Voros, "The Hungarian Ethnic Group," 49.
73 Interviews with István Takács and József Magyar, July 1980, Ajak, Hungary, and John Sipos, 4 March 1980, Hamilton.
74 Interview with Mary Gabura, January 1977, Toronto.
75 Interviews with Helen Czukár, March 1980, Hamilton; Mary Polyoka, 26 February 1980, Hamilton; Helen Süle, 9 December 1976, Toronto; Vilma Lőrincz, 11 June 1982, Hamilton; Erzsébet C., October 1982, Windsor; and Sándor Medgyesi, August 1980, Budapest; István Márkos, Memoirs, Szőke papers, Puskás collection, Budapest.
76 Interview with Sándor Gál, Delhi Project, MHSO.
77 Degh, *People*, xv–xvii and passim. *A dohányvidéki*, 16; *Kanadai Magyar Ujság*, 14 April 1932, 7 September 1933, 8 August 1939.
78 *Buffalói Híradó* (Buffalo Herald), 2 July 1921; Reverend Ferenc Kovács to Nicholas Istvánffy, 9 November 1928, Records of the Canadian Hungarian Association (CHA records), MG 28, V65, vol. 3, file 44, NA. Interviews with Helen Czukár, March 1980, Hamilton; Steven Gérus, March 1980, Hamilton; and Mr. Kemény, June 1982, Puskás collection, MHSO. Hoó, *Tiszakerecsenytöl Kanadáig*, 328–30, 337–54.
79 Interview with Mrs Béla H., Tape 34, Degh-Vázsonyi collection.
80 See, for example, Jenő Horváth, a miner in Timmins, to Canadian Hungarian Federation, 6 January 1931, CHA records, MG 28, V65, vol. 5, file 72, NA.
81 Report dated 6 March 1930, Hungarians Abroad, K 71 1931-I/1-20630, NAH.
82 See, for example, *Egyetértés* (Montreal), 20 June, 27 June 1931.
83 *Census of Canada*, 1931, 1941.
84 *A Montreal Magyar*, 52–3. Undated clipping based on account of Mrs Beatrice Steinmetz, wife of the Hungarian Presbyterian minister in Toronto, in Reverend Charles Steinmetz papers, MHSO.
85 *Munkás*, 15 December 1932.
86 Interview with Erzsébet C., October 1982, Windsor.
87 Report of Consul General Károly Winter, 11 July 1930, Hungarians Abroad, K 71, I/1-21735/30, NAH.
88 Interview with Steven H., Tape 51, Degh-Vázsonyi collection.
89 Letter from Port Colborne to *Munkás*, 23 February 1933.
90 Interview with József Jáger, 14 February 1981, Toronto.

91 *Munkás*, 3 March 1933.
92 Barna Hegedűs to Hungarian World Federation, 15 March 1934, Federation papers, P 965, Ka 44, NAH.
93 Sándor Hajas to József Hajas, n.d., Records of the Ministry of the Interior (Interior records), 651f2/1933-6047, IPH. Hajas's letters home were intercepted by postal officials because he belonged to the proletarian camp. The ministry kept a file on him.
94 *Ujság*, 31 July 1931.
95 Clipping dated 11 July 1932, source not identified, Steinmetz papers.
96 *Egyetértés*, 11 July 1931.
97 Interview with Mrs B.H., Tape 34/2, Degh-Vázsonyi collection.
98 Rózsa memoirs.
99 Ibid.

CHAPTER THREE

1 Interview with Margaret Wappel, 17 January 1977, Toronto.
2 For a thorough and concise discussion of ethnic neighbourhoods, see Conzen, "Immigrants."
3 Calculations based on data in *Census of Canada*, 1921, 1931, 1941.
4 Paizs, *Magyarok Kanadában*, 199–200; Bődy, "Travel Reports"; *Buffalói Híradó*, 25 December, 18 September 1920, 2 July 1921. The census of 1911 lists 355 Hungarians in Hamilton; that of 1921, 200.
5 See Tables A7 and A8 in the Appendix.
6 *Census of Canada*, 1921, 1931.
7 Canada, Dominion Bureau of Statistics, *Racial Origins and Nativity*.
8 Vecoli, "Contadini," 406–7.
9 Alexander, "The Immigrant Church," 149ff.
10 Harney, "Toronto's Little Italy"; Zucchi, *Italian Immigrants*.
11 *Kanadai Magyar Hírlap* (*Hírlap*) (Welland and Toronto), 24 July 1928; *Kanadai Magyar Ujság* (Winnipeg), 19 December 1925, 19 July 1929, 11 July 1944.
12 Interview with E.S.B., Tape 28/1, Degh-Vázsonyi collection.
13 *Hírlap*, 14 December 1928.
14 Interview with József Jáger, 13 September 1978, MHSO.
15 Smith, "Religion," 1171.
16 Records of the First Magyar Reformed Church of Montreal (Montreal Reformed records), MG 8, G76, NA; Records of Kelen, Alexander A., Ltd, MG 8 V52, NA.
17 Unfortunately, suitable records for this purpose are no more plentiful than sources for the study of regionalism and neighbourhood patterns. Roman Catholic parish records for the period are closed to researchers, while Protestant ministers did not always note the village origins of the couples whom they married.

18 Records of the First Hungarian Presbyterian Church of Toronto, Marriage Register 1937–78, MHSO.
19 Records of the John Calvin Hungarian Presbyterian Church, Hamilton, Register, MHSO; Montreal Reformed records, MG 8, G76, NA.
20 Degh, *Folktale*, 3–11.
21 István Vörös to Baron Zsigmond Perényi, n.d., Records of the Hungarian World Federation (Federation records), P 975, K 137, NAH.
22 Memoirs of István Márkos, Puskás collection, Budapest.
23 Interview with József N., Tape 39/1, Degh-Vázsonyi collection.
24 There have been remarkably few studies of these multi-ethnic neighbourhoods in Canada, and the ones that do exist concentrate on the last few decades. See, for example, Polèse, Hamle, and Bailly, *La géographie résidentielle*. For Toronto, see Richmond, *Ethnic Residential Segregation*. I have recently examined the immigrant quarter of Crowland, Ontario, during the Depression in *Relief Strike*.
25 Interview with Léna Váradi, 22 September 1968, Karcsa, Hungary, Puskás collection, Budapest. Interview with Mrs M.B., Tape 36, Degh-Vázsonyi collection. For a more general treatment, see Harney, "Ethnicity and Neighbourhoods."
26 Cited in Voros, "The Hungarian Ethnic Group," 162.
27 See Degh, *People*.
28 See Vázsonyi, "The Star Boarder."
29 Interviews with József Máté, September 1982, Montreal, and József Jáger, 14 February 1981, Toronto. On the institution, see Harney, "Boarding and Belonging."
30 Joseph Blaskó, Memoirs, Collection of Memoirs, World Federation of Hungarians, Budapest.
31 Interview with Mary Gabura, 31 January 1980, Toronto.
32 They received $25 to $28 a month from each boarder; full-time employment in industry would have earned them an average of $80 a month. *Wages and Hours of Labour in Canada, 1920 to 1930*, Report No. 14 (Ottawa: Department of Labour, 1930).
33 Interview with Gusztáv Lőrincz, 11 June 1982, Hamilton; *Kanadai Magyar Hirlap*, 28 May 1929; *Kanadai Magyar Ujság*, 17 April 1930.
34 Interview with Sándor G., Tape 30, Degh-Vázsonyi collection.
35 Interview with Ferenc Magyar, July 1980, Ajak, Hungary.
36 Interview with Stephen Bornemissza, 25 November 1986, Welland.
37 Interviews with István Szakszon, July 1980, Ajak, Hungary, and Steven H., Tape 51, Degh-Vázsonyi collection.
38 Interview with Mary Gabura, January 1977, Toronto.
39 Interview with Stephen Bornemissza, 25 November 1986, Welland.
40 Interview with József Gaál, September 1982, Montreal.
41 Interview with György Nóvák, n.d., Végardó, Hungary, Puskás collection, Budapest.

42 Blaskó, Memoirs.
43 See Vázsonyi, "The Star-Boarder."
44 Interview with István Szakszon, July 1980, Ajak, Hungary.
45 Report by Consul General Károly Winter, 11 July 1930, Hungarians Abroad, K 71 I/1-1929, NAH.
46 Voros, "The Hungarian Ethnic Group," 106–7.
47 Report by Consul General Károly Winter, 11 July 1930, Hungarians Abroad, K 71 I/1-1929, NAH; interview with Helen Süle, 9 December 1977, Toronto.
48 Interview with Helen Süle, 9 December 1977, Toronto.
49 Interviews with György Nóvák, Végárdó, Hungary, Puskás collection, Budapest; Mrs A.B., Tape 36, Degh-Vázsonyi collection; Margaret Wappel, 17 January 1977, Toronto.
50 Interviews with Alex Kelen, September 1980, Montreal, and Mr and Mrs Moos, 16 March 1980, Toronto.
51 Eisner Papers, N.F. Dreisziger Collection, Kingston, Ontario.
52 Interview with Alex Kelen, September 1980, Montreal.
53 N. Istvánffy to V. Subosits, n.d., and Istvánffy to D. Demetrovits, CHA records, MG 28, V65, vol. 5, file 81, NA; *Canadai Magyar Farmer* (Winnipeg), 15 May 1915; *Buffalói Híradó*, 26 February 1921; *Kanadai Magyar Ujság*, 13 November 1926.
54 *Canadai Kis Ujság* (Welland), 23 January 1936.
55 Interview with Henry Moos, 16 March 1980, Toronto.
56 Interview with Alex Kelen, September 1980, Montreal.
57 Ibid.
58 The most shocking case for the community was that of István Jánossy, see *Híradó* (Toronto and Hamilton), 26 April 1937; *Canadai Kis Ujság*, 26 April 1937.
59 Minutes, Records of the Windsor and District Hungarian Club (Windsor club records), Windsor, 15 May 1938, 5 January 1941, 9 January 1944. In 1982 one of the founders still spoke with pride of the ousting of Jewish members. Interview with J.H., October 1982, Windsor. Somewhat earlier anti-semitic attacks were also directed against Joseph Schwartz, a very successful steamship agent in Calgary. J. Colley to C.A. Van Scoy, 23 January 1928, CP-731, CPR records.
60 Park, *The Immigrant Press*, 7.
61 McLaren, *Ontario Ethno-Cultural Newspapers, 1835–1972*.
62 CHA records, MG 28, V65, vol. 6, file 89, NA; *Kanadai Magyar Ujság*, 21 August, 16 October 1926.

CHAPTER FOUR

1 On the role of voluntary associations in other immigrant and ethnic groups, see Barton, *Peasants and Strangers*, 64–90; Briggs, *An Italian*

Passage, 138–63; *Records of Ethnic Fraternal Benefit Associations*; Bodnar, *The Transplanted*, 120–38.

2 Ruzsa, *A kanadai magyarság története*, 372.

3 *Híradó*, 25 July 1936.

4 Interviews with Helen Czukár, March 1982, Hamilton; József Jáger, 14 February 1980, Toronto; Mr Kemény, June 1982, Puskás collection, MHSO.

5 Interview with József Jáger, 13 September 1978, Toronto, MHSO.

6 Incorporation papers, 25 August 1927, 02-85-85, Ministry of Consumer and Corporate Affairs (MCCA), Toronto.

7 Incorporation papers, 4 November 1926, 02-67-75, MCCA.

8 *Kanadai Magyar Ujság*, 12 January 1929; Dezső Andrássy to Nicholas Istvánffy, 13 March 1929, CHA records, MG 28, V65, vol. 5, file 107, NA.

9 Ruzsa, *A kanadai magyarság története*, 177, 195; Ledger, Records of the Brantford Hungarian Sick Benefit Society, Toronto chapter, MHSO.

10 István Jánossy to Károly Nagy, Director of Permanent Bureau of the World Congress of Hungarians, 28 December 1936, Federation records, P 975, Ka 4, NAH.

11 Incorporation papers, 7 March 1924, 02-34-67, MCCA; *Ujság*, 23 January 1926; Minute Books, Records of the Welland Hungarian Self-Culture Society (Welland society), MHSO; Ruzsa, *A kanadai magyarság története*, 254.

12 Interview with József Havrán, October 1982, Windsor; Letters Patent, 28 August 1928, Windsor club records; *Windsor and District Hungarian Society, Golden Anniversary Publication*, 2.

13 Minutes, 11 December, 26 December 1926. Charter, 10 December 1927, Records of the Hungaria Social Club (Hungaria), Montreal; *Kanadai Magyar Ujság*, 26 February 1927.

14 *Ujság*, 12 February 1932; interview with József Kovács, September 1982, Montreal.

15 By-laws, I(2) and II(1), Székely Kultur Egylet (Székely Club).

16 Interview with József Kovács.

17 Ibid.

18 *Ujság*, 30 June 1932.

19 *Kanadai Magyar Munkás*, 17 December 1931.

20 Hungary's first anti-Jewish law, restricting the number of Jewish students at Hungarian universities, was passed in 1920.

21 Ruzsa, *A kanadai magyarság története*, 311.

22 See above, chap. 3 note 59.

23 Béla Eisner to Rev. Eugene Molnár, 13 August 1942, Eisner Papers, N.F. Dreisziger Collection, Kingston.

24 Blaskó, Memoirs, 5–6.

25 *Ujság*, 16 January 1926.

26 *Új Előre*, 26 August 1927.
27 Constitution and By-laws of the Brantford Sick Benefit Society, 02-67-75, MCCA.
28 Interview with József Havrán; *Ujság*, 18 July 1939.
29 By-laws of the Welland society (1940), vol. 3, 3, Géza Kertész papers, MHSO.
30 John Exner to Baron Zsigmond Perényi, n.d., Federation records, P 975, Ka 9, NAH; By-laws, vol. 4, 9, and Minutes, 5 May 1929, Welland society.
31 Minutes, 19 January 1928, Hungaria.
32 Note from Women's Group of Székely Club, n.d., Federation records, P 975, Ka 53, NAH.
33 Minutes, 2 December 1927, Hungaria.
34 See, for example, ibid., 30 January 1931.
35 See the discussion of the Windsor club and of Béla Eisner in this chapter, above.
36 *Ujság*, 11 February 1932.
37 See, for example, Minutes, 2 February 1930, Hungaria.
38 Minutes, 6 December 1936, 6 February 1938, Windsor club.
39 Minute Book, Notes for January 1926, Welland society.
40 Ibid., 6 January 1924.
41 Charter, 10 December 1927, Hungaria. Report on Hungaria Club, n.d., CHA records, MG 28, V65, vol. 2, file 21, NA.
42 *Ujság*, 4 May 1934.
43 Charter, 28 August 1928, Windsor club.
44 Minutes, 5 September 1937, Windsor club.
45 *Ujság*, 16 January 1940.
46 Minutes, 8 March 1938, Hungaria.
47 Interviews with József Kovács, September 1982, Montreal, and Mrs Biró, Montreal, Collection of Rev. Aladár Komjáthy (Komjáthy collection), Montreal.
48 Interview with Margaret Wappel, Toronto.
49 Minutes, 3 May 1940, Windsor club.
50 András Zsidor to Hungarian World Federation, 3 January 1937. Federation records, P 975, Ka 112, NAH.
51 Lajos Szabó to President of Hungarian World Congress, 11 February 1932, Records of the World Federation of Hungarians, P 975, Ka 9, NAH.
52 Incorporation papers, 7 March 1924, 02-34-60, MCCA.
53 Incorporation papers, 24 November 1936, 04-25-77, MCCA; By-laws, Records of the Oshawa Hungarian Cultural Club, 1935–55, MHSO.
54 Minutes, 21 March 1930, 31 August 1938, Hungaria; Minutes, 5 January 1936, Windsor club; Minutes, 8 October 1939, Székely club.

55 For example, By-laws, vol. 5, 1, Welland society; Minutes, 24 March 1924, Welland society, By-laws, vol. 4, 7, Székely club.

56 Information compiled from membership figures for the Welland society, Géza Kertész papers, MHSO and from *Canadai Kis Ujság* (Welland), 5 December 1935.

57 Puskás, *Kivándorló magyarok*, 228.

58 See, for example, Minutes, 21 March 1930, Hungaria; Minutes, 1 March 1940, Windsor club.

59 Interview with József Kovács, Montreal, 1980.

CHAPTER FIVE

1 *Hírlap*, 16 November 1928.

2 Father Biró to the Most Reverend Fergus P. McEvay, 7 December 1908, Archbishop McNeil papers, Archdiocesan Archives of Toronto (AAT).

3 See, for example, Desiderius Nagy, Pastor, Holy Cross Roman Catholic Church, Detroit, Michigan, to Archbishop McNeil, 26 August 1927, McNeil papers, AAT.

4 Reverend Bonaventura Peéri, Rector, St. Stephen's Hungarian Church, New York, to Archbishop McNeil, 23 May 1923, McNeil papers, AAT.

5 *Catholic Register*, 7 January 1927. See also ibid., 30 August, 8 October 1925, 11 April 1928, and Columba Danny, Mount Carmel College Niagara Falls, to Reverend M.J. Nealon, 11 April 1934, McNeil papers, AAT.

6 Albert de Haydin to Archbishop McNeil, 10 July 1926, McNeil papers, AAT.

7 Father Barron to Reverend T.J. Manley, Chancellor of Archdiocese of Toronto, 10 June 1926, McNeil Papers, AAT.

8 Father Lipót Mosonyi to Archbishop McNeil, 5 July 1927, McNeil papers, AAT.

9 Father Nyiri to Archbishop McNeil, 11 August 1927, McNeil papers, AAT.

10 *Hírlap*, 16 November 1928.

11 Father Nyiri to Archbishop McNeil, 8 June and 5 July 1928, McNeil Papers, AAT.

12 *Szabadság* (Cleveland), 14 January 1928.

13 *Hírlap*, 11 September 1928. *Ujság*, 7 December 1929. Ruzsa, *A kanadai magyarság*, 154–61.

14 *Ujság*, 4 December 1926.

15 Records of Our Lady of Hungary Roman Catholic Church, (Our Lady records), Montreal.

16 *Magyarok Nagyasszonya Egyházközség, 1928–1978*; Ruzsa, *A kanadai magyarság*, 301.

17 Ruzsa, *A kanadai magyarság*, 302; *A Kanadai Magyar Ujság és Védő Iroda képes nagy naptára as 1926 évre*, 128; Recollections of Sister Mary, Our Lady records; Sister Ida Horváth to Baron Zsigmond Perényi, 11 June 1930, Federation records, P 975, Ka 23, and Sister Mary to Károly Nagy, 5 August 1934, Federation records, P 975, Ka 63, NAH. On relations with the Hungarian government and work towards revision of Trianon, see Vice Consul Domonkos Szent Iványi to Hungarian Ministry of Foreign Affairs, Report on Social Sisters Association, 26 February 1930, Hungarians Abroad, K 71, I/1, 20793, NAH; Margit Slachta to Permanent Bureau of the Hungarian World Congress, 3 December 1929, Hungarians Abroad, K 71 I/1-22220, NAH; *Ujság*, 6 March 1926.

18 *Ujság*, 12 September 1925, 6 February 1926.

19 Minutes, Presbytery of Hamilton of the Presbyterian Church in Canada (Hamilton Presbytery), 21 June, 3 November 1925, Archives of the Presbyterian Church of Canada, Toronto (APC).

20 *Acts and Proceedings of the General Assembly of the Presbyterian Church of Canada (APPCC)* (1937), 27.

21 *Ujság*, 1 May 1926.

22 *Amerikai magyar református árvaházi és aggmenházi naptár*, 104–7.

23 Ibid.; *Hiradó*, 6 February 1937. APPCC (1960), 590.

24 Interview with Beatrice Steinmetz (née Bernath), 27 February 1980, Toronto.

25 Hamilton Presbytery, 26 April, 3 May, 15 September 1927, 6 March 1928, APC; Minutes of the Presbytery of Toronto, 6 March 1928, APC.

26 Hamilton Presbytery, 26 April, 3 May, 15 September 1927, 6 March 1928, APC.

27 Report by Frank Kovács, n.d., AR.-7.5, Hung., APC.

28 *A Ligonieri Bethlen Otthon naptára*, 100–2.

29 Béla Bucsin to Nicholas Istvánffy, 29 May 1928, CHA records, MG 28, V65, vol. 2, file 31, NA.

30 Interview with Reverend Charles Steinmetz, 28 March 1979, Campbellford, Ontario.

31 *A Montreali Magyar*, 27.

32 Ibid., 17.

33 Reverend Colin Young, Associate Secretary of the United Church of Canada's Board of Home Missions to Reverend Forster, 23 June 1926, Reverend H.G. Forster personal papers, United Church Archives (UCA), Toronto.

34 Reverend Colin Young to Rev. H.G. Forster, 2 September 1926, 29 November 1927; John L. Papp to Rev. Forster, 20 October 1927, Forster papers, UCA.

35 *Otthon*, (Saskatoon), March 1925; Minutes of the Hamilton Conference of the United Church, 1965.

36 Ambrosius Czakó papers, Collection of Erzsébet Vezér, Budapest.
37 Report by J.I. McKay on the non–Anglo-Saxon work, 1928, Records of the Board of Home Missions, 1930–31, UCA.
38 *A magyar ágostai hitvallású evangélikusok emlékalbuma*, 2–3.
39 Ruzsa, *A kanadai magyarság*, 168.
40 Viczián, "Background," 23–4.
41 Interviews with Reverend Charles Steinmetz, 28 March 1977, and with Mrs Werle, 10 May 1977, Toronto.
42 Reverend Charles Steinmetz described how his parents, who became Baptists in the United States because they were disillusioned with the Hungarian Reformed Church, employed proselytizing techniques that they learned in the United States to convert Hungarians in Bihar county, Transylvania. They took back a suitcase full of musical instruments to help them with the task.
43 Ruzsa, *A kanadai magyarság*, 334. Baptists from Bekevar who moved to Welland were apparently also instrumental in the establishment of the Baptist congregation there.
44 *Ujság*, 6 February, 17 April, 12 June 1926, 19 November 1927.
45 Annual Report, 1938, All People's Mission, Niagara Presbytery, Foster papers, UCA.
46 Recollections of Péter Libas and György Nóvák, Puskás collection, Budapest.
47 Minutes of the Toronto Presbytery, 5 January 1937, APC.
48 Josef Barton, for example, shows that clergy were responsible for setting up US Slovak associations, yet he believes that "crucial to the understanding of ethnic culture is that it was the possession of agricultural labourers, peasants and artisans." *Peasants and Strangers*, 157.
49 Interview with Father László Forgách, 25 August 1978, Toronto.
50 Ibid.
51 Ibid.
52 *Református Hiradó*, May 1929. *A Montreáli Magyar*, 53; *APPCC* (1941), 26; interview with Imre Csatlós, Karos, Hungary, n.d., Puskás collection, Budapest.
53 Interview with Mary Gabura, 31 January 1977, Toronto.
54 Interview with Mrs A.B., Tape 36/2, Degh-Vázsonyi collection.
55 Recollections of Sister Mary, Our Lady records, Montreal.
56 *Hírlap*, 28 December 1928.
57 Fehér to A.G. Howell, Chairman of the Church of All Nations Committee, 25 February 1930, Correspondence, 1926, 1928–30, Records of the First Hungarian Reformed Church of Montreal (Montreal First Reformed records), MG 8, G76, vol. 1, NA.
58 Interview with Léna Váradi, 22 September 1968, Karcsa, Hungary, Puskás collection, Budapest.

59 Ambrosius Czakó, "A Kind of Autobiography," unpublished manuscript, Ambrosius Czakó papers, Collection of Erzsébet Vezér, Budapest.

60 Father Szöllősy, Minutes of the Montreali Magyar Római Katholikus Társas Egylet (Hungarian Roman Catholic Social Club of Montreal), Montreal, 17 February 1936. Reverend Fehér, Minutes, 15 January, 8 July 1928, 5 May 1940, 16 May 1943, Montreal First Reformed records, M-6481, NA. Ujság, 10 April 1945.

61 Father Rácz to Károly Nagy, Director of the Permanent Bureau of the World Congress of Hungarians, 22 July 1930, Federation records, P 975, Ka 22, NAH; Ujság, 26 June 1930.

62 Report by Károly Winter, Hungarian Consul General, 30 March 1930, Hungarians Abroad, K 71 1932-1/6-21334,NAH.

63 Recollections of Sister Mary, Our Lady records, Montreal. Magyarok Nagyasszonya Egyházközség, 1928–1978.

64 Report on the remigration movement from Canada, Consul General Károly Winter, 27 November 1930, Hungarians Abroad, K 71 I/1-1929, 20370, NAH.

65 Ujság, 24 November 1932.

66 Minutes, 1 February 1931, Montreal First Reformed records, NA.

67 Hírlap, 14 May 1929.

68 Minutes of the Church Council, 13 December 1930, Records of the First Hungarian Presbyterian Church of Toronto, MHSO. Reverend Kovács subsequently resumed pastoral work and was apparently able to form a more harmonious relationship with his congregation. See Minutes of the Hamilton Presbytery, 7 March 1939, APC.

69 Interview with Reverend Charles Steinmetz, 28 March 1978, Campbellford, Ontario.

70 APPCC, (1934), 18.

71 General Report on the Hungarian Church in Montreal to the Montreal Presbytery, 25 September 1929, Reports 1929–30, Montreal First Reformed records, MG 8, G76, vol. 1, NA.

72 Report by Reverend Frank Kovács on Hamilton, APPCC (1932), 25. Interview with Mrs Beatrice Steinmetz, 1980. Our Lady records, Montreal.

73 APPCC (1930), 35–6.

74 Hírlap, 7 December 1928.

75 APPCC, (1930), 36–8.

76 Farkas to Reverend Michael Fehér, 22 March 1930, Fehér Correspondence 1926, 1928–30, Montreal First Reformed records, MG 8, G76, vol. 1, NA.

77 Reverend W.A. Cameron, Secretary of the General Board of Missions, to Reverend Charles Steinmetz, 1 April 1941, Steinmetz papers, MHSO.

78 Sister Mary to Károly Nagy, 8 April 1935, Federation records, P 975, Ka 63, NAH.
79 Report on Hungarian Work in the Hamilton Presbytery, n.d., AR, vol. 7, 5, APC.
80 Memoirs of Joseph Blaskó, unpublished manuscript, Collection of memoirs, World Federation of Hungarians, Budapest.
81 Interview with Margaret Wappel, 17 January 1977, Toronto.
82 Rev. Fehér to Father Pál Sántha, 6 October 1932, Fehér Correspondence, Montreal First Reformed records, MG 8, G 76, vol. 1, NA.
83 Reverend Charles Steinmetz to Reverend W.A. Cameron, 13 September 1940, Steinmetz papers, MHSO.
84 Sister Mary to Károly Nagy, 5 August 1934, Federation records, P 975, Ka 63, NAH.
85 Interview with Imre S., Windsor, Tape 33, Degh-Vázsonyi collection.
86 APPCC (1933), 22.
87 Accounts, Records of the First Hungarian Presbyterian Church of Toronto, MHSO.
88 "Report on Welland, Ontario," Reverend C. Steinmetz, n.d., Steinmetz papers, MHSO; A Montreáli Magyar, 67.
89 Hamilton Presbytery, 20 February 1936, APC. APPCC (1937), 27. Amerikai magyar református árvaházi és aggmenházi naptár, 107.
90 Reverend János László Papp, in Hírlap, 13 June 1936.
91 Reverend Fehér to his father, 18 January 1937, Correspondence 1937–39, Montreal First Reformed records, MG 8, G76, vol. 1, NA.
92 Fehér to Mrs. Maxwell Loveys, Executive Secretary of the Women's Missionary Society, 11 February 1943, Correspondence, E. Bagossy, Montreal First Reformed records, MG 8, G76, vol. 1, NA.
93 Magyarok Nagyasszonya Egyházközség, 6.
94 Recollections of Sister Mary, Our Lady records, Montreal.
95 Report by Rev. M. Fehér, Képes nagy naptár (Winnipeg: Kanadai Magyar Ujság, 1930), 300; Minutes, 25 March 1934, Montreal First Reformed records, M-6481, NA, and Report, 25 March 1934, Montreal First Reformed records, MG 8, G76, vol. 3, NA; Ujság, 19 July 1925; Otthon, April 1926.
96 Ujság, 20 June, 11 August 1939.
97 A Montreáli Magyar, 36.
98 Sister Mary to Károly Nagy, 22 November 1935, Federation papers, P 975, Ka 63, NAH.
99 Interview with József Jáger, 13 September 1978, MHSO.
100 Catholic Register, 30 August, 8 October, 29 October 1925, 11 April 1928. J. Kidd, Bishop of Calgary to Archbishop McNeil, 8 January 1927, McNeil papers, AAT.
101 See note 17 of this chapter.

102 *APPCC* (1937), 26. Toronto Presbytery, 16 February 1933, APC.
103 See, for example, Hamilton Presbytery, Presbyterian Church of Canada (PCC), 5 May 1931; *APPCC* (1922), 9.
104 Foster, *Our Canadian Mosaic*, 135.
105 An outline of the speech appeared, in English, in *Otthon*, April 1930.
106 Rev. Harvey Forster to L. Vaczek, Hungarian consular official, Montreal, Montreal consulate, records, K 128 I/7367/2162, NAH.
107 Eighth Annual Report by Reverend Michael Fehér, 1934, Reports, Montreal First Reformed records, MG 8, G76, vol. 1, NA.
108 Reverend J. MacKay, "The Church's Responsibility for the Integration of Non-Anglo-Saxon People," Robertson Memorial Lecture, Records of the General Council, R6, Box 5, 1957, UCA.
109 Charles Steinmetz to Károly Winter, 23 March 1939, Montreal consulate records, K 128 I/4-16-cs., NAH. See also Report by Rev. F. Kovács, Hamilton Presbytery, 3 July 1928, *APPCC* (1928), 873–4.
110 Hamilton Presbytery, 27 June 1933, APC. For the great esteem for Reverend Kovács, see *Hamilton Herald*, 6 June 1930.
111 Fehér to Mrs. Maxwell Loveys, 11 February 1943, Correspondence, E. Bagossy, Montreal First Reformed records, MG 8, G76, vol 1, NA.
112 Minutes, 25 March 1934, Reports 1934–35, ibid.

CHAPTER SIX

1 Report by Consul General Albert de Haydin, 28 December 1926, PM records, K 28 ME-1927-T34, NAH.
2 Note, 30 May 1922, attached to translation of a Hungarian circular re Office for the Protection of Hungarian Immigrants and Emigrants; F.C. Blair, Secretary of the Department of Immigration and Colonization, to Sir Joseph Pope, Undersecretary of State for External Affairs, 1 December 1922, Papers of the Immigration Branch, RG 76, vol. 7301, 34274, NA; Invitation to the 20 December 1923 meeting of the Emigration Council, Records of that meeting, PM records, K28 363-1923-T-25, NAH. Ruzsa, *A kanadai Magyarság*, 323–32, 364–5.
3 Emigration Act, 1909, cap. 4, sec. 29. "Az iroda története és alapszabályai" (The History and Constitution of the Bureau), Records of the Emigrants and Remigrants Aid Bureau, 1932–1946, P 1256, NAH. Order 44-700, 30 May 1921, Ministry of the Interior, in Jenő Gaál, *A társadalom feladatai a kivándorlás ügyével szemben*, 47–53. Ilona Varga, "Magyar kivándorlás Latin-Amerikába," 118.
4 *Ujság*, 2 December 1924.
5 *A Kanadai Magyar Ujság képes nagy naptára*, (1926), 171, (1927), 30. *Ujság*, 10 March 1925; Report no. 494 to the Ministry of Commerce, 1927, Montreal consulate records, K 128 I/1-1-cs.; NAH; István Shefbeck to

Baron Zsigmond Perényi, 15 June 1931, Hungarians Abroad, K 71 1932 I/6-30-cs., NAH.

6 Jenő Gaál, *A társadalom feladatai a kivándorlás ügyével szemben*, 39–40; Report by Consul General Albert de Haydin, 6 April 1926, PM records, K 28 ME 1927-T34, NAH.

7 Confidential report on the subject of organizing Hungarians abroad, n.d., Hungarians Abroad, K 71 I/6-1934-36-cs., NAH.

8 Confidential report and Guide for the Minister of Foreign Affairs for budget discussions of the Parliamentary Committee on Foreign Affairs, from Department Nine of the Ministry of Foreign Affairs, (Guide) 10 April 1936, Hungarians Abroad, K 71 1936-I/1-61-cs., NAH; Ilona Varga, "Magyar kivándorlás Latin-Amerikába," 119; *Külföldi Magyarság* (Hungarians Abroad), the publication of the League of Hungarians Abroad, passim; Annual Report of the Permanent Bureau of the World Congress of Hungarians, 1932, Federation records, P 975, Ka 35, NAH.

9 Confidential report and Guide; message of István Antal, press director of the Hungarian Prime Minister's Office, in *Ujság*, 16 March 1933; Tibor Törs, speech to Hungarian Parliament, *Ujság*, 16 June 1936; Hungarian MP György Lukács, in *Hírlap*, 27 November 1928; Ödön Paizs to Rev. F. Kovács, 28 June 1929, Federation records, P 975, Ka 33, NAH; Ilona Varga, "Magyar kivándorlás Latin-Amerikába," 137.

10 Report on the jubilee celebrations of Hungarians in Stockholm, Sask., 21 June 1928, Papers, Department of the Permanent Undersecretary, Ministry of Foreign Affairs, K 60 1927-8-cs., NAH.

11 This objective is evident in the Records of the (Hungarian) Ministry of the Interior, BM 651f, Institute for Party History (IPH). The government's intention of preventing communism from making inroads among immigrants is also evident from the correspondence concerning subsidies to *Ujság*; see Hungarians Abroad, NAH.

12 Chief Commissioner of the CPR to F.C. Blair, 11 November 1922, RG 76, vol. 7301, 34274, NA. This comment was made even before the bureau was created, in response to a notice about plans for its establishment that de Hann was circulating among Hungarians.

13 Brief to Károly Nagy, Director of the Permanent Bureau of the World Congress of Hungarians, n.d., Hungarians Abroad, K 71 I/6-1934-36-cs., NAH.

14 By-laws of the Hungarian World Federation, Budapest 1938, vol. 2, 2. Federation records, P 975, 30 cs., NAH. The International Labour Office was given the impression that the League of Hungarians Abroad was "a sort of mutual aid society whose main function is, as its name would show, to assist Hungarian emigrants." International Labour Office, *Migration Laws*, vol. 1, 134.

15 See, for example, Baron Zsigmond Perényi to Count István Bethlen, Prime Minister of Hungary, 22 November 1923, in *Bethlen István titkos iratai*, 139.

16 Report on the activities of Department Nine, n.d., Hungarians Abroad, K 71 1932-I/6, NAH.

17 By-laws of the Hungarian National Federation (Budapest, 1923), vol. 2, 4; *Nagymagyarország* (Greater Hungary), publication of the federation, various issues, passim. See also Report from Department Eight of the Hungarian Ministry of Foreign Affairs to Prime Minister Gömbös, 20 October 1932, Hungarians Abroad, K 71 1932-I/6-21-cs., NAH.

18 *Ujság*, 19 July 1925.

19 Ibid., 2 December 1924.

20 Report on dissolution of the newspaper company, 1 February 1934, Hungarians Abroad, K 71 I/6-1934-1002/34, NAH; Inquiry by Márffy Mantuano, retired consul, June 1936, Hungarians Abroad, K 71 I/6-1936-1002, NAH. István Shefbeck to Zsigmond Perényi, 15 June 1931, Hungarians Abroad, K 71 I/6-1932-30-cs., NAH.

21 Report from Winnipeg Consul, István Schefbeck, 25 October 1928, Press Archives, K 66 1935-I/5-255-cs., NAH.

22 István Schefbeck to Minister of Foreign Affairs, 19 February 1934, Hungarians Abroad, K 71 I/6-1934-1002/34 NAH; Zsigmond Perényi to Lajos Szelle, Hungarian Consul in Winnipeg, 20 November 1937, Hungarians Abroad, K 71 I/6-1937-70 cs., NAH.

23 Report on *Kanadai Magyar Ujság* from the Winnipeg Consulate, 16 July 1937, Hungarians Abroad, K 71 1937-I/6-70 cs., NAH.

24 Report by Consul General A. de Haydin, 28 December 1926, PM records K28 ME-1927-T34, NAH; Zsigmond Perényi to Lajos Szelle, Hungarian Consul, Winnipeg, 20 November 1937, Hungarians Abroad, K 71 I/6-1937-70-cs., NAH; Report by István Schefbeck, 8 October 1931, Hungarians Abroad, K 71 I/6-1932-30-cs., NAH.

25 Béla Payerle to István Schefbeck, 21 February 1934, István Shefbeck reports, 19 February 1934 and 10 May 1934, Hungarians Abroad, K 71 I/6-1934-1002, NAH; Report on *Kanadai Magyar Ujság*, 20 December 1930 and 1931/32, Hungarians Abroad, K 71 I/6-1931-26 and K 71 I/6-1932-30-cs., NAH.

26 Report dated 11 March 1932, Montreal consulate records, K 128 I/7-1227, NAH.

27 *Ujság*, 5 December 1925.

28 Zsigmond Perényi to Minister of Foreign Affairs, 6 June 1929, Hungarians Abroad, K 71 I/6-1936-1002, NAH; Report on dissolution of the Canadian Hungarian News Stock Company, 1 February 1934, Hungarians Abroad, K 71 I/6-1934-1002, NAH.

29 This is evident form the pages of *Ujság*. The records of the Division in Charge of Hungarians Abroad (NAH) also contain many letters from Béla Payerle.

30 Béla Payerle to Lajos Szelle, Hungarian Consul, Winnipeg, 31 August 1937, Hungarians Abroad, K 71 1936-I/6-70-cs., NAH. *Ujság*, 18 July 1925.

31 Reports of students, Manuscript collection, Sárospatak College of Theology; I. Gábor Kovács, "A magyar kalendárium főbb tipusai a 19. században"; Ortutay, "Kalendárium-olvasó magyarok."

32 Ortutay, "Kalendárium-olvasó magyarok."

33 Béla Payerle to István Petényi, Hungarian Consul, Winnipeg, 28 February 1936, and Report on the *Young Magyar American* by István Petényi (Schefbeck), 23 March 1936, Hungarians Abroad, K 71 I/6-1936-20721, NAH.

34 Interviews with Mary Polyoka, 26 February 1980, Hamilton; Mary Kiskó, 3 March 1980, Welland.

35 Mihály Szűcs, *Ujság*, 24 February 1942.

36 Report by Winnipeg Consul Schefbeck, 19 February 1934, Hungarians Abroad, K 71 I/6-1934-47-cs., NAH.

37 Mrs Pál Morvay, *Ujság*, 21 March 1941.

38 *Ujság*, 10 April 1930.

39 Ibid., 26 December 1925.

40 Frank Frey, Hungarian immigrant in Flatbush, Alberta, to Editor, 5 March 1928, Records of *Kanadai Magyar Ujság*, MG 28, V19, vol. 2, file 30, NA.

41 Report by Winnipeg Consul Schefbeck, 19 February 1934, Hungarians Abroad, K 71 I/6-1934-47-cs., NAH.

42 Report from the Winnipeg Consulate, 12 June 1937, Hungarians Abroad, K 71 1/6-1937-1001, NAH.

43 Report on the visit of Baron Zsigmond Perényi, 25 April 1925, Winnipeg consulate records, K 139, 1930–1939, 55-1933; *Nagymagyarország*, 1 June 1928; *Winnipeg Evening Tribune*, 29 March 1928.

44 Czank to Perényi, 20 November 1938, Federation records, P 975, Ka 149, NAH.

45 Instructions on Examining the Content of Foreign Textbooks, 1933, Winnipeg consulate records, K 139 1933-3678 and K 139 1933-3842, NAH.

46 Ibid., marginal notes. Winnipeg Consul to Reverend F. Hoffman, 10 July 1930, Winnipeg consulate records, K 139 1938-1116, NAH.

47 Winnipeg Consul to Reverend Frank Hoffman, 10 July 1930, Winnipeg consulate records, K 139 1938-1116, NAH; letter marked "confidential."

48 Brief by Dr. Károly Nagy, Hungarians Abroad, K 71 I/6-1934-36-cs., NAH.
    See also Report by Consul General Albert de Haydin, 8 November
    1927, PM records, K 28 ME-1927-A, NAH.
49 Confidential report, Hungarians Abroad, K 71 I/6-1934-36-cs., NAH.
50 Report by Consul General Albert de Haydin, 28 December 1926, PM
    records, K 28, ME-1927-T34, NAH.
51 Reports, 19 December 1925 and 28 December 1926, PM records, K 28,
    ME-1927-T34, NAH.
52 Report on Communists in Canada, 9 April 1932, Interior records, BM
    651f, 2/1933-f-2286, IPH. See also Report from Consul General
    Albert de Haydin, 8 November 1927, PM records, K 28 ME-1927-A, NAH.
53 Confidential report.
54 Report by Consul General Albert de Haydin, 5 January 1931, Hungarians
    Abroad, K 71 I/6-1932-21334, NAH; Father I. Rácz to the Hungarian
    Ministry of Foreign Affairs, 10 October 1930, Hungarians Abroad, K 71
    1932-I/6-21334, NAH.
55 Report, 28 December 1926, PM records, K 28 ME-1927-T34, NAH.
56 Baron Zsigmond Perényi to Kálmán Kánya, Minister of Foreign Affairs,
    2 April 1935, Hungarians Abroad, K 71 I/6- 1935-55-cs., NAH.
57 Charles Steinmetz to Károly Nagy, 27 June 1933, Federation records,
    P 975, Ka 35, NAH.
58 Report by Consul General Károly Winter, 1940, Montreal consulate
    records, K 128 I/7-927/1940, NAH.
59 Zsigmond Perényi to the Ministry of Foreign Affairs, 14 June 1932,
    Hungarians Abroad, K 71 I/6-1933, NAH.
60 Report of the Permanent Bureau of the Hungarian World Congress,
    1929–1935, Federation, records, P 975, Ka 50, NAH.
61 Rev. Mihály Fehér to Permanent Bureau of the World Congress of
    Hungarians, 15 July 1930, Federation records, P 975, Ka 12, NAH.
    The bureau obtained 130 volumes at a 50 per cent discount for the
    United Church congregation.
62 Distribution of Calvinist Almanacs, 1938, Montreal consulate records,
    K 128 I/7-1938, NAH; Minutes, 3 February 1935, Montreal First
    Reformed records, MG 8, G76, NA. The Julian Association also sent books
    to Canadian Associations. See Reverend Károly Farkas to Dr. Paul
    Petri, Julian Association, 23 April 1930, PM records, K 28
    ME-1930-J-16387, NAH.
63 Iván Halász de Béky, "The Hungarian Consulates and the Educational
    Needs of Hungarian Schools in Canada, 1932–40. Documents,"
    Hungarian Studies Review 8 (Spring 1981) 119–26.
64 Memorandum from the Office of the Hungarian Prime Minister to the
    Ministry of Foreign Affairs, 18 February 1926, PM records, K 28
    ME-1927-T, NAH.

65 János Exner to Baron Perényi, 28 March 1930, Federation records, P 975, Ka 23, NAH.
66 Ferenc Kovács and János Czank to the Permanent Bureau of the World Congress of Hungarians, n.d., Federation records, P 975, Ka 9, NAH.
67 Imre Szikszay, President, and Gyula Minács, Secretary, to the Bureau of the Congress, 10 February 1937, Federation records, P 975, Ka 112, NAH.
68 Fehér to Perényi, 14 August 1928, Correspondence 1928–30, Montreal First Reformed records, MG 8, G76, vol. 1, NA.
69 Ladislaus Forgách to the Minister of Religion and Education, 30 April 1929, Hungarians Abroad, K 71 I/6-1930-21922, NAH.
70 See above, chap. 5.
71 Reports of students, Manuscript collection, Sárospatak College of Theology.
72 Interview with József Jáger, 14 February 1980, Toronto.
73 István Szalontay to the Hungarian World Federation, 1939, Federation records, P 975, K 154, NAH.
74 Minutes, 5 December 1930, Hungaria.
75 John Burkus to World Congress of Hungarians, 6 January 1934, Federation records, P 975, Ka 61, NAH.
76 Mátyás Lissauer to Director of Permanent Bureau of World Congress of Hungarians, 15 August 1932, Federation records, P 975, Ka 54, NAH.
77 Imre Furka to Hungarian Consul in Winnipeg, 13 January 1933, Winnipeg consulate records, K 139-1933/26, NAH.

CHAPTER SEVEN

1 Recollections of Emil Gárdos, Memoirs of Hungarian Communists Abroad, H-g-184, IPH (Budapest); *Munkás*, 21 July 1932.
2 Puskás, *Kivándorló magyarok*, 374; József Kovács, *A szocialista magyar irodalom*, 27–8.
3 Vörös, *American Commissar*, 198–9, 201; Gárdos, "Az amerikai magyar munkásmozgalom történetéhez"; Gárdos recollections, IPH; *Új Előre*, 31 March 1927; Subversive Activities Control Board Hearings, *Herbert Brownell Jr, Attorney General of the United States vs. Communist Party of the United States*, Lautner testimony, Washington, DC, typewritten record, 1951–53.
4 *Új Előre*, 11 June, 8 July 1926; Gárdos recollections, IPH.
5 Helen Czukár, 27 March 1980, personal communication.
6 *Új Előre*, 7 January, 6 December 1926, 19 March 1927, 17 April, 7 May, 16 October 1928.
7 Márkos memoirs, Puskás collection, Budapest.

8   Pásztor and Kristoff, "A Független Betegsegélyző." Memoirs of József Blaskó, 17, Collection of memoirs, World Federation of Hungarians, Budapest. The 25th anniversary booklet of the Benefit Federation makes no reference to American organizers at all.

9   Blaskó memoirs, 71; Pásztor and Kristoff, "A Független Betegsegélyző," 35; Memoirs of István Markos, 44, István Szőke papers, Puskás collection, Budapest.

10 Report of Hungarian buro (sic) to party plenum, n.d., Communist Party of Canada Collection, CP 9 C 0808, Archives of Ontario (AO). In Montreal, Hungarian party members had similar difficulties. See letter to J. Lovas, Hamilton, 15 April 1931, CP 2 A 1169, AO.

11 Vörös, American Commissar, 206. Subversive Activities Control Board Hearings, Brownell vs. Communist Party, Lautner testimony, 9174, 9177.

12 Új Előre, 10 March, 26 March 1927.

13 Ujság, 9 April, 17 May 1927.

14 Puskás, Kivándorló magyarok, 342.

15 Blaskó memoirs, 24; Ujság, 16 January 1926.

16 Új Előre, 2 April 1927; Minutes, 2 January, 3 April 1927, Hungaria Social Club.

17 Minutes, 3 April 1927, Hungaria.

18 Új Előre, 3 April 1927.

19 Minutes, 22 April 1928, Hungaria.

20 See below, chap. 8.

21 Minutes, 1 April 1928, Hungaria.

22 Hírlap, 24 August 1928.

23 Kanadai Magyar Népszava (Hamilton), 21 February 1929.

24 Munkás, 26 July, 2 August, 6 August 1935; Minutes, 26 February, 14 June 1935, Welland society, MHSO.

25 Blaskó memoirs, 10, 40.

26 Ibid.

27 Ibid., 18, 25; Pásztor and Kristoff, "A Független Betegsegélyző," 36.

28 By-law 21, re Branches, 5 August 1927, Canadian Hungarian Mutual Benefit Federation, 02-85-85, MCCA.

29 Blaskó memoirs, 18–19.

30 By-law 2, re Objects, 25 August 1927, Benefit Federation.

31 Munkás, 12 July 1934; Blaskó memoirs, 73.

32 Memorandum from Károly Winter, Hungarian Consul General in Montreal, to the Hungarian Ministry of Foreign Affairs, 22 November 1928, Press Archives, K 66 I/5-1935-255-cs., NAH. Minutes, 5 January 1929, Canadian Hungarian Association,Windsor CHA records, MG 28, V65, vol. 5, file 86, NA; Blaskó memoirs, 73–4; József Kovács, A szocialista magyar irodalom, 33; Munkás, 16 June 1932.

33 *Új Előre,* 18 February 1929.

34 Interview with Helen Czukár, March 1982, Hamilton.

35 Vörös, *American Commissar,* 206.

36 Ibid., 202–3.

37 Hoó, *Tiszakerecsenytöl Kanadáig,* 327.

38 John Lovas to Tim Buck, n.d., CP 4 A 2581, unsigned letter to John Lovas, n.d., CP A 1171, and letter dated 29 April 1931, CP A 1179, all in Communist Party of Canada Collection, AO.

39 *Munkás,* 29 January 1931, 21 July 1932; on attempts to recruit farmers, see 7 June 1934, 18 January 1934, 8 February 1935.

40 Ibid., 29 January 1931, 5 July 1934.

41 Ibid., 6 October 1932.

42 Ibid., 20 May 1931.

43 Ibid., 22 January 1933.

44 Pásztor and Kristoff, "A Független Betegsegélyző," 124; *Munkás,* 24 November 1932, 19 July 1934.

45 Blaskó memoirs, 101; *Munkás,* 5 July 1934.

46 *Munkás,* 1 June, 5 October 1933, 8 September 1936; Pásztor and Kristoff, "A Független Betegsegélyző," 124; Minutes, 11 February 1940, Central Committee of the Hungarian Workers' Clubs, Puskás collection, MHSO.

47 *Úttörő,* 27 November 1934.

48 For Workers' club, see *Munkás,* 5 June 1933; for Welland society figures, see Géza Kertész papers, series L, MHSO.

49 See above, chap. 6.

50 Report of the Hungarian Consulate in Winnipeg on the subvention to *Kanadai Magyar Ujság* in the fiscal year 1936–37, 12 July 1937, Hungarians Abroad, K 71 I/6-1937-70-cs., NAH.

51 "Notes on the number and organization of readers," Records of the Workers' Clubs and the Independent Mutual Benefit Federation, Puskás collection, MHSO.

52 Gárdos, "Az amerikai," 24–5; Puskás, *Kivándorló magyarok,* 377.

53 Rasporich, *For a Better Life,* chap. 6.

54 *Úttörő,* 15 October 1931.

55 *Munkás,* 19 July 1934. Figures on Hungarian immigrants in Hamilton are based on the 1931 census.

56 For Canada, see Schultz et al., *Politics of Discontent.* For the Communist party in Canada, see Avakumovic, *The Communist Party in Canada;* Avery, *Dangerous Foreigners.*

57 Interview with Sándor Egyed, June 1982, MHSO.

58 See Avery, *Dangerous Foreigners,* chaps. 4 and 5.

59 For a discussion of this question in relation to the US Communist party, see Glazer, *Social Basis,* 88–9.

60 Rev. Eugene Molnár to Nicholas Istvánffy, 30 May 1928, and Father Jeromos Hédly to Károly Winter, 3 January 1932, Montreal consulate records, K 128 I/1-1930-1-cs., NAH; *Canadai Kis Ujság*, 21 November 1935; *Ujság*, 16 November 1929; *Munkás*, 12 January 1933, 5 April 1934.
61 *Munkás*, 16 November 1933; Tóth, *23 év*, 208.
62 *Welland Tribune*, 27 October 1933.
63 *Munkás*, 6 November 1930, 29 October 1931.
64 Ibid., 25 January 1934.
65 Interview with John Sipos, 14 March 1980, Hamilton.
66 Interview with John Sipos. See also *Munkás*, 25 January 1934, and Blaskó memoirs, 43.
67 Avery, *Dangerous Foreigners*, chap. 5. For an account of the deportations, see Roberts, *Whence They Came*.
68 Memorandum for E. Bayly, Deputy Attorney General of Ontario, re "Vapaus," "Hungarian Worker," "Az Úttörő" (The Pioneer), "The Worker," Communist Party of Canada Collection, RG 4, Box 30 (30 L 0645), AO.
69 Notes from Sergeant R.E. Webster, Hamilton Detachment, RCMP, n.d., Communist Party Collection, RG4, Box 30, (30 L 06457), AO.
70 A.L. Joliffe, Commissioner, Department of Immigration and Colonization, to Károly Winter, Hungarian Consul General, 7 June 1932, Interior records, 651f2/1933-5-2283, IPH.
71 Report dated 21 April 1932, Interior records, 3971/pl., IPH. Interview with Mary Polyoka, 26 February 1980, Hamilton.
72 *Ujság*, 26 November 1931; *Munkás*, 25 May 1933; *Ujság*, 17 September 1940.
73 Interview with Sándor Medgyesi, August 1980, Budapest.
74 Károly Winter to W.H. Price, Attorney General of Ontario, 13 July 1931, Communist Party Collection, RG 4, Box 30 (30 L 0750), AO.
75 See below, chap. 8.
76 Hoó, *Tiszakerecsenytöl Kanadáig*, 324.
77 For a more general discussion of the importance of organizers in the success of the Communist party, see Glazer, *Social Basis*, 88–9.
78 See below, chap. 8.
79 By-law 19, 25 August 1927, Benefit Federation, 02-85-85, MCCA.
80 Blaskó memoirs, 54–5, 63, 83–4, 96; *Munkás*, 4 May 1933, 8 September 1936.
81 *Munkás*, 8 September 1936.
82 Ibid., 8 January, 18 January 1935.
83 Interview with Andrew Hertel, 11 July 1977, MHSO. The only Hungarian association in Driftwood, Ontario – a branch of the Sick Benefit Society – was also launched by an itinerant organizer. *Munkás*, 20 October 1932.

84 By-laws, Benefit Federation, MCCA.

85 *Úttörő*, 16 November 1933.

86 Ibid.

87 Minutes, 28 January 1934, Central Committee of the Workers' Clubs, Records of the Workers' Clubs, Puskás collection, MHSO.

CHAPTER EIGHT

1 See, for example, comments of Father Jeromos Hédly in *Hírlap*, 16 November 1928; Reverend J. Papp to the directors of the Julian Association, 29 April 1930, Hungarians Abroad, K 71 I/6-21403, NAH; *Református Híradó*, March 1931; *Canadai Kis Ujság*, 13 February 1936; András Zsidor, Oshawa Hungarian Cultural Club, to World Federation of Hungarians, 3 January 1937, Federation records, P 975, Ka 112, NAH; Reverend Charles Steinmetz to Károly Winter, Hungarian Consul General, Montreal, 23 March 1939, Montreal consulate records, K 128 I/416-cs., NAH; Minutes, 3 May 1940, Windsor club.

2 Minutes, 22 April 1928, Hungaria.

3 Reverend Mihály Fehér to Károly Nagy, Director, Permanent Bureau of the World Congress of Hungarians, 11 November 1935, Federation records, P 975, Ka 12, NAH. Reverend Charles Kovács to the World Federation, n.d., Federation records, P 975, Ka 146, NAH. *Kanadai Magyar Ujság* (Winnipeg), 6 March 1934. Comments of László Panczél, Canadian delegate to the 1929 International Congress of Hungarians in Budapest, in *A Magyarok Világkongresszusának tárgyalásai*, 208.

4 Comments of Reverend Mihály Fehér to the Petőfi Choir of Montreal, Records of the Petőfi Choir, 21 February 1931, Montreal First Reformed records, M-6485, vol. 3, NA; Reverend Charles Steinmetz, *Híradó*, 5 December 1936.

5 Sister Mary to Károly Nagy, 22 November 1935, Federation records, P 975, Ka 63, NAH. Mrs. Steinmetz to World Federation, 23 February 1934, P 975, Ka 35, NAH.

6 *Mail and Empire* (Toronto), 25 August 1931; *Toronto Daily Star*, 17 November 1939, 14 November 1941. Hungarian patriotic newspapers generally took note of such articles – for example, *Egyetértés*, 29 August 1931, and *Híradó*, 29 February 1936.

7 Mrs Fehér to Károly Nagy, 9 November 1935, Federation records, P 975, Ka 12, NAH.

8 Sister Mary to Károly Nagy, 22 November 1935, Federation records, P 975, Ka 63, NAH.

9 Minutes, 30 January 1937, Petőfi Choir, Montreal First Reformed records, MG 8, G76, vol. 3, NA.

10 *A Montreáli Magyar*, 39.

11 Interview with Sándor Birinyi, 8 December 1976, Toronto. *Kanadai*

Magyar Hírlap (*Hírlap*) (Welland and Toronto), 29 November 1928, 4 January 1929; *Ujság*, 1 May 1930.

12 *Hírlap*, 16 April 1929; poem submitted to *Ujság*, 30 January 1926; 27 April 1929; speech by Reverend Charles Steinmetz, 15 March 1938, on back of program, Steinmetz papers, MHSO.

13 *Ujság*, 12 March 1931, 12 January 1934, 20 August 1940; *Híradó*, 21 December 1935; *Református Híradó*, August 1930. B. Eisner, "Hungary and the League," talk given at Westmount YMCA, 9 April 1936, Eisner Papers, Dreisziger Collection, Kingston.

14 *Híradó*, 21 December 1935; *Református Híradó*, August 1930; telegram sent by Windsor Presbyterians to the League of Nations, *Ujság*, 13 June 1930, cable sent by Toronto Hungarians, *Ujság*, 19 June 1930; Béla Eisner to Walter O'Hearn, 25 April 1940, Eisner papers; *Hírlap*, 21 August 1928.

15 Report of Reverend Charles Steinmetz, First Hungarian Presbyterian Church, 1938, Steinmetz papers, MHSO; *Református Híradó*, December 1929; speech of Reverend Károly Szebik, Montreal, *Ujság*, 27 October 1933.

16 The case of the Windsor club is mentioned above. See also Győző Vietoris to Nicholas Istvánffy, 24 January 1929, CHA records, MG 28 V65, vol. 5, NA; and *Canadai Kis Ujság*, 31 November 1935.

17 *Hírlap*, 16 October 1928.

18 *Ujság*, 1 April 1938, 14 March 1941.

19 Ibid., 13 April 1937.

20 Ibid., 31 August 1937, 10 March 1939.

21 *Híradó*, 21 December 1935.

22 Béla Eisner in *Református Híradó*, October 1929; speech of Reverend Michael Fehér, *Ujság*, 6 March 1929, 15 October 1931; Reverend F. Kovács, *Hírlap*, 22 December 1928.

23 *Ujság*, 25 August 1932, 20 August 1937; *Hírlap*, 21 August 1928; *Református Híradó*, August 1930.

24 Father József Rácz to Ministry of Foreign Affairs, 10 October 1930, Hungarians Abroad, K 71 1932-I/6-21334, NAH.

25 István Karnay commenting on a performance by the St Antal amateur drama troupe in Windsor, *Canadai Kis Ujság*, 13 February 1936.

26 *Református Híradó*, July 1929.

27 *Ujság*, 7 November 1925, 31 August 1937; *Otthon*, June 1928; *Híradó*, 21 December 1935; report of protest meeting against Trianon in Hamilton, *Ujság*, 4 June 1931; cable sent by Hungarian Reformed Church of Montreal to Admiral Horthy, Minutes, 6 November 1938, Montreal First Reformed records, M-6481, NA; Annual Report for 1938, Reports 1937–39, MG 8, G76, vol. 1, NA; Rev. J.L. Papp, Windsor, in *Híradó*, 14 November 1935.

28 On the proletarian view of Horthyist irredentism, see below, chap. 9.

29 *Ujság*, 7 November 1925.

30 Minutes, 6 November 1938, Montreal First Reformed records, M-6481, NA.

31 See Table A3 in the Appendix.

32 Albert Kibédi to World Federation of Hungarians, 31 May 1932, Federation records, P 975, Ka 53, NAH.

33 Interview with József Jáger, 14 February 1980, Toronto.

34 Géza Kertész to Hungarian World Federation, 18 June 1939, Federation records, P 975, Ka, NAH.

35 *Ujság*, 12 March 1940. For comments on community response, see also Report on the Occupation of Upper Hungary and related celebrations, 28 November 1938, Montreal consulate records, K 128 I/7-138-4467, NAH; Mrs. Dezső Andrássy, Sudbury Hungarian Women's Association, to World Congress, n.d., Federation records, P 975, Ka 168, NAH; *Ujság*, 19 January 1939.

36 *Ujság*, 9 November 1934, 13 May, 26 July 1938, 15 April 1941. Father Matty, Windsor, in *Canadai Kis Ujság*, 20 October 1936.

37 *Otthon*, February 1925; E. Papp, recording secretary of the Hungarian Presbyterian Church in Hamilton, to Canadian Hungarian Association, 25 January 1929, CHA records, MG 28, V65, vol. 5, file 107, NA; Rev. Frank Kovács in *Hírlap*, 22 December 1928; *Egyetértés*, 7 November 1931; *Canadai Kis Ujság*, 24 December 1935; *Ujság*, 29 May 1930, stated explicitly that the treaty alone was responsible for slowing Hungary's progress towards democracy and social justice.

38 *Ujság*, 9 July 1929.

39 See above, chap. 7.

40 Minutes, 1 April 1928, Hungaria Social Club.

41 *Munkás*, 26 July, 2 August, 6 August 1935; Record of a recommendation to the Welland Hungarian Self-Culture Society, 14 June 1935, Kertész papers, MHSO.

42 *Híradó*, 14 November 1935.

43 Nicholas Hornyánszky to Károly Nagy, 4 April 1939, Federation records, P 975, Ka 167, NAH.

44 *APPCC* (1934), 20.

45 *Free Press*, 26 January 1938; *APPCC* (1934), 20. *Windsor Star*, n.d., clipping in Scrapbooks, Steinmetz papers, MHSO; *New Canadian*, 29 January 1938.

46 *Canadai Kis Ujság*, 4 June 1936.

47 *APPCC* (1930), 28; 1937, 26–7; *Glad Tidings*, June 1937; *Catholic Register*, 7 January 1927; A. Czako, "Hungarians," in Stephenson, ed., *That They May Be One*, 150.

48 Minutes, 5 January 1929, meeting of the CHA, Windsor, CHA records,

MG 28, V65, vol. 5, file 86, NA; Father P. Sántha to Rev. M. Fehér, 25 March, 31 August 1932, Montreal First Reformed records, MG 8, G76, vol. 1, NA; *Híradó*, 24 October 1935.

49 *Híradó*, 21 December 1935.

50 *Hírlap*, 28 December 1928.

51 *Őrszem*, September 1931. In 1923, before he left Hungary, Father Jeromos Hédly, editor of *Őrszem*, had praised the Bavarian Arrow Cross during a public meeting. Géza Ujvári, former member of parliament, to Count István Bethlen, *Bethlen István titkos iratai*, 139–40.

52 *Ujság*, 2 February 1929, 19 May 1932, 19 June, 22 June, 10 July 1934, 19 November 1937. See also *Hírlap*, 28 December 1928, and *Canadai Kis Ujság*, 31 November 1935.

53 Reverend J. Hammond, St. James Orthodox Catholic Church, Windsor, to W.H. Price, Attorney-General, Ontario, 15 August 1931, Communist Party of Canada Collection, 30 L 0866, AO.

54 Blaskó memoirs, 73–4; *Munkás*, 21 July 1932. *Welland Tribune*, 5 August 1931.

55 Report on Communists in Canada, 9 April 1932, Interior records, BM 651f 2/1933-1-2286; IPH; Béla Bucsin to István Schefbeck, 11 June 1932, Interior records, BM 651f 2/1932-1-8337, IPH.

56 *Hírlap*, 11 January, 18 January 1929; *Református Híradó*, January 1929; *Otthon*, January 1928; *Ujság*, 5 September 1925.

57 *Otthon*, January 1925, October 1926; *Ujság*, 27 January, 24 October, 21 November, 19 December 1925, 26 March, 23 April, 30 April, 8 October 1927, 2 February 1929, 30 January 1930.

58 *Ujság*, 23 January 1926.

59 *Otthon*, December 1925, January 1925. Rev. F. Kovács in *Ujság*, 14 January 1939; Louis White in *Ujság*, 16 June 1932. By-laws, CHA, CHA records, MG 28, V65, vol. 1, NA; Iván Hordossy to R.H. Hooper, editor of the *Winnipeg Tribune*, 25 January 1928, CHA records, MG 28, V65, vol. 2, file 30, NA.

60 *Híradó*, 21 December 1935. See also *Hírlap*, 28 December 1928.

61 Minutes, 10 March 1929, Hungaria Social Club.

62 *Ujság*, 13 April 1937.

63 *Református Híradó*, September 1929.

64 Text of speech given by Reverend Frank Kovács, leader of Hungarian delegation that visited Ottawa in an effort to change the status of Hungarians, cited in *Hírlap*, 30 March 1929. See also *Református Híradó*, January, December 1929; *Hírlap*, 12 February 1929.

65 Frank Kovács's speech in Ottawa, cited in *Ujság*, 30 March 1929; Minutes, 24 May 1929, CHA records, MG 28, V65, vol. 5, file 86, NA; *Híradó*, 15 February 1936.

66 *Ujság*, 25 December 1930; *Hírlap*, 9 November 1928, 30 March 1929; *Híradó*, 15 February, 3 October 1936.

67 See notes 13 and 14 to this chapter. See also *Református Híradó*, January
1929; *Híradó*, 5 December 1935; letter from Rev. Frank Kovács in
Hamilton Herald, 16 June 1926.
68 See above, chap. 4.
69 *Hírlap*, 23 October 1928.
70 *Egyetértés*, 22 August 1931; *Ujság*, 12 March 1927; Open letter to the
Hungarians of Montreal from the Hungaria Social Club, n.d.,
Montreal First Reformed records, MG 28, G76, vol. 3, NA.
71 János Balázs of the Brantford Hungarian Sick Benefit Federation, quoted
in *Ujság*, 9 April 1931; István K. Karnay in *Canadai Kis Ujság*,
15 October 1936.
72 See above, chap. 4.
73 *Híradó*, 23 January 1937; Nicholas Istvánffy, General Secretary of the
Canadian Hungarian Association, to the Association's President,
Baron Csávossy, 18 February 1930, CHA records, MG 28, V65, vol. 4, file
60, NA. Rev. L.J. Papp, Minutes, 5 January 1929, meeting of CHA,
Windsor, CHA records, MG 28, V65, vol. 5, file 86, NA; Louis White, president of the Hungaria Social Club, in *Híradó*, 21 November 1935;
Hírlap, 28 September, 28 December 1928.
74 *Canadai Kis Ujság*, 21 November 1935.
75 *Welland Tribune*, 5 August 1931.
76 *Ujság*, 6 March 1934; *Híradó*, 27 February 1937; Minutes, 6 January 1936,
Montreal First Reformed records.
77 Interview with László Forgách, 25 August 1978, Toronto.
78 See, for example, *Ujság*, 12 January 1937.
79 Ibid., 3 February 1937.
80 See, for example, *Híradó*, 2 May 1936.
81 Reverend Mihály Fehér in *Református Híradó*, July 1931. For advice to
be patient and endure, see also *Ujság*, 21 April 1932; Father Oliver
Horváth, Welland, in *Ujság*, 22 December 1932; *Egyetértés*, 6 June,
12 September 1931.
82 See Dreisziger, "In Search."
83 *Ujság*, 25 July 1925, 16 January, 3 July 1926.
84 See, for example, György Szabó, a Winnipeg steamship agent, to Rev.
J. Kovács, 27 April 1927, CHA records, MG 28, V65, vol. 6, file 104,
NA; Gyula Iszák in *Ujság*, 15 October 1927; Composition of preparatory
committee, *Ujság*, 20 August 1927.
85 *Ujság*, 11 February 1928.
86 See, for example, Minutes, 13 December 1930, Church Council, Records
of the first Hungarian Presbyterian Church of Toronto, MHSO; *Ujság*,
25 July 1925, 16 January 1926.
87 By-laws and constitution, CHA, CHA records, MG 28, V65, vol. 1, file 1,
NA; Iván Hordossy to R.H. Hooper, editor of the *Winnipeg Tribune*,
25 January 1928, CHA records, MG 28, V65, vol. 2, file 30, NA.

88 György Szabó to Gyula Izsák, 13 September 1927, CHA records, MG 28, V65, vol. 6, file 104, NA; Szabó to Jenö Molnár, 17 December 1927, CHA records, MG 28, V65, vol. 6, file 89, NA.

89 Pál Szabó, in *Ujság*, 5 November 1927; *Otthon*, March 1928; Report on meeting, Hamilton branch, CHA, *Hírlap*, 18 January 1929; Rev. F. Kovács to Nicholas Istvánffy, secretary of the CHA, 7 February 1929, CHA records, MG 28, V65, vol. 3, file 44, NA.

90 See, for example, in CHA records (NA), MG 28, V65: Rev. F. Kovács to G. Szabó, 2 January 1928, vol. 5, file 107; Nicholas Istvánffy to Father Csáky, 24 January 1929, vol. 6, file 96; Dezsö Andrássy, secretary of the Brantford Sick Benefit Society in Hamilton, to N. Istvánffy, 13 March 1929, vol. 4, file 53; and Zoltán Molnár to Istvánffy, 22 March 1928, vol. 2, file 30.

91 *Új Előre*, 26 August 1926, 27 February, 26 March 1928. The *Munkás* continued to attack the CHA; see, e.g., 10 October 1929, 24 July 1930.

92 *Ujság*, 11 February 1928; Rusza, *A kanadai magyarság*, 70–4; Dreisziger, "In Search," 85.

93 *Ujság*, 11 February 1928.

94 See, for example, letter signed N.N., CHA records, MG 28, V65, vol. 3, file 34, NA.

95 Minutes, 12 February 1928, meeting of Hungarian Roman Catholic Priests in Melville, Saskatchewan, Winnipeg consulate records, K 139 1936/438, NAH.

96 Győző Vietoris to Nicholas Istvánffy, 24 January 1929, CHA records, MG 28, V65, vol. 5, NA.

97 István Schefbeck to A. de Haydin, 27 March 1928, Winnipeg consulate records, K 139 1936/438, NAH.

98 Istvánffy to Jenő Molnár, 1 August 1928, CHA records, MG 28, V65, vol. 3, file 38, NA; Istvánffy to Ferenc Kovács, 1 August 1928, CHA records, MG 28, V65, vol. 3, file 44, NA. Apparently Szabó and Ujváry both launched complaints against the Winnipeg consul with Consul General de Haydin; see Schefbeck to Haydin, 27 March 1928, Winnipeg consulate records, K 139 1936/438, NAH.

99 *Szabadság*, 20 April 1928. Zsigmond Balla in *Családi Kör*, supplement to the bulletin of the Winnipeg Reformed Church. The Hungarian consul was also involved in settling the dispute between Hordossy and the CHA; see Rev. S. Csutoros to I. Schefbeck, 6 July 1928, Winnipeg consulate records, K 139 1936/438, NAH.

100 Nicholas Istvánffy to Ferenc Kovács, 9 August 1929, CHA records, MG 28, V65, vol. 4, file 51, NA.

101 Baron József Csávossy to István Shefbeck, n.d. [1929], Winnipeg consulate records, K 139 1936/438, NAH.

102 On financial difficulties experienced by Nicholas Istvánffy, see, in CHA records (NA), MG 28, V65: Istvánffy to János Ujváry, 7 March 1928,

vol. 2, file 30; Istvánffy to F. Kovács, 1 August 1928, vol. 3, file 44; and Istvánffy to E. Molnár, 1 August 1928, vol. 3, file 38; on the loans made to the CHA, see vol. 3, file 35.

103 Nicholas Istvánffy to Rev. Jenő Molnár, 11 September 1928, CHA records, MG 28, V65, vol. 3, file 38, NA; Dezsö Andrássy, Secretary of Brantford Sick Benefit Society in Hamilton, to Istvánffy, 13 March 1929, CHA records, MG 28, V65, vol. 5 file, 107, NA.

104 Istvánffy to Dezső Demetrovics, 11 October 1929, CHA records, MG 28, V65, vol. 4, file 54, NA.

105 Ruzsa, *A kanadai magyarság*, 186; *Híradó*, 11 April, 6 June, 20 June 1936.

106 Ruzsa, *A kanadai magyarság*, 186.

107 Ibid.

108 Minutes, 13 February, 13 March 1935, 2 February 1936, Hungaria Social Club; Ruzsa, *A kanadai magyarság*, 309.

109 Minutes, 21 February 1937, Hungaria.

110 Ibid., 26 February, 8 May 1936, 11 February 1937, Hungaria. *Híradó*, 22 February 1936.

111 Louis White, in *Híradó*, 22 February 1936.

112 Minutes, 18 October 1938, Hungaria.

113 Ibid., 25 October 1938, Hungaria.

114 *Canadai Kis Ujság*, 9 January 1936.

115 President's speech on the occasion of the choir's performance, Minutes, 30 January 1937, Petőfi Choir, Montreal First Reformed records, M-6485, vol. 3, NA.

116 Minutes, 26 February, 6 November 1938, Székely Club, Montreal.

117 Minutes, 31 July 1927, Welland Hungarian Self-Culture Society, MHSO.

118 Interview with István Bornemissza, 25 November 1986, Welland. *Munkás*, 15 August 1929.

119 *Gyertyafény*, 20 October 1935.

120 *Canadai Kis Ujság*, 23 January 1936.

121 Ibid.

122 Thus, for example, in 1928, when there were about one thousand Hungarians in Welland, according to the society's officers celebrations of 15 March at the society's hall drew approximately 600–700 people. Minutes, 1 April 1928.

123 János Exner to Baron Perényi, 28 March 1930, Federation records, P 975, Ka 23, NAH.

124 *Canadai Kis Ujság*, 4 March 1937.

125 *Ujság*, 13 September 1935. *Híradó*, 29 August, 5 September 1935.

CHAPTER NINE

1 *Új Előre*, 16 June 1928; *Munkás*, 24 July 1930, 24 August 1934.

2 *Munkás*, 24 July 1930.

3 *Új Előre*, 2 April 1927; *Munkás*, 3 July 1930, 20 October, 25 August 1932, 5 February 1935.

4 *Új Előre*, 16 June 1928; see also 29 January 1927. *Munkás*, 26 May 1932, 15 June 1933, 20 January 1937.

5 See, for example, *Munkás*, 12 February 1931, 3 February, 21 July, 22 September, 27 October 1932, 15 June, 17 August 1933, 15 February, 25 December, 28 December 1934.

6 Ibid., 22 January 1930.

7 *Új Előre*, 5 November 1926; *Munkás*, 5 June 1930, 5 March 1931.

8 *Munkás*, 16 July 1929.

9 On home work, see *Munkás*, 3 April 1930. On discrimination against immigrant workers, see *Munkás*, 9 June, 7 July 1932, 24 August 1934.

10 Ibid., 12 September 1929.

11 Schaeffer, "Munkássorsok gazdag Kanadában," 50.

12 *Munkás*, 5 September 1929.

13 Interview with Béla Vágó, November 1976, Toronto.

14 Interview with Helen Czukár, March 1980, Hamilton.

15 Interview with Mary Kisko, 3 March 1980, Welland.

16 Interview with Mary Polyoka, 26 February 1980, Hamilton.

17 Marczi, "Az utolsó állomás."

18 *Munkás*, 30 December 1929.

19 See above, 73.

20 Sándor Hajas to József Hajas, n.d., Interior records, 651f2/1933-6047, IPH. Because of Hajas's involvement in the proletarian camp, the ministry kept a file on him. The file contains copies of his letters home, which were intercepted by postal officials. It also contains a letter from Sándor's father to the Immigrant Aid Bureau in which he explains that he is very concerned about his son, who sent him a picture "and he is so thin, you can barely recognize him. This hurts a parent." Hajas humbly inquires whether the bureau could not help to bring Sándor home. He explains: "although we are very poor, if only we could see our dear child once more, we would be rich."

21 Blaskó memoirs, 70; Vörös, *American Commissar*, 203, 206.

22 See, for example, speech by Lautner, an organizer from the United States, to Windsor Workers' Club, *Munkás*, 13 November 1930; see also 20 July, 27 July, 12 October 1929.

23 *Munkás*, 14 January, 16 January, 25 January 1936.

24 Blasko memoirs, 107; Szőke, *We Are Canadians*, 80.

25 *Munkás*, 1 October 1936.

26 Ibid., 16 October 1936, 19 August, 12 June, 19 July, 14 August 1937.

27 Ibid., 26 August, 29 August 1939.

28 Vörös, *American Commissar*, 206.

29 *Új Előre*, 1 February 1929.

30 Ibid.; *Munkás*, 22 August 1929, 27 August, 20 May 1931, 14 September, 19 October 1934.
31 *Munkás*, 11 June 1935, 6 August 1931, 16 November 1934.
32 Ibid., 12 June 1930.
33 *Új Előre*, 8 January 1929; *Munkás*, 22 August 1929.
34 Speech given by József Dohány to Toronto workers, *Munkás*, 24 July 1929.
35 Ibid., 16 July, 24 October 1929, 2 August, 21 August 1934.
36 Ibid., 31 May 1934.
37 Ibid., 31 May 1934, 16 July 1929.
38 Ibid., 29 August 1929, 19 March 1931. István Szőke to World Federation of Hungarians, 14 August 1938, Federation records, P 975, Ka 139, NAH.
39 *Munkás*, 26 July 1934.
40 Interview with George Palotás, July 1980, Szamosszeg, Hungary.
41 Speech by Mihály Pásztor, Hamilton, *Munkás*, 10 October 1929; speech by József Dohány, Toronto, ibid., 24 July 1929; *Új Előre*, 11 February, 28 February, 28 December 1928.
42 *Új Előre*, 20 November 1925.
43 Ibid., 28 December 1928; *Munkás*, 11 October 1933; *Új Előre*, 19 April, 31 March 1928; *Munkás*, 24 July 1929, 13 March, 17 April 1930.
44 *Új Előre*, 26 August 1926, 27 February, 20 March, 26 March 1928; *Munkás*, 24 October, 24 July 1930.
45 Tóth, *23 év*, 156–7.
46 *Munkás*, 15 September 1932, 5 January 1934; *Úttörő*, 22 October 1936.
47 *Munkás*, 29 May 1937. Medgyesi, "Munkás kulturát," 99.
48 *Munkás*, 14 September 1934.
49 Ibid., 16 June 1932, 30 June 1932, 22 January 1930, 9 March 1933.
50 *Új Előre*, 7 May, 8 January 1928. See also *Munkás*, 29 August 1929.
51 *Munkás*, 29 April 1931, *Úttörő*, 3 October 1929.
52 *Új Előre*, 8 January 1929.
53 Interviews with Mary Gabura, 31 January 1977, Toronto, and Sándor Egyed, June 1982, Niagara Falls; *Munkás*, 25 May 1933.
54 *Új Előre*, 8 July 1927.
55 Ibid., 2 November 1927, 1 October 1928; *Munkás*, 21 November 1929, 13 March, 20 March 1930, 2 July 1931, 12 July 1935.
56 *Munkás*, 28 August 1934.
57 Ibid., 12 July 1934.
58 Ibid., 8 March 1935.
59 Minutes, 27 August 1933, Central Committee of the Workers' Clubs, Records of Workers' Clubs, Puskás collection, MHSO; *Munkás*, 27 March, 3 April 1930, 15 February 1934, 8 March 1935.
60 The *Munkás* had a special women's column. See, for example, *Munkás*, 1934, 1937; on the distribution of pamphlets by Communist women,

report on Mrs. János Lancsa, of Windsor, Interior records, 651f2/1936-4298, IPH.

61 *Munkás*, 16 August 1934, 15 October 1936.

62 Carr, *Twilight of Comintern*, 8.

63 *Munkás*, 21 August 1934, 30 November, 31 December 1930, 13 July 1933.

64 Ibid., 24 October 1929, 3 July 1930, 20 May, 21 July 1931, 17 November 1932, 24 May 1934, 2 January 1937.

65 Ibid., 28 April, 12 May 1932, 27 July, 23 February 1933, 8 January, 8 March, 21 June, 19 July 1934.

66 Ibid., 12 September 1929, 7 September, 2 October 1934.

67 Ibid., 5 September 1929, 22 January 1930.

68 See, for example, ibid., 18 September 1930, 1 April 1931, 21 July 1932, 12 October 1933.

69 Ibid., 4 September 1930.

70 See, for example, ibid., 10 July 1930, 17 August, 25 August 1932, 4 May, 24 August 1933, 7 September, 14 September, 21 September 1934, 19 April 1935.

71 Ibid., 12 February 1935, 16 August 1936.

72 Kovrig, *Communism*, 97, 99, 132.

73 *Munkás*, 5 March 1935.

74 Ibid., 18 February, 18 May 1937, 13 April 1932. For a discussion of CIO activities in Canada and the Communist party, see Abella, *Nationalism*, chap. 1.

75 *Munkás*, 22 October 1936, 23 January, 13 February, 20 May 1937.

76 *50 éves a Szent Erzsébet*, 10; Minutes, 6 February 1935, Church Council, Records of the First Hungarian Presbyterian Church of Toronto, MHSO.

77 *Munkás*, 15 March 1934; Minutes, 14 November 1934, Hungaria.

78 *Munkás*, 12 July, 19 July, 26 July, 30 July 1935, 18 July 1938; *A Kanadai Magyar Munkás Naptára* (1937), passim.

79 See, for example, *Munkás*, 18 January, 19 February 1935, 27 June 1936, 20 February 1937.

80 Interview with George Palotás, July 1980, Szamosszeg, Hungary.

81 *Munkás*, 18 May 1937.

82 See below, chap. 10.

83 *Munkás*, 8 September 1932.

CHAPTER TEN

1 *Munkás*, 4 June 1935.

2 Ibid.

3 *Munkás*, 28 December 1933.

4 Ibid.

5 Ibid., 29 December 1932.
6 *Welland Tribune*, 10 August 1933, Blaskó memoirs, 81; *Munkás*, 3 August, 17 August 1933, 4 January 1934. The charges against Pásztor were eventually dismissed.
7 See Minutes, Central Committee of the Workers' Clubs, 1932–1934, and Records of the Workers' Clubs and the Independent Mutual Benefit Federation, Puskás collection, MHSO.
8 These observations are based on an examination of the content of the libraries of the Hamilton and Toronto Workers' clubs. See also *Munkás*, 20 May 1931, for advice given by central committee on libraries.
9 *Munkás*, 27 March 1937.
10 Minutes, 2 August 1934, Central Committee of the Workers' Clubs. Smaller groups in outlying areas could not always comply with these directives. See, for example, *Munkás*, 11 January 1934.
11 *Munkás*, 26 April 1934.
12 Minutes, 28 January 1934, Central Committee of the Workers' Clubs.
13 Ibid.; *Munkás*, 30 July 1935.
14 I am aware of three "mass trials" during the interwar years – those of Béla Jánosik, Sándor Illés, and Juhász and Tirpák. For Jánosik, see Minutes, 5 October 1932, Central Committee of Workers' Clubs, and transcript of the trial, Puskás collection, MHSO, and *Munkás*, 13 October, 20 October 1932; for Illés, see *Munkás*, 2 July 1935; and for Juhász and Tirpák, see *Munkás*, 29 August 1935.
15 *Munkás*, 9 February 1933, 1 March 1934.
16 Ibid., 9 February 1933.
17 Ibid., 1 March 1934.
18 Ibid., 3 October 1929, 8 January 1930.
19 Ibid., 5 February 1933.
20 See, for example, letter from Hans Marchwitza, German worker correspondent, in ibid., 6 August 1931.
21 Ibid., 1 June 1933.
22 Ibid., 30 December 1929.
23 Ibid., 20 July 1933, 29 March 1935.
24 Ibid., 3 September, 8 October 1931.
25 Interview with Helen Czukár, March 1980, Hamilton.
26 Vilmos, "Műkedvelőinkhez," 204. Vilmos's discussion was similar to that of Lajos Egri in the *Új Előre*'s 1934 Almanac, 47.
27 See, for example, *Le théâtre d'agit-prop*; Innes, *Erwin Piscator's Political Theatre*; Willett, *The Theatre of Erwin Piscator*; Waterman, "Proltet: The Yiddish-Speaking Group"; Gruber, "Willi Munzenberg's."
28 Lists of plays available from the central committee appeared regularly in the *Munkás*.
29 *Munkás*, 22 February 1934.

30 Ibid., 2 February 1937.
31 *A Kanadai Magyar Munkás Naptára* (1937), 204.
32 Examples drawn from the Hamilton Workers' club's copy of *A betyár kendője* (The Outlaw's Kerchief).
33 Blaskó memoirs, 21; see also *Munkás*, 21 January 1937.
34 *Munkás*, 15 February 1934.
35 See, for example, ibid., 5 May, 22 September 1932, 28 September 1934.
36 Interview with István Weszely, 27 March 1980, Burlington.
37 Ibid.
38 Ibid.
39 *Munkás*, 20 July 1933.
40 Ibid., 26 March 1935.
41 Report from the Chief Constable of the District of Orosháza to the Ministry of Interior, Interior records, 651f 2/1936-4298, IPH.
42 *Munkás*, 23 April 1935.
43 Ibid., 18 May 1937.
44 Ibid.
45 Minutes, 4 July 1933, Central Committee of the Workers' Clubs, in *Munkás*, 20 July 1933.
46 *Munkás*, 23 April 1935; see also 12 March 1935.
47 Ibid., 4 January 1934.
48 Ibid., 29 June 1933. See also 13 July 1933, 19 July 1934, 8 March, 1935, and Blaskó memoirs, 41–2.
49 For Canada, see *Munkás*, 17 December 1931, 21 July 1932, 5 October 1933. Interviews with András Durovec, June 1982, Toronto, and Sándor Medgyesi, Budapest, 1980; Recollections of Sándor Hajas, H-h-172 and Sándor Mező, H-m-202, IPH; Minutes, 26 February 1934, Central Committee of the Workers' Clubs. For the United States, see recollections of Emil Gárdos, H-g-184, IPH.
50 *Munkás*, 21 July 1932.
51 Tóth, *23 év*, 156–7.
52 Interview with Sándor Medgyesi, Budapest, 1980.
53 *Munkás*, 12 February 1931.
54 Ibid., 25 June 1931.
55 Report No. 2, n.d., Hamilton, Communist Party of Canada Collection, Reel 5, 8 C 0058, AO. *Munkás*, 19 September 1929.
56 *Munkás*, 24 August 1934.
57 Ibid., 5 January 1933.
58 Ibid., 26 April 1934.
59 Ibid., 27 April 1933.
60 On neighbourhood councils in Canada, see Avakumovic, *The Communist Party*, 75. On organizing the unemployed in the United States and

the roots of this strategy in Russia, see Klehr, *Heyday*, 5off. and 423 note 2. On the Hungarian proletarian camp in Canada see *Munkás*, 13 January, 2 February, 10 March, 16 March, 27 April 1933, 26 April, 24 August 1934; Memoirs of Sándor Greczula, 14, István Szőke papers, Puskás collection, Budapest.

61 *Úttörő*, 15 October, 10 December 1931. On the International Workers' Order, see Draper, *American Communism*, 431. Klehr, *Heyday*, passim.

62 Blaskó memoirs, 65; *Úttörő*, 15 October 1931, 3 August 1933.

63 *Úttörő*, 15 October 1931.

64 Blaskó memoirs, 65.

65 *Uttörő*, 3 August 1933.

66 Ibid.; the association was still receiving aid from American Hungarian organizers in 1935, *Úttörő*, 19 February 1935.

67 Blaskó memoirs, 91.

68 Ibid., 66.

69 See, for example, *Új Előre*, 13 March 1929; *Munkás*, 26 March 1935; Nyerki, "Itt sincs jobb dolgunk," 87.

70 *Munkás*, 19 March 1931, 23 March 1933, 12 April 1935.

71 *Új Előre*, 13 March 1929.

72 Flyer for 1946 celebrations by Hamilton Workers' Club.

73 *Munkás*, 17 March 1932, 26 March 1935.

74 Ibid., 23 March 1933, 2 April 1935.

75 Ibid., 23 March 1933.

76 Ibid., 15 March 1934. Hungarian Communist organizers in Canada seem to have made such outwardly conciliatory moves towards the patriots even before the official announcement of the Popular Front policy by the Comintern. Before 1934, members of the proletarian camp attended, and attempted to disrupt, community functions organized by the patriots. See, for example, *Munkás*, 10 September 1931, 10 November 1932.

77 *Munkás*, 29 March 1934. Translation of Petőfi's poem from Nyerges, *Petőfi*, 173.

78 See, for example, Minutes, 14 November 1934, Hungaria Social Club. The Workers' club attempted to join patriotic organizations on 6 October but was turned away, because Hungaria members believed that the left had used the 15 March celebrations to make inflammatory propaganda.

CONCLUSION

1 Dreisziger et al., *Struggle and Hope*, 171, and Dreisziger, "Rise of a Bureaucracy."

2 Béla Eisner, "Towards a United Canada (Some Problems of the Hungarian-born Canadians)," 17 October 1944, Eisner Papers, Dreisziger collection, Kingston.
3 Kallen, "Multiculturalism," 56. See also Peter, "The Myth of Multiculturalism," 57, 63.

Bibliography

MANUSCRIPTS

Hungary

Budapest
COLLECTION OF ERZSÉBET VEZÉR
Ambrosius C•akó papers.

COLLECTION OF JULIANNA PUSKÁS
István Szőke papers.

INSTITUTE FOR PARTY HISTORY (IPH)
Memoirs of Hungarian Communists Abroad.
Records of the Ministry of the Interior (Interior records).

NATIONAL ARCHIVES OF HUNGARY (NAH)
Records of the Emigrants and Remigrants' Protection Bureau, 1932–1946.
Records of the Ministry of Agriculture (Agriculture records).
Records of the Ministry of Foreign Affairs, Division in Charge of Hungarians
  Abroad (Hungarians Abroad).
– Press Archives, 1914–1944.
– Records of the Consulate General of Hungary, Montreal, 1922–1941
  (Montreal consulate records).
– Records of the Consulate of Hungary, Winnipeg, 1927–1941 (Winnipeg
  consulate records).

- Records of the World Federation of Hungarians, 1928–1944 (Federation records).
Records of the Prime Minister's Office (PM records). Division of Nationalities and Minorities.
WORLD FEDERATION OF HUNGARIANS
Collection of memoirs by members of communist mass organizations in Canada.

Nyíregyháza
SZABOLCS-SZATMÁR COUNTY ARCHIVES
Records of the alispán (head of county administration).

Sárospatak
SÁROSPATAK COLLEGE OF THEOLOGY
Manuscript collection.

Canada

Calgary
GLENBOW INSTITUTE
Colonization Records of the Canadian Pacific Railway Company (CPR records).

Kingston
Eisner Papers, N.F. Dreisziger Collection.

Montreal
Records of Our Lady of Hungary Roman Catholic Church (Our Lady records).
Records of the Hungaria Social Club.
Records of the Saint Stephen Hungarian Cultural Association.

COLLECTION OF JÓZSEF KOVÁCS
Records of the Székely Hungarian Culture Club.

Ottawa
NATIONAL ARCHIVES (NA)
Papers of the Immigration Branch.
Records of the Canadian Hungarian Association (CHA records).
Records of the Canadian National Railways (CNR records).
Records of the First Hungarian Reformed Church of Montreal (Montreal First Reformed records).
Records of Kanadai Magyar Ujság Company Ltd.
Records of Kelen, Alexander A., Ltd.

Regina
SASKATCHEWAN ARCHIVES
Records of the Royal Commission on the Immigration and Settlement of Saskatchewan.

Toronto
ARCHDIOCESAN ARCHIVES OF TORONTO (AAT)
Archbishop McNeil papers.
National Parishes. Welland.

ARCHIVES OF ONTARIO (AO)
Communist Party of Canada Collection.

ARCHIVES OF THE PRESBYTERIAN CHURCH IN CANADA (APC), KNOX COLLEGE
Minutes of the Hamilton Presbytery.
Minutes of the Presbytery of Toronto.

MINISTRY OF CONSUMER AND COMMERCIAL AFFAIRS (MCCA) (ONTARIO)
Business and Partnership Registry.

MULTICULTURAL HISTORY SOCIETY OF ONTARIO (MHSO)
András Durovec papers.
Géza Kertész papers.
Lawrence Kovács papers.
Records of the Brantford Hungarian Sick Benefit Society, Hamilton Chapter.
Records of the Brantford Hungarian Sick Benefit Society, Toronto Chapter.
Records of the First Hungarian Presbyterian Church of Toronto.
Records of the Hungarian Baptist Congregation, Toronto.
Records of the John Calvin Hungarian Presbyterian Church, Hamilton.
Records of the Oshawa Hungarian Cultural Club, 1935–55.
Records of the Welland Hungarian Self-Culture Society.
Records of the Workers' Clubs and the Independent Mutual Benefit Federation, Puskás collection.
Reverend Charles Steinmetz papers.

UNITED CHURCH ARCHIVES (UCA)
Records of the Board of Home Missions.
Reverend H. G. Forster personal papers.
Reverend F. Hoffman personal papers.
United Church of Canada. General Council Records.

Windsor
Records of the Windsor and District Hungarian Club.

INTERVIEWS

Hungary

Budapest
Collection of Julianna Puskás (Puskás collection). 6 interviews.

Canada

Hull
MUSEUM OF CIVILIZATION. FOLK STUDIES CENTRE
Collection of Linda Degh and Andrew Vázsonyi (Degh-Vázsonyi collection).
110 interviews.

Montreal
Collection of Rev. Aladár Komjáthy. 2 interviews.

Toronto
Collection of Carmela Patrias. 60 interviews.

MULTICULTURAL HISTORY SOCIETY OF ONTARIO (MHSO)
Collection of Julianna Puskás (Puskás collection). 13 interviews.
Collection of Susan Papp-Zubrits. 5 interviews.
Delhi Project. 17 interviews.

NEWSPAPERS AND PERIODICALS

Buffaloi Híradó (Buffalo).
Canadai Kis Ujság (Welland).
Canadai Magyar Farmer (Winnipeg).
Egyetértés (Montreal).
A Falu (Budapest).
Figyelő (Toronto).
Híradó (Toronto and Hamilton).
Kanadai Magyar Hírlap (Hírlap) (Welland and Toronto).
Kanadai Magyar Munkás (Munkás) (Hamilton and Toronto).
Kanadai Magyar Népszava (Hamilton).
Kanadai Magyar Ujság (Winnipeg).
Kanadai Magyarság (Winnipeg).
Külföldi Magyarság (Budapest).

Magyar Kalendárium (Toronto).
Otthon (Saskatoon).
Református Gyertyafény (Toronto).
Szabadság (Cleveland).
Tárogató (Toronto).
Új Előre (New York).
Úttörő (Hamilton and Toronto).

ALL OTHER SOURCES

Abella, I.M., and Troper, H. *None Is Too Many: Canada and the Jews of Europe,*
1933–48. Toronto: Lester and Orpen, 1982.
Abella, Irving. *Nationalism, Communism and Canadian Labour: The CIO, the*
Communist Party and the Canadian Congress of Labour. Toronto: University of
Toronto Press, 1972.
"The Agricultural Labourers of Hungary." *International Labour Review* 1
(January 1921) 137–44.
Agulhon, Maurice. *The Republic in the Village.* Trans. Janet Lloyd. Cambridge:
Cambridge University Press, 1982.
Alexander, June. "The Immigrant Church and Community: The Formation of
Pittsburgh's Slovak Religious Institutions, 1880–1914." PhD dissertation,
University of Minnesota, 1980.
Amerikai magyar református árvaházi és aggmenházi naptár (Almanac of the
Hungarian Reformed Orphanage and Old Folks Home). Ligonier, Pa.,
1936.
"Amerikás dalok" (Amerikás Songs). In *Magyar népdalok* (Hungarian
Folksongs), ed. Gyula Ortutay and Imre Katona, 633–50. Budapest:
Szépirodalmi Könyvkiadó, 1970.
Avakumovic, Ivan. *The Communist Party in Canada: A History.* Toronto:
McClelland and Stewart, 1975.
Avery, Donald. *Dangerous Foreigners: European Immigrant Workers and Labour*
Radicalism in Canada, 1896–1932. Toronto: McClelland and Stewart, 1979.
Bácskay Payerle, Béla. "Kanadai magyarság" (Canadian Hungarians). *Magyar*
Szemle (July 1933) 218–26.
Bálint, Sándor. "Szeged alsóvárosi vallásos társulatok és egyesületek" (Religious
Confraternities and Associations in Lower Town Szeged). *Paraszti társadalom*
és műveltség a 18–20-ik században (Peasant Society and Culture from the
Eighteenth to the Twentieth Century). Vol. 1, 115–24. Papers presented at
the 1974 meeting of the Hungarian Ethnographic Association in Szolnok.
Budapest: Magyar Néprajzi Társulat, 1974.
Balogh, István. "A paraszti művelődés" (Peasant Culture). In *A parasztság*
Magyarországon a kapitalizmus korában, ed. István Szabó, 487–565. Budapest:
Akadémiai Kiadó, 1965.

– *A parasztság művelődése a két világháború között* (Peasant Culture between the Two World Wars). Budapest: Akadémiai Kiadó, 1973.

Balogh, Sándor. "A bethleni konszolidáció és a magyar 'neonacionalizmus'" (The Bethlen Consolidation and Hungarian 'Neo-nationalism'). In *A magyar nacionalizmus kialakulása és története* (The Development and History of Hungarian Nationalism), ed. E. Andics, 316–40. Budapest: Kossuth Könyvkiadó, 1964.

Banfield, Edward C. *The Unheavenly City Revisited.* Boston and Toronto: Little, Brown, 1974.

Barany, George. "Hungary: From Aristocratic to Proletarian Nationalism." In *Nationalism in Eastern Europe,* ed. P. Sugar and I. Lederer. Seattle: University of Washington Press, 1969.

Barton, Josef. "Eastern and Southern Europeans." In *Ethnic Leadership in America,* ed. J. Higham, 150–71. Baltimore: Johns Hopkins University Press, 1978.

– *Peasants and Strangers: Italians, Romanians and Slovaks in an American City, 1890–1950.* Cambridge, Mass.: Harvard University Press, 1975.

Béky, Iván Halász de. "The Hungarian Consulates and the Educational Needs of Hungarian Schools in Canada, 1936–40: Documents." *Hungarian Studies Review* 8 (Spring 1981) 119–27.

Berend, Iván T., and Ránki, György. "A magyar társadalom a két világháború között" (Hungarian Society between the Two World Wars). In *Gazdaság és társadalom* (Economy and Society) 319–67. Budapest: Magvető, 1974.

– *The Development of the Manufacturing Industry in Hungary, 1900–44.* Budapest: Akadémiai Kiadó, 1960.

– "Economic Problems of the Danube Region after the Breakup of the Austro-Hungarian Monarchy." In *Essays on World War I: A Case Study of Trianon,* ed. B. Király, P. Pastor, and I. Sanders. War and Society in East Central Europe, Vol. 4. New York: Brooklyn College Press, 1982.

– *Hungary: A Century of Economic Development.* Newton Abbot, Devon: David and Charles, 1974.

– *Magyarország gazdasága az első világháború után, 1919–1929* (The Economy of Hungary after World War I). Budapest: Akadémiai Kiadó, 1966.

Bethlen István titkos iratai (The Confidential Papers of István Bethlen). Budapest: Kossuth, 1972.

Bianco, Carla. *The Two Rosetos.* Bloomington: Indiana University Press, 1974.

Blumstock, Robert, ed. *Bekevar: Working Papers on a Canadian Prairie Community.* Ottawa: National Museum of Man, 1979.

Bodnar, John. *Immigration and Industrialization: Ethnicity in an American Mill Town, 1870–1940.* Pittsburgh: University of Pittsburgh Press, 1977.

– "Immigration and Modernization: The Case of Slavic Peasants in Industrial America." *Journal of Social History* 4 (Fall 1976) 44–71.

– *The Transplanted: A History of Immigrants in Urban America.* Bloomington: Indiana University Press, 1987.

– *Workers' World: Kinship, Community and Protest in an Industrial Society, 1900–1940*. Baltimore and London: Johns Hopkins University Press, 1982.

Bodnar, J., Simon, B., and Weber, M. *Lives of Their Own: Blacks, Italians and Poles in Pittsburgh, 1900–60*. Urbana: University of Illinois Press, 1982.

Bodor, Antal. *Falusi egyletek, körök címtára* (Directory of Village Associations and Circles). Budapest: Falu Országos Szövetsége, 1923.

Bődy, Paul. "Travel Reports on Hungarian Settlements in Canada, 1905–1928." *Canadian-American Review of Hungarian Studies* 2 (Spring 1975) 21–32.

Briggs, John. *An Italian Passage: Immigrants to Three American Cities, 1890–1930*. New Haven, Conn.: Yale University Press, 1978.

Brody, David. *Steelworkers in America: The Nonunion Era*. New York: Harper and Row, 1960.

Bukowczyk, John J. *And My Children Did Not Know Me: A History of Polish-Americans*. Bloomington: Indiana University Press, 1987.

Canada. Department of Immigration and Colonization. *Annual Departmental Report*. Various years.

– Dominion Bureau of Statistics (DBS). *Census*. 1921, 1931, 1941.

– Dominion Bureau of Statistics. *Racial Origins and Nativity of the Canadian People*, by W. Burton Hurd, Census Monograph No. 4. Ottawa, 1937.

– Select Standing Committee on Agriculture and Colonization. *Minutes of the Proceedings and Evidence and Report*. Ottawa, 1928.

Carr, E.H. *Twilight of Comintern*. London: Macmillan, 1982.

Chudacoff, Howard P. "A New Look at Ethnic Neighborhoods: Residential Dispersion and the Concept of Visibility in a Medium-Sized City." *Journal of American History* 60 (June 1973) 79–93.

Conzen, Kathleen. "Immigrants, Immigrant Neighborhoods and Ethnic Identity: Historical Issues." *Journal of American History* 66 (December 1979) 603–15.

Dahli, Jorgen, and Fernando, Tissa, eds. *Ethnicity, Power and Politics in Canada*. Toronto: Methuen, 1981.

Deak, Istvan. "Hungary." In *The European Right: A Historical Profile*, ed. H. Rogger and E. Weber. Berkeley and Los Angeles: University of California Press, 1966.

Degh, Linda. *People in the Tobacco Belt: Four Lives*. Ottawa: National Museum of Man, 1975.

– "Survival and Revival of European Folk Culture in America." *Ethnologia Europeica* 2 (1968) 97–107.

– "Two Hungarian-American Stereotypes." *New York Folklore Quarterly* 28 (1972) 3–14.

– "Two Letters from Home." *Journal of American Folklore* 91 (1978) 809–10.

Degré, Alajos. "A községi képviselőtestület súlyának hanyatlása az I. világháború után" (The Decline in the Power of Communal Assemblies after the First World War). In *Az állami és jogintézmények változásai a XX. század első felében*

Magyarországon (Changes in Hungary's Political and Legal Institutions during the First Half of the Twentieth Century). Budapest, 1983.

A dohányvidéki Magyar Református Egyház templomszentelési emlékkönyve (Dedication Album of the Hungarian Presbyterian Church, Delhi). Delhi, Ont., 1951.

Dorson, Richard M. *Folklore and Fakelore.* Cambridge, Mass.: Harvard University Press, 1976.

Draper, Theodore. *American Communism and Soviet Russia.* New York: Octagon Books, 1977.

Dreisziger, N.F. "Aspects of Hungarian Settlement in Central Canada." *Canadian-American Review of Hungarian Studies* 7 (Spring 1980) 45–53.

– *The Hungarian Experience in Ontario.* Toronto: Hungarian Studies Review, 1985.

– "Immigrant Lives and Lifestyles in Canada, 1924–1939." *Hungarian Studies Review* 8 (Spring 1981) 61–5.

– "The Rise of a Bureaucracy for Multiculturalism: The Origin of the Nationalities Branch, 1939–41." In *On Guard for Thee: War, Ethnicity, and the Canadian State, 1939–45,* ed. N. Hillmer, B. Kordas, and L. Luciuk. Ottawa: Canadian Committee for the History of the Second World War, 1988.

– "In Search of a Hungarian-Canadian Lobby: 1927–1951." *Canadian Ethnic Studies* 12 (1980) 81–97.

Dreisziger, N.F., Kovacs, M.L., Bődy, Paul, and Kovrig, B. *Struggle and Hope: The Hungarian-Canadian Experience.* Toronto: McClelland and Stewart, 1982.

Dumas, Evelyn. *The Bitter Thirties in Quebec.* Montreal: Black Rose, 1975.

Eckstein, Alexander. "The Economic Development of Hungary, 1920–50: A Study in the Growth of an Economically Underdeveloped Area." PhD dissertation, University of California – Berkley, 1952.

Eddie, Scott. "The Changing Patterns of Landownership in Hungary, 1967–1914." *Economic History Review* 2nd Series 20 (1967) 293–310.

Eisenstadt, S.N. "The Place of Elites and Primary Groups in the Absorption of New Immigrants in Israel." *American Journal of Sociology* 57 (November 1951) 222–31.

Az első világháború és a forradalmak képei (Pictures of World War I and the Revolutions). Budapest: Europa Könyvkiadó, 1977.

England, Robert. *The Central European Immigrant in Canada.* Toronto: Macmillan, 1929.

– *The Colonization of Western Canada: A Study of Contemporary Land Settlement, 1896–1934.* London: P.S. King, 1936.

Erdei, Ferenc. *A magyar paraszttársadalom* (Hungarian Peasant Society). Budapest: Franklin, 1942.

– "A magyar társadalom a két háború között" (Hungarian Society between the Wars). In *A magyar társadalom* (Hungarian Society), ed. Kálmán Kulcsár, 293–323. Budapest: Akadémiai Kiadó, 1980.

50 éves a hamiltoni Kálvin János Magyar Református Egyház, 1926–1976 (Fiftieth Anniversary of the John Calvin Hungarian Presbyterian Church). Hamilton, 1976.

50 éves a Szent Erzsébet Egyházközség (Fiftieth Anniversary Pamphlet of St Elizabeth of Hungary Parish). Toronto, 1978.

Faragó, János. "A kanadai magyarság" (Canadian Hungarians). *Közgazdasági Szemle* (1902) 593–8.

– "A magyar kivándorlók Kanadában" (Hungarian Immigrants in Canada). *Közgazdasági Szemle* (1901) 810–26.

Fejős, Zoltán. "Kivándorlás Amerikába, Zemplén középső vidékéről" (Emigration to America from the Central Region of Zemplén County). *Herman Otto múzeum évkönyve* 19 (1980) 293–327.

Fél, Edit, and Hofer, Tamás. *Proper Peasants. Traditional Life in a Hungarian Village.* Chicago: Aldin Publishing, 1969.

Forró, Marianne. "Vándormozgalmak a világháború után hazánkban és az utódállamokban" (Migration Following the World War in Our Homeland and in the Successor States). *Országút* (1936) 29–32.

Foster, Kate A. *Our Canadian Mosaic.* Toronto: Dominion Council, Young Women's Christian Association, 1926.

Fox, William. "Folklore and Fakelore: Some Sociological Considerations." *Journal of Folklore Institute* 17 (1980) 244–61.

Fox Genovese, Elizabeth, and Genovese, Eugene. "The Political Crisis of Social History: A Marxian Perspective." *Journal of Social History* 10 (Winter 1976) 205–20.

Frager, Ruth. *Sweatshop Strife: Class, Ethnicity and Gender in the Jewish Labour Movement of Toronto, 1900–1939.* Toronto: University of Toronto Press, 1992.

Frey, Katherine Stenger. *The Danube Swabians: A People with Portable Roots.* Belleville, Ont.: Mika Publishing, 1982.

Friedlander, P. *The Emergence of UAW Local, 1936–1939.* Pittsburgh: University of Pittsburgh Press, 1975.

Független Magyar Református Egyház Windsor, Ontario, harminc év, 1933–63 (Free Hungarian Reformed Church, Windsor, Ontario, Thirty Years, 1933–63). Windsor, 1963.

Gaál, Endre. "Válogatott dokumentumok a szegedi ipari munkások szocialista szakmai szervezkedésének történetéből, 1901–04" (Selected Documents from the Associational History of Szeged's Socialist Industrial Workers, 1901–04). *Acta Historica* (Szeged) 50 (1974) 3–103.

Gaál, Jenő. *Kényszerkivándorlás* (Forced Emigration). Budapest: Pallas, 1925.

– *A társadalom feladatai a kivándorlás ügyével szemben* (Society's Duties with Regard to Emigration). Budapest: Kivándorlási Tanács, 1926.

Gabaccia, Donna Rae. *Militants and Migrants: Rural Sicilians Become American Workers.* New Brunswick, NJ, and London: Rutgers University Press, 1988.

Galamb, Sándor. *A magyar dráma története 1867-től 1896-ig* (The History of Hungarian Drama from 1867 to 1896). Budapest: A Magyar Tudományos Akadémia, 1937.

Gárdos, Emil. "Az amerikai magyar munkásmozgalom történetéhez 1919–1929" (On the Hungarian American Workers' Movement, 1919–1929). *Párttörténeti Közlemények* 1963.

Gerencsér, Ferenc. *Sárváriak Belgiumban* (People from Sárvár in Belgium). Szombathely: Vas megye tanácsa, 1977.

Gergely, Ferenc and Kiss, György. *Horthy leventéi* (Horthy's Leventes). Budapest: Kossuth Könyvkiadó, 1976.

Glazer, Nathan. "Ethnic Groups in America: From National Culture to Ideology." In *Freedom and Control in Modern Society*, ed. T. Abel and C.A. Page. New York: D. Van Nostrand, 1954.

– *The Social Basis of American Communism*. New York: Harcourt, Brace and World, 1961.

Golab, Caroline. *Immigrant Destinations*. Philadelphia: Temple University Press, 1977.

Gould, J.D. "European Inter-Continental Emigration: The Role of 'Diffusion' and 'Feedback'." *Journal of European Social History* (Fall 1980) 267–315.

Greene, Victor. "Becoming American: The Role of Ethnic Leaders – Swedes, Poles, Italians and Jews." In *The Ethnic Frontier*, ed. M.G. Holli and P.D'A. Jones. Grand Rapids, Mich.: William B. Eedermand Publishing, 1977.

– *For God and Country: The Rise of Polish and Lithuanian Ethnic Consciousness in America, 1860–1910*. Madison: State Historical Society of Wisconsin, 1975.

Gruber, Helmut. "Willi Munzenberg's German Communist Propaganda Empire, 1921–1933." *Journal of Modern History* 38 (September 1966) 278–97.

Gunda, Béla. "America in Hungarian Folk Tradition." *Journal of American Folklore* 88 (1970) 406–16.

Gunst, Péter. *A paraszti társadalom magyarországon a két világháború között* (Peasant Society in Hungary between the Two World Wars). Budapest: Akadémiai Könyvkiadó, 1987.

Gyimesi, Sándor. "A parasztság és a szövetkezeti mozgalmak" (The Peasantry and Associational Movements). In *A parasztság Magyarországon a kapitalizmus korában* ed. István Szabó, 616–55. Budapest: Akadémiai Kiadó, 1965.

A háború utáni sürgős teendők a kivándorlás és a visszavándorlás tárgyában (Urgent Tasks with Regard to Emigration and Remigration after the War). Budapest: Kivándorlási Tanács, 1916.

Hajdu, Géza. *Vásárhelyi egyletek és könyvtárak, 1827–1944* (The Associations and Libraries of Vásárhely, 1827–1944). Szeged: Somogy könyvtár, 1977.

Hammerton, Elizabeth, and Cannadine, David. "Conflict and Consensus on a Ceremonial Occasion: The Diamond Jubilee in Cambridge in 1897." *Historical Journal* 24 (1981) 111–46.

Hanák, Péter. *Magyarország a Monarchiában. Tanulmányok* (Hungary during the Monarchy. Studies). Budapest: Gondolat, 1975.

Handlin, Oscar. *The Uprooted*. Boston: Little, Brown, 1951.

Harney, Robert. "Ambiente and Social Class in North American Little Italies." *Canadian Review of Studies in Nationalism* (Spring 1975) 208–24.

– "Boarding and Belonging." *Urban History Review* (October 1978) 8–37.

– "Chiaroscuro: Italians in Toronto 1885–1915." *Italian American* (Spring 1975) 143–67.

– "The Commerce of Migration." *Canadian Ethnic Studies* 9 (1977) 42–53.

– "Ethnicity and Neighbourhoods." In *Gathering Places: People and Neighbourhoods of Toronto 1834–1945*, ed. R.F. Harney, 5–24. Toronto: Multicultural History Society of Ontario, 1985.

– "Toronto's Little Italy, 1885–1945." In *Little Italies in North America*, ed. R.F. Harney and J.V. Scarpaci. Toronto: Multicultural History Society of Ontario, 1981.

Harney, Robert, and Troper, Harold. *The Immigrants: A Portrait of the Urban Experience, 1890–1930*. Toronto: Van Nostrand, 1975.

Harvard Encyclopedia of American Ethnic Groups. "Hungarians," by Paula Benkart. Cambridge, Mass.: Belknap Press, 1980.

Hazafias Szinpad (Patriotic Stage). Budapest: A Magyar Nemzeti Szövetség, 1928.

Hedges, James. *Building the Canadian West*. New York: Macmillan, 1939.

Held, Joseph. "The Interwar Years and Agrarian Change." In *The Modernization of Agriculture: Rural Transformation in Hungary, 1848–1975*. Boulder, Col.: East European Monographs, 1980.

– "Some Aspects of the Transformation of the Hungarian Peasantry in the Twentieth Century." In *The Peasantry of Eastern Europe*, ed. I. Volgyes, vol. 2, 141–59. New York: Pergamon Press, 1979.

Heron, Craig. *Working in Steel: The Early Years in Canada, 1883–1935*. Toronto: McClelland and Stewart, 1988.

Higham, John. "Current Trends in the Study of Ethnicity in the United States." *Journal of American Ethnic History* 2 (Fall 1982) 5–15.

– "Hanging Together: Divergent Unities in American History." 41 (1974) 5–28.

– ed. *Ethnic Leadership in America*. Baltimore: Johns Hopkins University Press, 1978.

Hofer, Tamás. "The Creation of Ethnic Symbols from the Elements of Peasant Culture." In *Ethnic Diversity and Conflict in Eastern Europe*, ed. Peter F. Sugar. Santa Barbara, Calif.: ABC-Clio, 1980.

Hoffman, Ferenc. "A magyar telepekről" (On Hungarian Settlements). *Magyar Gazdák Szemléje* 1911.

Hoó, Bernát. *Tiszakerecsenytöl Kanadáig* (From Tiszakerecseny to Canada). Budapest: Magvető, 1963.

Iacovetta, Franca. *Such Hardworking People. Italian Immigrants in Postwar Toronto.* Montreal and Kingston: McGill-Queen's University Press, 1992.

Illyés, Gyula. *Hunok Párizsban* (Huns in Paris). Budapest: Szépirodalmi Könyvkiadó, 1970.

Incze, Miklós, and Petőcz, Pál. *A dolgozó parasztság helyzete az ellenforradalmi rendszerben* (The Condition of Rural Labourers under the Counterrevolutionary Regime). Budapest: Művelt Nép Könyvkiadó, 1954.

Innes, C.O. *Erwin Piscator's Political Theatre.* Cambridge: Cambridge University Press, 1972.

International Labour Office. *Migration Laws.*

Iratok az ellenforradalom történetéhez, 1919–45 (Documents for the History of the Counterrevolution, 1919–45). Budapest: Kossuth, 1959.

Janos, A.C., and Slottman, W.B. *Revolution in Perspective: Essays on the Hungarian Soviet Republic of 1919.* Berkeley: University of California Press, 1971.

Jóború, Magda. *A köznevelés a Horthy-korszakban* (Public Education during the Horthy Period). Budapest: Kossuth Könyvkiadó, 1972.

Kalassay, Louis. "The Educational and Religious History of the Hungarian Reformed Church in the United States." PhD dissertation, University of Pittsburgh, 1940.

Kallen, Evelyn. "Multiculturalism: Ideology, Policy, Reality." *Journal of Canadian Studies* 17 (Spring 1982) 51–64.

Kamenetsky, Christa. "Folklore and Ideology in the Third Reich." *Journal of American Folklore* 90 (1977) 168–78.

– "Folklore as a Political Tool in Nazi Germany." *Journal of American Folklore* 85 (1972) 221–35.

Kanadai Magyar Bevándorló Védő Iroda naptára (Almanac of the Canadian Hungarian Immigrant Aid Bureau). Winnipeg, 1927.

A Kanadai Magyar Munkás naptára (Almanac of the *Kanadai Magyar Munkás*). Toronto, 1937, 1948–52.

"Kanadai Magyar Néplap" (Canadian Hungarian People's Paper). *Magyar Kisebbség* (1924) 355–6.

A Kanadai Magyar Ujság és Védő Iroda képes nagy naptára az 1926 évre (The Great Illustrated Almanac of the *Kanadai Magyar Ujság* and the Immigrant Aid Bureau). Winnipeg, 1926.

A Kanadai Magyar Ujság képes nagy naptára (The Great Illustrated Almanac of the *Kanadai Magyar Ujság*). Winnipeg, 1926, 1927, 1929, 1930, 1940.

Kantowicz, Edward. *Polish-American Politics in Chicago, 1888–1940.* Chicago: University of Chicago Press, 1975.

Kardoss, László. *Egyház és vallásos élet egy mai faluban* (Church and Religious Life in a Contemporary Village). Budapest: Kossuth Könyvkiadó, 1969.

Katona, Imre. "Átmeneti bérmunkaformák" (Transitional Types of Wage Labour). In *A parasztság magyarországon a kapitalizmus korában*, ed. István Szabó, 382–433. Budapest: Akadémiai Kiadó, 1965.

Kellner, P.J. "Canadian Slavs through the Mirror of Their Press." *Slavs in Canada* 1 (1966) 148–58.

Keresztesy, Sándor. *Utlevél, vizum és kivándorlási ügyekben tanácsadó* (Guide on Passports, Visas and Emigration). Miskolc, Hungary, 1927.

Kirkconnell, Watson. "A Canadian Meets the Magyars." *Canadian-American Review of Hungarian Studies* 1 (Spring 1974) 1–11.

Kirschbaum, J.M. *Slovaks in Canada.* Toronto: Canadian Ethnic Press Association of Ontario, 1967.

Kiss, Jenő. "Gazdakörök és olvasókörök a két világháború között" (Farmers Circles and Reading Circles Between the Two World Wars). *Népművelési Értesitő,* 172–203. Budapest, 1963.

"A kivándorló magyarok sorsa Kanadában" (The Fate of Hungarian Emigrants in Canada). *Magyar Szövetkezés* 29 (February 1926) 50–1.

Kivándorlók tanácsadója az Északamerikai Egyesült Államokba vagy Kanadába kivándorlók részére (Guide to Emigrants: For Emigrants to the United States and Canada). Budapest, 1913.

Klehr, Harvey. *The Heyday of American Communism: The Depression Decade.* New York: Basic Books, 1984.

Klymasz, Robert B. "Culture Maintenance and the Ukrainian Experience in Western Canada." In *New Soil – Old Roots: The Ukrainian Experience in Canada,* 173–83. Winnipeg: Ukrainian Academy of Arts and Sciences in Canada, 1983.

Kocsis, Rózsa. *Igen és nem. A magyar avantgard szinját́ék története* (Yes and No: The History of Hungarian Avant-garde Theatre). Budapest: Magvető, 1973.

Kodály, Zoltán. *Folk Music of Hungary.* Budapest: Corvina Press, 1971.

Komjáthy, Aladár. "The Hungarian Church in America: An Effort to Preserve a Denominational Heritage." DTh dissertation, Princeton Theological Seminary, 1962.

Kőrösfőy, János. *Kanadai magyarok* (Hungarian Canadians). Published by the author, c. 1940.

Kósa, John. "A Century of Hungarian Emigration, 1850–1950." *American Slavic and East European Review* 16 (December 1957) 501–14.

– "Hungarian Immigrants in North America: Their Residential Mobility and Ecology." *Canadian Journal of Economics and Political Science* 22 (August 1956) 358–70.

– *Land of Choice: The Hungarians in Canada.* Toronto: University of Toronto Press, 1957.

Kovács, I. Gábor. "A magyar kalendárium főbb tipusai a 19.században" (The Major Types of Hungarian Almanacs in the Nineteenth Century). *Történelmi Szemle* (1980) 150–64.

Kovács, Imre. *A kivándorlás* (Emigration). Budapest: Cserépfalvi, 1938.

Kovács, József. *A szocialista magyar irodalom dokumentumai az amerikai magyar sajtóban, 1920–45* (The Records of Hungarian Socialist Literature in the American Hungarian Press, 1920–45). Budapest: Akadémiai Kiadó, 1977.

Kovacs, Martin L. "Aspects of Hungarian Peasant Emigration from Pre-1914 Hungary." In *The Peasantry of Eastern Europe*, ed. I. Volgyes, vol. 1, 119–32. New York: Pergamon Press, 1979.

– *Esterhazy and Early Hungarian Immigration to Canada*. Regina: Canadian Plains Research Centre, 1974.

– "From Industries to Farming." *Hungarian Studies Review* 8 (Spring 1981) 45–61.

– "The Hungarian School Question." In *Ethnic Canadians*, ed. M.L. Kovacs. Regina: Canadian Plains Research Centre, 1978.

– *Peace and Strife: Some Facets of the History of an Early Prairie Community*. Kipling, Sask.: Kipling District Historical Society, 1980.

– "Searching for Land: The First Hungarian Influx into Canada." *Canadian-American Review of Hungarian Studies* 7 (Spring 1980) 37–43.

Kovácsics, József. *Magyarország történeti demográfiája* (Hungary's Historical Demography). Budapest: Közgazdasági és Jogi Könyvkiadó, 1963.

– "Történeti demográfiai áttekintés a Kanadába vándorolt magyarokról" (A Historical-Demographic Overview of Hungarian Immigrants in Canada). *Demográfia* 24 (1981) 243–69.

Kővágó, Sarolta. "Szavalókórusok a magyar munkásmozgalomban (1926–33)" (Speaking Choruses in the Hungarian Workers' Movement, 1926–33). *Párttörténeti Közlemények* 36 (1980) 77–102.

Kovrig, Bennett. *Communism in Hungary from Kun to Kadar*. Stanford, Calif.: Stanford University Press, 1979.

Kuropas, Myron B. *The Ukrainian Americans: Roots and Aspirations, 1884–1945*. Toronto, University of Toronto Press, 1991.

Lackó, Miklós. "Kulturális megújulás és népművészet" (Cultural Regeneration and Folklore). *Forrás* no. 16, 12 (1984) 251–61.

Landau, Zbigniew. "The Employment-Seeking Emigration from the Second Republic, 1918–39." In *Employment-Seeking Emigration of the Poles World-Wide XIX and XX c.*, ed. C. Bobinska and A. Pilch. Krakow: Jagiellonian University, n.d.

Lengyel, Emil. *Americans from Hungary*. The Peoples of America Series. Reprint. Westport, Conn.: Greenwood Press, 1974.

Levi, Carlo. *Christ Stopped at Eboli*. New York: Farrar, Straus, Giroux, 1963.

A Ligonieri Bethlen Otthon naptára. (Almanac of the Bethlen Home, Ligonier). Ligonier, Pa., 1937.

Lindstrom-Best, Varpu. *Defiant Sisters: A Social History of Finnish Immigrant Women in Canada*. Toronto: Multicultural History Society of Ontario, 1988.

– "The Unbreachable Gulf: The Division of the Finnish Community of Toronto." In *Finnish Diaspora I: Canada, South America, Africa, Australia and*

Sweden, ed. Michael G. Karni. Toronto: Multicultural History Society of Ontario, 1981.

Lischerung, Gáspár. "A kanadai magyarokról" (On Hungarian Canadians). *Magyar Kultura* (1926) 145–9.

Luciuk, Lubomyr, and Hryniuk, Stella, eds. *Canada's Ukrainians: Negotiating an Identity*. Toronto: University of Toronto Press, 1991.

Macartney, Carlile Aylmer. *October Fifteenth. A History of Modern Hungary, 1929–45*. 2 vols. Edinburgh: Edinburgh University Press, 1956.

Mackintosh, W.A. *The Economic Background of Dominion Provincial Relations*. Appendix III of the Royal Commission Report on Dominion-Provincial Relations, ed. and introduced by J.H. Dales. Carleton Library No. 13. Toronto: McClelland and Stewart, 1964.

McLaren, Duncan. *Ontario Ethnocultural Newspapers, 1838–1972*. Toronto: University of Toronto Press, 1973.

A magyar ágostai hitvallású evangélikusok emlékalbuma (Souvenir Album of Hungarian Lutherans). Windsor, Ont., 1932.

Magyarok Nagyasszonya Egyházközség, 1928–1978 (Our Lady of Hungary Parish, 1928–1978). Montreal, 1978.

Magyarok Nagyasszonya Egyházközség, Welland, 25 év jubileumi évkönyve, 1928–1953. (Our Lady of Hungary Parish, Welland, Silver Jubilee Souvenir Book, 1928–53). Welland, Ont., 1953.

Magyarok Nagyasszonya Egyházközség, Welland, 50 év jubileumi évkönyve, 1928–1978 (Golden Anniversary Souvenir Book, Our Lady of Hungary Parish, Welland, 1928–1978). Welland, Ont., 1978.

A Magyarok Világkongresszusának tárgyalásai (Conference of the World Congress of Hungarians). Budapest: A Magyarok Világkongresszusa központi irodája, 1930.

A Magyarok Világkongresszusának tárgyalásai Budapesten, 1938 (Second Conference of the World Federation of Hungarians, in Budapest, 1938). Budapest: A Magyarok Világkongresszusa központi irodája, 1938.

Magyarország története, 1890–1918 (The History of Hungary, 1890–1918). Budapest: Akadémiai Kiadó, 1978.

Magyarország története, 1918–19, 1919–45. (The History of Hungary, 1918–19, 1919–45). Budapest: Akadémiai Kiadó, 1976.

Marchbin, Andrew A. "Early Emigration from Hungary to Canada." *Slavonic Review* 13 (July 1934) 127–38.

– "The Origin of Migration from South-Eastern Europe to Canada." *Canadian Historical Association Report* (1934) 110–20.

Marczi, György. "Az utolsó állomás" (The Last Stop). In *A Kanadai Magyar Munkás naptára* (Almanac of the Canadian Hungarian Worker), 116–19, 134–6. Toronto: Kanadai Magyar Munkás, 1936.

Marlyn, John. *Under the Ribs of Death*. Toronto: McClelland and Stewart, 1957.

302   Bibliography

Marsh, Leonard. *Canadians in and out of Work: A Survey of Economic Classes and Their Relation to the Labour Market.* McGill Social Research Series No. 9. Toronto: Oxford University Press, 1940.

– "The Mobility of Labour in Relation to Unemployment." *Proceedings of the Canadian Political Science Association* 3 (1931) 7–32.

Martynowycz, Orest. *Ukrainians in Canada: The Formative Years, 1891–1924.* Edmonton: Canadian Institute of Ukrainian Studies Press, 1991.

Medgyesi, Sándor. "Munkás kulturát" (Workers' Culture). In *A Kanadai Magyar Munkás naptára* (Almanac of the Canadian Hungarian Worker), 96–102. Toronto: Kanadai Magyar Munkás, 1936.

Miller, R.M., and Marzik, T.D., eds. *Immigrants and Religion in Urban America.* Philadelphia: Temple University Press, 1977.

Milnor, Andrew. "The New Politics and Ethnic Revolt: 1929–38." In *Politics in Saskatchewan,* ed. N. Ward and D. Stafford, 151–77. Don Mills, Ont.: Longmans Canada Ltd, 1968.

Mitnitzky, M. "The Economic and Social Effects of Industrial Development in Hungary." *International Labour Review* 39 (April 1939) 459–89.

Mócsy, István. "Partition of Hungary and the Origins of the Refugee Problem." In *Essays on World War I: Total War and Peacemaking. A Case Study on Trianon,* ed. by Béla V. Király, Peter Pastor, and Ivan Sanders, 491–509. War and Society in East Central Europe, Vol. 6. New York: Brooklyn College Press, 1982.

Montgomery, David. "Nationalism, American Patriotism, and Class Consciousness among Immigrant Workers in the United States in the Epoch of World War I." In *Struggle a Hard Battle,* ed. D. Hoerder. Dekalb, Ill.: Northern Illinois University Press, 1986.

A Montreáli Magyar Református Egyház jubileumi évkönyve (Magyar Reformed Church, Montreal, Jubilee Album). Montreal, 1966.

Morawska, Ewa. *For Bread with Butter: The Life-Worlds of East Central Europeans in Johnstown, Pennsylvania, 1890–1940.* Cambridge and New York: Cambridge University Press, 1985.

Móricz, M. "Landless Agricultural Workers in Hungary." *International Labour Review* 28 (October 1933) 518–31.

Műkedvelő előadások céljára engedélyezett szinművek és szindarabok jegyzéke (List of Authorized Plays for Performance by Amateurs). Budapest: Magyar Királyi Belügyminiszterium, Egyetemi Kiadó, 1934.

Műkedvelők szinműtára (Plays for Amateur Performers). Budapest: A népművelési titkárok nemzeti szövetsége, 1932.

Nagy, Dezső. *Az amerikai magyarok folklórja* (Folklore of American Hungarians). Folklore Archivum 10–11. Budapest: MTA néprajzi kutató csoport, 1979.

– "A munkásszinjátszás hagyományai" (The Traditions of Workers' Theatre). In *Legujabbkori múzeumi közlemények* (Contemporary Museum Communications), 38–61. Budapest: Népművelési Propaganda Iroda, 1968.

Nagy, Géza. "A kanadai magyarok helyzete és a montreáli m. kir. főkonzulátus felálitása" (The Condition of Hungarians in Canada and the Establishment of the Royal Hungarian Consulate General in Montreal). *Közgazdasági Szemle* (February 1923) 111–22.

Nagy, Gyula. "Parasztélet a Vásárhelyi-Pusztán" (Peasant Life on the Puszta of Vásárhely). Békéscsaba, Hungary, 1974.

Nagy, Iván. "Hungarians in Canada." *Journal de la société hongroise de statistique* 15 (1937) 171–92.

– *Öt világrész magyarsága* (Hungarians on Five Continents). Budapest: Magyar Szemle Társulat, 1931.

Nelli, Humbert. *Italians in Chicago, 1888–1930: A Study in Ethnic Mobility*. New York: Oxford University Press, 1970.

Nyerges, N. *Petőfi*. Buffalo: Hungarian Cultural Foundation, 1973.

Nyerki, Gyula. "Itt sincs jobb dolgunk" (We Are No Better off Here). In *A Kanadai Magyar Munkás naptára* (Almanac of the Canadian Hungarian Worker), 87–91. Toronto: Kanadai Magyar Munkás, 1936.

Orosz, István. "A differenciálodás és kisajátitás" (Partition and Expropriation). In *A parasztság Magyarországon a kapitalizmus korában*, ed. István Szabó. Budapest: Akadémiai Kiadó, 1965.

Országos Mezőgazdasági Címtár (National Agricultural Directory). Kaposvár, 1937.

Ortutay, Gyula. "Kalendáriumolvasó magyarok" (Almanac-Reading Hungarians). *Tükör* 4 (1936) 7–9.

Ortutay, Gyula, and Katona, Imre, eds. *Magyar népdalok* (Hungarian Folksongs). Budapest: Szépirodalmi Kőnyvkiadó, 1970.

Paizs, Ödön. *Magyarok Kanadában* (Hungarians in Canada). Budapest: Atheneum, 1928.

Pálfi, Csaba. "A gyöngyösbokréta története" (The History of the Pearly Bouquet). *Tánctudományi Tanulmányok* 1969–70.

Palmer, Howard. *Land of the Second Chance: A History of Ethnic Groups in Southern Alberta*. Lethbridge, Alta: Lethbridge Herald, 1972.

Palmer, Howard, and Palmer, Tamara. "The Hungarian Experience in Alberta." *Hungarian Studies Review* 8 (Fall 1981) 147–208.

Papp, (Mrs) István. "Adalékok az alföldi olvasókörök és népkönyvtárak történetéhez" (Contributions to the History of the Reading Circles and Popular Libraries of the Hungarian Plain). *Az Országos Széchenyi Könyvtár Évkönyve* (Yearbook of the National Széchenyi Library). Budapest, 1958.

Papp, Susan, ed. *Hungarians in Ontario*. Special issue of *Polyphony*. Toronto: Multicultural History Society of Ontario, 1979–80.

– "The Organizational Development of the Hungarian Community in Ontario." *Hungarian Studies Review* 8 (Spring 1981) 85–99.

Park, Robert. *The Immigrant Press and Its Control*. New York: Harper Brothers, 1922.

Pásztor, Miklós, and Kristoff, Ferenc, "A Független Betegsegélyző Szövetség és a kanadai magyar munkásmozgalom története (The Independent Mutual Benefit Federation and the History of the Hungarian-Canadian Workers Movement). In *Kanadai Magyar Munkás naptára.* Toronto: Kanadai Magyar Munkás, 1936.

Patrias, Carmela. "From Emigration Save Us, Oh Lord!" *Polyphony* 9 No. 1 (Fall/Winter 1987) 17–23.

– "Patriots and Proletarians: The Politicization of Hungarian Immigrants in Canada, 1924–1948." PhD dissertation, University of Toronto, 1985.

– *Relief Strike: Immigrant Workers and the Great Depression in Crowland, Ontario.* Toronto: New Hogtown Press, 1990.

Perin, Roberto. "Writing about Ethnicity." In *Writing about Canada: A Handbook for Modern Canadian History,* ed. John Schultz. Scarborough, Ont.: Prentice-Hall Canada, 1990.

Perin, Roberto, and Sturino, Franc. *Arrangiarsi: The Italian Immigration Experience in Canada.* Montreal: Guernica, 1989.

Peter, Karl. "The Myth of Multiculturalism and Other Political Fables." In *Ethnicity, Power and Politics in Canada,* ed. J. Dahlie and T. Fernando. Toronto: Methuen, 1981.

Polèse, M., Hamle, C., and Bailly, A. *La géographie résidentielle des immigrants et des groupes ethniques; Montréal, 1971.* Montreal, 1990.

Potrebenko, Helen. *No Streets of Gold: A Social History of Ukrainians in Alberta.* Vancouver: New Star Books, 1977.

Puotinen, Arthur Edwin. *Finnish Radicals and Religion in Midwestern Mining Towns, 1865–1914.* New York: Arno Press, 1979.

Pozetta, George. "The Italian Immigrant Press of New York City: The Early Years." *Journal of Ethnic Studies* 1 (Fall 1973) 32–46.

Presbyterian Church of Canada. *Acts and Proceedings of the General Assembly.* Reports of the Board of Home Missions and Social Services.

Prpic, George J. *The Croatian Immigrants in America.* New York: Philosophical Library, 1971.

Puskás, Julianna. *Emigration from Hungary to the United States before 1914.* Studia Historica 113. Budapest: Akadémiai Kiadó, 1975.

– "A földtulajdonosok és a földet bérlők társadalmi rétegeződésének módosulásai az 1920 és 1930 évi népszámlálási adatok alapján" (Changes in the Social Stratification of Land Owners and Tenants, as Indicated by Census Data for 1920 and 1930) *Történelmi Szemle* (1964) 452–65.

– *From Hungary to the United States (1880–1914).* Budapest: Akadémiai Kiadó, 1982.

– "Hungarian Migration Patterns. New Research in Hungary." *Acta Historica* 29 (1983) 269–71.

– *Kivándorló magyarok az Egyesült Államokban, 1880–1914* (Hungarian Emigrants in the United States, 1880–1914). Budapest: Akadémiai Kiadó, 1982.

- "A magyar szervezetek Amerikában" (Hungarian Associations in America). *Történelmi Szemle* 13 (1970) 528–68.
- "A magyarországi kivándorlás sajátosságai a két világháború között, 1920–1940" (The Characteristics of Emigration from Hungary, 1920–1940). *Magyar Tudomány* 26 (October 1981) 735–45.
- "The Process of Overseas Migration from East-Central Europe: Its Periods, Cycles and Characteristics. A Comparative Study." In *Emigration from Northern, Central and Southern Europe: Theoretical and Methodological Principles of Research.* Krakow. Jagiellonian University, 1984.

Rácz, István. *A paraszti migráció és politikai megítélése Magyarországon, 1849–1914* (Peasant Migration and Its Political Assessment in Hungary, 1849–1914). Budapest: Akadémiai Kiadó, 1980.
- "Parasztok elvándorlása a faluból" (Peasant Migration Away from the Village). In *A parasztság Magyarországon a kapitalizmus korában, 1884–1914* (The Peasantry in Hungary during the Capitalist Era, 1884–1914), ed. István Szabó, vol. 2, 433–87. Budapest: Akadémiai Kiadó, 1970.

Radecki, H., with Heydenkorn, B. *A Member of a Distinguished Family: The Polish Group in Canada.* Toronto: McClelland and Stewart, 1976.

Radforth, Ian. *Bushworkers and Bosses: Logging in Northern Ontario 1900–1980.* Toronto: University of Toronto Press, 1987.

Ramirez, Bruno. *On the Move: French-Canadian and Italian Migrants in the North Atlantic Economy 1860–1914.* Toronto: McClelland and Stewart, 1990.

Ramirez, Bruno, and Del Balso, Michael. *The Italians of Montreal: From Sojourning to Settlement, 1900–21.* Montreal: Les Éditions Courant, 1980.

Rasporich, Anthony. *For a Better Life: A History of the Croatians in Canada.* Toronto: McClelland and Stewart, 1982.

Records of Ethnic Fraternal Benefit Associations in the United States: Essays and Inventories. St Paul, Minn.: Immigration History Research Center, University of Minnesota, 1981.

Roberts, Barbara. *Whence They Came: Deportation from Canada, 1900–1935.* Ottawa: University of Ottawa Press, 1988.

Romsics, Ignác. *A Duna-Tisza köze hatalmi-politikai viszonyai 1918–19ben* (Political and Power Relations in the Region between the Duna and the Tisza in 1918–19). Budapest: Akadémiai Kiadó, 1982.
- *Ellenforradalom és konszolidáció. A Horthy-rendszer első tíz éve* (Counterrevolution and Consolidation: The First Ten Years of the Horthy Regime). Budapest: Gondolat, 1982.

Rosenblum, Gerald. *Immigrant Workers: Their Impact on American Labor Radicalism.* New York: Basic Books, 1972.

Rothschild, Joseph. *East Central Europe between the Two World Wars.* Seattle: University of Washington Press, 1974.

Ruzsa, Jenő. *A kanadai magyarság története* (The History of Hungarian Canadians). Toronto: published by the author, 1940.

Saloutos, Theodore. "The Immigrant Contribution to American Agriculture." *Agricultural History* 50 (January 1970) 45–68.

Sántha, Paul. *Three Generations, 1901–1957: The Hungarian Colony at Stockholm, Saskatchewan*. Stockholm, Sask.: published by the author, 1957.

Sárközi, Zoltán. "A summások" (Seasonal Agricultural Labourers). In *A parasztság Magyarországon a kapitalizmus korában*, ed. István Szabó, 321–82. Budapest: Akadémiai Kiadó, 1965.

Schaeffer, Ádám. "Munkássorsok gazdag Kanadában" (Workers' Destinies in Wealthy Canada). *A Kanadai Magyar Munkás naptára* (Almanac of the *Kanadai Magyar Munkás*), 47–52. Toronto: Kanadai Magyar Munkás, 1936.

Schultz, H.J., Ormsby, M.A., Wilbur, J.R.H., and Young, W. *Politics of Discontent*. Toronto: University of Toronto Press, 1967.

Schwartz, Harry. *Seasonal Farm Labor in the United States: With Special Reference to Hired Workers in Fruit and Vegetable and Sugar-Beet Production*. Columbia University Studies in the History of American Agriculture No. 11. New York: Columbia University Press, 1945.

Seager, Allen. "Class, Ethnicity and Politics in the Alberta Coalfields, 1905–45." In *Struggle a Hard Battle*, ed. D. Hoerder. Dekalb, Ill.: Northern Illinois University Press, 1986.

Simeone, William E. "Fascists and Folklorists in Italy." *Journal of American Folklore* 91 (1978) 543–59.

Smith, Allan. "Metaphor and Nationality in North America." *Canadian Historical Review* 60 (1970) 247–75.

Smith, Anthony. *The Ethnic Revival in the Modern World*. Cambridge: Cambridge University Press, 1981.

Smith, Timothy L. "Lay Initiative in the Religious Life of American Immigrants, 1880–1950." In *Anonymous Americans: Explorations in Nineteenth Century Social History*, ed. T. Hareven, 214–49. Englewood Cliffs, NJ: Prentice Hall, 1974.

– "New Approaches to the Study of Immigration in Twentieth-Century America." *American Historical Review* 71 (1965–66) 1265–79.

"Religion and Ethnicity in America." *American Historical Review* 83 (December 1978) 1155–85.

Spira, Thomas. *German-Hungarian Relations and the Swabian Problem*. Boulder; Col.: East European Quarterly, 1977.

Stasiulis, Daiva K. "The Political Structuring of Ethnic Community Action: A Reformulation." *Canadian Ethnic Studies* 12 (1980) 19–45.

Stephenson, A.D., ed. *That They May Be One: An Introduction to the Study of the Work of the Board of Home Missions of the United Church of Canada*. Toronto, 1929.

Stolarik, Mark M. "From Field to Factory: The Historiography of Slovak Immigration to the United States." *International Migration Review* 10 (1976) 81–103.

Storey, Merle. "Hungarians in Canada." *Canadian Geographical Journal* 55 (August 1957) 46–53.

Studies in Ethnicity: The East European Experience in America, ed. C.A. Ward, P. Shashko, and D.E. Pienkos. Boulder, Col.: East European Monographs, 1980.

Sturino, Franc. *Forging the Chain: Italian Migration to North America 1880–1930.* Toronto: Multicultural History Society of Ontario, 1990.

Swyripa, Frances. *Wedded to the Cause: Ukrainian-Canadian Women and Ethnic Identity, 1891–1991.* Toronto: University of Toronto Press, 1993.

Szabad, György. "A hitelviszonyok" (Credit Relations). In *A parasztság Magyarországon a kapitalizmus korában,* ed. István Szabó, 184–246. Budapest: Akadémiai Kiadó, 1965.

Szabady, Egon. *Magyarország népesedése a két világháború között* (Hungary's Demography between the Two World Wars). Budapest: Közgazdasági és Jogi Könyvkiadó, 1964.

Szabó, Zoltán. *Cifra nyomorúság: A Cserhát, Mátra, Bükk földje és népe* (Ornamented Misery: The Land and People of the Regions of Cserhát, Mátra and Bükk). Budapest: Cserépfalvi, n.d.

– *A tardi helyzet* (The Situation in Tard). Budapest: Cserépfalvi, 1937.

Szabolcs, Ottó. *Munka nélküli diplomások a Horthy-rendszerben, 1914–44* (Unemployed Professionals during the Horthy Regime, 1914–44). Budapest, 1964.

Szántó, Miklós. *Magyarok a nagyvilágban* (Hungarians World-wide). Budapest: Kossuth Könyvkiadó, 1970.

Szászi, Ferenc. *Az Amerikába irányuló kivándorlás Szabolcs megyéből az első világháborúig* (Emigration from Szabolcs County to America before World War I) Nyíregyháza: Szabolcs-Szatmár megyei tanács, 1972.

Szél, Tivadar. "A külsö vándormozgalom újabb alakulása" (New Developments in Out-Migration). *Magyar Statisztikai Szemle* 21 (1943) 83–102.

Szendrey, Thomas. "Hungarian-American Theater." In *Ethnic Theater in the United States,* ed. M. Seller. Westport, Conn.: Greenwood Press, 1983.

Szent Erzsébet Magyar Katolikus templomszentelési emlékkönyv (Souvenir Booklet of the Blessing of the Opening of the Hungarian Catholic St Elizabeth Church, Toronto). Toronto, 1944.

Szőke, István. *We Are Canadians: The National Group of Hungarian Canadians.* Toronto: Hungarian Literature Association, 1954.

Le théâtre d'agit-prop de 1917 à 1933, ed. Claude Amey et al. Lausanne: La Cité–L'Âge d'Homme, 1977.

Thirring, Gusztáv. "Az elcsatolt felvidék újabb kivándorlási mozgalmai" (Recent Migration Movements in Czech-Occupied Upper Hungary). *Magyar Statisztikai Szemle* 11 (1933) 72–90.

– "Hungarian Migration of Modern Times." In *International Migrations,* ed.

I. Ferenczi and W.F. Wilcox, vol. 2, 411–40. New York: Bureau of Economic Research, 1931.

Thompson, John, and Seager, Allen. "Workers, Growers and Monopolists: The 'Labour Problem' in the Alberta Beet Sugar Industry during the 1930s." *Labour/Le Travailleur* 3 (1978) 153–74.

Timár, Leslie Joseph. *A Short History of the Hungarian People of Canada.* Toronto: Across Canada Press, 1957.

Tomasi, S.M. *Piety and Power: The Role of the Italian Parishes in the New York Metropolitan Area.* Staten Island, NY: Center for Migration Studies, 1975.

Tóth, István. *23 év Kanadában* (23 Years in Canada). Budapest: Kozmosz, n.d.

Vally, István. "A gyöngyösbokréta indulása" (The Beginnings of the Pearly Bouquet). *Tánctudományi Tanulmányok* 1976–77.

Varga, Ilona. "Adalékok az Argentinába kivándorló magyarok életének alakulásához a két világháború között" (Notes on the Life of Hungarian Emigrants in Argentina between the Two World Wars). *Acta Historica* (Szeged) 46 (1972) 45–60.

– "Magyar kivándorlás Latin-Amerikába a két világháború között" (Hungarian Emigration to Latin America between the Two World Wars). Kandidátusi értekezés, University of Szeged, 1977.

Varga, István. "A közterhek" (Rates and Taxes). In *A parasztság Magyarországon a kapitalizmus korában,* ed. István Szabó, 246–87. Budapest: Akadémiai Kiadó, 1965.

Vassady, Béla, Jr. "The 'Homeland Cause' as Stimulant to Ethnic Unity: The Hungarian American Response to Károlyi's 1914 American Tour." *Journal of American Ethnic History* 2 (Fall 1982) 39–64.

Vázsonyi, Andrew. "The Star-Boarder. Traces of Cicisbeism in an Immigrant Community." In *Tractata Altaica* (Wiesbaden, 1976) 695–713.

Vecoli, Rudolph J. "Contadini in Chicago: A Critique of the Uprooted." *Journal of American History* 51 (December 1964) 404–17.

– "European Americans: From Immigrants to Ethnics." In *The Reinterpretation of American History and Culture,* ed. W.H. Cartwright and R.L. Watson. Washington, DC: National Council of Social Studies, 1973.

– "Italian American Workers, 1880–1920: Padrone Slaves or Primitive Rebels." In *Perspectives in Italian Immigration and Ethnicity,* ed. S.M. Tomasi, 25–51. Staten Island, NY: Center for Migration Studies, 1977.

– "Prelates and Peasants: Italian Immigration and the Catholic Church." *Journal of Social History* 2 (Spring 1969) 217–36.

Vér, Imre. *A kivándorlás örvényében* (In the Whirl of Emigration). Cluj-Kolozsvár, Romania: Világjáró lapkiadó, 1924.

Veres, Péter. *Számadás* (Statement). Budapest, 1948.

Viczián, John. "The Background, Beginnings and Growth of Hungarian Baptists in Toronto, 1929–76." Senior seminar paper, McMaster Divinity College, 1976.

Vilmos, Imre. "Műkedvelőinkhez" (To Our Amateur Performers). In *A Kanadai Magyar Munkás naptára* (Almanac of *Kanadai Magyar Munkás*), 204–8. Toronto: Kanadai Magyar Munkás, 1936.

Voros, Geraldine. "The Hungarian Ethnic Group: A Focus on an Ontario Community." Master's thesis, McMaster University, 1975.

Vörös, Antal. "The Age of Preparation: Hungarian Agrarian Conditions between 1848–1914." In *The Modernization Agriculture: Rural Transformations in Hungary 1848–1975*, ed. Joseph Held. Boulder, Col.: East European Monographs, 1980.

Vörös, Sándor. *American Commissar*. Philadelphia and New York: Chilton Co. Book Division, 1961.

Waterman, Ray. "Proltet: The Yiddish-Speaking Group of the Workers' Theatre Movement." *History Workshop* (Spring 1978) 174–8.

Weinberg, David. "Ethnic Identity in Industrial Cleveland: The Hungarians, 1900–1920." *Ohio History* 86 (Summer 1977) 171–86.

Weis, István. *A magyar falu* (The Hungarian Village). Budapest: Magyar Stemle Társaság, 1931.

– *A mai magyar társadalom* (Contemporary Hungarian Society). Budapest: Magyar Szemle Társaság, 1930.

Willet, John, *The Theatre of Erwin Piscator*. London: Eyre Methuen, 1978.

Windisch, József. "Magyar kivándorlók Kanadában" (Hungarian Emigrants in Canada). *Köztelek* (1927) 938–9.

Windsor and District Hungarian Society, Golden Anniversary Publication. Windsor, Ont., 1976.

Yans-McLaughlin, Virginia. *Family and Community: Italian Immigrants in Buffalo*. Ithaca, NY: Cornell University Press, 1977.

Zágonyi, Sámuel. *Kanada egy europai bevándorló megvilágitásában* (Canada through the Eyes of a European Immigrant). Budapest and Bridgeport, Conn.: published by the author, 1926.

Zucchi, John. *The Italian Immigrants of the St. John's Ward, 1875–1915*. Occasional Papers in Ethnic and Immigration Studies. Toronto: Multicultural History Society of Ontario, 1981.

– *Italians in Toronto. Development of a National Identity, 1875–1935*. Kingston and Montreal: McGill-Queen's University Press, 1988.

Index